T. E. Rhine, M.D.
Recollections of an Arkansas Country Doctor

Runner-up for General Practitioner of the Year in the United States in 1950, at the American Medical Association convention, Washington, D. C.

T. E. Rhine, M.D.

Recollections of an Arkansas Country Doctor

Collected and Edited by Pat Rhine Brown

August House, Inc. / Little Rock

Copyright 1985 Patricia Rhine Brown.
Published 1985 by August House, Inc., publishers, Post Office Box 3223,
Little Rock, Arkansas 72203. 501-663-7300. All rights reserved. No part of this
book may be reproduced in any manner without the prior written consent of
the author.
Printed in the United States of America.

First printing 1985

Library of Congress Cataloging in Publication Data
Main entry under title:

T. E. Rhine, M.D.: recollections of an Arkansas country doctor.

    1. Rhine, T. E. (Thomas Edwin), 1876-1964—Anecdotes.
2. Physicians (General practice)—Arkansas—Biography.
I. Brown, Pat Rhine, 1928-   . II. Rhine, T. E. (Thomas Edwin),
1876-1964. [DNLM: 1. Family Practice—biography. WZ 100 R437]
R154.R385T16   1985   610'. 92'4 [B]   85-13559
ISBN 0-935304-94-0

With love and appreciation,

TO MY PARENTS

PRB

PUBLISHER'S NOTE

This book is an historical document. As such, it required the suspension of some customary editing rules. Among these were editing to omit racially-charged words and editing of diction. We believe that you will find the book easily readable and we hasten to assure you that racially-charged terminology does not permeate the text—it is rare.

Perhaps the most charming—and informative—single section of this book is Nanneitta Raines Rhine's memento of her husband's fifty-one years of general practice written in 1948. We suggest you begin your reading with it, keeping in mind the historical setting which it so richly illustrates.

For ease of reading, we have tried to minimize footnotes. The result is that there are two types of intrusions in the text: the first is the interviewee's afterthought, which we have placed in parentheses; the second is the interviewer's explanation, which we have placed in brackets. We hope this simple system will make your reading more fruitful.

Contents

Formula for a Happy and Successful Life

Live well; laugh often; enjoy the respect and companionship of good, intelligent men and women; and have a love for little children. I think this philosophy of life is correct. After all, the great values in life are not what we have materially, but those finer qualities which are developed in character building, the possession of virtues which create a spirit of brotherhood and help us to be intensely interested in the welfare of others.

T. E. Rhine, M. D.

(written with a purple typewriter ribbon on a prescription blank.)

PREFACE

The stories always begin, "I will *never* forget Dr. Rhine! Why, he—" either brought them into the world, perhaps even their entire family, or he came to their home in a time of great need and ministered to them without thought of personal gain or time or discomfort for himself. Having remained in South Arkansas, I am the frequent recipient of these stories, and I treasure each one. They are personal—laced with trust, love and humor. They are recollections (a word that he used often) of a time when life was simple, hard, pleasant, and, of necessity, one of sharing. They reflect a style of "doctoring" that was unique to him even in his day. His medical career spanned the years from 1898 to 1964—from the simple cures to very complex techniques. All but the first year, he practiced medicine in Thornton, Arkansas, caring for one generation after another, becoming a very real and close part of the lives of his patients, who were also his friends.

Many of the stories I heard were the basis upon which this "recollection" was begun. These have expanded to include many others, many of which I heard for the first time as I was taping the interviews for this book. I have tried to keep the flavor, the feeling, and the spirit of each interview intact by using as nearly as possible the exact words of the contributor. I have tried not only to tell about Daddy's life and practice of medicine, but also to give a bit of a feeling for the time as well—how people lived, worked and played in a small, rural community in South Arkansas during very bad economic times.

The gathering of these memories has not only been a labor of love, it has been a remarkable experience for me. I have renewed many friendships and awakened many long forgotten memories. More importantly, I have become more keenly aware of the tremendous heritage of caring, serving, learning and enjoying that my parents practiced for so many years. It is a heritage that I hope will be transmitted to others—friends, family, physicians and anyone else who finds joy and inspiration from this book.

It is twenty years ago today that Daddy had a massive stroke, dying three days later. To me, this is the day he died. I have found that he is still remembered with great affection and respect. That is the mark of a long and remarkable life—to be remembered.

All of the photographs reproduced in this book, with the exception of the pictures of Anna Tatum, her house and the Rhine home, were from the collection of pictures that were owned and cherished by my parents throughout the years they lived in Thornton.

My sincerest thanks to the 127 people who made this "recollection" possible and to Dr. Calvin Simmons and Betty Freeze who 'translated' the handwritten paper, "Conduct of Normal Labor." Also my thanks to Dr. Don Miller and to Julie Bridgforth of the AHEC Library who supplied the correct spellings of the medical terms and medicines referred to in many of the tapes.

I must also add my deep gratitude to Ed Brown, my husband, who has suffered through many re-tellings of the marvelous stories that have been related to me.

Pat Rhine Brown

September 20, 1984
Pine Bluff, Arkansas

T. E. Rhine, M. D.

51

HIGHLIGHTS OF FIFTY-ONE YEARS
OF GENERAL PRACTICE

NANNEITTA RAINES RHINE

A GLIMPSE OF THE DOCTOR

"Whoa!"

The doctor stops his car underneath a shade tree just outside the yard fence. The resounding exclamation accompanying this action had served the doctor well in days when one got about the country on horseback. While the horse has long since been exchanged for a faster, though not always more reliable, means of communication, the habit ingrained with years of use is not so easily discarded. Besides, where there are no doorbells, a loud "whoa!" is an effective substitute. It brings the whole family, that is, the well ones, onto the front gallery along with a flurry of dogs underfoot. Children and dogs descend on the doctor.

"Mawnin', anybody live here? Howdy, Frisky Jane, how's my girl today? Been good boys today? You have! Now who told you so?"

"Dr. Rhine, I picked you this bag of peanuts," and "Doc, I can blow the fox horn you gave me," and "You just ought to see how much our puppies have grown," as the youngsters follow the doctor into the house. "Come in, Doc, sure glad you didn't get stuck coming out. Granny ain't doin' so well today."

The doctor hangs his hat on a nail in the open hall-way and goes into the room where an old lady is in bed. "Good morning, young lady, now just what are you fussin' about this morning? Why a gal like you ought to be able to jump a ten rail fence backwards," and the old lady's eyes brighten in spite of the pain, as she reaches out to grasp his hands, the hands that have aided her, her children and grandchildren, the hands of the doctor who has served her family in five generations.

HIS BOYHOOD

Born on April 2, 1876, near Lexington, Mississippi, Thomas Edwin Rhine was the fourth of seven children in the farm home of Susan Elizabeth

Weeks and John Thomas Rhine. There is little that he remembers of his life in Holmes County, Mississippi, for he was only five years old when his parents brought their family to Cleveland County, Arkansas. This journey was made by train from Lexington to Pine Bluff, Arkansas. They travelled from Pine Bluff to their new farm home near what is now Pansy Post Office, in a two-horse surrey. This move was made in March, 1881, and farming operations were begun immediately. The family's belongings were brought to the new home-site in covered wagons, and the covered wagon is one of Dr. Rhine's earliest memories. It was by means of the covered wagon that the annual trips to Pine Bluff were made. "Pappy" Rhine and his neighbors took turns in making the long drive to this town to purchase the year's supply of staples for the families in the little community. Little Ed was allowed to go along with his father on these trips, and the adventures of camping out on the road or in the wagon lots, provided by the merchants for their customers, were the outstanding pleasures of his early years. Back on the farm there were rabbit hunts, and when he was a few years older, a neighbor initiated him into the thrills of the fox chase, the sport which is today his greatest joy.

Two of the Rhine children died before the family left Mississippi and the youngest, a boy, died in their Cleveland County home. Thomas Edwin, the only son, soon learned to do the many chores of a farm boy of those days. His father was a hard worker and a most exacting mentor for his son. School "kept" only about three months each year, and young Ed, with his three sisters, attended the one in their community. This one-room log schoolhouse was commonly known as "Seed-Tick School" in honor of the creatures which the children collected on their persons in considerable quantities making their way through the underbrush to the scarcely less cleared space occupied by the school. Many years later, Dr. Rhine returned to the site of this school, where a more impressive hall of learning had been built, addressed the students and gave them large boxes of candy and fruit. Such goodies would have been indeed a rare treat to him and his playmates in their school days there.

After having exhausted the educational possibilities of "Seed-Tick," Ed expressed a desire for more education; even at that early period in his life he knew that he wanted to be a doctor. The oldest girl, Betty, had married by this time and the parents decided to leave the farm place with her and her husband, and to go where better schooling was available. The family moved to Fordyce, in Dallas County. Young Ed and his two sisters entered the Fordyce Public school, Ed beginning his work in the ninth grade. In Fordyce, Rhine took part in the usual activities of boys of his age and day, the chief sport being "lawnball." Basketball, football and baseball were then unknown. On Saturdays, after all home chores were done, he delighted in squirrel and possum hunting, and roamed the bottoms of Moro and Cook's Creeks with his pals.

One event of these school days became a legend of the community. A drove of goats belonging to an old lady who lived nearby got into the school building one weekend and chewed up the entire library. Of course, this library had very few books in it, but it contained the only books these students had other than their very dull text books, and their destruction caused much consternation among faculty and students alike. In retaliation, the boys caught the goats, tied tin cans to their tails and drove them through town. Naturally the old woman was furious and with the goats bleating, the boys shouting and the old lady in hot pursuit, waving a stick and declaring in no uncertain terms just how she felt and what she would do when she got her hands on those "young scamps," the town was treated to an impromptu parade which has been recalled through the years. After one of the "little scamps," Ed Rhine, became a sedate man of medicine, he was in a wedding that this old lady attended. She inquired as to who the groom's man was and when told she exclaimed, "Ed Rhine a doctor, why he couldn't tote a chamber for me!"

Thomas E. Rhine was in the first graduating class of the Fordyce High School, receiving the diploma along with his eight classmates in 1895. Fifty years later, this class was honored by an invitation to participate in the graduating excercises of 1945. Six members of the 1895 class returned and took part in the graduation. Dr. Rhine introduced the members of his class and reviewed the changes in education during this fifty year period.

In the fall of 1895, young Rhine entered the Clary Training School of Fordyce. Some of his fondest memories go back to these days and to the counsels and influence of Mr. J. D. Clary, the headmaster of this private school. He was graduated in 1896. Following graduation, Rhine attended a Normal School for teachers at Princeton, the county seat of Dallas County. On the basis of this six weeks' training he was hired to teach a three-months' summer school. It was a typical one-room school of those days. School was conducted only in the summertime, so doors and windows were considered unnecessary. Six or seven grades were taught and about fifteen pupils were in attendance. While serving as school master, Rhine spent his leisure hours in the office of Dr. J. W. John of Princeton, gleaning a few precious gems of knowledge from medical books and by questioning the good physician in the ways of doctoring. There were other doctors who encouraged the young man in the early years of his medical study: Doctors J. A. Waters, C. J. March and B. H. Gallagher, of Fordyce.

MEDICAL SCHOOL AT THE TURN OF THE CENTURY

In the fall of 1896, young Rhine began his formal medical education in the Memphis Hospital Medical College at Memphis, Tennessee. Here he attended all lectures; no distinctions in those days were made in the lecture hall between first, second and third year students. Rhine did dissecting during his first year and some work in the various laboratories. Students spent the hours from 8 A.M. to 4 P.M. listening to lectures and watching operations. From 7 to 10 P.M. they did dissecting and laboratory work. Despite such a grueling day, young Rhine customarily spent another hour in intensive study before going to bed, and then arose at five each morning to resume his studies.

After six months of attendance at medical school, Rhine returned to his farm home and worked until June, when Normal School began. The young medical student attended a second session and taught another three months' school in Dallas County. From this venture, he saved the princely sum of fifty dollars. His savings paid about one-third of the expenses for his second year in medical school.

Second year medical courses were the same as in the previous term and at the close of this six months he went to Locust Bayou, Calhoun County, Arkansas, to assist Dr. E. L. Beck in his practice. Before he could begin work, it was necessary that he obtain a license to practice medicine. At that time, licensing was a function of the individual counties, and examinations were given by the local physicians.

Dr. Rhine was licensed in a most informal fashion. He went to the home of Dr. W. D. Sadler at Thornton, where he was questioned and told to go before two other examiners. Rhine encountered the second examiner, who ordinarily would have been twenty-five miles distant, making a call along the route that led out of Thornton. While their nags rested, the second doctor questioned the young student.

Rhine resumed his quest for the remaining member of his "Examining Board," riding his horse some fifteen miles cross-country to the home of Dr. W. B. Jones of Summerville. Learning that the doctor was on an obstetrical call, Rhine pushed on some five miles further, arriving just in time to give a practical demonstration of his medical skill. Dr. Jones was in trouble and needed some help.

The assistance rendered did not end Rhine's "inquisition." The older doctor invited the young man to hitch his horse on back and ride along in his buckboard. The examination proceeded with the journey. Dr. Jones weighed about 400 pounds and young Rhine was a scant 155. The balance in the wagon was therefore considerably one-sided. When the wagon would come to a slant in the road, the wheels of the buggy on Rhine's side would jump up. The older doctor kept the horses at a brisk trot, increasing the hazards which the weight unbalance had already created. Young Rhine passed most of this examination mid-way 'twixt heaven and earth. He has often wondered at his inquisitor's understanding many of the answers he proffered.

Nonetheless, at the end of the journey - and the examination - Dr. Jones assured the aspiring physician that, being under the tutorship of Dr. Beck, he might safely pursue the practice of medicine until "the examining board" could find a convenient time to meet, discuss his qualifications, and issue him a license. Rhine was examined in April; his license to practice arrived in September.

At Locust Bayou the young doctor rode horseback, carrying his pill bags across his saddle. The country was flat, flooded much of the time, and there were no bridges over any of the many creeks in this large rural area. Rhine's horse was unafraid of water and never hesitated to swim these swollen streams, bearing his rider perched high in the saddle. Much travel was done over paths through the woods, in order to shorten the distance between the patients' homes. Rhine visited the sick as far as twenty miles from Dr. Beck's office, riding horseback. Because of the bad roads, a buggy was used very little. During this summer's work of three months, he had only one night of undisturbed sleep. When this rugged "internship" began on March 27, 1898, Rhine weighed 165 pounds; when he returned to school, he weighed 135 pounds.

During this internship in Locust Bayou, Rhine treated and helped in treating the different types of pneumonia, malaria in all its forms, typhoid fever, erysipelas, all types of gastro-intestinal diseases (known then as "summer complaints") and many other diseases which, he avers, "They did not correctly diagnose in those days." Obstetrics and surgery were done in the huts where the people lived. Appendectomies, amputations, paracentesis and other similar operations were performed on the kitchen tables. At night, kerosene lights illumined the improvised operating pit. Instruments were sterilized in pots on the cookstoves or in the fireplaces. There were no gloves; the doctors' hands were scrubbed with soap and water and then immersed in weak carbolic acid solution. Bandages were made of whatever cloth was available and sterile gauze was purchased in jars holding five-yard lengths. Clean bed sheets, non-sterilized, were used in the operations. The operating site was scrubbed with soap and water and sometimes was wet with absolute alcohol after the scrubbing. Dr. Rhine characterized this six-months' experience as the best "internship" a young doctor could have. It netted him his expenses, the upkeep of his horse and one hundred and fifteen dollars.

On the first of October, he returned to medical school. The lectures were as in the two former years during the day. At night, he was now permitted to attend surgical laboratories where the students were taught to do all kinds of operations on the cadaver. Pharmacy was also taught and, in these lessons, the students learned to make pills, emulsions and syrups, and how to compound the liquids which were not incompatible. Though they have outlived their use, the Doctor still keeps his pestle and mortar bowl as symbols of the early "pill rolling" days in medicine.

Rhine graduated in April, 1899, and was awarded the second highest honor in his class of one hundred and eighteen graduates. With his diploma and one dollar and ten cents in his pocket, he returned to his home in Fordyce. After a vacation of one month, he located at Thornton, Arkansas, six miles south of Fordyce. Riding into town on his gray horse, on the seventeenth day of May, 1899, with forty dollars borrowed from a friend, as his capital, he began his practice.

THE DOCTOR "LOCATES"

At the time of the young Doctor's arrival, Thornton was a small mill town. Within the first month, he made calls in two homes, where he is still the family physician. The people who called him were then young married couples with several children. They are now quite old and their children's children have families in which Doctor continues to practice.

Two other doctors were practicing in Thornton when Doctor Rhine began his career, and there were thirteen doctors in the county. Medical fellowship was unorganized in those days, and Dr. Rhine still values his associations with these early practitioners. Their advice and consultations were invaluable substitutes for the lectures and the clinics that the present day Medical Society affords.

On January 1, 1900, Dr. Rhine was apppointed head surgeon for the Stout Lumber Company which operated a large saw-mill at Thornton. He retained that position until the mill discontinued in 1927. At the same time he continued to practice in the town of Thornton and in the surrounding rural communities. Frequently in these early years of practice when he would arrive at a call many miles from home, someone would have to unloosen his feet from the stirrups where they were hard frozen. In these horseback days, the Doctor wore a large gum coat, gum hat and high leather boots. These were tied to the back of his saddle at all times, for emergency use. The gum coat covered him, his saddle and most of his horse. Many times, in freezing weather, he would pull off that coat, covered with ice, stand it on the porch of the home while seeing a patient, and return to find it still standing upright as he had left it. On rainy days, he covered his saddle and horse with the slicker and made a dash to and from the house; in that way he had a dry saddle and horse for his return trip. Even today, a gum coat and high-top boots, along with a shovel, an axe, a couple of planks, several jacks, a lantern and pine knots are as much a part of his medical equipment as are his pill bags.

Log rollings and house coverings were social events which the young Doctor tried never to miss. Those were the days when fields were being cleared for farming. Huge trees were cut, made into logs, and these logs were carried and put in heaps for burning. A stick was placed under each end of the log; then four men, two grasping the ends of the sticks, raised the log and carried it to the pile. Much merriment and competition took place at these gatherings, but Dr. Rhine, though he was of slighter stature than many of the husky farmers, was never "pulled down" by any of them.

Occasionally, the Doctor took his fox hounds with him, sandwiching a chase between calls. Because of his fox hunts, his long rides in reaching his patients and his love of dancing, not many hours of his day were spent in sleep. He still maintains that if his folks will let him have four hours of uninterrupted sleep, he can hold his own with any of the young fellows.

Those early years of his practice were filled with many incidents which we who are accustomed to look on travel as pleasantly uneventful might well regard as "hair raising." In swimming a creek one morning in 1903, the Doctor drew himself up in the saddle to avoid being wet. His foot happened to touch his horse's back and immediately he was thrown into the middle of the stream. Wet, cold, and not in the best of humor, he returned home and changed clothes and horses before making the call.

One time his horses ran away with him. He was jerked out of the buggy and three of his ribs were broken. Luckily, he was near a house where he could get water to give himself a hypodermic. The man of the house went to another home about a mile away and phoned the Doctor's mother to have someone bring his other team of horses and also someone to drive the runaway horses in home. Doctor walked the two miles to his patient and back to the scene of the accident while waiting for his folks to come for him. This mishap kept the Doctor in bed a couple of days.

Oftentimes his calls were so urgent that he had to miss meals as well as sleep. On one occasion he ate his noon meal one day, and had nothing more until about ten o'clock the next morning. At that hour he was making a call at the home of an old lady. Apologetically, he inquired if she could give him something to eat. She wanted to cook him a good meal but he had no time for that, so she put on the table just what she had. The meal consisted of cold spare ribs, homemade cold collard kraut, cold cornbread and sweet milk. Doctor Rhine declares yet that this was the best, most appreciated and easily-digested meal he ever ate.

Typhoid fever was common in these years and in 1902 Doctor Rhine had ten cases of this disease in one family that lived eight miles from his home. In 1906, he had six cases in another family ten miles distant. He had to ride horseback in seeing these patients daily. He considers it "simply good fortune" that there was not a death in either family.

In his capacity as surgeon for the Stout Lumber Company, Dr. Rhine did all kinds of amputations under the most unfavorable circumstances. Once, with the assistance of Dr. C. T. Black, who gave the anesthetic, he did a disarticulation of the hip joint. This operation was done in a Negro's hut. In a week's time, the Negro was hopping across the floor on one foot.

In these early years of his practice, there were few hospitals. St. Vincent's of Little Rock was the nearest in Arkansas, but Dr. Rhine could get a patient to Memphis, Tennessee, quicker than to his home state hospital. Still, to make the long train trip to a Memphis hospital was impractical in most instances. All emergencies and most of the necessary operations were done in the homes of his patients or in the Doctor's office.

Dr. Rhine had added a sterilizer to his portable medical equipment, and this was placed on the stoves wherever and whenever sterilization was needed.

During these years and those that followed, he practiced medicine by walking, riding horseback and in a one-horse buggy (later using a two-horse buggy alternately with his saddle horses), by bicycle, on the old-time hand cars and by riding passenger and freight trains on the Cotton Belt and Thornton and Alexander Railroads. He often rode the cow-catcher of the engine on the log trains going out to the various logging camps. Sometimes he rated a seat in the engine cab. Many times he rode the log cars and the hand speeders up and down the log roads. At times he would either walk or ride his bicycle out into the country to see his patients and then catch one of these log trains back into town. Dr. Rhine has driven a buggy and ridden horseback as many as ninety miles in twenty-four hours visiting his patients, stopping only long enough to change horses. Many times, in order to save time, he would phone ahead, so that someone at his home could have another horse saddled or a fresh team hitched up and waiting for him. He always kept fine horses, and his older patients frequently reminisce about his favorite mounts, always calling them by name. The most well-known and best-loved of his horses was "Bill," a spirited, black, five-gaited horse. Doctor made a trip to Missouri to select and purchase this horse in 1906.

The years passed and another mode of travel became available. In 1913, Dr. Rhine purchased a model-T Ford car, the second one bought by a doctor in his section of the State. This contraption was a marvel of speed, and often, when giving the other fellows a "spin" in his auto, he admonished: "Hold your hats, boys, I'm going to run her up to twenty-five miles an hour." The Ford car lessened the time between calls on his patients and aided the busy physician in getting over his ever-expanding territory, *provided* he could get it over the muddy, rough roads in winter and spring and over the rough, sandy roads in summer and fall.

Most of his territory consisted of low, flat or swampy lands and in the rainy months it was almost impossible to drive a car over the ungravelled country roads. Some parts of his practice were among the hills - red clay hills that stuck like glue. This was just as much an obstacle to motoring as were the mud holes of the flat lands. In the summertime, the sand beds proved equally disastrous. Those small-gauge Ford tires in a sand bed would just spin and spin without budging an inch. Many years had to pass, many cars had to be bought and many roads had to be improved or built entirely, before the Doctor could depend altogether on a car. "Old Bill" and his successors continued to be the Doctor's most reliable transportation until 1923.

WORLD WAR I INTERRUPTS

Upon the entrance of the United States into World War I, Dr. Rhine enlisted for active military service. On the 4th of September, 1918, he was commissioned a First Lieutenant in the Medical Corps. He was sent to Chickamauga Park, Georgia, and assigned to Company 27-A, Seventh Battalion. He was ordered to leave Camp Greenleaf on the 13th of October, and he reported to the Transport Division at Hoboken, New Jersey. Ten days later, he sailed on the steamer "Leicastershire" as transport surgeon, landing at Liverpool, England, on the 8th of November, 1918. A few days after his arrival Armistice was signed, and on Thanksgiving Day he sailed from Liverpool. On the return trip he served as Assistant Transport Surgeon on the ship "Ascanius." Arriving in the United States on the 11th of December, 1918, he was assigned work with the Transport Division at Hoboken until his discharge on the 24th of December. Influenza was raging all over the country when Lieutenant Rhine arrived home. Thornton was no exception and his transition to the life of a civilian doctor was immediate.

THE TEMPO OF THE TWENTIES
MOVES FASTER

In September of 1921, Doctor Rhine interrupted his routine of work long enough to make a drastic change in his life: he was married to Miss Nanneitta Raines of Little Rock.

His first child, Virginia Elizabeth, was born on August 17, 1922. A second child, Susan Ethel, was born in October of 1923. In 1928, on February 7, another little girl, Patricia Edwina came, and so Dr. Rhine's family was complete.

There was a time in the mid-twenties when the Doctor, sick and discouraged, was introduced to a medical school class for examination. The professor described his patient with "Here is a man, who unlike Rip Van Winkle, has not slept for twenty years. Now, what's wrong with him?" Actually, the auto had not been an altogether unmixed blessing; the Doctor's territory had expanded and the tempo of his days had increased.

By the war's end Thornton's population had grown to about 1,500. The Stout Lumber Company was operating box and veneer factories in connection with the planer and saw mill. Dr. C. T. Black, who practiced with Dr. Rhine, now took over the drug store, and together they did this work and the growing mill practice in Thornton and in the many logging camps. Even though the mill practice was extensive, Dr. Rhine insisted on holding his town and country practice. In doing all this and at times relieving his partner for a few hours each day in the drug store, his four hours sleep period was often shortened or skipped altogether.

In late March 1924 there was much sickness and many days Doctor drove almost constantly with little sleep and eating only when he could find time. On one of these days, he left home at 4 A.M., after a hurried breakfast; at 4 P.M. he was in Millville, about eleven miles from home, making calls. A friend, noticing his haggard look, asked him if he had had lunch. Getting a negative reply, the man ran into his nearby home and came out with a piece of pie which the Doctor gratefully accepted and ate as he drove along to the next patient.

There was no abatement in the tempo of his work. One morning he was called out before daybreak, and with calls stopping him on every turn of his journey through mill quarters, he found it impossible to return for breakfast. Noontime came and just as he thought of lunch, an urgent call came from the log camp ten miles away over an almost impassable road. After prizing his car out of mud holes and being pulled out of the stickiest places by teams, he finally reached the camp and attended the injured man, along with seeing many sick folks who called on learning that he was in camp. Then the mill office telephoned him to go on to the Jim Steelman Camp. He did, and having a pneumonia patient in the nearby Chambersville community, he decided to make this call before returning to Thornton. He took a colored man, who was wanting to get to Thornton, along with him. Together, they drove, shoved, prized and pushed the little one-seated car over an almost impassable road in a downpour of rain. At 4 P.M., Doctor made it home. Just as he sat down to his first meal of the day, the company telephone operator called him to return to the camp. The Doctor contacted the manager of the mill, explained that he was not physically able to put a car over those roads again, and requested that he be taken out on a hand car. He made the trip by hand car, and returned home many hours later in the night, staggering with exhaustion.

This was on Friday and the following Sunday morning Dr. Rhine awoke to find that his right side was paralyzed. His greatest concern was for his patients and for his partner, Dr. Black, who answered an early morning telephone call the morning after Dr. Rhine was stricken, with "Now don't ring my telephone before seven o'clock. You've sent one doctor to the hospital with his toes turned up and I don't plan to let you send me too." During the first week of Dr. Rhine's illness, so many calls regarding his condition were made to the Stout Lumber Company office that an extra girl was assigned to the switchboard to handle the overload.

Dr. Rhine spent the next six months in hospitals at Little Rock and Hot Springs. Those were trying days for a person of action, and most discouraging, since the Doctor was given no hope of ever being able to resume work. The most optimistic pronouncement was that someday in the quite distant future, he might be able to do a few hours' office work each day. In a most abject frame of mind, Dr. Rhine then asked his doctor if he would ever be able to go fox-hunting again. Laughing, the neurologist promised only that he might eventually get to where he could sit on the side of the road and listen to the barking of the hounds. "Well, that's worth living for," and with this determination, his struggle to get well began.

During the latter part of this enforced rest period, the Rhines discovered one morning that their huge barn was on fire. Doctor rushed out and was soon working as hard as anyone to keep the fire from spreading. (He lost his saddle, a two-horse buggy and his prized saddle bags in this fire.) The next day Doctor announced that a man who could undergo that much strain was able to get back in harness, and off he went to work. Despite dire prophecies and his doctor's warnings, he made his comeback.

23

Dr. Rhine resumed his practice in September of 1924 and in March, 1926, during a flu epidemic, he treated sixteen patients in his office and drove one hundred miles, making forty calls from 7 A.M. to 11 P.M.—the greatest number of calls he had ever made or has yet made in one day.

On one occasion Doctor was called to a distant log camp to see a Negro who had been hit by a windlass. His skull was crushed over the right eye. The Doctor removed the shattered part, raised the depressed part and trimmed the sharp edges. He sutured up the incision after putting in a small drain. In two weeks time this patient was driving a Ford car and almost ran over the Doctor.

By the late 1920's hospital facilities were somewhat better, but even then, it necessitated a train journey of several hours to reach even the nearest ones. Dr. Rhine, therefore, continued to do surgery. Amputations of arms and legs, all types of fractures, tonsilectomies, appendectomies and the care of injuries were part and parcel of his day's work while he was surgeon and physician for the Stout Lumber Company.

These years enriched the Doctor's life in many ways. Contacts were made with people in all walks of life and, though many lived in Thornton only a short time, their friendship for the mill doctor continues in far places to this day. Each year brings him visitors from all over the country who like to renew acquaintance and recall "the good old days in Thornton" with their family doctor of years gone by.

In 1925 the saw-mill burned and in 1927 the Stout Lumber Company sold all its remaining interests. Dr. Rhine was offered more lucrative practices in larger towns but, though he realized that he and his family would be deprived of a substantial and steady income, he decided to remain in Thornton. His life had become too entangled with the lives of the people whom he served for him to leave them. "Why, these folks raised me," he said. "When I go to see them, they look at me with confidence in my ability to relieve their suffering; there's a lot of satisfaction in that."

With his town and country patients, Doctor reasoned there was still enough work to keep even such an energetic doctor as he happily employed, though he would miss the surgery which the mill practice supplied.

THE THIRTIES AND DEPRESSION

Doctor was called to be at the bank (he was at that time Vice-President) early one morning. Thinking he was only wanted in consultation as to a loan for someone, the Doctor forgot this matter entirely when called to see an urgent case. It was several hours before he got back to Thornton and found that the bank had closed its doors. Doctor soon discovered that he would be better off financially to put his car in the garage and make only those calls within walking distance. He vetoed that plan immediately with the remark that if he had to turn his friends down when they were sick and needed him, he would soon be crazy. Doctor borrowed six thousand dollars on his insurance and with this he was able to keep his car going.

Dr. Rhine sums up the hardships of the depression years in one terse statement: 25% of his patients paid some cash, about 25% paid him in produce and the others just couldn't pay with anything. He served them all alike, and took on many other duties, such as investigating for the Red Cross and serving on the "Committee for Government Loans." As County Health Officer he drove into all sections of the country, inspecting the canning kitchens which were part of the WPA program. Many times when these units would get without anything to can, Doctor would hustle out among his debtors, get in peas, collards, fruit, a hog or heifer – anything that might be canned – and haul it to the kitchen so that it might continue in operation.

Cans of food turned out in the kitchens were stored in Doctor's smokehouse. During the winter it was almost a daily occurrence for someone to appear at the Rhine home with a prescription blank, signed by Dr. Rhine. Usually it read, "Give Uncle Sandy (or many another whose needy condition was well known to the Doctor) a can of beef and a bunch of that other stuff from the smokehouse." Not one can of this food was used by the Rhine family.

One day a colored patient met Dr. Rhine on the road and told him that he was clearing a new ground and would like to have some pumpkin seed to plant on this land, come spring. Doctor got him some seed and the patient raised a bumper crop of pumpkins. The darkey asked Doctor to drive out and view the crop before he harvested the pumpkins. The ground was almost covered with them. There was no market for this product, and Doctor loaded his car with them, took them to the canning kitchen. Prescription-blank bearers received more than their wont of pumpkin the next winter.

Most people appreciated being able to use their produce in lieu of cash in paying their doctor's bill, but others took advantage of the privilege. One morning, after a hard wind the night before, a man came into the Doctor's house bringing two bushels of green, hard, undeveloped pears which had been blown off his trees. The farmer announced that these pears, at $2.00 a bushel, were to be applied to his account. The Doctor's wife told him the pears were not fit to use, and she did not want them. He became quite angry and said she would have to take that or nothing. Her reply was, "Well, I don't know whose hogs those are in the grove, but please empty your crates out there for them. I'll tell Doctor to give you credit for the amount."

Another time, a man brought a load of corn. The Doctor's cook went to the barn to show him where to unload his wagon. He began complaining to her about how difficult it was to have had to work so hard in raising this corn and that now he had hauled it all the way to Thornton just to "pay for a few pills." Placing her hands on her hips, with a withering look, Selma proceeded to give him a "sarmon." "Mister," she said, "You was a feelin' pretty bad when you called Dr. Rhine out that night las' winter, wasn't you?

He had to git out of his warm bed, drive dat ole Ford over dem slick, sticky roads to get to yo' house, an' time he got there you was a-hurtin' bad and a-wishin' he'd hurry up and come. Well, dem little pills sho' did help you out, didn't they?" "Aunty, I guess you're right," he said, as he drove his wagon out of the gate. "I guess I wouldn't have made a crop if Doc hadn't seen me through that spell of sickness, and he never once mentioned pay."

For Dr. Rhine, the depression was a means by which he found ways for serving people other than through his profession. In making a Red Cross investigation one day, he took with him his little daughter. This family also had a child of about the same age as the Doctor's. She was blind and she began to feel of her visitor, saying, "She has eyes, she has hair." Dr. Rhine was deeply affected by this incident. He felt humbly grateful that his own child had all her faculties, and he vowed he would take the Depression philosophically and he would never complain over losing money. Doctor became interested in this child's welfare and got her into a hospital. She had partially regained her sight when, in playing around an open fire, her clothes ignited and she was burned to death. Such incidents punctuate a doctor's practice with anguish. They are many when that practice extends over 50 years.

The old darkey's pumpkin seed was just one instance of its kind. Seed from all good products were carefully sorted, dried and saved by the Rhine's cook for re-distribution to the farmers around, and the seed for many patches of watermelon, cantaloupes, corn and turnips, to mention only a few, were passed out the Doctor's door.

At one time during the Thirties a back room in the Doctor's home was used as a distribution center for Red Cross supplies, and the members of his household devoted several hours a day for weeks, measuring off cloth to needy mothers.

In serving on the Committee to pass on Government Loans, Doctor Rhine had to drive the eighteen miles to Hampton. Always these trips were made at his own expense.

During these years, many accounts were never posted on the Doctor's books. He knew the patients could not pay him and that the time spent in writing up the account was probably wasted. One day a building next to Doctor's office burned. It seemed impossible to save the building housing the office. Dr. Rhine grabbed his account books and dashed for the door, past some boys who were helping remove his equipment. One little fellow, who evidently was most observant, said, "Jes' as well leave your books, Doc, 'cause ain't nobody gonna pay you no-how, 'less they just want to."

A patient came into Doctor's home one morning, handed him a $10 bill and said, "Doc, this gets me paid up for the first time since Sarah and me were married. Six of our ten children are now making their own money. The others are big enough to help out at home. Many times I would get almost even with you, then some of us would get sick again. I sure thank you for being so patient."

Doctor Rhine took care of his people through these hard years and went when they called, just as he did when they had the money. In fact, he has never inquired whether money awaited him at the end of the journey.

The rigors of medical practice had not lessened with the years. One cold winter night during the Thirties, Doctor had a very sick patient about six miles from home. There was a heavy snow and the trees were bent and broken with ice. In making this trip, Doctor's car became entangled in the fallen telephone wires. He had become quite ill since leaving home, and it was almost more than he could do to get out in the snow and cut poles to hold the wires down so that he could drive his car over them. He became so exhausted that he had to crawl back to the car and rest a while before driving home. This trip put him in bed for several weeks.

FIGHTING A SECOND WAR ON A DIFFERENT FRONT

When World War II was declared, Doctor immediately volunteered for service in the Armed Forces. He was rejected because of his age. But before the war's end he was declaring that to have been in the Army would not have been nearly so hard as the work he had to do on the home front.

The establishment of a naval ordnance plant near Camden, 25 miles away, trebled the population in Dr. Rhine's territory, and at the age when most men think of retiring, his need was for more hours in the day to meet the emergency.

Newly arriving people were living in tents, barns, even chicken houses, when more decent quarters could not be obtained. Under such living conditions disease was easy to contract and quick to spread. Yet the exigencies of the war required the absence of one after another of the territory's doctors. Dr. Rhine was forced to extend his own already large territory to cover other towns and counties left without medical service.

For five years, Dr. Rhine did the practice which ordinarily would have taken the time and efforts of three doctors. He did not get one full night's rest during those years of the war. On one day between 7 A.M. and 10 P.M., he took care of fifty patients in the office and made three long country trips as well as several town calls. In a record twenty-four period during the emergency, Doctor drove his car 217 miles attending sick folk. Many days he almost equalled that record. Dr. Rhine was so rushed that more often than not he went unshaven. One little girl whom he was attending remarked to her mother, "We have two Dr. Rhines." "No, dear, there's only one Dr. Rhine," her mother replied. "Oh, but there are two; one of them has hair all over his face and the other doesn't."

One morning early when the Doctor had not had a shave for over a week, he was feeding his fox hounds. He had on high boots, an old hat and a denim jumper which was badly worn. With a bucket of dog feed in each hand, he came out of his garage. A bum who was seeking food asked him where he might get a cup of coffee. Doctor directed him to his house. The bum knocked at the Doctor's door, and said, "Lady, your hired man said for you to give me something to eat." He got a good meal and Doctor acquired a new nickname.

Frequently during the last decade Dr. Rhine has driven the seventy-five miles to Little Rock to see his patients in hospitals there. Often, he looks after his patients in the El Dorado and Camden hospitals.

The Doctor's first and only car wreck happened in these strenuous war years. Many times he has almost gone to sleep while driving his car and on this early morning call to Harrell, he really did doze. The car hit a culvert, left the road and ran into a fence. Luckily, Doctor was not killed. He got out of the car, looked the situation over and decided there was nothing he could do. Taking his medicine case, he walked about a mile and a half to the nearest house. The farmer took him to Harrell, where he saw his patient and called for a wrecker.

TALES OF A FAMILY DOCTOR AND THE ELUSIVE DOLLAR

One night Doctor was called on a case of obstetrics in Bradley County, about twenty-five miles from home. It was a very nasty night and Doctor was not well, but he got up and went. When he reached the home, which was only a shack, he found a woman lying on a cot, dressed in a ragged dress, with a dirty quilt covering her. He found a rusty half-gallon bucket in which he boiled some water. He washed his hands and dried them on a child's dress, the only clean thing to be found. He received $1.80 for this call and always said he felt mean to have accepted that.

A patient tells this story of an incident which occurred during World War II years. She called Dr. Rhine to come to her house about 6 in the evening. It was 9 P.M. before he got there. He came in apologizing for his appearance. His regular clothes were hidden 'neath overalls and jumper, and he wore knee-length rubber boots and a hunting cap. He was muddy all over. He had driven his car the sixteen miles to Kingsland where he was met by a man on a log wagon and taken eight miles. For the final two miles he walked, trudging through woods over a narrow path to a one-room shack. Here a fourteen-year-old Negro girl gave birth to her baby. No fee was received or expected.

One morning Mrs. Elsadie Christian came to the Doctor's home and handed his wife $1.00 which she said she owed the Doctor. She had ridden the bus several miles for the purpose of paying him. She became so engrossed in giving Mrs. Rhine an account of her many trials and tribulations as well as her particular religious views that when she finally departed it was too late for her to catch her bus. Thereupon, she returned to the Doctor's house and requested the return of her dollar bill, saying she would

28

just wait and give it to the Doctor himself. She remained at the house for lunch and enlivened the meal with a discourse on her favorite topic of "what is to be, will be." When Dr. Rhine arrived home about the middle of the afternoon, Mrs. Christian presented him with her dollar. However, aware of her financial condition, the Doctor refused to take her money, saying, "Why, I got that much fun out of having you yell when I lanced that boil on the back of your neck." As she carefully put the money in her purse, she turned to Mrs. Rhine and said, "Now, you see, the Lord knew exactly what He was doing when He let me miss that bus."

Many times when called by some man who had never made any gesture of settling long overdue bills, despite his making a good living, Dr. Rhine would argue with him about going. Sometimes Doctor would say that he just would not make the visit but only once did he actually carry out such a threat. The Doctor had delivered the man's two children and tended both the children and mother during later illnesses. The man was making a good salary, but wouldn't pay his doctor bill. One day when the Doctor encountered the father and asked him about the overdue bill, he received a rather indefinite and surly reply. Thereupon, Dr. Rhine told him that though he would never refuse to attend his wife or children, if he himself ever became sick he had just better call another physician. Later one evening, during the extremely hectic war years, the Doctor was called to come to this home. "Who's sick?" Dr. Rhine asked. When informed that it was the man, he refused to go. Next morning, when Dr. Rhine arrived at his office he found the man's father-in-law sitting in the doorway. He not only had brought money to pay all the unpaid bills, but cash in advance, for a visit to the patient.

Many people remonstrated with Dr. Rhine during the time that the Naval Plant workers lived in the area because he did not charge them more for his services.

An incident occurred one night which demonstrated his feelings on this matter. Doctor was preparing to leave for a long trip, when a young Naval Plant worker and his wife brought their little boy to his home. The child had had a convulsion and the parents were frantic. Dr. Rhine put the child to bed on the living room couch, gave him some medicine and watched him for about an hour before telling the father and mother that he thought they might safely take him home. The young man asked the charges and when told $1.00, he said, "Oh, no, Doctor, here's five. I'd have had to pay at least that much anywhere else." Doctor insisted on the one dollar, saying, "Whenever I take up robbery as a means of making my living, I'll get me a gun, get out on the highway and do the job right."

An especially beloved old lady, for whom Doctor had practiced for over forty years, was in her last sickness. The family was much concerned about her mental condition and often related her actions to the Doctor, remarking that she was "just bound to be crazy." "Oh, no, she's just old and childish and wants her way," he would say. One day the old lady refused to take her medicine. Her niece remonstrated with her and said, "If you won't do as

Dr. Rhine says, he won't come to see you." "Huh!" the old lady said, "Just shake a dollar bill at him and watch him come a-trotting." Turning to her niece so that the patient couldn't hear, Dr. Rhine said with feigned seriousness, "Haven't I told you all the time that Aunt Mary wasn't crazy?"

One very bad night, Doctor was called to see a patient who was supposedly near death. This old lady had long been wont to play sick when things didn't suit her, and Doctor knew this, having been summoned on many occasions. Consequently, his first question was, "Has there been a family row?" "Well, Doc, she didn't like what happened today, but Ma sure ain't puttin' on this time. She looks to me just like she's dead." Dr. Rhine left the house and drove over the very rough roads to her home. He found the old lady in bed, scarcely breathing. Anxiety and distress were reflected in the strained faces of her family which was gathered around her. Doctor looked at her, winked at the children, and said, "Well, she is sure dead this time. Son, you should have called the undertaker instead of me – there's not a thing I can do," and turning to her son-in-law who was a minister, he said, "Preacher, I don't imagine you can think up many good things to say about her, but I know one thing: she would have made a wonderful actress." Immediately, the old lady sat up and, angrily shaking her finger at Doctor Rhine, she demanded some medicine. Doctor grabbed his bag, yelled "Ghost," and made a run for his car. Far down the road, he could hear the laughter of the preacher. The old woman was the first one up the next morning, cooked breakfast and lived to be many years older. She never again called Dr. Rhine except when she was really sick.

One fourth of July a young man and woman came to the Doctor's home very early in the morning. They had been to a dance in Pine Bluff and were returning to their homes in El Dorado. Evidently the young man had gone to sleep while driving the car. It was a total wreck. Luckily, the young folks were only shocked and bruised. The young lady was put to bed after Doctor had taken care of her injuries. The couple's greatest concern was to return home, but they were without funds. Doctor Rhine called the wrecker to take care of the car and placed calls to arrange for friends to come for them. These calls were on Doctor's telephone bill that month and he never heard any more from the youngsters.

Dr. Rhine has taken care of many people injured in car wrecks in and around Thornton, but he has never been paid a penny for his services. Once he even hired a driver to take a woman and her children to their home forty miles distant. Thoughtless, as many people are, they even forgot to say "Thanks."

The Doctor, who is always keenly interested in the athletic activities of the young folks, never accepts recompense for looking after any who receive an injury in a game played at the local school. About eleven o'clock one night the door bell rang. Doctor's youngest daughter, who had just returned from a basketball game, answered it. A member of the North Little Rock team, which had been playing in El Dorado, had suffered a heart attack near Thornton. Doctor got up, looked after the young man, and told his daughter to make some hot chocolate for the other members of the team who had accompanied the ailing youth. While their teammate was recuperating, the team enjoyed hot chocolate and fruitcake.

ODDS AND ENDS ABOUT A COUNTRY PRACTICE: FUN, FACTS, AND PHENOMENA

Doctor calls most of his patients by their first names, since he has known most of them all their lives. He knows the birthday of hundreds and can even recall the weather conditions when a number of them were born. One day the Police Matron of Little Rock called him to know the age of a girl. Her father claimed she was not of age and had caused her to be detained by the police. Doctor immediately gave the date of her birth and recalled the difficulties he had experienced the night she was born.

Sometimes Dr. Rhine has had to use a bit of ingenuity in rigging up apparatus to substitute for hospital facilities in the homes of his patients. A funnel, fashioned of pasteboard or paper and attached to a tube of an oxygen tank, has served for an oxygen tent. Any number of times a cardboard box, a hot pad and a pillow have been made into an incubator. With a chicken incubator thermometer affixed to determine the degree of heat, the ersatz incubator has been as effective and cozy as a more elaborate container.

In delivering nearly 4800 children during his practice, Dr. Rhine has had a number of unusual cases, and has set an assortment of records. Among Dr. Rhine's deliveries was one hydrocephalic after-coming head. Slipping his hand up beside the neck, he was able to puncture the skull through the ear with a sharp pointed instrument, thereby draining the water. The after-coming head was then easily delivered.

He delivered triplets where the mother had complete dilatation with no pains. The first two babies delivered were breach and were delivered by traction by two fingers in the groin. The third was a foot presentation and was delivered by grasping both feet with his hand. The first baby delivered could not be resuscitated, the other two lived.

One Negro girl gave birth to her baby while sitting on a slop jar. The cord ruptured about four inches from the body. The mother of the girl found the baby in the slop jar, took it out and wrapped it up in a blanket. Doctor was called and attended to the baby and mother two hours later. Mother and baby did well and the Doctor's "drop in the bucket" is now several years old.

He delivered one hydati-form mole of 13 months' duration and several others of this kind, ranging from four to seven months. He has had one small afterbirth expelled thirty days after a full-term delivery, another one

one week after full-term delivery.

He has delivered one baby weighing eighteen pounds and one weighing twenty. The eighteen pound baby was delivered by podalic version. The twenty pound baby was an easy normal delivery.

In the course of the nearly 4,800 deliveries, Dr. Rhine has had only two face presentations and has seen only one accidental hemorrhage.

The farthest the Doctor has gone to deliver a baby is thirty-six miles. The last three miles he rode on a log wagon on two planks from one bolster to the other. Many times he had to hold his feet high to keep them out of the water.

He once delivered four babies within twenty hours. These cases were miles apart. He delivered three babies in sixteen hours. The first and last born were twenty-five miles apart. He delivered three babies in thirteen hours. The first one, sixteen miles from his home, was born at 9:30 P.M., the second, at 6:30 A.M., was seven miles from home and the third was born at 10:30 A.M. and was sixteen miles away from his home. He made the trip back to his home between each birth. He delivered seven babies in four days, many miles apart, during the war period. At this time Dr. Rhine was past sixty-five years of age.

Many families in Arkansas are completely Rhine delivered. He has delivered ten children in four families; he has delivered eleven children, ten of whom are living, in one family; he has delivered the thirteenth child in three families, and he was called to deliver the seventeenth baby in one family, but couldn't attend this case. Dr. Rhine can claim fourteen families in which he has delivered three generations.

In World War II over two hundred of Doctor's "babies" served in the armed forces. They have formed an American Legion Post, whose charter members were all men at whose births Dr. Rhine had officiated.

Doctor often assists in operations at nearby hospitals. He assisted in operating on a man who was ninety-two years old. This man had prostatic cancer. He lived a year after the operation.

At one time he drew one & a fourth gallons of urine out of an old lady's bladder. She had cancer of the uterus.

One Sunday afternoon, Doctor was called to see a man in the Negro section of Thornton. The Negro's step-son, a boy of about fourteen years, had completely dis-emboweled his step-father with a butcher knife. The man was lying on two boards which formed a low bench. A dirty towel was spread over his abdomen. The doctor tried using one of the darkies as an anesthetist while replacing the organs and sewing the patient up. The anesthetist would become too absorbed in the operation, forget to administer the anesthetic, the patient would take a deep breath and out would come the entrails again. Dr. Rhine finally had to call in another doctor to help him, and they sewed the Negro up as best they could.

The next morning when Dr. Rhine visited the Camden Hospital, the head nurse told him of a similar case, then in the hospital. Two weeks later he learned that the hospital patient had died. Earlier that day he had encountered his own patient heading for the pond with his fishing pole over his shoulder.

He has seen one case of leprosy. He diagnosed the first tularemia case in South Arkansas. The case received considerable publicity and so many physicians came in from nearby towns that the patient declared he was going to start charging a dime for admission to his sick room.

In years gone by he often did the work of the dentist, and even today when a patient suffers from a bad ache and cannot reach a dentist, Dr. Rhine has recourse to his forceps.

Many are the jokes he tells of his experiences. Several of his favorites are repeated below.

One day a very well-dressed colored woman of portly dimensions entered his office. She was trying very hard to be "proper." In questioning her as to her condition, Doctor asked, "And how are your bowels acting?" "Not so sporty, Doctor, not so sporty," she replied.

Early one morning a colored woman knocked at the back door. The door bell rang at the same time. Doctor was dressing, and absentmindedly hurried to answer these calls clad only in his BVD's. The colored woman reported the incident to a white neighbor. "Dr. Rhine made me so 'shamed this morning. He made his 'pearance at de back do' in his BVD's and then transferred hisself to de front do' de same way."

A little boy had been quite brave while having some necessary work done. Doctor rewarded him by giving him a nickel. The child's mother said, "Now son, what do you say to the Doctor?" The little fellow looked puzzled, studied a minute, and then flashing an enlightened smile at the Doctor said, "Gimme another one!"

Dr. Rhine carries a large stock of all kinds of medicine. He fills most of his own prescriptions which he types out by the two-finger system upon an old-time Oliver of over forty years vintage. (One specialist to whom Doctor referred many patients wrote a letter of protest when Dr. Rhine stopped using a purple typewriter ribbon some years ago.)

Dr. Rhine gets many requests for medicine through the mail. Hardly a day passes that his post office box does not hold a letter from a patient requesting "Some of those pills like you gave me two years ago;" "Doc, please send me another bottle of that bad-tasting medicine you gave me for that pain I had in my shoulder," or "Doc, I'm just hurting all over, please send me whatever you think I need."

One morning he received some such request, boxed up the medicine and mailed it. Neither the rural mail carriers, the postmaster nor the postmistress could determine to whom it was addressed. Doctor happened to return to the office about the time they had given up. He was asked to whom he was mailing the medicine. He couldn't remember, looked at the address and said, "Let me run back to my office and read that card again. I can't read my own handwriting."

On May 17, 1946, his friends and patients honored him with a celebration, which was attended by an estimated 8,000 people. Doctor's former patients from many states availed themselves of this opportunity to renew old acquaintances and pay tribute to their physician of past years. Many members of the medical profession in Arkansas took time out of their busy lives to drive to the little town of Thornton to attend this testimonial to the "jack-leg country doctor" as Dr. Rhine dubs himself.

Even on his "day of days" Dr. Rhine spent the morning seeing patients and doing office work. After the festivities were over, he made a long trip to the country on a call.

When he became quite ill in February, 1947, at which time he spent nine days in the Baptist Hospital in Little Rock, his attending physicians advised him that his condition would necessitate a complete rest over a period of months. On his birthday, April 2, he returned to his office. He asserted that that was the best birthday celebration he ever had. His most valued gift that birthday was a collection of Happy Birthday greetings made by the first-grade school children, who presented them to him.

March 27, 1948 signalled the completion of fifty years in the practice of medicine. In September, he celebrated this event by entertaining the Ouachita County Medical Society and other doctors from all over the state at a home barbecue. On May 17, 1949 Dr. Rhine hopes to mark the end of his first fifty years of practice in Thornton.

Dr. Rhine, who had organized the Calhoun County Medical Society during his first year of practice, and helped to organize the Dallas County Society, was Calhoun County's representative at the reorganization of the Arkansas State Medical Association as far back as 1903.

As years passed and the number of doctors in Calhoun County became too few to merit a county organization, he joined the Ouachita County Medical Society, of which he served as president in 1943.

He has always appreciated the privilege of membership in these local associations, and values highly the opportunities the associations afford for medical fellowship. Although in order to attend meetings Doctor must make the twenty mile drive to Camden after a hard day's work, and then frequently has work that keeps him busy many hours after the meetings, he attends every meeting possible.

Dr. Rhine has been a member of the Southern Medical Association since its organization and a member of the American Medical Association for over forty years.

Dr. Rhine has served on the staff of the Camden Hospital, making the forty-mile round-trip to attend staff meetings.

The Doctor especially enjoys his association with young medical students whom he quite often takes along on his calls. He encourages them to examine his patients, asks their viewpoint, discusses the case with them and explains his diagnosis and treatment. He is always willing to lend them books from his library and has just recently given a young surgeon a large donation of instruments.

FIFTY YEARS OF MEDICINE IN RETROSPECT

In these fifty-one years of practice Dr. Rhine has taken few vacations. He took time off in 1904 to attend the St. Louis World's Fair. In 1906, with his mother, he made a trip back to their former home in Lexington, Mississippi. This was his last real vacation. Since then, fox hunts and family reunions have afforded what relaxation he has sought to take.

During his half-century as a general practitioner, Dr. Rhine has lost little time from his work because of ill health, and that he gave grudgingly – the six months' period in 1924 due to a paralysis of the right side, the six week period in 1947, and a few other times when a few days' or weeks' illness slowed him down. Even then, while he was convalescing, his patients often came to his home for medicine, which members of his family would dispense under Doctor's direction.

During his years of practice, Doctor has witnessed many changes in the ways and means of treating diseases. When he began practicing, only a few germs were recognized by the profession as causes of disease. They were typhoid, dyphtheria, and pneumonia. Very little tissue was examined to make diagnosis. The mosquito was not known as the carrier for malaria, which was thought to be caused by impure drinking water taken from ponds, lakes, etc., or from inhaling impure air wafted from swampy areas. No screens were used to protect people from flies and mosquitoes. No precautions were taken in the disposal of the secretions from typhoid, dysentary, tuberculosis or any other contagious or infectious disease. People were isolated only for smallpox, the only disease for the prevention of which vaccinations were given. Dr. Rhine has experienced the advance of medicine from such old pharmaceuticals as Dover's powders, paregoric, laudanum, mercury with chalk, calomel, quinine, powered opium, gum opium, tincture nux vomica, tincture of iron, Fowler's solution of arsenic, may apple, Norwood's tincture of veratrum, tincture of aconite, bromide of potash, chlorate of potash and chloral hydrate, to the modern miracle workers such as sulpha drugs, penicillin, streptomycin, auromycin, duomycin, and the wide range of vitamins.

In fighting ignorance and superstition among his people, Doctor has spent untold hours, pleading with them individually and in groups, begging them to screen their homes, to clean up and burn the rubbish which provided places for flies and mosquitoes. He has campaigned against the old-time open toilets and advocated the installation of the closed aseptic toilet. He has talked with mid-wives, trying to teach them the importance of cleanliness and how to care for the newborn infant.

One of his difficult tasks has been in convincing people of the necessity of vaccinations to prevent disease. They had a fear of such procedures, and it took years of counseling and actual demonstration before Doctor could convince many to have these precautions taken. Oftentimes he would make long trips to other parts of the country to hold clinics for the examination of pre-school children and to give the preventive shots for diphtheria. Not one person would come. In one community, soon after he had held just such an unsuccessful clinic, a child died of diphtheria. Then the people came in droves.

He has many stories of the things people used as "cures" for their ills. Children have appeared at his office with hair twisted and tied so tightly they could hardly close their mouths. Parents thought this a remedy that would hold up a "fallen soft palate" (sore throat). Once an old woman appeared with rusty nails on her person. She explained that the nails were "magnetized" and helped to keep her blood pressure up.

One of the Doctor's amusing experiences with the widespread ignorance of the times occurred when it became necessary to send an old fellow to the hospital. This old man was very dirty, and Doctor recommended that he be bathed. The patient offered strenuous objection. He finally permitted the scrubbing of all but his back. He feared that the application of water to his back would "rust out his back bone." Doctor finally overcame his resistance by giving him a bottle of soda-pop and by promising to apply a lubricant to his spine, should the joints of his backbone suffer any ill effects from the scrubbing.

To advance his own store of knowledge, Doctor did postgraduate study at New Orleans Polyclinic and Tulane University Medical School in 1902. In 1918 he attended New York Polyclinic. He has always tried to keep abreast of the newest and best methods of treatment. His medical library contains about seven hundred and fifty volumes, and he subscribes to *The Year Book of General Medicine, The Yearbook of Mayo Papers, Digest of Treatment,* Saunders' *Medical Clinics,* all yearly volumes, and other new books of special interest. He tries to devote some time each day to study.

These fifty-one years of practice have endeared "Doctor" to thousands of people. No family reunion around about is complete without Dr. Rhine. He feels a part of these families and they feel that he is one of them. Today, he is practicing in one family for which he has practiced during six generations, in one hundred and five families for four generations. He has one hundred fourteen patients for whom he has practiced for over forty years. Five of these have been his patients for over fifty years. There are fourteen families in which Doctor has delivered both father and mother and all their progeny.

On Christmas, 1945, Doctor Rhine presented a Christmas basket to the families for which he had practiced for forty years or more, where husband and wife or where either husband or wife were still living. There were eighty-five of these families, and he drove to each home and made the presentation personally.

The Doctor's territory today exceeds 2,000 square miles in area and at the age of seventy-three he continues "on call" twenty-four hours a day. He often says he "must be getting old," for he just "can't seem to be able to work but twenty-four hours out of the twenty-four." He rarely ever refuses to make a call, day or night, rain or shine, sleet or snow. There are very few homes in Calhoun County in which he has not practiced.

36

THERE WAS TIME TO BE AN
ACTIVE CITIZEN, TOO

Dr. Rhine, always civic minded, has untiringly worked to better the community in which he lives, and in many ways his influence and help have been extended beyond the territory in which he practices.

He was a director of the Bank of Thornton from its organization in 1905 until 1931, when it closed its doors. During many of these years he served as President and as Vice-President of this institution. His particular function was to render advice on the loans to be made by the bank. Knowing well all those who might have any dealings with the bank, he was familiar with their characteristics of thrift, honesty and ability. On the basis of the fact that farmers in his territory were bringing in their produce from the fields by sacks and baskets instead of by wagonloads, Dr. Rhine warned of the impending economic disaster long before the crash occurred.

Education and the betterment of the local, county and state schools have always been dear to his heart. He was a member of the board of directors of the Thornton School for thirty-five years, serving as president during fifteen years of that time. With the exception of one occasion when he was too ill to attend, Dr. Rhine has accepted with much pleasure the request of the graduates to participate in every one of the thirty-five graduation programs, at which he awarded honors, delivered the diplomas or addressed the class. He is always invited to the Junior-Senior banquet, and yearly the children of the lower grades ask him, usually with success, to attend their picnic – perhaps because Dr. Rhine always provides a special treat of fruit and candy on such occasions. On Halloween he is the person selected, by the students, to crown the Queen.

Having presided at the birth of about 75% of the student body at the present time and for several years back, he is called on in any and all activities. Many times he lessened the terrors of that first day in school for some little fellow. A reassuring pat on the head by Dr. Rhine, accompanied by a nickel to buy candy, soon dries the initiate's tears.

He is active in PTA work and is called on to address these meetings in all the schools of the county. The hot lunches for school children was a project he promoted some time before they became a part of the government program. He was instrumental also in peacefully bringing about the consolidation of school districts in Calhoun County. He has advocated better school buildings, and has spent hours of his time in talking, planning and working for better educational conditions. As a member of the school board, he sought qualified teachers and a curriculum that met the needs of the students. He contributed much toward introducing home economic and agriculture departments into the Thornton School. He has spent his time and money, freely, in supplying the educational needs in both the white and colored schools and has actively worked for higher standards of scholarship. Incidental to this, he has for years given prizes or medals to the outstanding students in each grade of Thornton School. Dr. Rhine has always evinced special interest in helping students of promise, and while he takes no credit for their success in life, he is happy to have afforded them aid and encouragement in the pursuit of their careers.

A joiner and active member of civic organizations, Dr. Rhine became a Mason in 1904 and is active in the local lodge. He recieved his 32° in October 1908 and was made a member of the Shrine in November, 1908. At one time he was a member of the Elks and Odd Fellows, and in his mill years of practice he was a member of HooHoo, a lumber organization.

Doctor has been a consistent advocate of wild life conservation and has been active in organizing game preserves throughout Arkansas. At one time he imported pheasants to increase the gaming possibilities of South Arkansas. While he is a member of the local deer hunters' club, his greatest sport is fox hunting, and he has been awarded an honorary life membership in the State Fox Hunters' Association. For the past several years, he has had little time for this sport, but he always keeps a few fox hounds at his home and enjoys raising pups for the other hunters to train and run. Formerly, he was an ardent fancier of bird dogs; some of his dogs won all-state prizes. He vaccinates his own and other people's dogs, doctors them in various ways, and says that when he gets too old to doctor folks, he will take up veterinary medicine and grow wealthy. Recently, a friend's fine dog got run over by a car. Both legs on its left side were broken. A veterinarian was not available, so Doctor set the dog's legs and put him in a swing.

Doctor has seen much service as a veterinarian in other capacities. He has vaccinated as many as seventy-five hogs for cholera in a day – and horses and cows also have recuperated under his ministrations.

Naturally, good roads have been one of the Doctor's greatest needs and he has done much towards their improvement in South Arkansas. When the State was building Highway 79 between Fordyce and Bearden, Doctor Rhine was able to secure the right-of-way for several miles without cost to the State. Many people along this route were contentious about granting the right-of-way through their land. Doctor persuaded them to cooperate and cancelled their doctor bills in payment. He has made many cash donations towards building roads and keeps the proper persons informed as to the condition of the roads in his territory.

Doctor is very much interested in the forestry program in this State and never misses an opportunity to give his assistance in rebuilding the forests of South Arkansas.

Always on the alert for means of improving the living standards of his people, he has encouraged and contributed to community and county fairs. For a number of years Dr. Rhine kept the finest of Duroc Jersey hogs, using them for breeding to raise the quality of livestock in the community. One of his hogs, weighing over 1,000 pounds when dressed, was declared the grand champion at an Arkansas State Livestock show some years ago.

For a number of years the Doctor has kept high grade chickens, giving the eggs to anyone who wanted to improve their poultry flocks.

Dr. Rhine is a member of the local Methodist Church and contributes to the twelve white and colored churches in his immediate community. He helps in keeping up five cemeteries and in years past, before burial associations were formed, he contributed to the burial of many poor people. Many times after having practiced for a patient over long periods without pay, when death finally came, the Doctor bought the clothes and casket, thus, as he says, "burying his own mistakes."

Doctor avoids petty politics but always takes a firm stand when convinced of the rightness of a measure. His influence throughout his large territory is a commodity much sought after by political aspirants. He rarely takes an active part in any campaign, preferring to do his "politicking" in a quiet way, putting in a good word for "his" candidate here and there on his professional rounds. During this past year, however, he departed from this rule by assuming the chairmanship of a club boosting a young man for a state office. Doctor had known this gentleman all his life. He believed in him, worked for him, and was gratified in seeing him win by a record majority, carrying seventy-four of the seventy-five counties in the State.

Family doctor, citizen, and friend, T. E. Rhine, M. D. compounds these three words into an enviable life that has had abundant reward in friends, fellowship and professional stature.

Ed Rhine, a member of the first graduating class of Fordyce High School in 1895.

Dr. T. E. Rhine in 1900 when he became physician and surgeon for Stout Lumber Company in Thornton, Arkansas.

Early days on horseback—Dr. Rhine astride his favorite horse, Bill, bought in Missouri in 1906. Pill bags and slicker can be seen behind the saddle.

Time out for a picnic with friends in the early 1900's.

Dr. Rhine with his nephew, Rhine Condray, about 1911.

The original Rhine home, built in Thornton around 1905. Dr. Rhine is standing on the porch.

The black string tie became the only tie that he would *ever* wear throughout his life. He was in his late 30's when this picture was made.

First Lieutenant T. E. Rhine, 1918, served in the United States Army Medical Corp and was stationed in England for a short time.

An afternoon outing in the early 1900's. Dr. Rhine is on the back row.

Dr. Rhine raised hunting dogs . . .   and hogs.

His favorite picture of the girls, Susan and Virginia in the back, l. to r., Pat in the basket.

Dr. Rhine (right) with his good friends, Roy Wise, the postmaster and John Harris, a Primitive Baptist preacher; the identity of the man standing next to Dr. Rhine is not known.

The everpresent pill bag and Mr. Asbury Stell, grandfather of the Hunter Parham children and the Tom Stell children.

The Bank Building in Thornton. His office occupied two rooms at the back of the building.

The Thornton Deer Club was founded in 1936. Dr. Rhine was a charter member. This picture is of the camp near Princeton, 1944. The members are: (standing, from left) Kitchen Brandon, John Tomlinson, Hastings Marks, Fred Tomlinson, Edward Womble, C. Scott, Frank Scott, Billy Tomlinson, Larry Warren and Woodrow Manning, (kneeling) Earl Scott and Sidney Holmes.

An early reunion photograph of the Billy Hearnsberger family. Dr. Rhine is standing in the middle of the back row.

The same Hearnsberger family and more at a reunion in 1939. Dr. Rhine and Pat (face showing) are sitting on the left. Mr. Jim Easterling is the tall gentleman on the right.

The Bus Hearnsberger family about 1936. Dr. Rhine delivered all eleven children and got paid for all of them. All are still living except the youngest, who died at birth. Mr. and Mrs. Hearnsberger are in the back row on the right.

Jim and Betty Easterling.   Mr. and Mrs. Howell Easterling.

The Cone family gathering. Dr. Rhine is seated third from the right. Victor Cone is standing in front of the tree. Sue H. Hodnett is standing on the extreme left.

"It really isn't what the flowers cost or even if they are arranged properly, it is the love behind them that matters."

JO ANN JAMES CAYCE

THORNTON, ARKANSAS

I am fifty-three years old and my memory is not as good as it used to be, but I think Dr. Rhine was a person can't any of us really forget. We all have our own memories of him. Some of 'em are very personal, some are very touching and some are very funny.

Dr. Rhine didn't deliver me. I was six years old, almost, when we moved to Thornton. The first person we got acquainted with was Dr. Rhine and then the preacher. My mother and daddy [Jewel and Gurt James] were just almost flat broke when they moved to Thornton with me and my brother, Bill T. He was a year older than me. This was in 1939. They put in a little grocery store. My daddy used to laugh and say he had forty-four dollars to go in business on when they came, but that was more than they left behind, because they moved from Holly Springs to Thornton and their business had just gone broke over there.

Dr. Rhine was a regular customer for gas in his old car. He used to pull up at the pumps, and when my mother or daddy saw him pull up, they got out there as quick as they could, because they knew he was on the way somewhere to doctor somebody sick. All the time they were putting gas in his car, they were telling him the complaints they had or complaints with us children. Dr. Rhine would sometimes reach in the car and pull out a bottle of pills. I wondered years later, when I got a little sense, if maybe he pulled us out some dog medicine 'cause he always carried his dog medicine and his people medicine in the same bag. He never did give us anything that hurt us, I don't guess, because we grew like weeds.

I had a lot of kidney problems when I was a child. My mother would have me put a specimen in a fruit jar, and that was before the days when we knew he just needed four, five or six drops. She would send me to his office

47

carrying this fruit jar full of urine in a five pound paper sack. I would go over there, and we always took the last chair in Dr. Rhine's office, and every time he saw somebody, we moved up one chair. The ones that were left standing without a chair if his office was full would line up around the wall to the door. If there were more people than would go in that line, then the rest of them would stand outside.

Dr. Rhine never got in a hurry. He always had to take so much time fussin' at everybody. He'd call out and say, "What are you fussin' about?" But it wasn't the patient that was fussin' when they got to his office, it was him. I always carried my big jug of urine in, and he would take one look at it. He never did tell me, "You don't have to bring this much." He would go to the back door and pour most of it out. Then he would shake it once or twice and come back in with what was left. I used to think, as a child, that he didn't even know what he was doing. I used to tell Mother, "It's no use in me taking that urine. (I always said 'pee.') He just goes to the back door and pours it out." When he came back in, he would shake a little bit on a slide, and he would do his little test. He always gave me the same medicine.

If I went over there for something else, I always used to think he gave me the same medicine he gave me when I had kidney problems. Of course, he didn't. He knew what he was doing, but it was a big joke in town that Dr. Rhine gave everybody, pregnant women and impotent men medicine out of the same bottle.

I used to get so tickled at him when I would take my younger brother and sister to see him. My younger brother, Jimmy, was born when I was fourteen years old. My little sister, Barbara Sue, had been born the year before that, and Dr. Rhine delivered her and her twin, who died, at home. My mother had such a hard time and Dr. Rhine was growing older. My mother's heart had begun to bother her, (she was forty years old) so she went down to Dr. R. B. Robbins at Camden to have Jimmy. Dr. Robbins examined her all eight months of care, and he delivered him in the hospital at Camden.

I used to take my little brother and sister over when they would get an ear infection or a bad cold, and he would get my little sister up and he would just talk to her and love her and hug her and ask if she was being a good girl, because he delivered her. But my little brother, whom he didn't deliver, a year after my little sister, he'd just ignore him completely. He would finally look at him with what he called his "mean eye" and would ask, "What's the matter with you?"

We would get a kick out of it, because he was jealous to the day he died of any other doctor seeing any of his patients. If you went to a doctor out of town, even if you couldn't get Dr. Rhine or he was down sick in bed, and it wasn't your fault that you had to go to somebody else, it would make him mad if he found it out. Those were some of the best kept secrets in town, how many times people slipped off up to Dr. Atkinson at Fordyce to see if what Dr. Rhine had told them was true. Usually, when Dr. Harry Atkinson found out that Dr. Rhine was your doctor, he'd say, "I don't want nothing to do with you. I'm not going to get in no war with Dr. Rhine. You believe what he tells you. Go on back home and quit worrying about it and take his medicine."

When the war hit, my mother and daddy put in beer over to their grocery store and started selling hamburgers, and they even had a dance floor over there. Dr. Rhine wouldn't come over and buy his gas anymore because he said he didn't patronize places that sold beer. My daddy was a big fox hunter and about the only time he ever spoke to Daddy was when they were fox hunting, for the longest time. He finally got over his little mad spell about Daddy putting in beer. He said he knew a man had to make a living, but as big and healthy as my daddy was, he thought there was better ways to make a living. Dr. Rhine didn't stay mad at anybody long. Everybody was his friend and everybody loved him, and we all depended on him.

Kids over at school would get down sick, and it was nothing for Dr. Rhine to come to the school and see about them or sew them up. If a kid fell on the seesaw or slide, they'd just leave him there on the ground and call Dr. Rhine. It never dawned on anybody to pick the child up and take him to Dr. Rhine's office.

Dr. Rhine was always after some good driver in town that was sober enough on Saturday night to take him on his emergency calls. My brother, after he got big enough to drive, he drove Dr. Rhine a lot. People in Thornton used to feel very honored if Dr. Rhine called 'em and asked 'em to go with him on a call, when he got older. Before he began to ask someone to drive him on his calls, it was a big joke that if you saw a car coming on the shoulder of the road or halfway in the ditch, usually with only one headlight burning, everybody knew it was Dr. Rhine. He stayed on the country roads so much that the gravel kept his lights out half the time. He drove nearly in the ditch, because he had doctored so many drunks from accidents that he knew how many there were on the highway, and he wasn't taking any chances.

One time a state trooper stopped Dr. Rhine. He was a new officer in the county, and he didn't know how Dr. Rhine drove, and he didn't know how tired and haggard he looked all the time. He stopped Dr. Rhine, and Dr. Rhine got out of the car and in his usual gruff voice asked, "Whadda ya want? Whadda ya want?" He sounded like he was about half drunk, and the policeman pushed him up against the car and was going to search him. It got out that the policeman had handled Dr. Rhine pretty rough and boy, the people got riled up. The county judge was called and he put so much heat on the state police commissioner that he transferred that policeman right quick. He had accused Dr. Rhine of being drunk! I don't know if he smelled his breath or what they did in those days. That's been forty years ago. Anyway, that policeman wasn't around here very long.

I was just a young kid, maybe eight years old, when the war broke out. There were a lot of soldiers in a camp outside of town, doing maneuvers. A lot of the soldiers came in town on Friday and Saturday nights to play the music and dance and drink beer. There was always some trouble going on over there at my mother's and daddy's place. When one of the soldiers got in a fight or got hit or one of the black people got cut or had stab wounds or even shot, my daddy always put them in the pick-up truck and took them down to Dr. Rhine's. He would come in Dr. Rhine's yard blowing the horn, and, of course, the house would be dark because it would be midnight or later. Finally, Dr. Rhine would turn on the light and he'd come to the door in his BVD tops and pulling up his pants. He would be so mad when he would find out it was some drunk or some fight that could have been avoided if people was home in bed where they ought to be. I never heard him cuss, but he could say more ugly things not to use cuss words than anybody I've ever heard.

One night, a man named Rich Avery, who lived in town, shot his wife. She had been doing what she ought not to have done, I guess, I don't remember. I just remember the event. She was coming down the alley toward the store, and Rich was up in a tree. He shot her with rat shot all in the stomach. Us kids heard her hollering. We were out at the back of the store, playing, even as late as it was, and the music going and cars were parked everywhere. We went up the alley and there she lay, pulling up her clothes and crying, "I'm shot! I'm shot bad! Get me Dr. Rhine!"

My brother and I went back down to the store. It was probably midnight. Daddy and Mother were really busy on Saturday night, Mother making hamburgers and Daddy selling and collecting and serving people. We finally got them to go up to see about her, and Daddy said, "We have to put her in the truck and take her to Dr. Rhine." He backed up his little pick-up truck, I think it was a '41 model, to where she was and loaded her in it and took her to Dr. Rhine's house. Mrs. Rhine had a quilt box just inside the screened-in porch, so a couple of men got her under the arms and laid her up on the quilt box.

She was bleeding like a stuck hog. Dr. Rhine was fussing and mad. Us little kids was watching and thinking that was the greatest thing in the world. Dr. Rhine told Mrs. Rhine to get him a pan and put some water in it. He took a thing that looked like a thing to pull teeth. He pulled up her clothes, and she was shot with rat shot all in the stomach—the little pellets was just right under the skin. She was hollering and screaming, "Am I gonna die? Am I gonna die?" Dr. Rhine was digging those shot out and putting 'em in the pan Mrs. Rhine was holding. As he kept on digging, he'd say, "Yeah, you're gonna die. You probably won't even live to get home." He was so mad at being woke up at that time of night, and he knew it was all uncalled for. When he got through, she was as bloody as she could be, and he was, too. Blood was running all down the quilt box and on the floor. Of course, she didn't have any money, and she looked up at my dad and said, "Mr. Gurt, would you loan me two dollars?" Dr. Rhine says, "You don't owe me a thing, but don't you come down here any more in this condition." He just preached her a long sermon about how she ought to be at home where she ought to be.

That's the way that everybody that Daddy took over there from the place that ever got hurt fighting or doing something they ought not to do, Dr. Rhine always preached them a sermon before they left, on morals—how they ought to live and how they ought to do and they was old enough to have some sense and he was tired of fooling with them, and the next time they got in this condition, he wasn't going to touch them, he wasn't going to do one thing in the world to save their life. He'd just go on and on about it. When they would start off the porch, he'd turn out the light before they hardly got down the steps.

Another time, in the afternoon, a black man got knifed in the stomach at our place. They laid him out on a bench in front of the cafe. Dr. Rhine happened to drive by, saw the trouble and stopped. He cleaned the cut and clamped it together right there without any anesthetic. The man begged Daddy to please pay Dr. Rhine for him, because he knew that Dr. Rhine would not take his word that he would pay him later. But before Daddy could say, "No," Dr. Rhine said there would be no charge, because he didn't have to make a special trip, and also, because he knew the man didn't have money to pay him or Daddy either. Besides, the man was so ornery, he deserved the pain and suffering.

The cook at the cafe had lived with her boyfriend for many years. He mostly just lounged around the back door of the cafe. During World War II, when it appeared that he might be drafted, Daddy suggested to her that if he went to war and something happened to her friend, she would receive no benefits, unless they were married. With that, she told him to go home and put on a clean shirt. When he got back, Daddy had Brother John Harris, a Primitive Baptist preacher to come marry them. Just as the ceremony was about to begin, Dr. Rhine stopped in and stayed for the wedding. He bought a sack of flour for the bride and groom as a wedding present.

The socializing in those days was going to church revivals in the summer. If you were lucky, your boyfriend would walk home with you, or boys and girls would sit on the church steps for a while and visit. My brother was lucky enough to have an old A-model car. One night after church, we all went down to Dr. Rhine's house, hoping he would let us come in. Sometimes, he would have watermelons where people had paid him. It was always our greatest thrill if Dr. Rhine had gotten a load of watermelon or cantaloupes and he would let Pat bring us in the yard, and he would cut melons for us to eat. This particular night after church, we drove by the Rhine's and Dr. and Mrs. Rhine were sitting on the porch. Pat stuck her head out the window and yelled, "Daddy, can I go with the crowd to get something to drink?" Dr. Rhine answered, "There's plenty of water in the well!"

We have laughed about this for years. Everytime anybody suggested going for a cold drink, we would always say, "There's plenty of water in the well." The years passed and I met Hartsel Cayce. His father was C. H. Cayce, a Primitive Baptist or Hardshell Baptist preacher. [He was the editor and publisher of the Primitive Baptist paper.] I had really known

Hartsel all of my life, but not well until he came out of the army in 1947. We went together a couple of years and then we married. I didn't find out until I started going to the Primitive Baptist church that Dr. Rhine was a strong supporter of that church. He would find out that they were having a church meeting and would come up by the printing office and he would always slip a twenty dollar bill to Mrs. Cayce. He would tell her that was to help with the meeting. A lot of times, he would bring a ham or whatever he wanted to give for the meeting. He never got to come to church, but he was always giving. I don't know if he gave to other churches or not. [He financially supported every church in the area, both black and white.] He passed a lot of compliments on that church. He always said that church had a lot of good people, and he wanted to do anything he could to help 'em with their meeting.

Dr. Rhine really did mean a lot to this town. To somebody that had absolutely nothing and was down, destitute and ill, Dr. Rhine would come, and they knew that he would give them the best help and the best care and give them the best medicine that he had. Even if he paid $75.00 for the bottle of medicine that he poured out of, he would only sell it for 50 cents, for a big bottle. I don't know how in the world Mrs. Rhine put up with it, when he could have been a rich man, and she could have lived in a mansion. As far as I know, she never fussed at Dr. Rhine about all the people in this town that owed him, or the little dabs that he charged. If a widow-woman went in there with nothing and when she started to leave, she'd ask, "Dr. Rhine, how much do I owe you?" Dr. Rhine would say, "You get out of here!"

I don't know how many times the crippled and the blind and little children with itch and maybe some little boy with his dog that had stepped on a piece of glass would get comfort and care from him. It was nothing for black and white to wait together with sick animals or whatever in his office. Nobody ever thought about it in those days that he had an integrated waiting room and office. He saw everybody alike. When it came your turn, you went in and got doctored. If a little boy sat in front of you with an old mangy hound dog for Dr. Rhine to see his foot or whatever, well, Dr. Rhine took the dog.

The only thing that came first was emergencies. I have been in his office waiting with my little brother and sister and maybe a call would come on the telephone from someone needing Dr. Rhine right quick, and he would tell you, "Y'all can wait right here, or y'all can come back after lunch. I've got to go see Miz So and So out here—about to have a baby," or this, that and the other. Dr. Rhine was just out and gone. You would be left sitting there or you could go home and come back, and he could remember just exactly whose turn it was. If his office was full at lunchtime and Mrs. Rhine had lunch ready, he didn't quit and go home. He'd just keep right on working 'til he got that bunch worked off, and then he'd pull the door to and run get him a bite to eat. He never had any regular office hours. You just knew when his car was out front, he was there, and when his car wasn't there, well, he wasn't. In later years, he began to walk to the office and walk back home for the exercise. He had an old bare light bulb hanging on a long cord from the ceiling. The room had real high ceilings. When he went in, he always turned on this light, and you could see it through the window. You would know that he was there.

He had a little old typewriter that used to fascinate me as a child to stand and watch him. He had his reading glasses down on his nose, and he used the hunt and peck system with two fingers, but he could go like light'nin' on that typewriter. All the time he was typing the label for a medicine bottle, he was whistling through his teeth. He never quit his silly whistle unless he asked you something. I've been in there a lot of times and he would say, "Now, you tell me where it hurts." While you'd be telling him where it hurt and how you felt, he'd be whistling (no tune) through his teeth.

The woman who told me this story is still living here in town, and she is probably eighty years old. She had a next door neighbor who was a very sophisticated lady, and she always had on her corset with her hair fixed and her make-up on just right. She was a school teacher, and she was just a very proper lady. She said that one day her neighbor told her, "I've got hemorrhoids so bad, I just can't hardly stand it. I don't know what in the world I'm going to do."

"I'll tell you. Dr. Rhine is the best with hemorrhoids that ever was."

That was nothing new for people to say that. Whatever you had, somebody was bound to say, "Dr. Rhine is the best you ever saw at getting rid of migraine headaches" or "Dr. Rhine is the best you ever saw at getting rid of head lice" or "Dr. Rhine can cure the itch when can't anybody else." Just whatever you had anybody would tell you Dr. Rhine could cure it. So she said to her, "Why don't you go down to Dr. Rhine? He can get rid of those hemorrhoids in nothing flat." So her neighbor went down there. It wasn't but about an hour 'til she came back, and said, "Dr. Rhine wants me to bring a woman with me, so he can examine my hemorrhoids." So she went to the office with her and when they went in, Dr. Rhine just laid back his old chair. (He had an old chair and when he pushed a button, it leaned back, and when he pushed another button, it would just fall down flat. He could almost disjoint you, because he never thought to tell you he was fixing to lay you back. He just jerked the button and the chair fell back. It used to be our delight, when Dr. Rhine left his front door open, to slip in and us kids would lay back on Dr. Rhine's old "collapsible" chair-that's what we called it. If we heard him stop out front, we would beat it out the back door of his office.)

Anyway they went down to his office. Dr. Rhine put her up in his old collapsible chair and he got her legs all up and looked at her hemorrhoids. He turned around to his old pot that he kept all of his knives in, and she said he just got him a scalpel in his hand and while he had her behind all turned up, he just cut her hemorrhoids off right quick. The blood was just pouring, and he took his old towel that he used for everything. (If you went there and had a risin that had bursted, he used that same old towel. At least it seemed that way—they were always dirty looking. I'm sure that he took them home and Mrs. Rhine washed them. I think she is a saint for just having done that one thing.) Anyway, he grabbed up his dirty old towel and started sapping up the blood. He finally let her up and told her, "You go home and stay off your feet for two or three days, and keep that corset off." He had told her when he sent her after another woman, he says, "You go home and take that corset off." She couldn't get up. He had just paralyzed her! He had done a hemorrhoidectomy right there without any anesthetic or anything, and she was in tears. When Dr. Rhine punched the button and the chair came up, and she was in a sitting position, she said, "Aaaahhh" and fainted right there. Dr. Rhine didn't get excited or anything. He held a bottle under her nose until she came to. They had walked down to Dr. Rhine's office. The patient couldn't even hardly get to the front door, much less walk up the hill home. She told Dr. Rhine, "We walked down here. I don't believe she's going to be able to make it home." Dr. Rhine told them, "Get in the car out there, and I'll take you home." He let them out at the gate, and she got her in the house and got her to bed. She said if her neighbor ever had any more hemorrhoid trouble, she didn't know it. It was possible she had some and was too scared to tell anybody about it, afraid that word would get back to Dr. Rhine.

It was nothing for him to perform major surgery in his office. Sometimes he would give you a shot and sometimes, he would just go right at it. One time, when he sewed up my foot, he didn't give me a shot to deaden it. My mother told him, "Dr. Rhine, you've got to deaden that foot! She can't stand to have that foot sewed up." (I had stepped on a broken coke bottle, barefooted.) Dr. Rhine said, "The shot will hurt just as bad as sewing it up, so you just hush. I know how to do this job." He then sewed up my foot, and it like to have killed me, and I hated him after that for the longest time, 'til I needed him again.

He did things that, I'm sure if we had a record of it, that they didn't even do in hospitals, under anesthetic. He was that kind of person. If he saw a job that needed to be done, he didn't think or even entertain the idea "Can I do it?" He'd say, "We're gonna do it, and that's that."

With his determination and his confidence in hisself, he was just about a super doctor, that's all. He would do anything that needed to be done, and he did it without a nurse, without a receptionist. He didn't have an accountant or a bookkeeper. He never made an appointment. He answered his own telephone. How could any doctor do the things you saw Dr. Rhine do every day? It seems, today, looking back, like it was impossible, and you ask yourself, "Was he really like that? Is it true—all the things I remember about him? Was he *really* like that?" I know all of the memories I have of him, and all of the things he did, even the little things I saw him do, it seems like he was one of the most unusual people that I knew and was a profound example to me in my teenage years. His belief was that you could do anything if you made up your mind and if you were determined.

Dr. Rhine would go days without sleep—maybe get home and just barely get in bed and some women would call him that she was in hard labor, and off he would go, way over to Holly Springs or anywhere. It wasn't the distance, it was the time it took to get there that worried him. In those days, people would fall with a heart attack, and when he would get there, their heart would be running away. (I saw him do this on my mother.) My mothers heart was just about to tear out of her body, and he put his thumb on her whatever on her neck on one side and his fingers on the other side, and he held that so tight that he quieted her heart down. Every once in a while, he would let up, then he would hold it tight, then let up. I know that was something he discovered he could do for hisself. But if he ever told anybody about the things he discovered or even wrote them down, or was impressed by his own heroic deeds, I never knew that. He just did what he did and went on about his business. He didn't even surprise hisself with what he could do. That's the only thing I could say about it.

He could wrastle a baby out that should have been born by Caesarean. He could just put his hands up around that little body and guide it right out—the woman having all kinds of complications and not being near big enough to deliver. He would, by his sheer willing it out, bend and twist that baby, and it would arrive safe, all because Dr. Rhine was determined that baby was goin' to be borned and borned all right, and the mother was goin' to survive. You could hardly fail with Dr. Rhine managing your case. He fought so hard for you that you had to fight for yourself.

Mrs. Cayce, my mother-in-law, went with him to help deliver babies in a lot of cases. One was an illegitimate baby of a young girl here in town. The girl had played a basketball game the night before. She had kept her pregnancy hidden from the town. This girl was a tiny girl, and she had kept herself laced down with a corset and went to school every day. So when her time came for delivery, she had kept herself so confined, the muscles hadn't had time to expand like they should have, and Dr. Rhine had to practically will that baby out.

My own mother had twins. One of the babies was dead and in a capsule. The other one was borned alive. Had Dr. Rhine not got that little baby that was in a capsule and dead for several weeks out without bursting the membrane, it would surely have killed my mother with renic or septicemic poison.

I remember Mrs. Cora Strickland when she fell up to her house on her sleeping porch. She fell over backwards and hit her head. She was out cold. They sent for Dr. Rhine, and he came up. The first thing he wanted was cold water. He poured that cold water all over that woman and shook her about three times and blowed in her face and gave her a shot of something. She was up and cooked supper that night. He knew just exactly what to do.

In the late 1950's, my husband and I sponsored a young couple to come over from London, England. We found them a house and gave the man a job at the printing office. He and his wife had a young baby. They hadn't been here four or five weeks when the young woman developed a small risin on the side of her face. As the days went by, this risin got larger and larger. It looked like she had half an orange on the side of her face, it was so big. She didn't know a doctor, of course, and they didn't have very much money. She wanted to know what she should do. I told her, "We have a local doctor here in town. He's old, but you won't find any better." I took her to Dr. Rhine's office, and when wc got there, there was the usual large bunch waiting to see him. I told her we would have to wait our turn.

We sat down in the chairs. I could see her looking around at the old books, the old desk piled high with papers that had been there so long they were turning yellow. Dr. Rhine always had invoices for medicines stacked in boxes. Whether he ever looked at an invoice and checked to see if he had really gotten the stuff, I don't know. I don't know how in the world he ever made out his income tax return, because he didn't have time to keep books. I never thought about those things until I went into business for myself.

I could see this young girl from London, England taking in all of this stuff. The old basin was sitting on a table in the back, and Dr. Rhine was the town dentist, too. If you needed a tooth pulled, you went over to Dr. Rhine's and if you didn't watch out, he'd pull all of them out and tell you, when he got through, "I got them all, and you'll be better off." She was looking at some teeth in that pan where Dr. Rhine had put them. I could tell she was getting scareder and scareder. It finally came her turn to go back there, and she was so scared and so nervous, all she could do was stick her cheek up when Dr. Rhine asked her what was the matter.

Dr. Rhine said, "It ain't nothing serious. I can fix that." He turned around to the kettle thing that was half full of rusty water and got a scalpel, like he used to remove those hemorrhoids. Then he got an old dirty towel, probably the same one he wiped those hemorrhoids with, and it was stiff as it could be. He shook it two or three times and put it up on her shoulder and twisted her head around. He opened up the side of her face with that scalpel before you could say "Scat." You never saw as much stuff running down her face and onto this towel. He'd just squeeze and wipe and squeeze and wipe. It looked like a teacup full of stuff that run out of her face. She was screaming and crying with pain. When he got through, he said, "It won't be necessary for you to come back. I think this will be fine. You just give it a good squeeze before you go to bed tonight and a good squeeze in the morning." He never gave her a bit of antibiotic to put on it—he didn't even bandage it!

There she was, getting up to go, with bloody corruption running down the side of her face, and she didn't have a thing to wipe with. I asked Dr. Rhine, "How much does she owe you?"

"Who is she, anyway?" He didn't even know the girl's name, because he didn't keep any records. I told him that she was from London, England, and her husband was working for my husband, and they had not been living in town very long, and they had a new baby. Dr. Rhine looked at her and said, "Since the Cayce's are contributing what they are contributing, giving y'all a start in the United States, I'm going to contribute something, too. There won't be any charge." He reached out his hand and shook hands with her and said, "And welcome to the United States." She was so touched. When we got back up to the house, I got some bandages out and bandaged up her face. She said, in her London brogue, "I never saw anything like that in my life! I *never* saw anything like that in my life." She was very impressed with the first doctor she met in the United States. They were here working for us four or five years, and Dr. Rhine doctored the whole family the whole time they were here. It seemed like she fell more and more in love with Dr. Rhine, and when they left here, he had delivered one baby for her, and they hated to move, because she didn't know how she would do without Dr. Rhine. She had fell a victim to Dr. Rhine-a feeling of dependence on someone she felt she could trust.

I never will forget when Dr. Rhine got seriously ill. The whole town was just in mourning. It was something we had dreaded. For many, many years we had dreaded for the day when Dr. Rhine would get unable to work, but he kept on going on and going on just like he was indestructible. There was no getting him down. He would get a little sick, and then he would get back up. When he really, really got bad sick, all of us were in mourning, deep mourning and in deep prayer that Dr. Rhine would recover. Of course, he didn't. He passed away. You could hear a pin drop all over town because people didn't know what on earth was going to happen to them. A lot of them were taking medicine that their very life depended on, and they didn't even know the name of the medicine. He would just hold up a bottle and pour a little medicine out of this bottle and that bottle and mix it up like he wanted them to have it. They were fearful they would die, because they couldn't live without their medicine. Dr. Rhine never kept a record on a patient or wrote anything down about the medicine he gave.

After he died, the girls were going to clean out the office and get things straightened up down there because people were coming from everywhere for his funeral. I thought I would drive down there and see if there was anything I could do at the office or any junk I could carry off for them—anything they would need me to do. I went down pretty early that morning, but evidently they had got through the day before because there wasn't anybody at Dr. Rhine's office. I walked up to his door, and I don't believe I have ever been more touched about anything in my life. On the sill of his door sat a fruit jar full of zinnias. The flowers were not arranged in any order at all. Some of them were tall and short and long. Some of them were half dried up, but a fruit jar full of flowers.

It touched me so deep to know that somebody who had no money for store bought flowers wanted to show their love for Dr. Rhine, so they brought a fruit jar full of flowers from their own yard and set it on his door step. It seemed to me that there was plenty of flowers at his house and a big bouquet pinned up on the door facing, to show that someone in that household had died, but his office, where he had spent his life and wore hisself out, had no flowers or nothing there to show that a man that everybody loved had fallen. But there sat that fruit jar, there on the threshold of the door. I went down to the house and told the girls about it, and different ones walked up to the office and saw the flowers. No one knew who had brought them.

A week or so after Dr. Rhine was buried, we found out that it was Ludie Orr, a retarded lady, who was almost as old as Dr. Rhine, but he had taken care of her for a long time. She was a little bitty dried-up lady that lived about two miles out of town. She would walk in, sick, and Dr. Rhine would doctor her and then take her home. She had absolutely no money. She had picked those flowers and put them in that fruit jar. She had come up there before daylight that morning to set them on the doorstep of his office. I think someone made a picture of that. I believe I saw a picture of it. I really don't know if I saw a picture of it—a really sure-enough picture of it—or if I just carry a picture in my mind and heart of how humble it looked sitting there. I've thought a lot of times since then, when I would go to buy flowers for someone who had passed away, that it really isn't what the flowers cost or even if they are arranged properly, it is the love behind them that counts. To me, I always go back and remember the flowers in the fruit jar when Dr. Rhine passed away.

"The doctor's personality was a lot of the treatment ... It was almost a faith healing."

DR. HENRY HEARNSBERGER

LITTLE ROCK, ARKANSAS

He had his office in the back of the bank building, which later became the post office. There were three little rooms, probably ten by twelve, ten by ten and a nine by ten. The most vivid thing was the roll top desk with papers piled high. It was also littered with journals and books, and he always had some new books. All around the wall were bookcases. The medicine bottles were over in the corner on the floor in the office. He'd take a small bottle and pour it full from a big bottle, saying, "Take a tablespoon of this. Make you feel good."

At about the ninth grade age, I became interested in studying medicine. During the summertime, I would go down and stay all day with Dr. Rhine, ride with him and work in the office with him. I recall what was shocking to me on calls with him—a woman who was in bed, she'd had a fever and a cough. He had a stethoscope, but if he couldn't hear what he wanted to hear, he would just put his ear down to her breast, stripped down, and listen. Here I was in the ninth or tenth grade. I had never experienced such a thing, but it really worked better. You didn't have a loss of sound, because stethoscopes weren't all that great then.

I remember Harris Brothers Store in Thornton. It occupied about half a block. In size, it was the biggest store I had ever seen in my life. I didn't think there was anything in the world as big as Harris Brothers Store. You would go in there and think you could see one of everything that there was in the world that was ever made. It was near Dr. Rhine's office.

I was Master of Ceremonies at the State Fox Hunters meeting in 1956, when Dr. Rhine was named Arkansas Fox Hunter of the Year. It was the only fox hunting gathering that I had ever been to, and it was enlightening to see the people there, the entertainment, how they worked with the dogs

59

to get them up for showing and for running, and how well they took care of them. His interest in hunting was a recreation for him. Another recreational activity that helped when he was fatigued and worried was to stop along the road and walk through the woods and pick up pine knots. He had pine knot piles like Mexican pyramids in his back yard.

When he was out on calls, he would be flagged down like you would a bus, and he would stop. This thing of not ever knowing what he was going to face or get into—complicated obstetrics cases, with no one really to assist you, just whoever was there—could be very exhausting.

The big event for him was the National Doctor of the Year Nomination in 1949. Dr. R. B. Robbins of Camden was influential in publicizing Dr. Rhine's work through his involvement in the American Medical Association. He was a Vice-President at that time.

Dr. Rhine and Dr. Joe Shuffield of Little Rock were great friends, both medical and fox hunting. Dr. Silas Fulmer, the internist in Little Rock, received a lot of patients on referral from Dr. Rhine, for diagnostic evaluation. Doctors would remark that he always had the diagnosis when he sent them the patients. All they did was to confirm it.

He knew the family medical history of his patients for at least three generations. He also knew the culture and the socio-economic status of the family. And the fees—if someone came in—"What do I owe you, Doctor?" "Maybe fifty cents. You probably can't pay that," or "Why do you ask what you owe? You may not ever pay me anyway."

Back during the Depression, when other doctors would not go to see sick people who could not pay them, he would go anywhere. If a physician during those times made nine or ten thousand dollars a year, they were doing good. They did not have much overhead, except for automobile expenses. There was no concern about medical-legal things, that is, being sued by someone. Now you dare not do things that he did, except in the presence of someone.

When I graduated from medical school in 1944, the only specific drugs we had were digitalis, one of the sulfa drugs, Mapharsen and Salvarsan for the treatment of venereal disease and quinine and quinidine for cardiac rhythm. There were no others. When he was in practice earlier, there was nothing except symptomatic relief. Your treatment was the doctor-patient relationship and the doctor being supportive of the patient's immune system; of sitting with the pneumonia patient until they would go through the crisis and of sweating it out—going every day, and to do what? There were no specifics. It was a different kind of medicine then than we have now. The doctor's personality was a lot of the treatment, and this was what Dr. Rhine's personality did, dealing with those people. It cured a lot of them. It was almost a faith healing. They would come in moaning and groaning and go out smiling and feeling better already.

I never heard him grumble or complain other than the fussing that was part of his way of helping the people. Today, if a physician talked to his patients the way he did, he would run them all off. They would never come back to that crazy fool. The people expected this from Dr. Rhine. His remarks to people who came in went like this: "What are you here for? Is your husband not treating you right?" Having no bathroom facilities in his office, he'd say, "Use this and give me a specimen." He might turn his back and he might not. He would then check for sugar or albumen or look at it through the microscope.

He kept no charts. He had such recall. That was amazing to me, how he would know that much about his patients. As we would drive around, he would relate the various illnesses that had been in the family and what had happened to them. The placebo factor that the physician can have with his patients—he was an example of that.

Before he had an automobile, when he rode horseback, he had to be young and tireless to do the kind of work that he did. It was always amazing to me, when he would get these calls that would sound like a crisis to me, but he never moved. Of course, he knew the people and how they would report it in order to get his attention, but he was never rushed. When he was treating you, he never made you feel like he was rushed, no matter what he had to do. He paced himself, and this probably is the thing that made for his longevity in practice. He did not stress himself, except in the matter of hours.

His close association with his patients made it easier for him to know all about them, because he did all of it. His office demeanor was an outstanding characteristic, and a stranger might think this joker doesn't know what he is doing, but apparently, he did, because he was successful. He doctored the same people for a long, long time, and he got results.

He did not have the facilities to do the diagnostic workups—the new things that were coming along. One time, I remember, he had a book on laboratory procedures. His laboratory was a water bucket, a couple of test tubes, and a microscope. But he knew what was going on in medicine, although he didn't have the facilities to practice it. When he had difficult cases, he would refer them, but as far as diagnosis was concerned, he was expert. He knew the medical community, and they knew him—T. E. Rhine.

(Dr. Hearnsberger practiced medicine in Stephens, Arkansas from 1946 to 1965. He finished his residency in psychiatry in 1968 and is now Director of the Greater Little Rock Community Mental Health Center.) PRB

S A D I E   B A I L E Y

THORNTON, ARKANSAS

Ever since I've been old enough to remember anybody, and I'm eighty-five years old, I remember Dr. Rhine. I say just a good doctor is not enough, he was one of the best. I won't say he was *the* best, there may be some more like him, I don't know. Always, when I would get sick, and this is the truth, I would say, "If I could just see Dr. Rhine." And just the sight of him would help me. I was able to walk down to Thornton sometimes, but he stopped me. We lived out by the Stells, next to the Council place. He said, "I'm gonna stop helping you at all, if you don't stop walking down here." You see, I had high blood. He said he could keep it down if I wouldn't be hard-headed. It was about two-and-a-half miles, and it would be hot sometimes, but just the sight of Dr. Rhine, or if I could just hear him, would make me feel better.

He always teased me about my kitchen. I always liked for the kitchen to be the cleanest place in my house. My husband would tell him that was where he would take company, because it was the cleanest place in Sadie's house.

One time I was sick. I had typhoid fever, and Dr. Rhine cured me, and I was sick, I mean. One day he came, the kids thought I was passing and Lam Braswell's wife, too. That's my husband's sister, she was there. They were standing around. I wanted all the children to come around the bed. He teased me so much about this, after he got me well. He would tell me, "Sadie, I tell you the Lord is letting you stay here for some good purpose."

I would answer, "Well, Dr. Rhine, I hope so. I hope it's some good purpose."

And then he would say, "It's something good or something mighty bad."

"Dr. Rhine, I hope it's something good, because I want to do something good like you. I know I can't near reach you, because you've done so many good things for people, and you have done so much for me. I hope I do have a chance to do something for somebody."

This was in the late forties, and my youngest boy was five or six years old. I couldn't look but one way. I thought maybe I was passing, too, but I wasn't scared. I couldn't take my eyes off the corner. He said I had my eyes set. I wanted all the children to come around the bed. Dr. Rhine was sitting by my bed, and he was waiting patiently. He wanted to hear what I was going to tell them on my death bed. I told the children—"Children, *keep your kitchen clean.*"

Dr. Rhine told me not to start my youngest boy to school when he turned six, because he had something like bronchitis. He couldn't hardly breathe, and it was too far for him to walk. In the winter time, in the bad weather, it would be bad on his breathing. "It won't hurt him to wait until he gets seven, because the next year you'll have a school bus," Dr. Rhine said, and you know, we did. They gave us a school bus, and he didn't have to walk! The bus picked him up right at the gate. Dr. Rhine knew well ahead about the bus. I never dreamed of us getting a bus, but we sho' got it. And so many things he could tell me ahead of time.

And with all of my kids, when they were born, nobody but Dr. Rhine. All born here at home. We didn't have insurance and welfare stuff then. I wasn't able to go to a hospital. I didn't have the money. He would come to the house. Then we lived at Hopeville. My husband worked for the Anthonys, down below Mr. Hunter Parham's. That's where we got to go, to the nearest phone, to call Dr. Rhine. He'd let us call the doctor from his house.

I think about him so much. I told him so many times I didn't want him to leave me here. He told me he was my grandmother and my great-grandmother's doctor. My grandmother was Lucindy Johnson. We called her Grandma Cindy, and her mother's name was Peggy. Dr. Rhine would say to me, "I'll never forget old Aunt Cindy Johnson as long as I can see you. You are so much like her. You look like her, and you've got her ways." He also delivered some of my sisters and brothers, but not me. That's five generations he doctored on us.

Dr. Rhine told me one time he could pick out my kids among all the school children. "I know them by the way you brought them up. You've got a fine bunch of children." I had nine to get grown and the retarded one that died. He delivered all except one. I think he was sick or gone somewhere. He told me that I had a retarded baby, and she lived almost twelve years. He told me at the beginning that she might live twelve years. He told me one time, "Sadie, if that had been anybody else's baby, she never would have lived that long. You are so particular with everything."

He helped me in so many ways. He did so much for me. My husband went off one time and stayed for a long time. He had got in a little trouble, you know, and Dr. Rhine called those people in Hampton and told them he was going to send me down there and to put me on relief because I had all those children. I didn't know that until I got down there, and they said Dr. Rhine had told them all about it. I thought that was just wonderful. They gave me commodities and a little money. The children were all little. I wasn't able to work except a little washing and some ironing. I ironed for Mrs. Newton for years. She'd have the clothes already washed and bring 'em to my house. I wasn't able to go there.

Just before he died, I went to his office, and he gave me a double portion of medicine to last a long time. He said, "I want to give you this Sadie, for the same price you been paying for the other." It was for the high blood and some other little ailments. He told me if I needed a doctor, if he was gone, to go to Dr. Harry Atkinson, and you know, after he died, that's who I went to. I told Dr. Atkinson about that, and he said, "I try my best to be like Dr. Rhine, because you so crazy about him." He would tease me, too. He was more like Dr. Rhine. He'd say, "Why I came up under Dr. Rhine. He taught me."

Dr. Rhine told me not to go to funerals because I had a bad heart, too. I wanted to go to his funeral, but my husband said, "You know Dr. Rhine stopped you from going to funerals, and now you going to disobey him that much! He don't want you at his funeral!"

Thanks to Dr. Rhine and the good Lord, I'm still here.

JOHN BAILEY

FORDYCE, ARKANSAS

I'm the baby kid of Sadie Bailey. Dr. Rhine was my doctor, and when I went to him to get a blood test to be married, he asked, "Are you the same ugly kid that came along a long time ago? When you were born, you were so ugly I hit you in the face, thought it was your behind." I started out, and he said, "You not going to pay for that blood test?"

"I've got about three dollars."

"Well, since you were so ugly when you were born, I'm not goin' to charge you nothing." That was in 1960.

(Mr. Bailey is president of the Fordyce Club of Fordyce, which is affiliated with the Fordyce Clubs in Las Vegas, Los Angeles and Oakland.) PRB

MAURINE SHOCKLEY CATHEY

PINE BLUFF, ARKANSAS

I couldn't say nothing about him but something good. Mama, who is ninety-four, remembers when he rode a bicycle when he first come to Thornton, before he married. Then he rode a horse. I've heard my husband's mother talk about him riding in a horse and buggy. He went all out where the Catheys lived. I grew up in Thornton. There was two of us born in Thornton.

When I was born, Dr. Rhine was supposed to deliver me, but when the time come, he was out in the country, so the other young doctor there, Dr. C. T. Black, come and delivered me.

My father's sister was married to Dr. Robinson, who practiced in Thornton before Dr. Rhine.

When my baby, Bill, was born, I was living in Fordyce. Dr. Rhine had delivered the two older boys. Walter was working for the Cotton Belt Railroad and was gone. It was a terrible night. I finally got hold of Dr. Rhine, and he come on. It was just him and me there, and then the baby.

When you would go to see him at the office, he would take a little bit of this medicine and a little bit of that medicine, mix it up, but it would always cure you. I used to have one of his old bottles.

There's his picture that I admire so down at the Fordyce hospital. It hangs on the wall. He just looks like he orta talk, and just about anywhere you get, he's looking at you. It's a nice picture.

WYNNE, ARKANSAS

Dr. T. E. (Ed) Rhine, as I was priviledged to know him, was a professional man dedicated to ministering to and for physically ill people at any hour of the day or night, however situated or remotely located—time nor weather being a deterrent. It was an assurance afforded the ill or members of the family that "we have called (or sent for) Doctor Rhine." It afforded relief and was a comforting assurance, as his arrival and presence was anticipated and soon welcomed. He would enter with his customary comforting light-hearted greeting to those persons present; yet approaching the patient with concern. His approach usually involved some form of banter, especially toward some child or elderly person, his voice usually couched in a slightly nervous type of hacking cough.

Dr. Rhine lived a life of and in strict accordance with that of Free Masonry—a dedicated Blue Lodge Mason for years. He was the moving spirit of the Thornton Lodge, ever demanding and affecting strict adherence to the tenets of masonry life and practices, rightfully dividing the day into three equal parts, the twenty-four hour day being devoted to eight hours for the service of God and man, eight hours for refreshment and sleep, and eight hours for the pursuit of a vocation. I wonder how many eight hours of sleep might have been his lot!

I witnessed his arrival at one home where there had been prolonged illness and perhaps not so well provided for. He was carrying a crate of some six or eight frying-size chickens for the family use.

I also remember my first sight of Dr. Rhine when I must have been three or four years of age and ill of some fever. He was standing on the porch of our home talking with my father, discussing me, and though I did not understand or now remember what was said, I recall that he was young, erect and slender, wearing an attractive type suit and the most impressive narrow string bow tie and white stiff collar. It was the first sight of such for me and was my early impression of a doctor, a vision I can yet recall.

Dr. Rhine had a sudden attack of illness at Thornton. Mr. Will Chamberlain and Mr. Niemeyer of the Stout Lumber Company, on the advice of Dr. C. T. Black, arranged hospitalization in Little Rock for him. I accompanied him from Thornton to Fordyce. He was on a single iron bed in the back of a truck. At Fordyce, the iron bed was placed in the baggage car of a Rock Island passenger train, accompanied by a woman nurse (a very large person not much to the liking of our doctor) and myself. I went back later to check on him just a day or so before he returned home.

In 1981, my brother, John Randolph "Teannie" Gardner and myself, opened a new subdivision of twenty-seven lots in Wynne, Arkansas. The three streets are named Rhine, Bradley and Calhoun. Calhoun Street is for the home county of the Gardner family. Rhine Avenue is for Dr. T. E. Rhine, our family doctor, and Bradley Street is named for our oldest sister's husband. We did not dare use the name Thornton, as I have too frequently passed along tall tales of it and some of the individual originally endowed personalities I had known there.

BERT WALTON

FORDYCE, ARKANSAS

The second time I ever went to his office, in Thornton, there was a little man in the waiting room and he was there to see Dr. Rhine. I know they were good friends 'cause when Dr. Rhine came out of the door to the waiting room, the man beat him to the draw. He said, "Hello there, Ugly," talking to Dr. Rhine. "Ugly? I'd call somebody ugly if I looked like you! Come on in here and let me kill you!" I knew they were good friends, because I could hear them talking together in the office.

ALPHA BARNER WALTON

FORDYCE, ARKANSAS

There were no heaters in cars in the early days, and Dr. Rhine would heat bricks and put in a bucket and set down by him in the car to keep his feet and hands warm. He never knew what was going to happen, and he had an ax, a lantern and everything he thought he might need because the roads were so bad. He had these bricks in the car; it was cold, and they called him to come see this colored woman who had triplets. She didn't have a thing in the world. He got the bricks out of his car and warmed them in the fire and wrapped them and put them between those babies to keep them warm. He came back by our house, and he said, "I've made my first incubator. I dared 'em to let those brick get cold, and I dared 'em to burn those babies. We've got to have something to put on them." So Mama and I tore up every old sheet and flour sack and anything we had and made diapers and something to wrap 'em up in. He gathered up things and took over to them, and they grew like anything. It was ten miles up in the country from where we lived in Ramsey. I expect it was fifteen or twenty miles from Thornton, way out in the woods. And he had to walk part of the way. He couldn't get there in the car.

My mother grew pansies, and Dr. Rhine would always stop to see them. He would say, "They are the prettiest things! They look just like little dirty faced young 'uns." My parents were Morris Barner and Anna McCall Barner. Her grandfather, who raised her, was Dr. McDonald of Ramsey, and Dr. Rhine practiced with him when he was a young doctor. My mother just died in December, 1983, and she was ninety-four years old. She was here with me, and she begged for Dr. Rhine, after her mind got bad. Every night, she would beg me, "Call Dr. Rhine, and I'll be all right." She really did. It was so touching. She thought if he came everything would be all right. It always had been.

When he knew there was something wrong with you, he didn't wait for you to call him. If he was in the community, he'd stop by. That is what my mama liked about him. She'd save up all of her complaints, and when he'd come by she'd tell him about them, and they all got fixed. She knew that he would be passing by every few days. I grew up in the Ramsey community. I lived in Dallas County, got my mail from Ouachita County and went to school in Calhoun County. Can you beat that?

I knew one family that lived in our community that had seven children. Dr. Rhine delivered every one of them. He would come by and get Mama to go help him deliver them. He'd say, "We aren't going to get any money out of this, because I never have. But I've got to take care of this woman."

Dr. Rhine took my tonsils out, in his office, when I was a little girl. Dr. Atkinson, Sr. administered the anesthetic. When I woke up, I was at Dr. Rhine's house in the bed, and Pat was a little baby girl. Dr. Rhine was standing at the foot of the bed, dancing, with the baby in his arms when I woke up. I'll never forget it.

Mercille McMurry and I went to a graveyard working the day that her little brother, Rhine, was born. She was so miserable. She knew there was something going on, but she didn't know what. When we got back to our house that afternoon, they called and said she could come on home, that Rhine was there. She couldn't stay at home while the baby was being born.

My husband, Bert, had a brother nineteen years younger than he is. His mother told him when the baby was going to be born that he was going to have to spend the night with Granny because the doctor was coming to pull her tooth! Nineteen years old! They didn't take nature as it was back then.

If you were sick, Dr. Rhine really was going to be with you. He would come to your house and stay all night. You'd fix him a bed, if he thought that patient needed him, and he'd stay the night. We had a telephone, and Mama would know if anyone was sick because we did the calling for them. Often, Mrs. Rhine would call and ask if we had seen Dr. Rhine pass by, there were other calls for him to make.

Bert had an attack of kidney stones, and Dr. Rhine came. He was passing blood, so he knew he had kidney stones. He sent him to Dr. H. Fay H. Jones in Little Rock. They x-rayed him and Dr. Jones said, "Now Bert, I don't find a kidney stone. But you had a kidney stone. Dr. Rhine has never been wrong. We never argue with his diagnosis."

The night that he delivered our child, Dr. Rhine told Bert to get him a pan of hot water. Bert went and got the hot water. Dr. Rhine asked, "Is it hot?"

Bert ran his finger through it and said, "Yes."

"Go pour that water out! I want clean water. I don't want water you've taken a bath in!"

He was short spoken. Everybody took it, but he'd tell you quick what he thought.

Our child had an allergy. He sent me to Scott-White Clinic in Texas, and he sent me to Dr. Cazort in Little Rock. Dr. Cazort gave me a prescription for some shots. When I got back here to the drug store, they didn't have the medicine. I called Dr. Rhine and told him they didn't have it, and he asked what it was. I couldn't read the prescription, so I handed it to the pharmacist. He told him what it was, and Dr. Rhine said, "Oh. I've got that. Come on down here. It's at the house in the refrigerator." That's why we depended on him. He had everything we needed.

MERCILLE MCMURRY SUMMERS

FORDYCE, ARKANSAS

Dr. Rhine delivered me and the other children in my family, and most of the McMurry grandbabies—all of those who lived in the Temperance Hill community. My mother had lost a little girl when I was ten years old, and when my brother was born, three years later, they just had to name him Rhine. At the time Mother lost the little girl, they almost lost her, too. She was in bed for several months, and the family thought that Dr. Rhine saved her. He did save my brother because he was born without any breath. Dr. Rhine was there all day long. They did not think that Rhine was going to live. They dipped him in cold water and in hot water, and he still didn't breathe. My mother told me that Dr. Rhine said, "I don't like to do this, but I'm going to blow breath into this baby." He did, and that expanded his lungs, and he lived. So he had to have the name Rhine. We named him Alton Rhine, and we were going to call him that. When he got big enough to talk, and we would ask him what his name was, he would say, "'ine." He dropped the Alton himself. He chose Rhine for his name.

We thought Dr. Rhine could cure anything. Many times my family carried me down to his house in the middle of the night, when I couldn't breathe. He would come, day or night, anytime we called. It was about six or eight miles to our house.

My uncle Tom McMurry was about Dr. Rhine's age, and he outlived Dr. Rhine. One of his brothers would always say, "Tom will live as long as Dr. Rhine lives." He had high blood pressure and all of those things.

Our school, Bluff Springs, consolidated with the Thornton school when I went into the ninth grade. We thought if Dr. Rhine said it was so, it was so. He was interested in the schools, the community affairs, everything that went on. Our family loved him dearly.

68

Dr. Rhine always gave out diplomas at graduation. He was chairman of the school board and always made a speech. I know that he gave me my diploma when I graduated from high school.

I remember at Halloween we raised money for the school by each class sponsoring a candidate for queen. We had a sock social to raise money for it out in our community, and Dr. Rhine nominated me for queen of that event. Nobody else would have. I never was much for beauty, but I won it that night. A sock social is a gathering. The girls fill one sock with good things to eat, and the other sock is auctioned off to the highest bidder. Whoever bought the sock would also get the one with the goodies, and get to eat with the girl who brought it. A box supper is similar to a sock social. Boxes are decorated as pretty as they could by the girls and filled with good food. They, too, would be auctioned off to the highest bidder. You didn't know whose box it was, except the boys would find out their particular girl friend's box and buy it. Sometimes they would have to pay a big price, if they really wanted a certain girl's box. Others would bid them up. Dr. Rhine was often the auctioneer, and if he wasn't, he was the one who was bidding on the boxes to get the price up. He always had lots of fun at these socials.

In our community, we used to make friendship quilts. Everyone in the community would embroider their name on a block. We made one for Dr. and Mrs. Rhine just to show our love for them. [This quilt is now owned by Mr. and Mrs. Reese Parham, and is back in the Temperance Hill community.] That community gave me a friendship quilt when I graduated from high school. That was something they liked to do.

We had a telephone at our house, but there was a switchboard in the Ramsey community. Mrs. Mattie Wheeler took the calls and would locate Dr. Rhine when there was another call in the area. Mrs. Rhine always knew where Dr. Rhine was. We always talked about what a good companion she was for him. Any time you called her, she knew where he was and about how long it would be before he would be back. They were a team. Without her, he couldn't have done so much. He would call her if he was delayed, too.

On off hours, he just used his home for an office. He would invite you right in there on the back porch and give you a shot or a handful of pills. Then you didn't get a prescription to be filled. He just handed the pills right out to you. He always gave children candy, too, and it took the dread out of going to see the doctor, because you wanted to get that piece of candy.

My husband, Mike Summers, and I decided when we moved to Fordyce that we would not use Dr. Rhine so much because he was overloaded. Mike had a pain in his back, and we went to another doctor. The doctor told Mike he had a kidney stone and gave him some medicine. The next morning, Sunday, Mike said, "Dr. Rhine has never told me I have a kidney stone, and I'm going to see him." So we drove to Thornton on Sunday morning, because he always was at the office then. When Mike gave his ailments to him, he said, "Well, boy, you have a kidney stone." I laughed at Mike because he would never have believed that he had a kidney stone if Dr. Rhine hadn't told him. Dr. Rhine had also given him some pills and I asked him, "Whose medicine are you going to take?"

Dr. Rhine was not the Summers doctor all the time, because they lived in Bearden. But if they thought they were really sick, they always came to Thornton to see Dr. Rhine.

VICTOR WHEELER

RAMSEY, ARKANSAS

The thing I remember the most about Dr. Rhine was my mother used to have severe nose bleeds, and Dr. Rhine came out one night, and he couldn't get it stopped. He was going to send her to El Dorado the next day, and she did go. About two o'clock that same night, we heard a car drive up, and it was Dr. Rhine. He had gone home, and instead of going to bed, he had studied about the latest in nose bleeds, and he had come back to stop her nose from bleeding. The next day, at El Dorado, the specialist said that had beat anything he had ever seen, for an old man, as old as him, to be up on the latest methods, and use it, and to make an extra trip at two o'clock in the morning.

There was *one* time when Dr. Rhine's office was locked. Virginia gave a scavenger hunt, and one of the things on the list was a human skull. Of course, there was only one in Thornton. Since I was the lightest one in our group, they helped me up through the back window to get it from Dr. Rhine's office. To my delight, it was already gone. That was one collection I was happy not to make. I would guess that there were about twenty-five young people at this party. Dr. and Mrs. Rhine never served 'light' refreshments. They served huge, and let me stress *huge*, servings of homemade ice cream and cake on a tray with a big red rose on each tray, out of their rose garden. It must have taken gallons of ice cream—so much work and expense, back then.

The Ramsey telephone switchboard was operated by Mrs. John Wheeler. She was the first that I remember. I believe I've heard that Mrs. Nannie Barner was the first operator. Mrs. Wheeler died in 1939, and the switchboard had been placed in the Hawkins home about the mid-thirties. Mrs. Bay Starks, a daughter of the Hawkins' was the operator for a long time. Mrs. Edgar Sisson got it, and then Mrs. Bob Barner. She died in 1952, and the telephone system died about that time, too.

There were about four lines that ran into the switchboard. One served the people west of us. Our line served the people near the switchboard. One line went west toward Eaglette, and another went toward Fordyce. The dues were about $2.50 per *year*. The operator received about $10.00 per month. The men of the community kept up the lines. That was extremely cheap even then for the service rendered.

The operator handled all the calls for the doctor, so when someone from the other lines needed a doctor, she would know if he had a call anywhere in the community and could contact him there, saving time and trips for the doctor. She also would call Mrs. Rhine and let her know Dr. Rhine would be longer. I don't suppose though that Mrs. Rhine became alarmed when he was on a call for a long time because Dr. Rhine never left a patient as long as he felt needed, sometimes for hours.

When Dr. Rhine got a call in our area and then got another one around Fordyce, Mrs. Rhine would call him, and he could make better time going directly toward Fordyce since the road to Thornton was somewhat rougher.

We didn't have telephone numbers. Our ring was two short rings and a long. Mrs. Bob Barner was one long ring. Mrs. Forest Barner was two longs and two shorts. Mrs. Anna Barner was a long and two shorts and a long. Mrs. John McMurry's was four longs. A call rang every phone on the line, so there was a lot of eavesdropping that went on. Sometimes a half dozen women would visit nearly an hour or more. More service! However, if you should happen to want to borrow a thousand dollars, you had to go to the bank, or everyone in the neighborhood would know your business.

Dr. Rhine delivered more babies than any doctor ever did, I suppose. In our community, either Mrs. Anna Barner, Alpha's mother, or my mother aided him. Another community service.

When my sister, Martha Ruth, was born in 1936, Dr. Rhine was called to see my eleven-year-old brother, Jack. When he had doctored Jack, Jack was sent to Mrs. Bob Barner's and Martha Ruth was delivered. On that day, Mrs. John McMurry and Mrs. Tom McMurry and another neighbor rode the school bus over to our house to spend the day with Mother, not knowing anything unusual would happen that day. Mrs. John McMurry assisted Dr. Rhine in delivering Martha Ruth.

Dr. Rhine took great pride in his chickens and eggs. He once gave me a setting of eggs, but I suppose the school bus was too rough. They didn't hatch. Then I'll never forget the big platter of eggs Mrs. Rhine fixed for us at three o'clock in the morning on the day of our Senior Trip. Such a gracious hostess. I felt a little bad, and she really doctored me instead of the doctor doing it.

ALICE DEDMAN RUSSELL

FORDYCE, ARKANSAS

One time, Dr. Rhine was giving my husband, Harry, some shots. He was not feeling good, and he thought Dr. Rhine could get him straightened out. We'd go down to Thornton late in the afternoon after Harry would get off from work. One day he asked Dr. Rhine, "What kind of shots are those you are giving me?" "Oh, doodle bug juice." We all had so much confidence in Dr. Rhine that we would have taken anything he dished out.

He doctored my daughter, Pat, when Harry was in the Navy. She kept having chest colds, and finally he told me one day, "Alice, what's the matter with her is she's got asthma." So he started doctoring her for asthma, and when we'd see an attack coming on, we'd give her one of those pills, and it would stop it right away. Sometimes I would run into Mrs. Rhine, and give her some money for Dr. Rhine because he never would bill me.

He used to come to our home to see some of us, and he would get the well person to go out to his car with him. He'd open the back end of his car and get a bottle out and pour some pills into a cup. You never went to the drugstore. They tell me that whenever he treated anyone, he would put it on his books, but he never sent out any bills. He just depended on your goodness to pay him.

I have heard my mother say—his home in Fordyce when he was a boy was across the street from my parents—that on his way to school he would stop at their home and draw him some cool well water. He told her one day, "If I have a wife like you, I'll put her up on the mantle and feed her stick candy." His family moved here from Cleveland County about the time my parents married, 1889. My parents were Mr. and Mrs. John Dedman, and I was the youngest of eight children. My Daddy loaned him the money to buy his first horse when he started practicing medicine in Thornton in 1899. It was forty dollars. He mentioned that at Dr. Rhine's Day, when he made his speech.

My sister Pauline knew that he saved her life. He discovered she had diabetes, and he doctored her for that. Pauline and Gee always remembered Dr. Rhine's birthday. Another sister, Herris Garner, made him his last birthday cake. He liked just plain angel food cake without any icing. That's what Herris did. She made his cake and sent it down when they carried the roses.

I'll tell you right now, he saved Mama's life. My daddy worked at the lumber company. Mama was using the company doctor, and she was just in bed. She had a real bad case of pneumonia. Herris said, "We're just going to call Dr. Rhine." He came and told us what to do, and she began to get better. He was really good on pneumonia.

He often stopped at Mama's house to call Nita to see if he had any more calls to make in Fordyce before he went back to Thornton. Nita was certainly a good doctor's wife. He never got a call that she saw to it that he knew about it. She stayed at home and stayed on the job and helped him. You always felt so welcome in her home. She had so many good chairs to sit in.

Maurine Shockley Cathey was living in the house I had moved out of. Her husband worked for the railroad, and he wasn't at home all the time. It came time for Maurine to have her baby, and so, just Dr. Rhine and Maurine delivered that baby. Maurine told me after that, "Dr. Rhine almost sent for you." I was so glad he didn't, because I would have been bound to have gone if he wanted me to come. I would have done the best I could.

Dr. Rhine wrote everyone a penny post card to thank them for the roses. My sister Gee got the idea of everyone getting a red rose bud for Dr. Rhine for his 88th birthday—his last birthday. You know how many they wound up with? 243 roses!! Two great big baskets full of roses. She and Verda Barnes and Susie Campbell took the roses down to him in Susie's station wagon. That was Gee's idea. He was so happy to know that so many people remembered him. No one has anything but good memories of Dr. Rhine. Our problems were his problems.

S U S I E   W I L L I A M S   C A M P B E L L

FORDYCE, ARKANSAS

I was in the flower business for forty-two years in Fordyce. I can't think of any person that typified that old saying of 'Give me my flowers while I live' better than Dr. Rhine, and he got them. Dr. Rhine was the kind of person that when one person got a good idea about doing something for him, everybody else wanted to do it, too. On the occasion of his eighty-eighth birthday, it was Miss Gee Dedman that had the idea. She called Verda Barnes. At the time they came to me I don't think there were more than seven or eight people involved. By the time Verda Barnes called all the Easterling family it added to the list quite a little bit. By the time the Easterling family called all of their in-laws, and Gee Dedman's friends and other parts of her family called theirs and other people who had known and loved Dr. Rhine for so many years, there was a large group. The idea was for each family group to send him one red rose. They first had us order about seventy-five roses. (It started out that they were going to get a dozen, just a pretty vase of roses.) Seventy-five was going to be more than we could put in one basket. They wound up about two weeks later with somewhere between 250 and 300 roses. We had roses coming in on every bus. No person bought more than one rose. Everybody wanted it to include more people than roses. I do know they had to be put in several radiating type baskets so each rose could show its beauty best.

After we took them down there, Mrs. Rhine got tickled and said, "What are we going to do with all these roses, and where are we going to put them at night." She knew that everybody in Calhoun and Dallas Counties, and possibly Ouachita, were going to come there to see them. She came up with the idea of setting them in the bathtub and putting water in the bathtub. She kept them in the bathtub every night and would lift them carefully out and drain off the water and set them in the living room each day as long as they were pretty. There were other floral gifts at that time, but the roses

73

were the big thing. The rose was called "Forever Yours." It was a rich, red rose. There have been some popular doctors around, but never anybody that a whole area of the state was glad to call their own. Can you think of any one person that that many people came by or called in, saying, "I want in on it. I want in on it!" It just snowballed. We had to buy roses in bunches of twenty-five. We thought in the beginning they would get it up to two dozen. That would be a pretty basket. But it was more than ten times that many. Then we finally told people they couldn't order anymore. I was embarassed to order more roses. People kept coming in, one after the other. I know that Dr. Rhine got a bang out of that birthday present.

On the occasion of the anniversary of his sixtieth year of practice in Thornton, in May of 1959, that started off kinda mildly, like the day of the roses did. But it ballooned, too. I know that there were doctors there from everywhere. We had to double park at the house with the station wagon to get in to deliver the flowers. We made trip after trip after trip. A week or two before the day, those orders started coming in. I had never had an order before to please make a doctor's bag! Regulation size bag out of flowers. I finally cut it out of styrofoam and covered it with yellow and white pompoms. Each one was pinned on and glued on, all over it. Allen Lightfoot was the person who ordered that, and he was so proud when that was delivered.

Jane Bell's brother, Earl Glasscock, had left his practice in Bearden a long time before. He came there from Pine Bluff. I saw Earl, and I said, "What in the world are you doing down here?" I knew he didn't care much for rural areas. He answered, "I'd go anywhere to honor Dr. Rhine."

There really were more flowers sent that day, a lot more, than on his birthday—the eighty-eighth. It was amazing. Not a single person said, "Send some flowers to Dr. Rhine." They all came by and described what they wanted. They knew exactly what they wanted. They knew the event was coming up for a long time, and they had it all planned out in their minds, what they wanted to send. To me, that showed an especial affection for him.

I used to respect his wisdom a lot, and back during the war, there were people around that we didn't know. We didn't know whether to trust them or not. One day he came by and sat down on the front steps and talked to me. I brought up one name of someone who had moved to town, but I was a little skeptical about them, and I had been asked to trust them on a business deal. He told me, "I'll tell you Susie, I don't think I would. He may be a pretty good man, but he just don't 'stay hitched.' " I thought about that a lot of times, and I look at a business person that comes into this town, if they are somebody that moves around a whole lot and can't stay "hitched," I take Dr. Rhine's advice on that.

"Our Doctor Rhine"

STEWART GARDNER

CROSSETT, ARKANSAS

The title I gave this little thing is "Our Doctor Rhine." I suppose that every little boy picks his ideal as he grows into manhood. In my case, it was our Dr. Rhine: a man that loved his family, his country, his friends and *children*. I remember that so many times I would make rounds over the country with him, and as we drove along in the old T-model Ford to see his patients, the children would run out and yell, "Hi, Dr. Rhine. Goodbye, Dr. Rhine." He would always yell back, "Be good boys and girls now and don't fuss." And down the road we would go, kicking up dust, to see the next patient. The next one might have chills, fever, malaria, or diarrhea. Lots of the sickness back then was "lack of proper diet," he said. More or less a case of "missed meal" cholic. A dollar was hard to come by then, and most of the good people back then were honest with good intentions, but they were seldom able to pay for his services. A lot of it was paid for with produce. Many times our sweet NeeNee* worked so hard to "put it up" with her pressure cooker.

Our Dr. Rhine said he never kept books only on the ones he knew would pay him. Those that he knew couldn't pay him, he never put on the books. He'd go on and doctor them though. Doctor said that back then it was hard to raise a baby. "The reason," he said, "was we had no screen doors, no sewers, no refrigeration, and so much harsh and sour food. But someday that will all be taken care of." As I drive the rural sections now and see the power lines with all the good things he predicted, I sadly think back, how wonderful it would have been for those hard working people if they could have just had part of what we have now.

*A pet nickname for Mrs. Rhine, who had lived as a young lady with the Bradley family, whose children had given her this name. Her grandchildren also call her NeeNee. PRB

75

I stated in the beginning that Dr. Rhine loved children. I'll never forget when I was in the first grade, our teacher would tell us one day, "Be good boys and girls because we are going to have a big, wonderful surprise." During the day, in would slip our Dr. Rhine with two big sacks of red apples and peppermint stick candy. Now if you don't think peppermint stick candy and a red apple is good, try it some time. Back then, we didn't get fruit, only on Christmas.

As Doctor and I drove out to the Little Bay area one dry, hot summer day, we stopped to visit an old coot, who said he was sick—Jed Bass. We drove up to his place. Mrs. Bass was out in the old garden, burnt up, but she was trying to salvage a mess of dry beans or something there to eat. The old wagon was still parked down at the barn with twelve or fifteen fishing poles on it. About seven or eight young 'uns were out there playing baseball. Old Jed was sitting on the porch, didn't look like he was sick, in his rocking chair. Doctor went in and thumped around over him, gave him some pills and had a little conversation with him. He picked up his bag to leave, and Jed said, "Doc, I wish you could have been here the other night. We shore had a good fish fry." Doctor wheeled around and in his sternest voice said, "Jed that baseball club you got out there, about half those youngsters, like to starved to death last summer. If you don't change your ways, they all gonna starve this year," and grabbed that black bag and went on. We visited some rough ones in those days. Oh, he'd make them all. He knew he'd never get nothing out of it, but he went on anyway.

This old character from the Crawford family lived just below us out near Punkin Hill—the old man, the old lady, Elsie and the boy, Eke. Eric was his name, but they called him Eke. Dr. Rhine and Mr. Wilson, the school superintendent had some bad words over Eke. During World War I they were drafting boys, and Dr. Rhine and Mr. Wilson were on the draft board. Dr. Rhine said, "There is no sense in sending that boy up. I've got him where he's doing all right now, living with his mother and dad, the only dependent they got. He can stay there on that farm and work, but if you send him to the army, he's not going to take that drill and roughness, and he's going to be right back on the people and back down here where he can't do nobody any good."

Mr. Wilson declared, "No! He's going like the rest of 'em."

He and Doc had some pretty hard words over it, but Eke went, and he never got farther than Little Rock. He come back on a stretcher and lay around there just swelled up with rheumatism. Back then a hundred and fifty dollars was a lot of money. Eke got a hundred and fifty dollars the first day of every month, and him and his pa got in that T-model Ford and they went places! Didn't go no further than Camden and maybe Pine Bluff—just the suburbs. They didn't get much into town. But they were in the road every day. Mrs. Crawford had passed away. That old man would get his pipe and him and Eke would go! They lived like two kings.

Now, Dad and I called this one Dr. Rhine's masterpiece. On a Saturday afternoon, as happened quite often, Zell Hearnsberger and his boys would come into town, two little fellows, come into doctor's office and we'd visit. I'd come back and meet 'em there. We were standing there that afternoon talking about our dogs, and the hogs and what-have-you. This old boy lived neighbor to us, Eke Crawford, he lived there with his father. The old man had a bad case of indigestion or a struggle someway there. Eke come running into doctor's office. "Doc! Come quick! Pa's just about dead! May be dead by now!" Dr. Rhine grabbed his black satchel, told Zell we had to get away, we'd see him later. I jumped in the old Ford with him, and away we went out to the Crawfords'. We jumped out, I snatched the old gate open, Doctor run in and looked up. Old man Crawford was sitting on the front porch in his rocking chair smoking his pipe—that old home grown tobacco. That home grown tobacco was enough to kill anybody. We walked up to the porch, and old man Crawford said, "Hi, Doc. Come in and have a chair." I could tell then that Doctor was about out of snuff [patience]. "What's the matter with you, old man? I thought you were about to die." "Doc, by George, I thought I *was* going to die there for a minute. I was just walkin' the floor, just a-gaspin' and foaming at the mouth, but you know, I 'pooted' a coupla times and got all right." Boy, that Dr. Rhine grabbed that black satchel, kicked that gate open, jumped in the T-model and ran off and left me. I went home and Dad was sitting on our porch when I got there, and I was still laughing. I had to tell him the story. For years after that, Dad and I would be working around the place and we'd mash a finger, stump a toe or something, and Dad would say, "That's all right. Just apply old man Crawford's antidote to it, and you'll be better in a minute."

Once Dad got blood poisoning in his hand. It swelled so bad—you've seen Irish potatoes with knots on them—that's the way his hand looked. Those fingers looked like knots. They didn't have anything to kill the pain. Dad would sit there and drops of sweat would pop out on him. It looked like a river running down his face. Dr. Rhine stripped the vein down his palm and would take iodine on a swab and stick it between those fingers to get it into his blood stream.

Doctor and I were big buddies. He loved hound dogs and so did I. I was pretty much associated then with one of our friends, Zell Hearnsberger, who took care of doctor's dogs, and we hunted together. I wanted a coon dog. My Dad was never too much on me getting a coon dog. I went to Dr. Rhine and asked him if he wouldn't get me one. "Yeh." He'd see if he could find one. He ordered this dog from Sam Stephenson, Covington, Tennessee. I met #1 passenger train and even #4 in the mornings, looking for that dog every day for a week. Finally, this old white and black dog came in a crate. Oh! I latched on to him. Well, a year or two following that, I followed that dog up in the Wabbaseka Scatters. Nobody had told me that running water could be contaminated. I contracted a case of thyphoid fever. Doctor came out and diagnosed it as thyphoid, started me on castor oil, with very little food. I laid up for several weeks, and finally came out of it.

That coon dog had cost thirty-five dollars, and Dr. Rhine would never let me pay him for it. That was a lot of money in those days. Now, he's

77

treating me for thyphoid fever, and there was a doctor bill of fifty dollars on that. So it rocked on, and I grew into manhood, got a job working around. I never did pay Dr. Rhine. I told him a couple of times I wasn't going to pay him until he came to see me. Well, knowing our doctor like we did, he never had time to visit. He had to be there to look after those sick folks around Calhoun County. Well, he passed away, bless his old heart, before I ever paid him. One day I went to see NeeNee and told her this story. It was at our Marks family reunion. I said, "NeeNee, I don't feel bad about not paying doctor that bill because if I had given it to him, you wouldn't have got any part of it. Some other little freckled faced young'un would have asked him to buy him a coon dog, and he would have taken that money and bought him one. So, I want you to take this hundred dollar bill and put it where you can use it to your best advantage because thirty-five dollars for a coon dog and fifty dollars for a doctor bill isn't very much."

The Stout Lumber Company Mill burned on Christmas Day in 1925. I left Thornton the next year, 1926, when I was eighteen or nineteen years old. I went to Crossett and worked in a drug store with Bob Marks. In 1931, I started working for Crossett Lumber Company and worked for them until I retired in 1972.

LOIS THORNTON TOMLINSON

THORNTON, ARKANSAS

No, Dr. Rhine didn't deliver me. He had just come here, and he was a young man. Mama was a little shy, and she didn't want a young man to doctor her. He did deliver my younger sisters, Lillian and Edith. She was more used to him, and he had gotten a little older and she had, too. She was Emma Payne Thornton. There's six and a half years between me and Lillian and fifteen years between me and Edith. I was so embarassed when Edith came. Things are different nowadays.

When the mill was here, there were about 1500 people here at one time. We had a Main Street full of stores. There was a Sullivan had a drug store on the corner. Later on Uncle Jim Thornton had a dry goods store there. Next was Mr. Ezell's livery stable, at first. When cars came in, it was a garage. Later, Rufus and Virgie Hollingsworth had a cafe there. Mr. John Cone had a store, and there were two or three other stores on down the street to where Lionel Robertson had his store. Grover Turner had a store there before Lionel. The bank building was on the next block. There was a little house next to it that Joe Shaddock lived in. His father was postmaster as far back as I can remember. The post office was built in front of their house. Then Harris Brothers store was next. Mr. John Harris who was a preacher; Mr. Charlie Harris who married Sweet Alston; and Mr. Will Harris. Nell Gresham was a Harris, too.

During World War II, Dr. Rhine gathered up scrap iron. He was out on one of his trips and he came across an old hayrake. He put it in his car and brought it home and threw it on the scrap pile. Later on, the farmer come and got it. Well, Mina Stall was down at the doctor's office one day after that to get some treatment. Dr. Rhine got after her, because her apron was dirty. She answered him by saying, "My apron may be dirty, but I don't go around stealing people's hayrakes."

Here is a little thing that shows Dr. Rhine's complete dedication to his work. I witnessed similar occurences at least twice. I was sitting in his office and he had a call from down around Eagle Mills [about 12 miles, between Bearden and Camden]. A pregnant woman was ready to deliver. She was not Dr. Rhine's patient. I heard him ask, "Who is your Doctor? Why can't he come? Why do you think that I will come if she can't pay him?" After he hung up, he began to tell me how unthoughtful people are and his resentment that he was called out at the last moment. All the time he was letting his resentment out, he was packing his bag to get on his way to see the patient.

MAGGIE BRASWELL COLLINS

THORNTON, ARKANSAS

He would come anytime you sent after him. Ever since I was six years old, I remember him. I'm eighty now. He was the Company doctor. When he was young, I remember he was riding hosses. He had a—we called it "ole rusty bag"—leather bag done had been rained on so much. It crossed the horse, and it had a pocket on each side, and you put medicine in the bag like. It fit right behind the saddle. He also had a buggy, a one-seated buggy. He used to travel like that when I was a kid, and I remember he used to come to our house.

When you went to his office, he'd be sayin', "What you come here for?" "I'm gonna kill you." "I'm mean this mawnin'." "I'm gonna kick you folks out of here." I was so scared of him. I'd say, "Papa, don't carry me to see Dr. Rhine. He's goin' to kill me." But he'd give us children some candy. You know he'd jump and kick and make like he was dancin'. "Can't you get up and do this?"—all that stuff. He was just carryin' on, you know, foolishness. But I was as scared of him as I was a bear, when I was young. But later, I knew he didn't mean a word. He was having fun. We'd say, "Lord, Dr. Rhine's got started now." There'd be a big bunch in the office. He'd come in and say, "I'm mean this mawnin', I'm mean. I'm gonna kill all of you."

When my husband Jonah's father was sick, Dr. Rhine would come three times a day to see about him. He'd come after he made his rounds to the horspital, go to the office and turn them out, go back home and come at one o'clock, and then he'd come back at six. He was real sick, and he died here.

Dr. Rhine wouldn't send you to no horspital unless he had it to do. He doctored on my daddy, too. He'd come to see him three times a day, and he did it clean on up 'til he passed. Dr. Rhine got up in his eighties, and he still was goin'.

ILA AND GEORGE HEARNSBERGER

CHAMBERSVILLE, ARKANSAS

George: I'm one of the ten kids that Dr. Rhine waited on my mother when every one of us was born, and he got paid for all of them, too.

Ila: Twenty dollars, maybe. It wasn't ever over that.

George: Clarence was the oldest. I was next. He was born in 1904. I was born in 1906. Really there was eleven of us, but the last baby was born dead. All ten of us are alive today, and all of the in-laws except one. Mr. Zell Hearnsberger was my uncle and my brother-in-law. He lived on Grandpa Hearnsberger's place. He was Papa's baby brother. Ila and his wife, Lucille, are sisters. My father was G. W. Hearnsberger. Bus was his nickname. My mother was Lizzie. Right where I'm living at right now is where I was born and raised. When I retired, I came right back to the old home place. My grandfather was Billy Hearnsberger, and he lived one mile due south of here. That's where all the Hearnsberger reunions were held.

Ila: Dr. Rhine was always there.

George: He always brought the lemons, sugar and ice and made the lemonade in a tin tub and served the whole entire bunch. At that time, Stout Lumber Company was the only place that made ice, and he was the doctor for Stout Lumber Company when they were established at Thornton.

My daddy had a sorghum mill down by the creek. He made ribbon cane syrup, too. We raised the cane here. The crusher, or mill, crushed the juice out of the stalk. The juice ran out into a pan, which was over a fire, and that's where it was cooked. Mules turned the pulley to make the mill crush the stalks to press the juice out. When the raw juice was put into the pan to be cooked, it started at one end. There was partitions every so often, and it had to make the circle. When the juice reached the back end of the pan, it was syrup. It took twenty to thirty minutes, maybe an hour after you started cooking it. We used wooden paddles to stir and to test the syrup. You would dip into the syrup and hold the paddle up and when it dripped off right, it was done. We, also, had skimmers, because the syrup accumulated quite a bit of foam on the top, and that was skimmed off before it became syrup. As far as I know, all the syrup that Dr. Rhine sent to his doctor friends all over came from our mill. Our boy, G. E., had a little billy goat. That billy goat was bad about staying around the mill. He got into the juice one day, and it made him sick, and we lost the goat on account of it.

I remember a lot about Dr. Rhine and the fox hunting. At one time, I had thirteen dogs of his and my brother-in-law, Zell, had about twelve. We had about twenty-five dogs that we kept for him.

Ila: Of course, he furnished the food.

George: He would come out to fox hunt at night, and sometimes, he would have to leave to go see a patient. I know several times people would come get him while he would be hunting and he would have to go. I can remember when we would fox hunt on horses.

When the Hearnsbergers came here to Arkansas, they homesteaded here close to Chambersville. The first Hearnsberger came here with ten children. My Grandpa Billy Hearnsberger was the youngest boy. They came in 1843, I think. Our ancestors came from Switzerland and Germany to the United States in 1717. Hearnsberger was such a hard name to spell; you find it spelled six or seven different ways. Mr. Buddy Hearnsberger was the son of one of my grandfather's brothers. His place was where the Fordyce Country Club is now. He had a brother named Rob.

I remember an instrument he used in his office that had a crank and two cylinders that spread out when he turned the crank. He used it to test urine. I have one of his gallon medicine jugs, too. I have seen him take his hand and lay it on the neck of that bottle and lay it on his shoulder and pour it into a small bottle, without a funnel, and never spill a drop. Instead of prescriptions, you got your medicine right there.

I went to a basketball game one night in Bearden, and on the way home, the car turned over with us. Broke my collar bone. He fixed me up that night before I come home. Albert McGuffey was driving the car. We come around a curve and hit some loose gravel, threw the car, a Ford roadster. It turned over. I was on the bottom. Albert was on top of me, and the car was on top of him. There was gravel in my side. We had to pick the gravel out of me.

Ila: I fully believe we would have lost my sister, Lucille, Zell's wife. She had pneumonia and Dr. Rhine was sick at the same time, so we had to have another doctor, Dr. Ellis from Fordyce. Lucille was about to die. Dr. Ellis thought she was. Dr. Rhine got better and came to see her. When he walked in the door, you could see a different expression on her face. That helped her feelings when he walked in the door, and you can't tell me it didn't. She looked different just when he got in the door. He hadn't done a thing for her except come. He really wasn't able to come when he came out there to see her.

George: I've known him to come at night when you really wouldn't be expecting him, to see sick folks. Zell and I were sitting up with Mr. Reese Holmes there in Thornton one night. He was in real, real bad shape—pneumonia. It was right at midnight when Doc come walking in. No one had called him. He said he just had Mr. Holmes on his mind and wanted to see how he was. He come several times during the day, but this was around midnight.

When he had the stroke in 1924, he didn't know whether he was going to get over it or not. The thing that he did to help hisself was to get a double bit ax, and he went to cutting up pine. He had an enormous pine pile at his house. He taken this exercise and got hisself back in shape. He was a great believer in working. He worked hard. Being a doctor, too, you see, he knew what it would take. Those rich pine stumps—back in those days, they cut the timber pretty high. He would chop those stumps at the bottom and split 'em off. He hauled very bit of it in his car.*

His doctor, when he had the stroke, was Dr. Pat Murphey of Little Rock. I remember him coming down to bird hunt every season. We sure did enjoy him. We always would have a big bunch to hunt, and then we would have a big dinner for him. He really enjoyed eating our country food. This area is where they hunted for quail.

There wasn't nothing else to do around here but farm. I finally got to work with the State Highway Department through Dr. Rhine's help. I went to work when I was nineteen years old for fifteen cents an hour. That would be 1925. I was working with 'em when they opened the right-of-way from Thornton to Hampton. The old highway come off down through Chambersville. I helped clear the right-of-way, clear the stumps, and work with the road. I was with the highway department for sixteen years before I decided to go to Texas to do sawmill work. There wasn't any blacktop at all then. It was years later that the road was blacktopped. It was gravel until then. I maintained it with a motor patrol. Just raked them rocks back and forth to fill up the holes. Back then, they didn't realize they should put a crown in the middle of the road so the water would run off. Then the water just stayed in the road. Now, gravel roads have a crown. County roads now are better taken care of than we were able to take care of the state roads.

Dr. Rhine was with me all the way through my Lodge training. It was at the Thornton Lodge. It has a small number because it was organized years ago. [The Thornton Lodge was originally the Chambersville Lodge, established in the 1850's.]

Ila: Our son, G. E., got sick out in Garrison, Texas. We were visiting our daughter, Helen. Helen had to drive us home to Bernice, Louisiana, he was that sick. The next morning, we tried our best to get him to see a doctor in Bernice. "No." He wasn't going anywhere but to see Dr. Rhine. We came up here and it was the day Mr. Ples Steelman died, and Dr. Rhine thought so much of Mr. Steelman, but he did examine G. E. and told him he probably had arthritis of the spine. He gave him some pills that just really helped his back. He was nineteen or twenty years old at the time. We had good doctors in Bernice, but we had to bring him all the way up here to see Dr. Rhine.

George: We all come from Texas to be here for Dr. Rhine's Day in 1946. It was a wonderful day for us all. It was a gathering of, I don't know, thousands of people there—a large, large crowd. To have room, they had to

---

*He continued this practice of cutting up pine into splinters, especially when he was worried about a patient. PRB

have it on the school grounds. We had been gone quite a while, and it was just wonderful to meet all the people we hadn't seen in a long time. Our entire family was here, because we were introduced on the platform as being Dr. Rhine's prize family. He delivered all eleven of us and got paid for all of us—that was the remarkable part. Back then there was mighty little money. Folks just lived on what they raised—no cash crop hardly at all, a little cotton, but not much.

When Dr. Rhine died, we come for his funeral. Momma and Papa come with Walter, and Zell and Lucille come with us. Most all of the family come.

I come back here in 1972. I was sixty-five years old. I had been a sawfiler and mill foreman all over East Texas, wherever the sawmill was.

RUTH SISSON CATHEY

FORDYCE, ARKANSAS

I was born in Thornton in 1907. Dr. Rhine was with my mother when I was born. My father was Will Sisson. When I was a small child, Dr. Rhine would give me money to buy candy. He would get it out of his pocket. He called me "Cottontop." He would say, "Cottontop, here's you a dime. Buy you some candy." In those days a dime would buy a big sack of candy.

I remember when he bought his T-model car. I think it was one of the first cars in Thornton. My brother got snake bit, and Dr. Rhine asked my grandmother, Nanny Shockley and me to go to Princeton with him to visit my brother, who was his patient. We went, and I just cried. I was afraid we were going into the ditch. He said, "Now Cottontop, you just sit still and be quiet. We'll make it all right," which we did. It was my first automobile ride.

He was with my mother when she had pneumonia and passed away. I was two years old. We were living in Thornton, not far from his office. Dr. Rhine and a Mr. Murry were the ones who told Mr. and Mrs. Oliver Anthony about me needing a home, and I went there to Hopeville to live with them. I was eight years old.

Dr. Rhine used to come see Grandmother Best on his horse. He would always go out to her persimmon tree and eat all the persimmons he wanted before he came in. He knew that she kept candy by the bed, and so he would ease over and get a piece of her candy and just die laughing.

Dr. Rhine was always a guest at our family gatherings, and we always went to his celebrations. He was a doctor that never turned you down. If you had money, that was all right to pay him when he came to see you, but if not, that was all right, too. My husband used to carry him a load of pine or some wood. He would deliver a baby for $20.00.

He delivered my first four children. When my second baby was born, he said, "Now Ruth, I'm going to name this baby of yours."

"What are you going to name him, Dr. Rhine?"

"Let's see. Mr. Cathey's name was what?"

"Dan."

"Oh, Daniel."

"Yes."

"What was your Dad's name?"

"Will."

"Let's see. I'm going to name this baby Oliver Daniel."

"You are not! I don't like that."

"Yes, I am."

So that baby is O. D. today.

Once he asked me, "Ruth, do you remember your mother and daddy?"

"No."

"Well, sit down. I want to tell you a few things. You had one of the sweetest mothers I ever knew. I was with her when you were born, and I was with her when she passed away. She was such a good woman, such a hard working woman, who kept you children clean and pretty." No one knows how much I appreciate Dr. Rhine telling me that. It was after I was married.

Dr. Rhine and Mr. Cone and some other men in Thornton hunted all night long for my daddy, who had gotten killed by the T. and A. train that ran through Thornton. He worked for the lumber company. He was on the dock at the back of the mill. They hunted all night and found his body the next morning.

You know, he always said what he thought. I was in his office one day. A girl came in. Her heart was just a poundin' and beatin' hard. She had come from Harrell. He said, "Why didn't you stop and wait until you got better to come?" He looked at her and said, "You may live 'til morning, but I don't know." I had let her have my place to see Dr. Rhine. I could see her little heart tickin'. She died before morning.

I often wondered how he knew which medicine to give. He would pour some medicine from one bottle, then another one. He'd say, "Now, Ruth, don't be scared. I'm not fixing to kill you." He was so patient.

He treated Robert Dorey's son for blood poisoning in the leg. He would put one or two pounds of epsom salts in real hot water and put the leg in it, and that cured it. I use epsom salt water for my toenails, which give me trouble. Dr. Rhine taught me to do that, and I keep two or three pounds of it on hand. I use it for everything. Dr. Rhine taught us to do that, and I'm still doing it.

THORNTON, ARKANSAS

When I was eight years old and goin' to school, (I'm eighty-two years old now) Dr. Rhine would pass our house in Thornton, and I'd hear the horse a coming, and I'd run for the front to hear him call out, "Hello, Junebug! How are you today?" He always called us Junebug, and I thought that was the funniest thing for a doctor to be doing. He rode a big, black horse. There wasn't any cars, you know. We were just crazy about him, now we were *really* crazy about him. He was dating my school teacher. He'd buy five gallons of ice cream and bring when we would have a picnic. I know one time we had a picnic, (we always had them on the old road, across the creek, going to the Paynes) big shade trees was there and Dr. Rhine would always come. We kids thought he come on account of us, but it was on account of his sweetheart. Anyway, we enjoyed it no end. He'd help the teacher put the lunches out. Then, everybody brought a whole lunch. Dr. Rhine, one day, oh it just thrilled me to death, opened my box. He thought the lunch belonged to a little girl whose mother ran the hotel. Mine was steak sandwiches. He said, "Oh, I'll bettcha this is Ruth's box." I was so happy to tell him, "No, it's mine." "It is sure nice." It was great big pieces of fried steak. Oh, I don't know what all Dr. Rhine did do for us children back in that day. That was a long time before he got married.

My parents were Martin and Emma Cathey. She and Dr. Rhine were about the same age. Mama was visiting me one day, and we were sitting on the porch, and Dr. Rhine came down to the house next to me. They had a sick dog. He got out of the car, and oh, he just danced up a storm, really danced. Mama was just looking at him and smiling all over. "I wish I could do that." Our house was bricked up around the porch, and he didn't notice Mama sitting there, I'm sure. He went on and doctored the dog, and when he come back, he looked over and saw Mama, and he come over to visit. That's one way he kept going, prancing around.

Dr. Rhine went out to Chambersville to wait on a woman who was having a baby. Back then you didn't know 'til they got there, how many there was goin' to be. It was two, and they couldn't take care of one. Dr. Rhine come right back to town and bought clothes and carried out there. The woman told me about it.

I remember his mother, Mammy Rhine. She was frail. Mammy thought she had a fine meal if she had turnip greens and scalded cornbread (where you put your finger prints in the bread before you cooked it). Dr. Rhine told me that. Her whole life was Ed. She had daughters [Betty Strait, Ethel Condray and May Hardman] but he was at home, and he was the only boy. I've heard Mammy say, "We didn't have much meat when Eddie was going to school, but I saw to it that Eddie got the meat. The rest of us would do without." I imagine she told them to do without! They all worshiped him, his sisters and his parents, and he was good to them.

Over across the road from Dr. Rhine's house was where Aunt Puss Cone lived. She was an old lady and was fat. We lived down the road a bit. Every time it looked like the weather was going to be bad, Mama would make us kids go over to Aunt Puss's and get in her wood, carry in enough wood to last her during the bad spell, so it would be dry for her. Now Aunt Puss Cone, there was a good old woman. She raised Jim Thornton.

The night that Earl was born, he had a date with Miss Nanita Raines. He told us that he had told her he couldn't stay out late, because Mrs. Harper was sick, and when he come, he stayed all night. He didn't leave.

Larkin, my husband, had pneumonia five times, and that was back when, if you lived nine days with the doctor treating you, you got well. If you got worse on that day, you died. They called it the "crisis." They would call Dr. Rhine. They had their old telephone you would ring yourself, hanging on the wall. Larkin would get worse every night after dark, Mrs. Harper said. Dr. Rhine would come down there, and the boys was always ready to go out and more or less cut him off the horse. He would be frozen to the horse. He had a slicker and an overcoat made for that purpose. It come back over the horse's hips, and all that would freeze, and they would help him to tear it loose, to get him off so he could get in to the fire.

I told him one time that Larkin was afraid to be around pneumonia, afraid that he would catch it. He said, "Well Ona, I don't blame him. That boy can have it the quickest of anybody I ever saw. The Harpers and the Easterlings, they have pneumonia if they have a bad cold."

During that time, Larkin got better, and they thought he was doing all right, but he got to hurting in his chest and a big knot was under his arm. Dr. Rhine come out and told Mrs. Harper, said, "I'm going to have to go in with a needle and draw the puss off his lungs." We didn't have hospitals then. He went in and hit a rib, and it just like to have killed Larkin. Larkin was fat. He was just a boy. Mr. Harper said, "Dr. Rhine, don't try to go in any more. I can't stand it." "I wasn't going to." It went on a few days, and Larkin was still sick and hurting. Dr. Rhine come back and said that it was abscessing under his arm, and in a few days, he lanced it. Mrs. Harper said that puss flew nearly to the top of the house, it had such force behind it. Oh, it smelled bad! That was the awfullest thing. Dr. Rhine thought it was awful, and that made Mrs. Harper uneasy when she saw Dr. Rhine was scared. Now, she really believed in him.

When my son, Earl, died, (he had leukemia) he was twenty-five years old, was married and had two little children. Dr. Rhine would come out there, and he gave us the dope, syringe needle, and he would say, "Just keep him comfortable." He didn't tell us to be sparing on him or nothing. The day came that Earl was dying. All that night, I sat there by him, and I couldn't rest, because Dr. Rhine wasn't there. The next morning, he wasn't any better, and I told Larkin, "Larkin, I tell you, I want Dr. Rhine!" I was crying. Larkin jumped up and said, "I'm going to get him."

There was a big snow on the ground, terrible big for here. Larkin walked up to Thornton, about two miles, and told Dr. Rhine, "You don't know how

86

bad I hate to ask you to go out there in weather like this."

Dr. Rhine said, "Larkin, I'd go if I had to walk. She wants me, and that will comfort her if I go. I'm agoin'."

He did come, and I felt better. He got around there and talked to me. "Ona, I thought you'd be more prepared when it come than this."

"Dr. Rhine, you don't get ready for a death in your family. You think you're prepared, but you never are."

"I guess you are right."

I had a heart attack about thirty-one years ago. Larkin got up at three o'clock in the morning and went after Dr. Rhine. He knew there was something bad wrong for us to call him out at night. He jumped out of bed and just slipped on his britches and his houseshoes. He still had his pajama top on when he come to see about me. He give me a shot, and it didn't do me a bit of good. He was standing by my bed just staring at me. Ruth asked, "Is she any better?"

"No. Don't you see how she's got her gown gripped? When her hand relaxes, she's better."

I heard them a talking, but I didn't realize I was that sick. All of a sudden he whirled around and went out to his car and brought something else and gave me another shot. Ruth asked again, "Is she any better?"

"She's asleep now. Let's get her back on the bed."

Ruth took aholt of my feet and Dr. Rhine caught me under the shoulders, and they lifted me back on the bed, and I was gone.

Later on in the morning, I was allergic to something, and I had clawed myself something awful. I got up the next morning to go to work. Larkin come in and said, "What in the world do you mean?"

"I'm fixin' to go to work."

"You're not fixin' to go anywhere but in that bed, and you get in there. Dr. Rhine's goin' to be here any minute, and he'd kill you if he thought you were up like this."

I crawled back in the bed, and no sooner had I got in there, Dr. Rhine knocked at the door. He told me to stay in the bed all day. He stopped in four times during the day to see how I was doing. Before he bedded down for the night, it must have been about ten o'clock, he come back out to see me.

We got Earl's children, Peggy and Bobby, to raise. I'll always believe Dr. Rhine had something to do with us getting the children. You know he always done good things for people, but wouldn't tell it. The children wasn't getting the benefit of their Social Security, not any of it, not even beans. The little children was having a hard time, and Dr. Rhine knew it. He said, "Ona, it takes all of my time and all of yours when they come, to get them able to go back."

Peggy was in the bed, had a sore throat. They was always sick, her and Bobby both, when we would get them. Peggy had a little puppy, a little bulldog. That night that little dog cried and cried. I got up and Peggy was sitting in the middle of the floor just a-crying. I said, "What's the matter, Peggy?"

"I can't get this little puppy to hush crying."

"Put him back in his box and he'll hush. We'll wrap him up good, and you go back to bed and go to sleep."

He got awful quiet. Everything was too quiet. I went to see. She had that little dog in bed with her, his little head up on her pillow. Larkin thought it was a disgrace—having a dog in the bed. Dr. Rhine come to see Peggy the next morning. Larkin had to tell Dr. Rhine what an awful thing Peggy had done. Dr. Rhine told Peggy, "That's all right. You love your little dog and any time he cries, you get up and get him and put him in the bed, I've seen nastier things than a puppy in the bed."

I'll tell you this about Dr. Rhine, there's nobody aliving that can say anything good enough for him. That is the truth if I ever told it! And when you had sick folks, you could depend on him. Now he knew what was going on in all the families. He knew if anybody was having a hard time. I never did understand it altogether, but he did know.

"If there ever was a person looked up to and worshipped, it was him. Black and white, everybody loved him."

VERDA EASTERLING BARNES

FORDYCE, ARKANSAS

My father was Howell Easterling. He had a brother, Jim. I was only six months old when Dr. Rhine started practicing medicine for our family. I'm eighty-four now. He was our doctor from then on, as long as he was able to practice. I can just hear that horse's feet now, coming. Boy, when you were sick, it sounded good, too. The horse was named Bill, and he was the prettiest thing.

I was a sickly little child. He took my adenoids out sitting up in a straight chair in his office at Thornton, and I rode home in a wagon. I got along just grand. He told me I needed my tonsils out, and he fussed at me as long as he lived about not having them out. I wished a thousand times that I had.

He practiced on five generations in my family, starting with my grandparents, Jones Easterling and Matt (Martha was her name). She and Dr. Rhine had some terrible arguments. She was a Primitive Baptist, you know, Hardshell. Dr. Rhine would tease her about her religion. She said to him one day, "Doctor, you don't really believe you can save life, do you?" "No, but I can sure make 'em sick." That just tickled her to death. He never would charge them anything, my grandpa or grandma, either one. He never took a penny from either one of 'em. She'd say, "Now, doctor, how much do I owe you?" "I don't know. You're going to have to sell old Pied to pay me," talking about the old cow.

I know I'm the only person he died owing. When I was little, we had an orchard and all kinds of fruit trees. All the kids was eating apples. I wanted an apple, and he said, "Verda, you can't have an apple. You know that."

"Well, Dr. Rhine, they're gonna eat 'em all up while I'm sick."

"If they do, I'm gonna bring you a bushel of apples."

89

I fussed at him as long as he lived about owing me the apples. He never brought me the apples, but the apples weren't gone when I got up, either.

I remember one time he came. I had tonsillitis all the time in the wintertime. I'd miss a week of school, go back, miss another week. So one day he came, and my tonsils were all enlarged. He went out and cut a limb off a peach tree and whittled it down real sharp. He punctured one of my tonsils, and that tonsil never bothered me to this day.

We lived at Chambersville. We lived in a house that my daddy built when he and Mama married, and all four of us children were born there. The first children were twins, Byron and Abbie, then Vernon and five years later, me. Most of the neighbor women were younger than Mama, and they had children on down, some of 'em, as many as seven. Dr. Rhine would call Mama and he'd say, "Alice, get ready. I'm coming. So and so's in labor." Mama was at more places when kids were born than anybody down there. I was such a baby, I wouldn't sleep with nobody but my Mama, and it would make me so mad. I'd say, "I wish these women would quit having babies." If anybody was real sick in the community, he wanted Mama to go with him. He'd drive a buggy with two horses, and Mama was scared to death, because he would just fly. If he didn't ride old Bill, well, he went in that buggy.

This nephew of mine, Raymond Hudson, and two other babies, twins, Dr. Rhine delivered them on the 11th of September in 1918. He left to go to the service on the morning of the 12th. He would go from one house to the other. My sister, Abbie Hudson, lived about half a mile from us, just below the schoolhouse, but the Wrights lived close to the Ebenezer Church. He would go over there to see her, then he'd come see the other one. All day long he did that. My nephew was the last one to be born. He laughed at them. "You all got scared. You knew I was leaving in the morning, and all of you went and got sick at the same time." He told me he kept count of the babies he delivered to over 6,000, then just quit keeping count.

He told us about an old colored man who lived out of Thornton toward Chambersville. He got sick, and they called Dr. Rhine. He went out to see him and came back to town. That was when Harris Brothers had their big store. He went to Harris Brothers and told them, "That old man is not sick. He needs cleaning up, and he needs food. Load up your truck with groceries, and new sheets, towels and pillowcases and pajamas and send them out there. That's what he needs." There's no telling how many others he did that way. I don't know how in the world he made a living. He wouldn't charge people—no widow, no preachers. He never charged any of them anything.

My husband, Newell Barnes, had grown up in the Bucksnort community. They had used Dr. Simmons. When we married, he was manager of the Cities Service station in Fordyce. Dr. Rhine drove in there one morning; he had been to see Mammy Easterling. It was when she taken sick to die. Newell said, "Dr. Rhine, how is Mammy this morning."

Dr. Rhine looked up and said, "Who are you?"

90

"I married Verda."

"I don't think she'll live through the day." She did live a few days after that.

Uncle Jimmy fell and broke his hip. Dr. Rhine came. My daughter, Peggy, was taking nurse's training. She took Papa, Mama and me down to see him at Chambersville. Dr. Rhine was there. He gave him a shot and said, "Ira, this will last 'til midnight. You'll have to call me at midnight to come back." He had already called the hospital in Little Rock, and the doctor was going to see him the next morning. He asked. "Is anybody here who can give him a shot?"

Peggy said, "I can. I'll stay down here." Of course, we thought that if Dr. Rhine got there, we was going to get well. Anyway, Dr. Rhine sent him on to Little Rock, but he died the next night. I wouldn't tell Papa, because his health was bad. Jack Gray was living with us at that time. I said to him, "Jack, what must I do about telling Papa?"

"Call Dr. Rhine and tell him to come by here and let him tell your daddy." He came and told Papa, and he took it real good. If anybody else had told him, he'd probably'd gone to pieces, but Dr. Rhine made it sound like he was so much better off, which he was.

Dr. Rhine gave me my first car ride—in a little Ford roadster. We always had what we called a "graveyard working." Everybody would go and take hoes and rakes and brooms and clean the graveyard. They didn't have grass then. It was at the Chambersville Baptist Church. After they cleaned up, we would have picnic lunch, and everybody would spread lunch on a table there.

After lunch we would go down to the schoolhouse to the baseball field. Thornton and Chambersville had a team together. There wasn't enough boys at Chambersville, so they had Thornton boys come out and play. Dr. Rhine bought all the equipment, their suits, bats, balls, gloves. He loved baseball. He played some that afternoon. He told all of us little girls to come get in the car. Some were on the fender, some were on the seat with him, and some were standing up on the back, holding on to the seat. That was our first car ride, and we thought we had really done something—rode in a car. It was in 1913, and I think it was the first car I had ever seen.

My brother, Byron, when he went as far as he could go in the Chambersville school (tenth grade) went to Thornton to school. Papa bought him a horse. The boys wanted a football team, so Dr. Rhine had bleachers built, the field fixed, he ordered all the equipment, suits and everything, paid for every bit of it himself, and they had a football team. I used to have a picture of the football team. It was kinda quaint looking. That was long about the time John Strait was there living with Dr. Rhine.* He was older than them. Ira, Uncle Jimmy's boy got his nose broke. Uncle Jimmy was very much opposed to them playing football. He didn't want them to get hurt. They played on Saturday. Ira come back to our

*Dr. Rhine's nephew, who lived with him in order to attend school. PRB

house and spent the night. Mama washed his shirt out, dried and ironed it. They doctored his nose, and Uncle Jimmy wasn't any the wiser. He kept on playing football.

They used to have log rollings. They would clear the land to farm. They would cut the trees and saw them into logs, like building a house. All the men would come and help. Dr. Rhine would always come by for noon and eat with them. He was always invited to every one. House coverings, too. If a house needed covering, the men would come. Those that knew how to cover a house would do that. Others would carry the shingles up to them. The women would come and help cook dinner and maybe bring part of the dinner.

They was having a log rolling at our house. We had moved over on the Chambersville and Hampton road and built a new house over there. Mama called Dr. Rhine and said, "I want you to come and eat dinner with us today. We are having a log rolling."

"All right. I'll be there. Could I bring somebody with me?"

"Why sure. Bring anybody you want and as many as you want to."

When he came, he brought Miss Nanita Raines. He introduced her to everybody as his fiancee. They were getting married in two weeks. That was our first meeting of Mrs. Rhine.

Her father, Mr. James Raines, was County Agent (I don't know what they called them then) in Dallas County. Papa planted wheat one year. They didn't grow wheat very much. It was such a beautiful crop. He went to Fordyce and told Mr. Raines he wanted him to come out and see his wheat crop. He came out and brought a camera and made a picture of it.

My family, the Easterlings, was all musically inclined but Ellen, Charlie and me. None of us could play a tune on anything. My granddaddy was in the Civil War, and his commanding officer taught him to play the violin. He was as good as I ever heard. He would sit so erect and hold that bow just so. He said that officer was so particular about how they performed. He taught Uncle Jimmy and he taught Papa to play the violin. Willie didn't learn to play the violin, but he played the guitar and the mandolin. Ira played the violin. Clyde played the violin. Vernon played the violin, and Byron played the piano. They also had a bass violin. They'd get together, and they just had a string band. Dr. Rhine just loved that music. He'd come out there, and sometimes would just stop by and want them to play for him.

He loved to dance, too, and he was a good dancer. Uncle Jimmy was going to let them have a dance. He had a great big house, four rooms upstairs and four downstairs. It was built before the Civil War. Uncle Jimmy called Dr. Rhine and told him they was gonna have a dance. He and the Alston girls, Candy and Sweet, Nell Harris and her sister, Ruth, and one or two boys came down. They were on their way to Fordyce to a concert or something. It was Christmas week, and the dance would start early. They came by and danced a while before they went on. Dr. Rhine had on a tuxedo, and it was the first time we ever saw anybody with a tuxedo on. We just thought that was really something. The girls were dressed up in their party frocks. Oh, he loved to dance. He said that music was just what he loved to dance by. It was waltzes and two steps. I miss that music so much.

On my sixteenth birthday, Papa sang "Sweet Sixteen" to me and played the guitar. That was a thrill for me.

Bill Brandon was traveling for some tractor company, and he went to Hot Springs. That was when they started that radio station there. He made an appointment for the Easterling boys to play on the radio. They wouldn't go.*

Dr. Rhine, when he was in service overseas, wrote a postcard to the youngest member of his closest families. I got a card from him, and I treasured that card. I loved it. I thought that was the grandest thing in the world—getting a card from Dr. Rhine. He had his picture made with his uniform on. I've got one, and I'm giving it to Raymond, because he was born the day before Dr. Rhine left for the army.

Everybody around always went to Uncle Billy Hearnsberger's house on the twentieth of September. That was their wedding anniversary—Aunt Pat and Uncle Billy. Everybody would go whether they was kinfolks or not. They had a big shady backyard and a table out there. We all had to wait dinner until Dr. Rhine got there. I had a picture of Uncle Billy and Aunt Pat and one of his brothers and one of her brothers and all of the children. I also had one of all the Hearnsberger grandchildren, but Lord, that wasn't a tenth of what there was before it was all over. But Dr. Rhine was in the picture. You know, a lot of times, I think about that on the twentieth of September now. I'll tell you, that family of girls, Aunt Betty and Ruth Gray and all of that bunch, were the best cooks!

If there was anything to do at school, Dr. Rhine always had to come out and make a talk to us, and tell us how to do and take the opportunities that was offered to us. We didn't all of us do it. The Chambersville School was a two-story building. He helped to get good teachers for the school. They had up through the tenth grade, and then you had to go to school somewhere else. I was going to Fordyce to school, live with my aunt, but that was the year of the flu epidemic, and they didn't have any school.

The flu was so bad, a lot of people that died in Fordyce was brought to Chambersville to be buried. Nearly every day they come by our house. Mr. and Mrs. Bowe didn't have a funeral home. They just had a building there on Main Street. She would go on one funeral and he another. Benton's was the same way. There was just so many people died.

All the boys was in service except Vernon and Nelson Jones. They went with Papa and Uncle Jimmy up to Camp Pike in North Little Rock to see Byron and Ira before they went overseas. They got to the river bridge going

*A string band from Thornton called the Thornton Merrymakers, whose theme song was "Down Yonder," did play on the Hot Springs radio station. People from all around came to listen to them on the radio at our house. This was in the mid-thirties. PRB

over to Camp Pike and they stopped them, saying, "You can't go because of the flu." They went by the train station then, and they said caskets were just stacked on top of caskets. It was a terrible time.

These wars we are having now—maybe there are so many more people killed than there was then, but they don't have the hard times that our boys had when they were over there, and they didn't have the hard time that my granddaddy had when he was in the Civil War. They had to furnish their horses, their clothes. (I think they gave them their uniforms to start with, but he said they wore out before the four years was over with, and they had to wear just whatever they could get.) They would pass a cornfield, and they would stop and gather corn for their horses. They would gather fruit to eat. They had to furnish their own bedding. He said one night they was camping up on a high hill, and it was warm when they went to bed. They had oil cloth they would spread down and then their blanket, with a blanket over them and then oil cloth over that, if it rained. They woke up the next morning, and he said he was so warm and comfortable and he threw his cover back and six inches of snow had fell that night. Out in the open! But they were healthy, tough men. They could take it.

Ed Hawkins, his family all used Dr. Rhine. They lived up in the Ramsey community. He was working for my husband, Newell. They were going fishing down below Hampton, and Newell had burned his hand, just his fingers, real bad. Ed said, "C'mon. I'll take you to a doctor that can fix you up." Newell and I hadn't been married very long, and he didn't know Dr. Rhine very well. So they stopped down at Dr. Rhine's and went back in the office. He said that Dr. Rhine took a paddle, dipped up some stuff that looked like axle grease and put on it and wrapped it up and said, "Go on fishing."

Newell said he told Ed when he got in the car, "That stuff's not going to do my hand any good."

"You just wait."

He wore that bandage awhile and when he took it off, it was just healed over. It really made a believer out of him. We all believed in him. Not only us, but everybody in the community. The Parham families out at Temperence Hill, the Easterling family here and the Hearnsberger family, the Dedman family up at Ramsey. These families just lived and breathed by Dr. Rhine. I guess if there ever was a person looked up to and worshiped it was him. Black and white, everybody loved him.

ELLEN EASTERLING BRANDON

THORNTON, ARKANSAS

When Dr. Rhine came to Thornton, he learned about my father's, Jim Easterling, love for fox hunting, and they became close friends. My father lost his first wife a little before Dr. Rhine came to Thornton. His parents broke up housekeeping and came to live with him. He had five boys. Later he married my mother, Betty Jones. She originally was Betty Hearnsberger, a sister of his first wife.

I guess that I was the first patient at our house that he had. He delivered me—seventy-five years ago. When I was a few years old, I can barely remember it, Dr. Rhine came and asked my grandmother, we always called her Mammy, would she get him a gallon of chinquapins. Of course, he told me I could help her. I got the credit for gathering them, but she did most of the work. We had three big chinquapin trees in our big field. No one else had any. At that time, we lived on the Fordyce road in Chambersville. He told me that he would give me something if I would do it for him. He brought me material for a dress. It was blue. That was a high spot in my life, because Dr. Rhine had given it to me.

When I got old enough to go to school, I didn't want to go. I was timid. Dr. Rhine told me that if I would start to school, he would bring me some more material for a dress. That's the only way they could get me to go to school, was to let me wear that dress. It was a little lighter than royal blue. I can see that dress now. I thought he had hung the moon, because he did that. My half-sister, Vera, did the sewing. Mama could sew, but Lord, she had her hands full feeding such a crowd. When we would sit at the table, before we started marrying off, there were thirteen of us. Mama's kids and Papa's kids, Mammy and Pappy Easterling and me.

We raised all of our food, and we had good food. Mama set a big, good table every day. I have never wanted for good food. We raised pork. Mama canned every kind of pickle, every kind of vegetable, every kind of meat. I don't know how she did it. She did the cooking and the girls did the dishwashing, cleaning and clothes washing. Mama kept tea cakes *all* the time, ever since I can remember. As the grandchildren came along, they expected them. She made a cobbler pie might near every day. My Papa liked them, and she also kept pound cake for him. Mama and Papa both died in 1951.

We had a rough life, but I wouldn't exchange it for the world. It wasn't all roses, there was a lot of hard work, but there were a lot of rewards. Kids didn't run around at night. We played cards, popped popcorn—just had a party at home every night. Finally, we got a radio. Papa had the first one. A lot of the neighbors would come in to listen to it. Everybody had to be so quiet then.

Dewey Brandon and I eloped. Dr. Rhine had delivered Dewey, too. He delivered our first baby, which will be fifty-seven years ago. He delivered seven of our children—all the boys. We lost two boys, the fourth one at six months, he had diptheria and pneumonia, and the seventh son at two days. When I got pregnant with Kay, our only girl, Dr. Rhine was old, and I was old. I was forty-five, and I even had three grandchildren at that time. My three boys who were married were about to have a fit. They thought I ought to go to the hospital. Dr. Rhine said that if I wanted to go, all right, but he wouldn't go with me, and he just cried. It broke my heart, too, and I cried. We went to Warren though, and I don't think Kay would have made it because I had a lot of complications. But he did deliver me, my husband and seven boys.

The way we would call him, there was one phone in the community, and that was Mrs. Garrison's. We would send for him to come, and if I knew that they had gotten in touch with him, I felt like we were all right now. We would get well. I thought he could raise the dead. I loved him like a father image, besides being my doctor. I didn't know there was another doctor in the world but him—didn't want to know it.

CLAUDIE B. GARRISON, E. D. D.

FORT SMITH, ARKANSAS

Our home was at the crossroads of three intersecting roads in the Chambersville community. Consequently, we were somewhat the center of activity in our community. More particularly, for a number of years, ours was the last telephone on the party line, which meant that people for miles around from six different directions, would often come to our home to use the telephone. In more cases than not, the use of the telephone was to call the doctor. In those days, "the doctor" was Dr. Rhine. I am sure I was near my teens before I realized there was any other physician in the world.

A typical incident would happen somewhere around midnight or after when a loud voice from the middle of the road would holler out, "Mr. Garrison, Mr. Garrison." After considerable confusion trying to get the dogs quiet, my father would answer in just as strong a voice that could be heard for miles around. Having ascertained the identity of the party, they would make known they wished to call the doctor. In our house the telephone was on the wall in the master bedroom. So, any such activity became a household affair. Even though I slept across the gallery, it was the case that a youngster could not afford to miss whatever excitement exists, particularly in the middle of the night.

Once the person was in the house, it usually became my mother's task to "ring the doctor." As you know, the phone on the wall was still an awesome piece of equipment for most people in those days. Having reached the doctor on the phone, everyone in the room could hear his response. Needless to say, he had a reputation, at least on the phone, of being a bit gruff; who could blame him, for the number of calls he received in the middle of the night. I suppose that most people delay contacting the doctor until after dark, and certainly it was no exception when I was a child. The call invariably resulted in some loud exchanges. It was still the case in those days that most people thought, since it was so far away, you had to talk real loud regardless of the efficiency of the instrument. It was, however, a standing tradition that shortly after the phone was hung up, you could hear a car coming around the curve. Again, in those days, it was not likely that any other car would be out at one o'clock in the morning. You could be reasonably sure that when you looked out across the field and around the curve and saw the lights, that it was Dr. Rhine coming.

During the interim time, of course, there was considerable visiting about who was sick and what was wrong. It became my task, as the youngest in the family, to wait in the road and flag down Dr. Rhine so that the party calling could ride back home with him and tell him the problem. As I indicated earlier, it was understood, and tradition, that regardless of the tone of voice or response from Dr. Rhine, shortly after the phone was hung up you began to watch for the headlights. Invariably, he was there. In retrospect, I cannot understand how he physically withstood the hours and the service that he rendered for years and years, knowing full well our telephone at the end of the line was only one of the telephones at the end of the lines of communities he served.

I remember, too, some personal privileges I had in being around his home as a teenager. His second daughter, Susan, and I were classmates, and the seven or eight of us that made up the junior and senior play staff, the assembly committee, the FFA and home economics banquet, etc. used Dr. Rhine's house as a hang-out. At that time, Dr. Rhine had an old 1928 Chevrolet which at times he would make available to us to make trips to ballgames or to places that other people during that day and time could not afford. Dr. Rhine, for some reason, always suggested that on a trip out of town, I drive the car; should this sound too sophisticated, a trip out of town would have been to Hampton or Bearden or some place within a fifteen mile range. Nevertheless, I was always honored that he suggested that I drive the car.

I remember, also, a number of things around the house that impressed me over a period of years. One of which was that Dr. Rhine apparently kept little or poor records relative to payment for his services. I was always impressed with the amount of firewood that he had stacked up around the house and other in-kind payments which he received for his services.

I was also impressed with the fact that in spite of Mrs. Rhine's attempt to shield him from any activity which interrupted the few times that he had to rest, that he found time to visit with us as young people in his home. He was one of the (if not the sole) supporters of the school system there for years and years and years. It was almost a tradition that he visit the school assembly program and talk to the youngsters. Without embellishment, it certainly was the case that Dr. Rhine was an inspiration to me and a number of other young people.

(Dr. Garrison is superintendent of the school system in Fort Smith, Arkansas) PRB

DR. CECIL EVANS

TEXARKANA, ARKANSAS

My dad was Jim Evans and my mother was Sarah Ellis Evans, and Dr. Rhine delivered all nine of us at home. We lived down in the Providence community. I guess he did a good job, because eight of us are still living and the youngest is in her forties.

I still have, in my office, though I don't use them, the forceps Dr. Rhine gave me when I graduated from dental school. Evidently, I was the only dentist that he ever delivered. When I got out of dental school, I went by to see him, and he said, "I don't take out teeth anymore. There are dentists around now, and I don't need these. I want to give them to you." I treasure them.

There was a big bunch of us kids and mostly boys, so fighting was a matter of survival. Just before school started, Clifford, my oldest brother, and I got into a scrap, and in the confusion (we were shucking corn fodder and it was dark; I couldn't see to dodge), I got a lick in the eye. It made the white of my eye completely red. I didn't want my parents to know that we had been into it. When I was in the house, I would look to the right all the time, and you couldn't see the red. Finally, days later, my mother saw it.

When school started, of course Dr. Rhine *was* the school board, and as he came down the aisle before the program began, I stopped him and showed him my eye. I thought he could just tell me something to do or give me something that would clear it up at once, and I'd be off the hook. He said, "Rinse it out with warm salt water." I wanted something more specific than that and quicker.

We just almost worshiped him because he came regularly to deliver a baby. My mother was an Ellis, the sixteenth of seventeen children. She lived to be seventy-two. Thirteen of them lived to be grown and had families. John D. Ellis, Robert Ellis, Dr. Walter Ellis of Fordyce were some of her brothers.

LOUISE WRIGHT SIMPSON

JACKSON, TENNESSEE

My youngest brother, Jack, was a special pet of Dr. Rhine's. There really are not enough or adequate words for me to describe Dr. Rhine, and our families feeling for him. Jack was little more than a baby. In fact, Dr. Rhine delivered Jack. Before he was school age, he had pneumonia. At that time, there was not much to be done for it. He was real sick. They took him to Texarkana to the hospital (my Dad worked for the Cotton Belt Railroad), and they had to operate. When he got back, he just continued to go down. I remember that Dr. Rhine had to perform a little operation. He went in and inserted a tube and drained his lungs. He had my mother to leave the room because he knew she couldn't take it. From that day on, he began to improve, and Dr. Rhine nursed him back to good health.

Immediately after that, Jack had a facial stroke, which Dr. Rhine discovered. He treated him and gave him what therapy they had in those days, and today you cannot tell that he ever had a stroke.

Dr. Rhine doctored on all of us—six children, Mother and Dad. I went to him even for my warts. He removed eighty-seven of them from my hands and three on my mouth. We went to him for everything, and we loved him and his family better than anything or anybody we knew. We frequently had Dr. Rhine to our house for meals, and Mother baked him a fruitcake every Christmas. He was just special.

"A stethoscope is a very simple instrument . . . What really is important is what is between the ears of the guy that is using it."

DR. GEORGE MORRISON HENRY

LITTLE ROCK, ARKANSAS

The relationship that I had with Dr. Rhine, I would have to categorize in three ways. First, just as a young child in the community. Second, the more intense relationship which occurred between the ages of fourteen to eighteen for myself when I would do a lot of his driving, especially in the afternoon, evenings and week-ends. I had always liked to drive an automobile, and at age fourteen, that is 1949, there weren't all that many cars, and I thoroughly enjoyed driving him, if for no other reason than the fact that I was the one boy in town who got to do a lot of driving. I was never paid anything for doing this. It never entered my mind. I was asked to do it once, probably by my grandmother, and I kept on doing it. Actually, it would have been awkward for me if I had been offered money. I would not have known what to do or say. Besides, when someone asked you to do something for them, you were glad to do it, to be of help. I was glad to be a part of something that I knew was good. The third part of the relationship would be after I left high school and would return periodically throughout the years as a college student and then as a medical student.

As a young child, I felt admiration for him as someone in the community who was obviously a person who commanded a lot of respect from all of the adults in the community, and I did not know exactly why he commanded so much respect. I was too young to understand that, yet I knew it.

As I became his driver from 1949 to 1953, before I graduated from high school, I would visit with him many of his patients, especially the house calls and in his office. Also, I then began to have first-hand experience, though a little distant, and began to understand better what the relationship was between Dr. Rhine and his patients, and would understand why

100

they had so much admiration for him as a physician and also as a person in the community. At the time I was driving for him, I was not going to become a doctor. Actually, I was a senior in high school when I decided what I was going to do, and then changed it the first year I was in college. I was originally going to be an engineer, and I'm sure that I told him that, so my young age, plus the fact that I was not going to be a doctor made me a little bit more distant from him in his practice than, say, my next oldest brother, Pat, who had already decided to be a doctor. Still, I thoroughly enjoyed observing him in his practice.

The anecdotes that I might bring to bear could be many, but I want you to understand that I was just fourteen to eighteen years old, so my observations were those of a very immature young man trying to make some observations of a serious and mature relationship between a much older man and his patients. So with that in mind, my observations are as follows.

I was always taken by the enormous respect that Dr. Rhine had for his own patients, and the respect that they returned to him. That relationship was always one that they respected greatly, and he respected greatly. Anything that the patient told him, that would be the end of it. It never went any further than that, and I quickly understood that that was the way that it was, and I was not to discuss that any further either. I was not even to discuss it with him. That was just not a point of conversation from that point on. Even if we left that house and went to another, any conversation that came up had nothing to do with what the patient had said, except maybe the illness was described. The same was true at the office. Anything that the patient told him, that was the end of it. It never went any further with me, and I'm sure, that it never went any further with him, even with his family.

In looking back and knowing how important that is in a physician's life, I now have even greater admiration for the way that he conducted himself in his practice than I did at that time. I'm sure that he learned this very early in his practice, because he carried it out so well, almost as if there was nothing to it. He handled it with such ease that it makes me look back now and have such admiration for his seriousness in his attitude toward the practice of medicine, that I could not come near understanding at my age then.

I always admired him because he seemed to do his work with such ease. I'm now talking about the practice of medicine—making a diagnosis and deciding what to do. I thought that he moved about his work with such ease and with so much fun that practicing medicine must not be as hard as folks propped it up to be. Now again, I didn't recognize the kind of medicine he was practicing was any different than anybody else. I hadn't had any other exposure to medicine. Looking back and reflecting upon it, it was easy for him only because he had done this for so long, and that he had done it in a very consistent way. He was never trying to second guess himself, he knew the limits of his knowledge, and he knew how to apply the knowledge that he had. He knew exactly what to do if it was going beyond his knowledge. The knowledge of the medical histories of his patients helped too, in the respect that if you know not only their medical history, but their psychological adjustment, then you can understand a lot of the things a patient is going to tell you, because you can put it in perspective. Knowing the patient, knowing the family helps a great deal. It was an important piece of knowledge that he had. It was a very large amount of knowledge, because he knew so many people and so many families and had known them for such a long period of time.

The only records that I ever saw him keep were actually records on charges. He did have a record in the office on which he would jot down certain charges. I have no idea as to what made him jot some down and not jot down others. As a young man it never dawned on me to assess "is he not jotting it down because he knows the patient doesn't have the money and never will, or is he not jotting it down for some other reason?" I never questioned it in my own mind, so I can't give you an answer as to why he recorded some debts and did not record other debts. But I do know that on occasion someone would ask him, "How much do I owe you from the last time I was here," and he would look that up, on some people at least. That is the only kind of record that I ever saw him keep.

I don't think that he kept any patient medical records, except in his own mind. I do know that he kept that very well, because if someone came in with a laceration on a given day, he could remember when the sutures were to come out.

If anyone would ask him "how much is my bill today?", a common response that he would have would be, "Well, how much do you have?" I think that he only said that to people who fully understood what he meant, which was, "How much of what I would charge can you afford to pay today?" If they would say, "I have a couple of dollars" or "I have fifty cents" or "I have a dollar," he would always say, "That's O.K." and that was the end of it. Whatever the patient answered was what he accepted in payment. I assume that he had been doing that for so long that the patient knew about what an office call was, and that he knew that the patient was going to be honest and say how much of that the patient could actually afford to pay.

In looking back, I don't quite know how he made a living, because he charged a certain amount which I strongly suspect, in so many cases, was far below what the charge should have been compared to what other doctors were charging in that vicinity of the state. It amazes me now, looking back, that he always had a nice home for our community. I would hesitate to say nice cars, because he never took care of his cars, but he had two functional cars, and his children had what I'm sure they wanted. At least, what he felt like they should have without spoiling them unduly.

Again, in respect to charges, even when a patient paid him for something, he never put it in a billfold; he didn't put it in a cash register or a lock box or a zipper bag of any kind; or hide it. He simply put it in his pockets. It might be his coat pocket or it might be a trouser pocket, but it would just go into a pocket. Even then, I would wonder, "How does that man know how much money he has in his pocket?" I don't know if he ever counted it, but periodically he would say, "We need to go by the bank." In our rounds we would end up at the bank, and I would wait in the car. He was never gone more than a few minutes, and I assume that he would make his bank deposit at that time.

Back to the medical practice. I remember that if we were going to a house where some woman was in labor, there was always a separate bag, rather than his usual "black bag," which was brown. This separate bag had the material in it that he used for delivering babies, such as stirrups, forceps, suture packs and things like that. I never witnessed him deliver any babies, and I'm glad that I didn't, because I don't think I was old enough to be privy to anything like that. I was always told to sit in this room, which was usually what we referred to then as "the front room," and be patient until the delivery transpired. It could be twenty minutes or it could be a number of hours.

Another observation that I made about deliveries is that if he got there and found out after his inspection that this was likely not going to take place for another two, four, six hours, then we would simply start the circuit again. He would already have decided ahead of time when he would return, but in the meantime, if we happened to stop at someone's house that had a phone, then he would try to connect again with where we had been, just to make sure that the labor was progressing according to plan. If the people where the person was in labor did not have a phone, they were told where we would be going, and they could call from a neighbor's phone and catch us if it was needed. It all seemed so casual, but in his own mind, it was very well organized, but he didn't convey this organization to anyone except the parties immediately involved. I often wondered what would happen if the baby went ahead and was delivered in his absence. Now I know there was probably someone there who could actually deliver it. But it never actually happened in my experience with him. He always got back and things always seemed to be under control. If he anticipated that things would not be under control, he would not have left in the first place. His time was never wasted in sitting there with someone in a prolonged delivery. It amazes me now to realize that he was able to carry out a house call practice for the most part, and yet carry out house deliveries at the same time.

Another aspect of his practice that amazes me now, and I had some understanding of it then, was the number of people that he would see on house calls and the amount of time that was actually spent, and yet, at the end of the day, the total number seen would not have been great because of the enormous distance that had to be covered between calls and the amount of time that he would actually spend with the individual patient in the home. He was not one to cut short those conversations. I strongly suspect that many of those conversations could have been abbreviated by the patient, but he did not insist upon that. He allowed the patient to take whatever time that was necessary.

To come back to the office practice, the way that I was involved with that was that if we were through making a certain number of house calls, that is, we were through with a territory, so to speak, and now we would "swing back" by the office. That was always his comment, "Let's swing by the office." That implies that he is going home if there is no one at the office, but, of course, there was always someone at the office, so we would have to stop. In his office practice, I probably was a little more privy to what was actually going on between him and the patient, because he would always ask me to come back to the inner office where he was doing his work.

In reference to his medicines, it amazed me even then, how he knew what was in those big bottles. Of course, all of his medicine was stored in big brown bottles. That is, the liquids. The pills were all sorts of colors, and each was certainly labeled. I would never want to say that he was guessing what was in them. Those with liquids in them, the liquid had dripped down the side and you had to look hard to figure out what the label really said. He knew exactly what he was doing in pouring up his medicine and in putting pills into white envelopes. I recognized back then that he had a terrible handwriting—illegible. He was always very careful to type his labels for the medicine that went into the bottles. He wrote the instructions on the white envelopes, that he put the pills in, but always told the patient clearly what it said, because I don't think the patient could actually read it. In typing the labels, he was using the kind of typewriter that the keys came from the sides. It was certainly one of the first ones and obviously lasted longer than things last nowadays.

His door was never locked. A patient would come to the door, knowing that it would be unlocked, and come in. Most likely he is not there. In the winter, if the gas stove was not lighted, they would light the stove and sit down and just sit there because sooner or later he would show up. The patient never had to wait outside in inclement weather. When other patients came in, one always would remember where one was in line because there was no place to sign in, and Dr. Rhine would simply say, "Who was here first?" They also knew that if there was a more urgent problem, they could pick up the telephone in his office and call Mrs. Rhine and she would give them some idea of when he would be back. She would get in contact with him if there was something urgent. Most of the time, urgent things never came up very often. Things tended to occur on schedule, even though it looked like things were at random.

His medications were just out in the open. His office was unlocked, and in the second part of the waiting room, his medicines were just spread out all over the room—on the floor and on a few shelves in the back. Even in the third room, which was the room in which he examined the patient and talked to them, that room, also, was not locked. What equipment that he had that he did not carry in the car was in that room—syringes, sterilizer. His total practice was open to the world, if the world wanted to inspect it, and, to my knowledge, nothing was ever taken or ever even vandalized.

In his practice of not having a segregated waiting room, his patient was a patient. He had no social rank-order or financial rank-order. (We would all have had trouble getting in line with Garland Anthony.) Black and white was not a rank-order either, nor age nor specie.

Here is an anecdote about a person who would be taken aback about some of his practices. This really illustrates how he handled different kinds of people. The person I speak of is Mary Wise, who was my great aunt. She was reared in a separate family than my grandmother. They had a little more than my part of the family, so she always thought of herself as being a little better than others. She always insisted upon bringing her own medicine bottles to the office. She thought that Dr. Rhine's medicine bottles were not clean—at least not clean enough for her. She would mention that if she was going to the doctor she would certainly take her own bottle, because his were not clean. My grandmother, Aunt Mary's sister, Mama Pearl [Morrison] who lived with us, never questioned whether or not he was clean in his work, because she knew that he was. She would not ever take any medicine bottles back to have her medicine put in them. She would, however, return her medicine bottles because she never wasted anything.

Also, Aunt Mary never wished to expose her complete buttock, if she had to have a shot. She always insisted on being a little more private, and he understood and accepted that. Neither attitude bothered him, or at least he didn't let it show. After all, it was such a small thing.

Insofar as examining equipment, his stethoscope was not a current one, but a stethoscope is a very simple instrument, so it doesn't have to be new to be good. What really is important is what is between the ears of the guy that is using it. What amazed me then and amazes me even more now, is that he commonly used his ear to examine a patient's chest. We just don't do that now, probably for propriety's sake. The diaphram of the stethoscope does add a little bit of amplification, but in all honesty, not much. His ophthalmoscope always worked, which is all that is required, good batteries in it and a light bulb that worked, and his always did. His suturing equipment always came out of the sterilizer. I don't know when he would turn that thing on and sterilize things. I never actually saw him do it. It must have been sterile, because his patients never got infections. The suture materials and clamps (he used a lot of clamps) were easy to sterilize. I did see him sewing up faces in the office. I remember one man who had been beaten up (he was drunk), and how difficult it was to take care of a drunk, yet he did it with a lot of ease, not that it wasn't difficult to get it all done, for the fellow was as drunk as he could be. It's much easier to work with some anesthesia. It doesn't take much, but he didn't use it.

What I observed about Dr. Rhine on returning was how current his information was and what he could do in his own practice himself and what he should do once the patient's problem exceeded his own knowledge—the referring of the patient to the proper physician and the efficiency of the referral. Oftentimes when we leave home to go away to college or medical school, we think that everything in our background probably ought to be forgotten, because it can't be current. That was not the case with him because I would go back as a skeptical college student or medical student. I would have all of the answers—just home from the mecca—all the answers to all of the problems, and I would find that both Dr. and Mrs. Rhine were quite current. That is like finding out that your parents really do know something after all.

In medicine and, for her, in music, they could talk about the same things that you had just learned, either the same book you had just read or the same idea about which you had been thinking or researching. In his case, it was currently used medications. He had them right there—in a brown bottle. You might be writing prescriptions to a drug store, but he had the same medicine, pouring it out and prescribing it appropriately.

Dr. Rhine had an understanding of what the consultant should do. Physicians to whom he referred patients were consultants to him. He knew what he could expect from them from a medical standpoint, and he knew what he could expect from a behavior standpoint. He selected the doctors based upon those two things—that they were current in their field of medicine and knew how to apply it, and that they also conducted themselves in a proper way with the patients.

While I was driving for him as a boy, I once drove Dr. Rhine to a meeting in Little Rock. It was a postmaster's meeting and Mr. Roy Wise, the postmaster at Thornton, Mrs. Wise and my mother, Lois Henry, who was a postal clerk at the time, were all there. The speaker for the banquet was to be Dr. John R. Steelman, and I did not know Dr. Steelman personally then. I just knew who he was—he was Assistant to the President of the United States, and he was from Thornton. I was to drive Dr. Rhine, and I thought, "This is really high cotton that I'm going to be in." I drove him in Mr. Wise's car, and I thank the Lord that it was Mr. Wise's car, because I usually kept it clean for the Wises. (That was another chore that I had.) I knew that Dr. Rhine's car probably would not be clean. I learned when we got there why we took the clean car, and the reason was that Dr. Steelman was going to return to Thornton with us, and I really was in 'high cotton' then.

The things that I observed were that going to Little Rock, Dr. Rhine slept most of the way, and I understood that because you could just carry on a limited amount of conversation with a teenager driving a car of any value. But returning, Dr. Rhine talked the entire way back with Dr. Steelman. I knew that Dr. Steelman had spent some years in Dr. Rhine's home going to school in Thornton. I knew that that was the connection between the two. What had transpired between the time Dr. Steelman had actually left Thornton and ultimately landed this very good job, I didn't know. I recognized that Dr. Rhine was not overly impressed by Dr. Steelman's position. They just talked about ordinary things like Dr. Steelman's brothers and sister, what was going on in Thornton, which was really nothing compared to what was going on in Washington. I was carried away

106

with my position of driving the car for the Assistant to the President, but here Dr. Rhine was entertaining him and not being impressed at all. To Dr. Rhine it was the friendship between the two that was important, not the station of the man coming from Washington, just as his relationship with a patient was based on the individual and not the station of either Dr. Rhine or the patient—whether higher or lower by someone else's standards.

I came to realize that Dr. Rhine was not flaunting his own position or giving undue respect to the position of Dr. Steelman. They were just two people talking entirely on their own merit or accomplishments. What Dr. Steelman had accomplished was not the basis for their friendship, and therefore, Dr. Rhine could admire what Dr. Steelman was doing, and I'm sure that he did, but that was not the original basis for their friendship.

I had a longer and closer relationship with Mrs. Rhine than I had with Dr. Rhine. In taking piano lessons from her until I graduated from high school, I would see her on as many occasions in those years as I would him. I was able to understand her participation in his practice and something about her own life. I always knew that her life as a piano teacher was only a portion of her life in the community, and it had nothing to do with him. That was her endeavor, and she was able to keep that going while she was carrying on other endeavors. My lessons were commonly either before or after school. She was always on time and looking back, I don't see how she was able to accomplish that, knowing how he ran his practice. The lessons were at her house.

If the phone rang during a lesson, she would say, "Please continue," or she would simply say, "Please hold for just a moment," and she would answer the phone and it would always be about his practice. (I don't think that she ever received social calls during the times of piano lessons.) Sometimes it was Dr. Rhine calling to give her a message as to where he would be for the next stops. If it was a patient calling, she would give advice like, "He is on a call now, and he is going from there to thus and so" or "He will be back in the office in approximately forty-five minutes to an hour"— something to that effect, so the patient could then make plans accordingly. If it was a house call, she would know the vicinity where he was, and if the new call was close by where he was, she would say, "I'll try to reach him before he gets out of that neighborhood." She would return to the piano, and we would resume the lesson. I don't recall ever feeling like the music lesson was being interrupted because she did all of this so calmly. I do know that my piano lessons were important to her and important to me, but I never got the feeling that our activity was being disrupted by the calls and the transfer of information.

If Dr. Rhine came in during the lesson (he would never come in to that area of the living room where I was having my lesson), he would always come in the back door, into the kitchen, the dining room, to the living room. Most of the time he would look at a note pad sitting by the telephone and get his messages off of it. If something was not self-explanatory, it was not Dr. Rhine who asked about it, she would already have volunteered the informa-

107

tion. Again, I was hearing information about his practice, but I knew full well that whatever I was hearing was none of my business. If he had no calls, and especially in the winter, he would commonly sit down, and I don't know if he read or listened to my music lesson or what; he was always totally quiet.

I had some understanding then, but more understanding now of what her life must have been like to have to try to meld teaching piano lessons and rearing children into his kind of practice, but she had been doing it long enough, by the time I came along, that it seemed that there was nothing to it. Yet her life was very confining. She was confined to that house, commonly twenty-four hours a day, day on end, and yet she didn't come across as a person whose life was at all restricted. "I have a life. I'm enjoying it. Whatever it is that I am doing, that is my total life for right now, and I'm very happy with it." From my observation, she always appeared to be very happy—happy in her work, happy in her children. I never saw any indication of any unhappiness in anything, and I don't think that was false. She was not a social butterfly, putting on an air about something. What you saw was what it was, and what I saw was happiness.

My own appreciation of classical music I attribute to Mrs. Rhine. I feel sure that I was a good piano student for her. I was always a compulsive kid, and if I set about doing something, I always did it to the best of my ability, so I did practice, as opposed to my brother, Pat, who did not practice. And I did enjoy my lessons, and I did not use the lessons to talk about anything else. At recital time, I was always worried about it, but I had always practiced my pieces and I was ready for it technically. Emotionally, I never learned how to relax for a recital. I love classical music to this day, and to her I would have to attribute the reason that some of that fire has been lighted. Music remains a very significant part of my life. I still play some, though I mostly listen to music now.

My desire to learn classical music was not shared by any other student in school. I always felt a little alone in that. For a teenager, feeling alone is not a comfortable feeling, and yet, I liked music well enough that it didn't bother me that much. Too, I was always a little bit embarrassed to be on a piano recital, but not enough that I wasn't on them. I was a six-foot-two teenager with all those little girls. I was not the only male, but you could count them on one hand, and it would take several hands to count the females. I don't remember if she influenced how I handled this embarrassment.

She and I had a few discussions about whether or not I should continue music after high school. Her advice to me was fairly direct. I won't forget it, because I made a decision based upon it. I was still undecided about what I was going to do with my life. I was sixteen or seventeen when I discussed with her going further with piano. She advised me that it was extremely difficult, *extremely* difficult to be good enough to be a concert pianist, and to make a living at that. Starting at that point in my life would be almost impossible. I didn't understand that then, but with other things as they were, I let music go as a career. Now, I know that if you want to be a concert pianist, you don't start at seventeen, you start at three. She may have meant that I really didn't have the talent, I don't know. In any case, her advice was good, and she did give it to me fairly directly—as directly as you can give it to a sixteen or seventeen-year-old and get them to act upon it. After that, there was no longer any question about it.

The ease with which she went about handling her part of his practice, which was primarily the receiver of information about patients, and the ease with which she transferred it to him and pulling the practice together day in and day out—twenty-four hours a day—it is truly amazing what she did, and did it in such a self-effacing way. It is amazing that a person can adjust to that amount of unknowns. She would never know what time he was coming home. You know that he is going to come home when he is through. He is not going to play cards or checkers or shoot the bull with someone or go to Mr. Robertson's store and whittle, like some of the other gentlemen in the community. You know that he is going to come only after he is finished, and you can't predict when he is going to be finished with his work. That is such a hectic schedule to adjust to, but by the time I came along, she was so adjusted to it, that you didn't recognize there could be any problem with it. Her total life was that way. So much of her life was given to seeing that his practice moved along, and yet she was able to have her own areas of interest, which never really waned in spite of it, and she was able to work it around what she had to do in his practice. There were her children, her music and her reading.

I recognized her strong inner resources after I went away to college and would return. She was able to carry on conversations with me about the things I was doing, and after I met Jo Ann (my wife) she would converse with her without any prior knowledge of her development, because she was not from that area—what she was choosing to do in college, her teaching career. Mrs. Rhine always carried on an intelligent conversation. One would never suspect that most of what she was talking about she had actually assimilated sitting in her own house, reading or talking with other people.

(Dr. Henry is a neurologist and an internist, but practices neurology only.) PRB

"I got the idea from him of working long hours. He never knew when to quit."

DR. JOHN ROY STEELMAN

NAPLES, FLORIDA

I inherited something from my parents, something worth more than millions, namely, stamina. I can outwork anybody my age on this earth. I am eighty-four years old. My father got me into this, and Dr. Rhine had a hand in it, too, because my father said it, and Dr. Rhine not only said it, but did it. I got the idea from him of working long hours. He never knew when to quit. My father told me when I went off to work, way back, probably 1914, "If you will outwork everybody there, you'll come out on top." As I said, he said it and Dr. Rhine exhibited it to me. It got so ingrained in my mind that all my life, everywhere I went, I had to outdo the other fellow. So when I went to Washington—here I am, just a country boy from Arkansas—I figure the only way to go up is to outwork every son-of-a-gun in town, and I did. Finally, at the White House, too.

In order to go to high school, I lived with Dr. Rhine for at least two years. I watched him work day and night. He was honest and sincere. He wanted to serve the people. He didn't think too much about what he was going to get out of it. He just wanted to *do* it. From him I got the idea of doing it right, and he sure did. No matter how many hours it took. Between him and my father, they caused me to lose a lot of sleep along the way. I got a lot out of him. I learned a lot from him.

When I think of him, one or two things always come to mind. One of them was that he was my Grandma's doctor, Grandma Steelman. Now she was a chronic complainer—what you call a hypochondriac, and Dr. Rhine knew nothing was wrong with Grandma, but he said, "She thinks there is, so I've got to give her medicine." He would come home and say to his mother after dinner (he was usually late), "Mammy, bring me a tablespoonful of flour." He would get out the capsules, and he would sit

110

there packing some capsules for Grandma Steelman. Just plain flour! He said, "This will fix her right up." So he would give her those. She would take them for a while, and she would say, "Oh, that's fine. I feel so much better."

Later on she would see the doctor, and she would say, "Doctor, this medicine you gave me played out. It just doesn't work anymore. I got to have something else." So then he would get something real bitter and put it in with her flour. I don't know what it was. She'd take it and say, "This is terrible stuff, but it helps." So she'd take that a while and come back complaining again. He'd say, "I've got some capsules here that are a little different, but I believe that it will cure your pain." And he'd give her some more flour. It went on and on. I think that all the time I lived at his house, he was doctoring Grandma with one thing and another, saying, "There's nothing wrong with her. She just thinks she's sick."

Another thing I remember about him—I don't think he ever sent anybody a bill. They could pay him if they wanted to, and he would come home with a sack full of beans or potatoes or apples or something. People would say, "Doc, I got no money, but we sure got some beautiful beans here. You take these home."

Dr. Rhine had this horse he rode. He'd ride the horse a great round, miles and miles, and he'd come back home and change over to the buggy. He had two smaller, faster horses that would pull the buggy. When he would come to our house, when he would turn left at Little Bay, he would go to sleep. There was a branch that ran across the road. Just before he got to that branch, there was something, which we never could find, that would scare the horses, making them jerk, and waking him up. But he would get a nice nap from Little Bay to that creek.

(Mr. Roy, as we called him, was an advisor to Presidents Roosevelt and Eisenhower and was the Special Assistant to President Harry Truman. That job is now called Chief of Staff.) PRB

ANNIE STEELMAN DAVIDSON

THORNTON, ARKANSAS

Sometimes Dr. Rhine couldn't get all the way to the house in the car. He had boots to walk across a stream. This time he got as far as the Robert Ellis old place, and his car stalled. He walked from there to the house, across the stream. When he got ready to come back, there had come this big rain, and Mr. Joe Jones was there. Dr. Rhine asked, "Is there any way I can get back to Thornton? My car has gone dead, and I've got to get someone to come and fix it." Joe Jones said, "I'll take you. I had to leave my car on the other side of the stream." They had to walk to the cars, and Joe said, "Dr. Rhine had boots and I didn't, and I got my feet and legs wet."

Dr. Rhine delivered all of my babies down at home in the Providence community—four children, three girls and a boy. Johnny, my husband, and Dr. Rhine hunted together all the time, and he kept a bunch of Dr. Rhine's dogs. Dr. Rhine delivered all but one of my brothers and also me. Roy [Dr. John R. Steelman] was born a few months before Dr. Rhine became our family doctor in 1900, but the rest of us were born on that same farm where my children were born. My brother Jewel's children were all born there, too—five boys—all born on that same farm.

He delivered my daughter Pat's children, too. She had her first baby at the Camden Hospital. Dr. Rhine went there to deliver it. Sue, another daughter, just took over when Pat got sick. She thought she had to do everything. It was in the night, and she got dressed, put on her high heeled shoes and went for Dr. Rhine. Dr. Rhine said that when she came up that brick sidewalk (they slept in the back sleeping porch) he could hear those heels popping along. She called to him, and he said to carry her on to the hospital. He would be there soon. Pat's next baby was born at Hampton, and Dr. Rhine delivered that baby. When the third baby was born, she was somewhere else, but she told the doctor there that she wanted Dr. Rhine to be there, and she didn't think he liked that very much, but she had him there anyway.

My father, Mr. Ples Steelman, was a great friend of Dr. Rhine. The Rhine family was always asked to any family dinners we had. During the summer, when we had every kind of vegetable, watermelon and such, Papa would just load him down when he would come. He wanted Dr. Rhine to have some of everything he had. Johnny did, too, after he came in the family. We continued on with that great friendship. Johnny drove the school bus, and he spent a lot of time with Dr. Rhine.

I have never been sick. I never did have to go to a doctor, except when my babies were born. I was in a hospital only once in my life, and I'm nearly 81 years old. I think it's because I have always eaten good home grown vegetables and meats.

Mrs. Watt Files told me about when her oldest daughter, Kathryn Sue, was born. They lived out past Little Bay in the Providence community where they still live. Then Watt and Clemmie lived in an old log house. They called for Dr. Rhine to come deliver the baby, but when she was born, she didn't seem to have a breath of life in her. He called for a tub of water, which someone had to draw from a well with a bucket. Dr. Rhine soused the baby down in that water, and then began slapping her in the face. She began crying then. Clemmie says if Dr. Rhine had not done that, she didn't think the baby would ever have caught her breath.

In the Dr. Rhine days, it was something else! He was so good. He would get up all hours of the night and go all night long with no sleep. He would deliver babies to whole families, knowing he would never get a dime. He never did refuse. He just loved to help people; that was what it was.

112

I remember so well one night, Dr. Rhine had been in service, and this was his first night at home. My parents had to call him to come see me. I believe that was the time I had thyphoid fever. We thought that if we could get Dr. Rhine, we would be all right. My mother, Mrs. Bunn Ezell, really swore by him. When she would be here in Bearden visiting me, after they moved to Little Rock, and she got sick, he was the first one we called. He always came without a murmur, and she immediately felt better afterwards. He was really something.

At the time I broke my arm, he was in service stationed in England, and, of course, we couldn't have him. That threw us for a loop. Even after I came to Bearden, I called him for people when we couldn't get a doctor here. He always came right on.

After my husband, Raymond, retired, I retired. I told him one day, "Dr. Rhine, I just want to tell you that I have retired."

"What did you do that for?"

He didn't believe much in retirement. He was going to work 'til he dropped.

I grew up in Thornton. I finished school in 1923 and worked for Stout Lumber Company until 1926, when I married and came to Bearden. As a little girl, I would go to Mammy Rhine's. We bought milk from her. I was curious and would go all over the house. She never said anything to me. It was all right for me to go. Dr. Rhine's dancing slippers were sitting under the table in one of the rooms, and that's where they stayed all of the time. They were black patent slippers with a grosgrain ribbon bow across the toes.

For a while he drove a horse and buggy, then when he got a car, he would drive up in front of the house and yell, "Whoa!" I can just hear him saying that now.

Most of the time he called me "Miss Jennie." My name is Jennie Vance. Everybody else called me Vance, but he called me "Miss Jennie."

One time he took some warts off my hand. I was a grown girl then, working. They got to hurting pretty bad after I got back to the office and began to swell. They were bound. I went back to his office, and he started unwrapping them, and I just keeled over. He said, "Oh, Miss Jennie, I didn't know you were going to do that."

There was a huge crowd at Dr. Rhine Day, and I remember so well what I took to eat. They had the meat, and we took salads and desserts. I baked a jam cake. Friends of ours that we ran into there, that we saw occasionally, not that often, were Harry and Aleene Littrell. I told Harry, "I want you to get a piece of that jam cake." But when we got to the table it was gone. So many people! It was a wonderful day. He just loved people, and everybody truly loved him. He never seemed to get out of sorts. He was always the same, everywhere you saw Dr. Rhine.

My mother and Dr. Rhine's mother were real good friends. Both families were very close. Mama had kept her invitation to Dr. Rhine Day and the note from Dr. Rhine, with a picture of him speaking to the crowd, thanking them for coming to the celebration, all of these years—since 1946. [This note was typed with the well-known purple typewriter ribbon.]

T. E. Rhine, M. D.
Thornton, Ark.
Nov.10,46.

Mr. & Mrs. Bunn Ezell
Little Rock, Ark.
Dear Friends:—It was a great pleasure to have you both down to help celebrate my day and make it a happier day for me. That was sure a great dy for all the family but I feel that I was not worthy of that much honor its true I have worked day and night for the people of Thornton and surrounding country and twons adjacent to thornton territory. So am sending you a snap shot of me while trying to talk to my many friends.Now rats, mice, roaches, termites and all other bothersome pests around the house will disappear immediately. Its just a small remembrances your faily every since I came to Thornton. Hope you accepts it as such. When down be sure and come around to see us. All the girls are away from home from New Your City to San antonio, Texas.

Your friend,

T. E. Rhine, M.D.

ELLIE MCCLAIN

FORDYCE, ARKANSAS

When I commenced working for the telephone company in Fordyce in 1925, then we knew everybody's number. Reading the directory was just something people didn't do. They would call in and say, "I want so and so's number," and we would tell it to them. We gave out the fire alarms, and sometimes we would get a bad weather report, and we would ring out on the rural lines to warn them if a storm was coming. All of the doctors would call in and say, "If I get any calls, I will be at so and so." Each operator would pass that word to the others. Of course, there weren't but three of us. We did this until 1956. Also, if a woman was at a neighbor's house, and she heard her phone ringing, she would call in and ask us to connect the call to where she was. Then you could tell who was talking, because the lines would be plugged in. We would do that. Every Christmas all of the doctors would bring us boxes of candy. Dr. Thomas always brought chocolate-covered cherries, and my daddy, John McClain, was going to have those. Other people in town appreciated us, too, merchants and others. I did everything at the telephone office but climb the poles and dig the holes. Mr. Orie Bryant did that. I worked forty-four years to the day for the phone company—one company. I'm eighty-one years old now. I started work for $30.00 a month. After four weeks, I got a raise to $35.00. I just danced all over the rest room when I got $2.50 more in my pay check.

For several years, Mama fed Dr. Rhine's fox dogs, until a mad dog came in and bit them, and we had to kill them all. They didn't have any dog food then. She made cornbread for them, and we had home ground meal and there would be lots of bran left that she would put in the cornbread. If she boiled any meat, she would take that juice and pour over the bread, and, of course, there were table scraps. We had some dogs ourselves, too—fox dogs.

Back when Dr. Rhine was riding a horse, a good while before he married, he came by our house one night and said to my mother, "Miss Molly, have you got a bed that I can sleep on? I have gone 'til I can't go any farther. If they call and Mammy knows where I am, she'll tell them, because she's not going to lie. And if I get the word that somebody needs me, I'm going. I'll not turn them down." So Mama fixed a bed, and he told Daddy when to wake him up. He went across the hall, which was open, a dog trot, they call it. When he woke up, Daddy had taken his horse to the barn, given it feed and water and curried it down. That horse was as tired as he was. Mama had his breakfast fixed when he got up, so he ate and then went on home.

Another time he stopped by our house just to get warm. He stretched his feet out in front of him and went to sleep. That is one time the McClain kids kept quiet. Mama took us to the kitchen. When Dr. Rhine woke up, he had a whole lot to say about sick folks that needed him, and he needed to have been on his way. Daddy said to him, "That rest will do you and your patients more good than the medicine you'd give those sick folks."

"I guess you are right."

When Mama was sick the last time, she was in bed for nineteen weeks. She had a heart attack. Dr. Rhine didn't think that she would live through the night. He would come by our house and call Mrs. Rhine to see if he had any calls. Some days he would be there twice. Maybe more, but everyday Dr. Rhine had a call to Fordyce, and he would come use the phone and check on Mama—for nineteen weeks. He never charged us, except for the few times we called him to come when Mama was worse. There never was a person like Dr. Rhine.

One Sunday afternoon, Orie Bryant had been fishing and brought us some fish. We got out in the yard to clean the fish and a spider bit me. I didn't pay any attention to it. I had to work that night, all night, by myself. After I got to work, it began swelling. All I could do was put ice water on my throat. By morning, you couldn't tell where my chin was. It was just level with my throat. Dr. Rhine came to the Fielder's house that morning to see a sick child, and Mama called him to come see me. Daddy was at work, so Dr. Rhine went to town and got my medicine and brought it back to me. That afternoon around four, Dr. Rhine came back to see me, and before we went to bed, he was back again. The next morning, before we got up (he had been somewhere and was going home) he came. He came five times from noon of one day to the next. That's how he felt about his patients!

He not only doctored you, he advised you and you could go to him with your troubles.

We used to go to these big dinners, and all the women knew that Dr. Rhine liked chicken gizzards. "Dr. Rhine, I brought you some." "Dr. Rhine," and he'd have a plate full of chicken gizzards to eat.

There were just nine days difference in my dad's and Dr. Rhine's birthdays. Dr. Rhine would always say, "When I get as old as John McClain, I'm quitting work."

When my daddy died (he died instantly of a heart attack), Dr. Rhine tried to take all four of us in his arms at the same time, and we were all grown. They were great friends. He called him John Mc, like so many did.

Dr. Rhine and Jack Wright, one of his special children.

Sara Brandon Cathey, whose father was the first white patient Dr. Rhine saw. He delivered Sara and her sister, and in 1960, delivered Sara's oldest daughter and was to have delivered a later baby in 1962, but an ice storm prevented that.

Allen and Lillian Lightfoot and their four sons, Jimmy, Johnny, Bobby and Gerald. Dr. Rhine delivered both parents and the children.

Mary Theresa and Jerry Atchley, children of a Methodist minister and his wife, both delivered by Dr. Rhine.

Pat and Morrison Henry. Both drove Dr. Rhine on calls, both were piano students of Mrs. Rhine and both are now doctors.

Ed and Verna Gresham and their son, Junior. Ed was the third baby that Dr. Rhine delivered. He also delivered Verna and Junior.

This child was born in a slop jar. Dr. Rhine attended him several hours later.

Dr. Pat Murphey of Little Rock. He was the first neurologist in the state and was Dr. Rhine's doctor and a very close friend.

Dud Crosby, a fox hunting friend of Dr. Rhine's, blowing a hunting horn.

Anna Tatum Crosby in 1984

and the house she built in 1944.

Dr. John Roy Steelman (left) and John Strait. Both lived with Dr. Rhine in order to attend high school. Both ended up in Washington, D. C., Dr. Steelman as a presidential advisor and Strait as manager of the office of Sun Life Assurance Company of Canada.

Dr. Steelman with the Truman family and other advisors on vacation in Key West, Florida, in 1950.

Dr. Rhine amid part of the scrap iron that he collected during World War II.

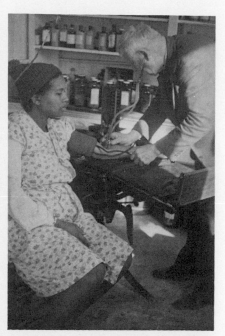

Doctor Rhine ministering to his patients.

Doctor dispensing medicine.   Reflecting on a problem.

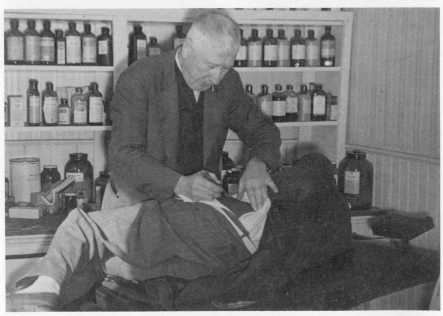

A shot in the rear—of the office.

"We did have a political horizon in the state at that time, in which local influencial citizens did have an especially great influence on the outcome of elections. Dr. Rhine was an example of this."

FEDERAL JUDGE OREN HARRIS

EL DORADO, ARKANSAS

I grew up in Hempstead County, but I settled in Union County, El Dorado, Arkansas, in 1930, having received my certificate to practice law. Just a young man, trying to get along during the Depression, I had a background about political matters and public service because my granddad was a county judge of Nevada County back in 1882 to 1886. My own father was elected Tax Assessor in Hempstead County and served four years. Then in the 1920's, my older brother was elected to county offices, first county clerk for four years and then county treasurer for four years. Coming to El Dorado, Arkansas, I went into the law office with Mr. John E. Harris, (no relation of mine) and General Compere, who was very active in state politics, especially during the period of time just before the Depression and during the Depression. He was Chairman of the State Democratic Committee. Therefore, I came into an office, both interested in politics, and from that base, after two years in the practice of law, doing the best I could to make a living, I went in the prosecuting attorney's office as a deputy in Union County, Arkansas. This is the 13th Judicial Circuit of Arkansas, composed of Union, Columbia, Ouachita and Calhoun Counties. You know, Thornton is in Calhoun County. I was designated by the Prosecuting Attorney to take over the business in Calhoun County, and among those I met early during that time, 1933, was Dr. T. E. Rhine. I knew about him before I met him.

Back in those days, we didn't have municipal courts like we do now. The Justice of the Peace in each township, what we called the J. P. courts, held court. For misdemeanor and small crimes and hearings on bonds and

123

things of that sort, we went to the J. P. court. Thornton did have a J. P. court at that time, and I attended the court and looked after it.* Through that experience, I met Dr. Rhine, became acquainted with him, and we did form a very close friendship, a relationship that lasted throughout his life. I never knew of anyone who did not have a lot of respect for his counsel and advice.

Back in those days, throughout Arkansas, we did have the good fortune of having good people interested in politics, and we did have a political horizon in the state at the time, in which local influencial citizens did have an especially great influence on the outcome of elections. Dr. Rhine was an example of this, as well as (in our area) Hendrick Alphin and Joe K. Mahony of El Dorado, who was a very good friend of Dr. Rhine. He knew him when he was Prosecuting Attorney back in the teens. He used to comment, "Those like Dr. Rhine and others"—the people you could depend upon.**

When the occasion arose, I would consult with Dr. Rhine, requesting information about the type of person I would be dealing with. As an example, there was an individual, John Fultz, who wanted to be a public official and lived nearby in Bearden. He was a deputy sheriff in Ouachita County and was charged with breaking the dam in a pond. (I sent that fellow to the penitentiary for life later on for killing his first cousin and his wife.) He did this because he wanted to have a fish-fry, and he wanted to get all the fish out of the pond. I went to Dr. Rhine for some confidential information, and he told me all about it.

There was a postmaster in Thornton, Roy Wise, and he looked towards Dr. Rhine as though he was his son and had great confidence in him, and he and I would talk, too, from time to time. I would go into Dr. Rhine's office, I wouldn't impose upon him at all, because he was a very busy doctor, and he would give me information. From all of this, the friendship and relationship increased. As time went on, I had friends in Harrell, Hampton,

---

* Mr. Ben Murry was the Justice of the Peace for Caswell Township, and court was held at his general store in Thornton. PRB

**from *Southern Politics*, by V. O. Key, Jr. (Chapter Nine, page 196):
"A second category of voters consists of those controlled by local leaders (in sub-county areas usually) who will not sell their influence. There are many such leaders, our practical politician assures us. They would be insulted if you offered them money. It would be 'like waving a red flag.' They throw their support to the candidate they believe to be 'the best man' for the office. Much of a candidate's task is to reach and sell these leaders the idea that he is the 'best man'. Such a local leader, of more than average stature, several politicians say, is Dr. T. E. Rhine, of Thornton in South Arkansas. The good doctor is a beloved and respected local practitioner in whose honor the community declared a holiday and conducted festivities on the forty-ninth anniversary of the beginning of his medical career in the community." 23Note 23: *Arkansas Gazette* (Little Rock) June 18, 1948. The doctor, one politician says, backs a candidate on the basis of merit and his people vote as he votes. "He won't trade out; you wouldn't dare suggest it to him."

Tinsman, and Dr. Rhine was very familiar with the county. He was a student of politics and of people. He knew people. He was willing to tell you about things and conditions, whatever they might be and what was good for the community.

At the end of four years as deputy prosecutor, I ran for Prosecuting Attorney. Listen, I had no trouble at all at Tinsman. I carried that vote by a big vote. In fact, I carried all of Calhoun County.

Out at Ellisville during that time, this man, almost like an animal, killed his wife. He strangled her with wire. I prosecuted that case. [It was written up in *True Detective* magazine.] Later, when I went to Ellisville, Dr. Rhine told me who the people were to remember, and we were investigating this murder at that time. The result was—I never was too proud of the several people I sent to the electric chair. I took a bunch of people down to that old store in Ellisville, and for about ten or twelve dollars, we treated everybody around there. When I ran for Prosecuting Attorney there were about ninety-four votes cast in Ellisville, and I got ninety-two of them.

During all those years I was associated with people there, Dr. Rhine was the central figure that I would always go to, because I knew he was dependable. He knew what he was talking about. He would give you information about the community, the environment of the community and the people that lived there, their nature. He was really magnificent in a field of this kind. I enjoyed this relationship, and I'll tell you the kind of man that he was. When Captain Wade Kitchens was elected to Congress in 1936 there were some things, like appointing Roy Wise to the postmastership, that Captain Kitchens followed the advice of Dr. Rhine, and I can understand why. Although we had formed a close relationship, Captain Kitchens had done some favors for them at Thornton. [Judge Harris ran for Congress against Captain Kitchens in 1940 and won.] Dr. Rhine didn't take any active position against me, but he told me outright what his situation was toward Kitchens and me. He thought personally, that he would like to be for me. He thought I was the man for the job, and he wasn't going to do me any harm. I knew what he meant. He was telling me that he became obligated to this man, even though he was not anything like as close friends as we were, but he felt obligated, and he was going to honor the obligation. I respected him for it. I thought it was one of the finest things. I knew he didn't do anything against me, because I got most of the votes there that time, too.

From then on, we enjoyed many years of very close relationship, and that is the first time I heard of and knew John Steelman, because Dr. Rhine was a prime sponsor of John Steelman. I thought it was a good thing, too, because John Steelman was an outstanding individual.

Dr. Rhine was first of all a good man, a good citizen, dependable, and he was a country doctor. He went to see the people in a horse and buggy in the early days. The night never got too dark or too rough when someone would call for him to go. He was known throughout all of that area. He was one of the most honorable individuals—honest. A great individual to analyse people to tell what they are. He knew who they were—he was a student of human nature.

I was fortunate to be there at his big celebration [Dr. Rhine Day, May 17, 1946]. It was a great day. One of the humorous notes—Dr. Shuffield, Joe Shuffield, from Little Rock was there, and he made some remarks. Having known me a lot longer than anybody there, he said that when I was a youngster, in about the third grade he and his wife taught school where I lived, at Belton, in Hempstead County. He told of me sucking my thumb and what he tried to do to keep me from sucking my thumb.

Dr. R. B. Robbins was there, a great friend of Dr. Rhine. Dr. Shuffield was a great friend, too. There were many doctors throughout the state there that day.

I was one of the principal speakers, among others at Dr. Rhine Day. Ham Moses, president of Arkansas Power and Light Company at that time, was another one. He grew up in Hampton. It was an occasion that I was thrilled to share all the joy that came out of it. It was a great day for him, and he deserved it.

To me, my relationship with Dr. Rhine, was one of the finest experiences of a public relationship that I have enjoyed during all the years. I shall always cherish the feeling, the warmth, the friendship, in the numerous times that I visited Dr. Rhine in his office, sharing some of his experience. Advice about what he thought public servants should engage in. I know it helped me, not only in my objective, political service, but it helped me personally, in my own life. I shall always remember it.

I was present, and one of the honorees, at the party for Distinguished Arkansans, held at the American Medical Association Convention in Washington, in 1949. Ruth was there with me. That honor given to him was publicized throughout the nation through the American Medical Journal, and I know he received letters and all kinds of communications, from doctors, principally. This honor became known as one of the major events of the AMA meeting that year. [He was not the winner of the General Practitioner of the Year Award. He was the runner-up.] We talked about the health insurance legislation, and he wasn't too crazy about making speeches, unless they were impromptu and among friends.

I was there at the dedication of the hospital addition in Fordyce in 1965. I made the principal address. That hospital meant a lot to Dr. Rhine. It was part of the Hill-Burton program. It came out of the committee that I worked on, and later on, I was the sponsor of legislation that extended that program. They called it then the Hill-Burton-Harris program. Before I left Congress in 1966, we had one of those hospitals in every county I represented—twenty-eight counties—except one.

On February 3, 1983 in El Dorado, the Court of Appeals of the Eighth Circuit met and held some hearings. It was the first time in the history of the Court that had ever happened. They had a ceremony beforehand and hung my portrait in the courtroom to celebrate my fifty years of public service.

BILL T. JAMES

We were having a fox hunters' gathering down below Thornton. Sid McMath was running for governor, and he came to the supper. There were a lot of people there. Dr. Rhine told him he could speak for five minutes, and when that time was up, Dr. Rhine stopped him saying, "We came out here for fox hunting, not politics." Dud Crosby then got up and talked for thirty minutes. He told about how bad the dog food was during the War. So bad, in fact, that his children wouldn't even eat it. We knew he was lying.

Dr. Rhine was color blind as far as black or white. He didn't care. A fellow moved into town, and he was a KKK [Ku Klux Klan] man, but no one knew it. Dr. Rhine was fixin' to have a party [to celebrate his sixty years in Thornton] and black and white and all were invited. This fellow put KKK signs on trees across from Doctor's house. We thought he did it, didn't know for sure. Claud Arnold and Bill Parker looked into it, and the fellow left town. He was the only one we knew who could have done it. He had joined the Assembly of God Church in Hopeville, a church in Fordyce and the Baptist Church here. He was really trying to get the KKK thing started here. Claud and Bill Parker was goin' to put that man in the river, but he left. Claud would have killed in a minute for Dr. Rhine. Claud was a Dr. Rhine baby. Claud was bad to drink, fight and cut-up, but Dr. Rhine helped him to quit that. I was young and wanting to get into something—craving excitement—and I followed Claud and Bill all the time.

Claud and Bill both kept dogs for Doc, and I had two or three. He gave me two horns, too.

After Dr. Rhine got to where he couldn't drive at night (he was always a bad driver anyway), I drove him a lot. If he was delivering a baby, maybe he would be there two or three hours, he would get out and chop wood or carry rocks and fill up a hole, or do something. He was never idle. He didn't appear to be nervous or restless, but it seemed like he was trying to do something constructive all the time.

We boys used to hitchhike to Fordyce every Saturday. There weren't many cars in Thornton—Dr. Rhine, of course, Jessie McManus, Johnnie Tomlinson had one and Skinny—Mr. Lionel Robertson. We'd watch for Dr. Rhine, because we knew he would pick us up. All of us were scared to ride with him. There were so many bags and bottles in that old car, you couldn't hardly find a place to sit. It was always filthy dirty. I don't guess he ever washed it.

LITTLE ROCK, ARKANSAS

I remember meeting Dr. Rhine at a fox hunting dinner. This was a big event for that section of the state. There were several people making talks, and Dr. Rhine, who was presiding, ran a tight ship. When my five minutes was up he, figuratively speaking, used the shepherd's staff to pull me off the podium. He was the greatest.

He had tremendous influence politically and was one of the last of the great family physicians who made house calls and provided medical attention, counsel and even financial help to those of his patients in need.

I recall vividly attending the meeting in Washington when he was runner-up for General Practitioner of the Year, which was a great honor for him and a distinction for the State of Arkansas.

In addition, he was an avid fox hunter and could sound a fox horn with the best.

(Governor McMath was the governor of the State of Arkansas from 1949-1953.) PRB

"Usually, when we went on those trips to Little Rock, Dr. Rhine would send the doctors something, maybe a bucket of molasses..."

VICTOR CONE

COLUMBIA, TENNESSEE

There was a closeness and special friendship between the Rhine family and the Cone family. Dr. Rhine was more than a friend to me, and I will always treasure that friendship as long as I live. As a boy growing up, I can remember my mother telling me about Dr. Rhine and how much she loved him and thought of him and what friends he and my father were. Dr. Rhine was a friend to everyone. Color didn't make any difference to him. If someone called him and needed him, and he could get there, he would go. I've been with him when he has gone over roads that I didn't think a wagon could get over. I've been with him on trips from one end of Calhoun County to the other, in Dallas, Cleveland, Bradley and Ouachita Counties, on roads, back at that time, that you wouldn't believe.

One night, he came by the house, picked me up and we started toward Fordyce. About four or five miles up the highway, he turned off to the right, and we started off through the woods to an old darky's house. We came to a big mud puddle. He stopped, looked at it for a few minutes and told me to hold on. We started through it, and when we did, we hit a high place in the center of the road. It shoved the radiator back into the fan. We got out of the car and walked the rest of the way, with his lantern to light the way. After he had seen the darky, the man of the house hitched up his team and drove us down to the car in the wagon and hitched a chain to the car, pulled it out, turned it around and pulled us back to Thornton to Scott's garage to have the car fixed.

I can remember how he would laugh when he would tell about the old darky who was in his office and said to him, "Dr. Rhine, don't you die 'cause you is the only colored doctor that we got."

One cold winter night, he came by to pick me up to go with him to Star

129

City. One of the girls came along, too. Somewhere between Rison and Star City, as we were driving along, there was a man walking down the road. Dr. Rhine stopped and picked him up, and he got in the back seat. This fellow had a body odor that I don't believe anybody could have stayed in the car with. I was in the back seat with him. I rolled the glass down to get some fresh air. After we had let him out, we made our call in Star City. Sometime in the night, I took the earache. It was so bad, that my mother sent me down to Dr. Rhine's to get something to help me sleep. I got him out of bed. He said, "Good gracious alive! I'm sorry about that. It was that cold wind that caused it."

One night he came by and wanted me to go fox hunting with him. We left out and went to Calaway Cemetery down between Thornton and Hampton and parked the car. We got out. We could hear the dogs running. Dr. Rhine took out across a sage field, and it was cold that night. He would hit those persimmon bushes, and they would fly back and hit me in the face or upside the head. We ran until my tongue just rolled out. We got to the other side of the field. Those dogs turned around and started right back across that same sage field. Dr. Rhine turned around, and here we started back again. We got nearly back across, and he stepped in a hole and fell. It just so happened that it didn't hurt him, but I never was so glad in my life to see someone fall because I was just absolutely given out.

On another fox hunt, he had me to take Mrs. Rhine's car, fill it up with fox hounds, and drive down below Thornton toward Hampton. It was cold that night. We got to smelling something, and when we got down to where we were to unload the dogs, we found the dogs had gotten sick in the car, and you talk about a mess! I drove the car down to a creek, and we found a bucket and took water from the creek and washed the car out. I think that was my last fox hunting trip.

We made so many trips to Little Rock taking the girls to have their teeth straightened and taking patients to see doctors in Little Rock and other places. These trips were such happy times. The children would always play games. One trip, the sky was cloudy and the game was to find enough blue in the sky to make a Dutchman a pair of britches.

On another trip, it was just before I went in the army in 1942 when tires were hard to get. We had so many flats going up there and coming back. I'd change that flat, get the spare on and get some service station to fix it, wouldn't go far, have another flat.

When we got back home, Virginia said to Mrs. Rhine, "You ought to pay Victor plenty of money for all this trouble that he had." I laughed, and told Mrs. Rhine, "You don't owe me one penny. I was paid a long time ago." I can remember my mother telling me, "Any time that Dr. or Mrs. Rhine or the girls need you to drive them or do something for them, don't you *ever* turn them down," and that's something I always tried to do because I always enjoyed every bit, even going to those Shirley Temple movies on Sunday afternoon in Fordyce.

Usually, when we went on those trips to Little Rock, Dr. Rhine would send the doctors something, maybe a bucket of molasses or a country ham, or a big bundle of kindling that he would chop up. He had a big pine pile out behind his house. I told him one day, "You have enough pine knots to start a fire in every stove in Calhoun County." He got the biggest kick out of that. But he would bundle it up, and when we would go to Little Rock, he would send some to his doctor friends.

One doctor stands out especially in my mind—Dr. Pat Murphey. I would go, after I let Mrs. Rhine and the girls out at the Donaghey Building to see Dr. Henry Mahoney, to Dr. Murphey's office on Scott Street to deliver the molasses, ham or whatever. There the receptionist would have me to wait, and I didn't have to wait long because Dr. Murphey would come out, and he would tell me how much he appreciated me doing that for him for Dr. Rhine, and to tell Dr. Rhine how much he appreciated it. Dr. Murphey always came down to Thornton every fall when Dr. Rhine would have a big bird hunt. I went a time or two on that hunt, and I just enjoyed the fellowship so much.

On one of our trips to Little Rock, I had several gallons of molasses in the back of the car to take to different doctors. Between Sheridan and Little Rock, we started smelling something. I pulled over to the side of the road, stopped, went back and raised the back end up, and lo and behold, the top was off of one of those buckets of molasses and molasses had spilled all over the trunk of the car. How those molasses did smell and what a sticky mess!

When some of Dr. Rhine's patients needed to go to Little Rock, he would find me and have me to drive them up there. I took Kenneth Hardman, Dr. Rhine's nephew, to the hospital. I took Rhine Condray, another nephew, to Claremore, Oklahoma, for him.

One day I walked in his office. He heard me come in and hollered at me, "Come here a minute." I went to the back room and the old darky, Tom Campbell was in the chair, and Dr. Rhine was trying to pull his tooth. Dr. Rhine would get ahold of that tooth and yank and pull, but he couldn't budge it. Finally, he told me, "Victor, put Tom in my car, and take him to Fordyce to Dr. Patterson and see what he can do." I did that. I parked by the window at Dr. Patterson's office, and he called me to come in. "I want to show you something." I walked in. He couldn't pull the tooth out either. He reached into his cabinet and got out something that looked like a chisel and a hammer, and he had to bust that tooth to finish pulling it out. Then, he took something that looked like a hay hook to get the roots out.

One trip I made with Dr. and Mrs. Rhine was to an American Legion Convention in Hot Springs. There was a public wedding at noon on the grounds of the Arlington Hotel. There was a huge crowd there. Coming back, we stopped at Lake Catherine at the home of Arkansas Power and Light Company president, Harvey Couch. He had a beautiful home there with lots of wild animals.

As a boy growing up, I had a jaw tooth on each side that ached. My mother sent me to Dr. Rhine. That was in the early 1920's, when he had his

131

office with Dr. C. T. Black up at the drugstore near the mill—Stout Lumber Company. I walked in and told him what was wrong. He pulled a straight-back chair out and told me to sit down. He looked at my teeth. He said, "Yes, they need coming out." He got ahold of one and when he did, he said, "Now you grab me around the leg, and you squeeze just as hard as you can." I know I nearly pulled his leg off, because I thought he was going to pull my head off, before he pulled those two teeth out. Back in that time, they didn't give shots to deaden the pain when they would pull a tooth.

One time, as a boy, I was going to town, my mother gave me ten dollars and told me, "Go by Dr. Rhine's office and give this to him on my bill." I took that ten dollars, went to his office, walked in and handed it to him. "What's that for?"

"Mama said this is to put on her doctor bill."

He smiled and told me, "Victor, as long as I live, as long as your mother and you live, your doctor bills will never cost you anything." That's the kind of a man he was.

The last trip I made with Dr. and Mrs. Rhine was after I came out of the Army in 1946. Genevieve and I had moved to Fordyce. I was working for Cities Service. He stopped by one day and told me he would like for me to go with them to Tyronza, Arkansas. I told him to let me know the day, and I'd get off work. Sure enough, later he told me when they were going, and I made arrangements to be off that day. Early that morning, he and Mrs. Rhine picked us up, and we went to Tyronza for a medical meeting. Dr. Rhine had such a good time. Dr. McDaniel was entertaining the doctors. It was the year Dr. Rhine was Doctor of the Year in Arkansas, 1949. I was so proud of him, and we had a wonderful trip that day.

I have three pictures of Dr. Rhine that I value very highly. One he gave me was of him and a pair of his prize fox hounds. Another was made at a family reunion just a short while before my family came to Tennessee. During that reunion, that day, we had gotten in touch with Dr. Rhine and that afternoon he came by and stopped. Alexander's of Fordyce came down to make pictures of the family. He was included in with our family, and it's a wonderful picture. We were so proud to have him in our family picture.

The other picture he gave me in the office one day is of him while he was in Washington, D. C. during the time that he was nominated for National Doctor of the Year. It shows him with the stethoscope and that big smile on his face—December 5, 1949. He was being interviewed by the Washington News Herald. We were all so proud of him. I just wanted him to win that award worse than anything in the world, but there was another doctor that beat him out by just a few points, but he was still my National Doctor of the Year.*

* Mother said that he would have refused the award when he found out in Washington that he would be expected to travel around the country, speaking against President Harry Truman's National Health Insurance legislation. He said that he could not leave his patients unattended, and furthermore, because of his close friendship with Dr. John R. Steelman, President Truman's Assistant, he could not speak against Truman's health program. PRB

I still have a letter from Dr. Rhine, after we moved to Tennessee, telling us how much he missed us and telling us if we ever needed him to just let him know, and I knew he meant that.

On another occasion, Dr. Rhine made me feel so good, and I felt very close to him at that time. It was when I took my master's degree in Masonry. I didn't know he would be there that night but he showed up, and I was so glad to see him. He knew there was a lot that I didn't know or understand during that degree, and he would look at me and smile but never said a word. After it was over, of course, he was called on to make a speech. He said, "About this young man, he and I have been very close through all these years. He and I and our families have been close." That just made me feel so good to know that he would think that much of me to say that and to take off from his work to come up there that night and be there when I received my master's degree. I'll never forget that.

PATRICIA MURPHEY ROSTKER

PASADENA, CALIFORNIA

There is one thing that's connected up in my mind with Dr. Rhine. Whenever my father either returned from a visit to Thornton, or whenever he got that nailed-up sorghum can delivered to him, it meant pancakes and gingerbread, a real treat as far as I was and am concerned. I use an old recipe today that was handed down to me, and it's titled, "Dr. Rhine's Gingerbread with Sorghum". I'll bet no one knew that when he was Doctor of the Year.

I have another fond memory of being in Thornton, probably at the age of ten or eleven, and going with Dr. Rhine and my father to visit some town folks. Not a medical call, but a compare-notes-on-hunting call. After hearing all the jollity and joking that went on, I remember thinking, "they're just like kids." But on the way home, Dr. Rhine began telling me the names of shrubs, trees and flowers, and joking about how he had to learn them in medical school. Then I realized he was constantly teaching as he went along.

As I look back, I doubt that my father had a better friend than Dr. Rhine. And I'll also bet that he enjoyed—really enjoyed—that friendship above any others. It really seems remarkable to me now, because I never heard Dr. Pat say so, but I bet his visits and hunts and all were a real highlight to him, more like his early growing up in the country.

(Patricia and I are named for the same person, her father, Dr. Pat Murphey). PRB

MARKS HINTON

HOUSTON, TEXAS

I must have been around ten years old, and I was spending a few days with Nita and Doctor in Thornton. (Nita and I were first cousins.) I was a city boy from Little Rock. Doc and I were going to Chambersville to visit some sick people. Along the way, he began bending my ear with comments about how those Chambersville fellows were the toughest around those parts and about how they just loved to fight. Needless to say, when we got to our destination, I didn't get out of that car. I knew that he was pulling my leg, but I wasn't taking any chances.

Around 1928 or 1930, I spent some time in Thornton with the Rhines, periodically. On one of those visits, I was available to drive the family to Little Rock. As was his custom, Doctor often sent country goods to his city friends. This time it was sorghum molasses. As I rounded the corner of the hallway in the Donaghey Building, a gallon of molasses in each hand and several country cousins trailing along behind I ran into a girl I had dated early in high school. Her name was Elsie Smith, and the expression on her face said, "What's going on here?" I had to laugh, and she did, too, after I explained about the children and the gifts of molasses.

During my summer visits to Thornton, I would play baseball on a team with the local boys. I was the catcher. On one hot, dry Sunday afternoon we were playing a team from Holly Springs, up in northern Dallas County. We had been told that they had two brothers on the team who were *fast*. During the game, one of those boys got on base. He called 'time out', sat down on the bag and proceeded to remove his shoes and socks. To me, the catcher, that was a very clear signal that he planned to steal second. When play was resumed, I called for a pitch-out, in order to pick him off. He took off running and ran into second base standing up. He didn't even have to slide, he was so fast. The fastest runner I had ever seen, by far.

JOE BRANSFORD

WEST HOLLYWOOD, CALIFORNIA

The first time I met Dr. Rhine, my eye was swollen to a tiny squint, my nose was swollen and tender. There were imprints of baseball stitches on my also swollen cheekbone—and my new shirt was bloody. My handerchief had long been discarded at the cow pasture baseball field where it all began.

When he asked why I was catching without my mask, I replied with all the sure logic of a twelve-year-old boy, that my only other alternative was right field. And everyone knows that nothing ever happens in right field—

especially if it happens to trail off into thick underbrush.

The fact that I happened to be left-handed as well made him laugh. He pointed out to me that he couldn't recall, offhand at least, any southpaw catchers in the major leagues. Anyone who liked baseball enough to catch without a mask must really want to play major league baseball.

Now, at the risk of being accused of 'good old days' syndrome, I must point out that the major league teams of the mid-40's were classics—Pete Rose, Johnny Bench, Sandy Koufax and their peers notwithstanding. (Ask G. T. Griffin. We grew up together in Bearden, and he could cite name and number and averages of all the teams and their individual players.)

At that moment, however, my mind was not on the game; but on some kind of excuse to take home along with my slightly altered appearance and bloodied shirt. My permission to travel to that particular game had been given to me with extreme reluctance, since I invariably came home with a torn shirt, torn pants and no good excuse. Today I had out done myself.

Dr. Rhine added the finishing touches to my fear by asking for our phone number. He wanted to advise my parents to have my eye checked— just in case. Of course, I had no choice. But I think he saw my quiet turmoil, because he softened the blow for me. After assuring them that I was in perfect health (he had, by now, checked my heart, lungs, legs, ears, and probably my height and weight. "As long as I was there," was his answer to my asking why the additional attention.) he, somehow, failed to mention to them about my catching without a mask. I supposed, at the time, that he simply forgot to do so.

If memory serves me, it was Ralph Bryant who drove me back to Bearden. Usually Ralph found the time to take us kids to our ballgames, be it Holly Springs, Thornton or Harmony Grove. He and Nig Bowen and Ben Arnold did a lot for those of us who wanted to play baseball. I don't believe that Ralph ever mentioned the incident to my Dad. Of course, as in all such things, my parents learned the facts. But not before Dr. Rhine had mitigated the worst of my fears by a convenient lapse of memory at the right time.

I took Dr. Rhine's observation about left-handed catchers to heart, and I learned how to pitch a baseball. Later, I pitched for Bearden when it had an independent baseball team—back in the late 40's and early 50's. I pitched for the Camden American Legion ball club in 1951, I believe. We nearly won the state championship, losing in the playoffs. I also played for the Camden Kraftsmen baseball team. Then, after joining the army, I pitched for our regiment—along with many other fine ball players. We were fortunate enough to win the European Championship in 1956.

Ironically, in 1953, after my father's sudden death, we moved from Bearden to Abilene, Texas. I enlisted in the army and was sent to Ft. Bliss, Texas. The irony of the situation came in the form of a letter from the St. Louis Cardinal chain. (I had attended a tryout camp sponsored by the Cardinals that same year.) They were offering me a chance to sign with one of their farm clubs. The letter was dated June of 1953, and I received it in

January of 1954, while in the hospital with hepatitis at William Beaumont Army Hospital. The letter had first been sent to Bearden, then to Texas and then into the military mail system—and lost for seven months.

I mention this personal incident because it clearly points out the manner of man the doctor was and his insight into a young boy's silent dreams—and quiet fears, on a hot summer day in the 1940's.

KNIGHT JOHNSON

THORNTON, ARKANSAS

The first twin girl and boy that Dr. Rhine caught were Lethal and Lee Maxwell, March 25, 1922. They were born by Maggie Johnson, my first cousin.

In the '30's up to '41, I was the one that raised the garden and kept the lawn mowed at the Rhine house. We didn't have no power mower. We pushed the mower, and *that was a big yard*. I kept the wood in, 'cause we didn't have no gas. We were burning wood, and I helped take care of the fox dogs and the yard dog named Queen, a German Police dog. I went on calls a lot with Dr. Rhine in the winter time, in case he would get stuck on those country roads, he would have someone with him—Big Hill to Harrell and Hampton. He used to tell me all about when he rode horseback. He had two horses—a black and a red horse. When I first knowed him, he was driving a Model-T Ford car. I worked with him and worked for him, worked around his place until 1941, and I went into service. He give me a little '28 model Chevrolet. He said, "Knight, when I get my new car, you can have this old car," but the Army caught me, and I didn't get my car. I was in the service for four years, eight months and twelve days. I come back here, and that's what I got! [Pointing to his wife, Mattie Bell Hemmitt, who also had had Dr. Rhine for her family's doctor, but in the Jonesboro community.]

"He told us that we were going to miss him, and that's the truth."

ED RHUBARB

THORNTON, ARKANSAS

I think about him so much. We still talk about him, been gone twenty years. We always go by to see his picture every time we go to the hospital. It's just like him. He told us that we were going to miss him, and that's the truth. Everybody in this country, they miss him.

I remember in 1936, I had gotten hurt on the job. I worked for Fordyce Lumber Company for thirty-three straight years. He come out here and examined me, and told me, "Ed, if you don't go to the hospital (he'd been trying to get me to go to the Veterans' Hospital) they are going to carry you to the cemetery." I told him I was ready to go. He wrote me two letters to the Memphis Veterans' Hospital. I stayed there three months. He wrote to me, "When you get able to come home, I'm going to put you on pension." I come home on number three passenger train. I got in around two or three o'clock in the morning. Me and Minnie sat up 'til day and talked. We went down to Dr. Rhine, and he examined me, and said, "I'm ready to put you on pension." I said to give me a chance and let me work, and I did.

In my younger days, I had indigestion a lot of times. I sent for Dr. Rhine at twelve o'clock one night. When he got here, I was better. He said, "I ought to charge you ten dollars," and I said, "I don't care if you do." Well, he just charged me two dollars. He was a fine doctor. He done a lot of good things for the people of Calhoun County.

Once I had the pneumonia. I come from the mill. I thought I had a cold. I told Dr. Rhine I had a cold, and he give me something for it. Two or three days later, I got worse, and I sent back for Dr. Rhine. I never will forget it. He'd drive up out there and get that little black bag, come on in.

"Well, what's the matter? What you fussin' about?"

I was hurting, too. I had the pneumonia bad. He opened up my collar, put his ear down there.

"Yeh, you got a little taste of pneumonia."

I had a big taste, the way I hurt. He told Minnie to get a glass of water, and he put two tablets in that water, let them dissolve. At ten o'clock he said to give me another two. And you know, at ten o'clock I wasn't hurting a bit. Them tablets knocked that pneumonia out. I got all right, but he wouldn't let me go back to work for two or three weeks.

He waited on my mother and my daddy, too. He said that my daddy was the oldest man that he ever waited on that he didn't have to draw his water. His water never did stop on him.

People would send me for Dr. Rhine. I remember one night, the ground was froze, the road was bad, and I went after him. It was after twelve o'clock. I didn't much want to go after him that night. It was too late. I knowed where he slept at. Me and two other men went. I sat out there in my truck and put them up to go wake him up. I knew he was going to fuss.

G. C. Smith went first and knocked on the door. "Dr. Rhine?" he said in a very small voice.

Dr. Rhine called out, "WHO IS THAT?"

"This is G. C."

"What do you want?"

"I want to get the doctor to go see Bob Weathers. . ."

"You go on home. I ain't studying about it."

And so, Willie Green, he was next. Willie Green went up there and said, "Dr. Rhine?" He talked easy.

Dr. Rhine knew his voice. "What do you want, Willie?"

"I want you to go see Bob. There's somethin' wrong with him." He run him away.

I said, "Lord, it's my time now." Me and Dr. Rhine was just as close as two fingers together. I told him, "Dr. Rhine, this is Ed."

"What is it, Ed?"

I says, "Something's wrong. I wouldn't be down here if it wasn't. Bob's mother wanted me to come get you. Bob is dead. I don't know what it is, but he's just dead as a nit. He wasn't breathing."

He said, "Ed, I can't get down in there with my car. You get him and bring him to your house."

The boys went down and got him. By the time we got back there, it wasn't but a few minutes before Dr. Rhine come in. He stuck him all over with a pin, and Bob didn't even grunt, but in a few days, he had Bob where he could talk.

Now Dr. Rhine would lay with you any time of the night. You go down and get him. Dr. Rhine, if you didn't have the money, he was comin' anyhow. He wouldn't charge you over two dollars for comin' out here and that was the medicine, too. That's all he would charge you. You be done got the medicine, too.

[Ed Rhubarb is ninety years old.] PRB

MINNIE RHUBARB

THORNTON, ARKANSAS

He was our family doctor, too. My name was Wright. I was born and reared up here in Thornton. We don't know nothing but Dr. Rhine. My father had heart trouble for years, and he patched him up. He said that's what he was doing. He said, "I can't cure him, but I can keep him alive for awhile longer."

We had a boy that we raised, and he had pneumonia. We had carried him to the company doctor, and they wasn't doing nothing for him. So I said, "Send for Dr. Rhine. Dr. Rhine will know what to do." He come out here and he looked at him and said, "This boy has got pneumonia." The other doctors never did tell us what was wrong. He gave him some pills and said, "I'll be back after awhile." He come back, and he was better. Dr. Rhine made two trips a day until he got that child up. He sho' did.

RUTH JOHNSON JACOBS

THORNTON, ARKANSAS

When I first remember him, he was on a horse. Later on, he had a car. He always had a saw, hammer, ax, all those kind of things in his car, so if he happened to run across a tree over the road, he could get out and cut it and get it out of the way.

Each time he would come if some of us had pneumonia. Not only us, anybody in the community. You just had to send for him one time. The other times he would come until he felt like the pneumonia was all right on the patient. You didn't ever have to go and say, "You come this day. You come back tomorrow." No, he came on his own. When that pneumonia was over, he knew it, and he didn't use all of these different instruments. He used his ears. He'd lay his head against your chest or your back, and he could tell if your lungs were clear.

I went one time to get a tooth pulled. That was terrible, because you knew what the pain was going to be.

He said, "Yeah. I'll pull it."

"O. K. It's got to be pulled, because it's killing me."

He pulled it that day, and I said, "I will *never* let him pull another tooth."

That night, I had another toothache. I went back. He pulled it, and it had a big abscess under it. It all came out with the tooth. "Now this was your trouble. The other tooth was affected by the tooth with the abscess."

We walked to school every morning, about a mile and a half, but we were on time every morning. I remember him coming to the school ever so often and speaking to the children. Mrs. Rhine was so good about sending magazines to the school, so children would have pictures and something to read. He had such high regard for the principal, Elsie Johnson. She would come to school mornings, and children who didn't have food, she would start two or three big pots of soup, and they would have a cup of soup and some crackers around eleven and that helped them. He came to the school often, where all the kids would be able to hear him. It made a difference, because he touched everybody.

I've never seen, since or before, a person like him. He was just all that was in a doctor, and all that was in a person's care. To doctor on an individual—"What's the medicine?" "Fifty cents," or "A dollar". How he could do it, we don't know. He probably went in debt over some of us. He knew the ones that were able to pay and the ones that were not able to pay. It didn't make him any difference who the person was, he would give you just as much care as the other individual.

He liked to sit down and talk. "I doctored on your daddy. I doctored on your granddaddy. That makes me to have been here a long time." "I always remember my people. I never forget them." And he didn't.

He'd get terribly upset when people would meddle with his business, because he knew he was out for the thing that was right. "What did I tell you to do?" There were a lot of things in him that you won't ever find in any other person.

It's not an individual around here that remembers him, that don't speak something about him. I know Credell Green from Pine Bluff was here for a family reunion last summer. He said, "Ruth, guess what I have. Look in that album." On the first page was Dr. Rhine's picture that he had gotten out of the Hampton paper not too long ago. "I still subscribe to the Calhoun County paper. That picture was there, and I wouldn't depart from it for nobody." The picture was of Dr. Rhine on his horse. Every write-up that was in the paper telling about the number of years he practiced I cut it out, and I still have them.

WILLIAM SYPHO & NANCY THROWER

THORNTON, ARKANSAS

Sypho: I remember one time he fixed my hand up. I tell you, we wuz working on the WPA, and this man was—oooh, I got so scared. The train wuz comin'! I tell you who it wuz, Mr. Frank Cathey. He wuz drivin' the truck. I seen the train acomin', and I just dropped off and skint my hand and arm and he fixed it up. Ooooh woman! My wife got a needle in her hand, and she went up there three times. Miz Hemmitt told her, "Don't go no mo'." Dr. Rhine sent her up to have an x-ray of her hand, and Dr. Jamison

140

went in and got it out. Now wasn't that wunnerful? Oh yeah, that's the truth. He loved us, what you talkin' 'bout! Oh, we loved him, too, I'm tellin' you. No mistake, he wuz som'in, awright. We miss him.

Nancy: Phil Thrower was my husband. His wife, Ola, died in 1959, and me and Phil married in 1960. My home was at New Edinburg, but Dr. Rhine was our doctor. We used to come to Thornton to see him. It was about thirteen miles to our home. Phil died in 1982, and he was my husband's doctor 'til he died. He would always be funny when you would go to him.

Sypho: That's the truth.

Nancy: He'd tell you "Come on in here and let me kill you."

Sypho: Yes, he would.

Nancy: He'd go and get them big ole bottles of medicine settin' round there and he'd pour a little of this in a bottle and another little bit in the bottle. Finally, he'd have your medicine fixed up. We wondered did he know'd what he doin', but he know'd what he doin'!

Sypho: That's right!

Nancy: He didn't kill us.

Sypho: He pour medicine from them bottles and he wouldn't drop a bit. He had a good memory, all them bottles. He could remember. He wuz som'in!

Nancy: He told us all the time, said, "Whenever I die and leave y'all, y'all goin' to pay for yo doctor bill."

Sypho: He sho' did. That's the truth.

Nancy: He wouldn't ever charge us very much.

Sypho: That's right.

Nancy: He always had sympathy with us, and we cared a lots for him. I have some clippings from a paper at the house—som'in 'bout him.

Sypho: He say to us we could go to those hi-fa-lutin' doctors after he wuz gone.

"I never saw anybody pursue the practice of medicine like he did."

DR. LOUIS R. MCFARLAND

HOT SPRINGS, ARKANSAS

I practiced in Hampton, Arkansas, from 1946 to 1950, and I first met Dr. Rhine the day before I opened my office. He came in and said that he wanted to talk to me. As I remember, he had about a four day growth of beard, he had on a pair of pants and a coat that didn't match, no tie, (in fact, I don't think I ever saw him with a tie on). He came in and sat down. I was still doing some painting, was anticipating opening the office the next day, and we talked for an hour and a half. When he introduced himself, said he was Dr. Rhine, I thought he was kidding. He looked a lot more like one of the farmers in the area than he did a doctor. We talked for a long, long time about the area, and he told me how pleased he was that I had decided to come there, because of the acute doctor shortage. At that time, there was one other doctor in the area, and he was an eclectic, whom Dr. Rhine didn't think a whole lot of.

I'll never forget, when he left my office, he said, "I'm going to give you some advice you didn't ask for, but I'm going to tell you anyhow. When you open your office tomorrow, you had better set it up just like you'd like to have it the day you retire."

"Dr. Rhine, what do you mean?"

"Son, you think about that."

He never would tell me. I laid awake half the night trying to figure out what the man meant and finally figured it out. He meant that it just better be like I would like to have it when I was ready to retire because I never would be able to change it. It greatly influenced the way I have practiced medicine ever since. I did set it up like I wanted it. I'm probably the laziest working doctor you ever saw. I get in the office about four and a half hours a day, and I've done it that way for thirty years, plus. I think it has made my practice much more enjoyable for the unasked for advice I got.

142

I saw Dr. Rhine on lots and lots of cases. His opinion I valued highly. I think he was probably the best read general practitioner I've ever known and especially from a small town. And, believe me, Thornton was a small town.

I recall one child that I saw with him one time. The child was a diabetic. She was about fifteen years old. I got called to her home. She was supposedly in a coma. I checked this kid over and couldn't find a thing in the world the matter with her. She was breathing normally, she had no diabetic breathing. She had no symptoms of her diabetes. She was just 'out' in the bed. I could not get any response. I tried painful stimuli. I finally called Dr. Rhine and asked him if he would meet me at the kid's house. This was way up in the night. I just didn't know what I was dealing with. He came. It was about halfway between Hampton and Thornton, on one of the back roads. (There wasn't anything but back roads in Calhoun County. There was only one paved road in Calhoun County, highway 167 to El Dorado, and I didn't have a patient that lived on it). He met me there and checked this little girl over. I remember she was as fat as a little butterball.

He said, "Let's walk out on the front porch." We stood there. "What do you think about her?"

"Dr. Rhine, I'm at an absolute loss. I have no idea what's the matter with her."

"Well, I can't find anything the matter with her either. I have an idea that she is faking."

"Maybe. I can't prove or disprove it."

"I think I can."

I never will forget. He went back in the house. We rolled her over on her tummy, and he raised up her night gown and her bare fanny was sticking out, and he popped her across the seat with his bare hand, and that kid jumped two and a half feet out of that bed screaming. He had cured her diabetic coma instantly.

As we were leaving, I said, "Dr. Rhine, what if you had been wrong?"

"I guess I'd a got sued."

He was a very kind person, a very beautifully read person. He loved the *Journal of the American Medical Association*, and I believe he had it fully read within twelve hours of the time he received it. His office had stacks of 'em, where you didn't have room to walk, but he could tell you every article in every one of them, and if something new came out, he was using it within a week. I never saw anybody that pursued the practice of medicine like he did.

There was nothing more impressive in my mind than this. Here was a man in a little town of 600. Hampton had only 800, and it seemed so much smaller than Hampton. I believe the first year they ever had Physician of the Year in the United States for the American Medical Association, Dr. Rhine from this little town finished runner-up. I thought this was absolutely incredible.*

* A picture of Dr. Rhine taken at this time in Washington was in Dr. McFarland's office.
PRB

I remember the celebration they had in 1946. God knows how many thousands of people were there—several thousand. I was always impressed by the number of people he had met and contacted.

We delivered some babies together, obviously the tough ones.

I thought I knew enough to cure the whole world, but I learned an awfully lot from him. I told him when I came to Hampton (I was just out of the service and was broke) that I did not intend to practice general medicine all my life, that I was going back into residency. I thought, at the time, I was going back into obstetrics.

He asked, "How long are you going to stay?"

"I don't know, probably two or three years." I wound up staying four and a half.

There was no hospital in Hampton at that time. My first office there was behind the barber shop. It was the only vacant building in town— behind Pete Oliver's barbership. We had no drugstore, either. I dispensed medicine just like Dr. Rhine did. I'm still using a drug that Dr. Rhine introduced me to. It's still on the market—called bentyl with phenobarbital. It's the greatest thing for colic in a baby there ever was. I never heard of it until he told me about it. He used to make a mixture of syrup of bentyl plain and syrup of bentyl with phenobarb and mix them half and half, which cut the dose of the phenobarb in half and would give a teaspoonful to a colicky baby. And I still use it. I sure do. I do let the druggist mix them now.

I've still got my daybook from my office the first year I practiced. We charged a dollar for office calls, that included your medicine. We charged two dollars for house calls. It's amazing that we could live on that, but I actually saved money—enough money to go through my residency in pediatrics. That says something for the value of the dollar.

The other thing is that I compared percentage of expenses between that daybook and my present one, and they are still about the same percentage-wise—rent, secretarial help, nurse, medicine, drug and cleaning supplies are virtually the same percentage of the fee as before.

I made the biggest fee I ever made in Calhoun County on a veterinary case. I was also Hampton's vet at the time, with Mr. Lyons. He would often help me with my practice, and I'd help him with his. It was a cow. The fellow called me, because he, himself, was sick in bed. He had had a cow jump a fence and had ripped her belly open, down through the udder and right out. She was the best milk cow he had, and he was afraid he was going to lose her. He asked me if I would sew her up. I had to get out there, saddle a horse, ride to a back pasture, rope her, bring her to the barn, throw her, tie her up and anesthetize her before I could sew her up. As I was leaving, I asked if he needed anything for his problem, and he said, "No. Just get my cow well." I never did see the patient that was laying in there with the flu. I charged him a hundred and fifty dollars, unheard of, but it took me all day long. I had to throw that cow by myself.

I know that Dr. Rhine never had segregated waiting rooms, and I never did either. I had a patient once complain bitterly that I took in a black baby before I saw her baby. I asked her if she could show me any way that black baby was less sick than her white one. If she could, I would take her white one first. I never had another complaint. We had a big black population, probably sixty-five to seventy percent. That's when I first learned about 'fall terms.' There were a number of families there who maintained the black families who worked for them—paid their bills at the end of the year. You would carry them on your books, and they would guarantee them, and pay you when they got the crops in.

I remember delivering a baby one time in a tent, with snow on the ground. I never took my boots, coat or anything off. The woman was black. She had on a slip, period. I caught the flu, and the mama and the baby did well. The baby, by the way, died one year later, on its birthday, with whooping cough. We innoculated babies then, but they didn't do it. They took better care of their hogs in Calhoun County than they did their babies. They rarely gave immunizations to the children, even with all the insistence you could give. Of course, we didn't have anything but DPT (diptheria, pertussis, tetanus) then.

This is one of the little things I enjoyed doing in Calhoun County. I'm sure there is many a school teacher who has cursed me for years on end. Black people loved for the doctor to name the babies. My name was Louis Richard, so I named all the male babies Louis Richard. I named all the female babies Jane Elizabeth, because that's what my mother wanted me to be. Calhoun County is now full of Jane Elizabeths and Louis Richards. I've often wondered what happened at the first grade in school. That little baby that died that I was talking about was named Jane Elizabeth. I took her to Warner-Brown Hospital in El Dorado, but she died. The El Dorado hospital was the one I used, because the roads were better—that was down highway 167.

I had a Jeep down there. I put 125,000 miles on that Jeep in three and a half years. I remember the ice storm in 1949 that was so devastating to the county. We were without electricity for thirteen or fourteen days. I borrowed a generator from a fellow named Hollis Reep, who was the International Paper Company representative there. I put this generator in the back of my Jeep and backed it up to my office in the day time and ran electricity there and took it home at night and ran my house then. During that time, I was the only one that could get through (I had the only Jeep in the county), so I was carrying the mail to El Dorado. I'd pick it up at Mr. Biggers' post office and take it to El Dorado.

Effie Gresham, who had a boarding house in Hampton, had a son who went to medical school, and he came home in his senior year during the holidays. He went on calls with me several times. I had a Negro patient that lived down in the Ouachita bottoms. The river was flooded. We got in my Jeep and went down through this place. He had epilepsy, and he was in a status of epilepsy, and they couldn't get him out of it. We went down to see him that night. We drove through water for about five miles without ever seeing the road, and I think Dr. Gresham decided right then that if that was what family practice was, he didn't want any piece of it. We drove, it seemed like hours, at night, in water. It came clear up in the Jeep, in wintertime.

Dr. Rhine gave me a present once, and he told me how to use it. It was a pair of forceps about sixteen inches long. He told me that when I had an uncooperative woman to deal with, all I would have to do is get out these forceps, unsterilized, and bang them together several times where she could see them. Without fail, she would ask what I was going to do with those. When you replied, "Use them," you would get instant cooperation. I have never used them, because I am a pediatrician, but I still have them.

I used to go by in later years and see Dr. and Mrs. Rhine. I saw him during his last year. I never went through Hampton, that I didn't stop at two places—Dr. and Mrs. Rhine's and Jack Ethridge's beer joint because there I could get all of the news of everything that was going on in Hampton for the last six months.

"I don't believe there was a lazy bone in that guy. He believed in doin' somethin', and he believed in you doin' somethin'."

ED AND VERNA GRESHAM

CHAMBERSVILLE, ARKANSAS

Verna: I didn't have no better friend than Dr. Rhines. He was just such a good fellow. He was so kind and good to everybody.

Ed: And another thing he'd do, he'd go to see ya. It made no difference about the woods, the thickets you lived in or whatever, he went. He'd come.

Verna: Whatever time of night.

Ed: I've saw him go out after midnight to see people. Get up out of bed. He did that for a long time.

He stopped me one day and said, "Folks are going crazy up here."

"What?"

"Fixin' to have a Day up here."

"Yeah."

"If my records show right, you are the first baby born when I come to Thornton."

But he went back and relooked, and he found I was the third one. A fellow named Hopkins was the first and Harry Gray's wife, Lottie, was the second. He had an old book, I mean it was an old one. He said I was the third one he delivered here. I'm eighty-four years old. I remember one night, it was late in the night. Our son, Junior, had a stone bruise from going barefoot. He had one there on his foot, and it was a-hurting bad. I drove up there to Dr. Rhine's house, and the lights were out. I honked, and a light come on. I said to myself, "Dr. Rhine may run me off from here." I went to the door and told him, "Junior's out in the car with a stone bruise, and it's killing him. I don't know what to do about it. He's just crying."

"Bring him on in here."

He got up out of the bed and come to the door in what we wore then, what you call BVD's-altogether. He put Junior in a chair, and I held his

147

head and he lanced it—right there. I never saw a kid go to sleep any quicker when we brought him home.

When Junior was born here—right in that room there—there was a sick kid who died right near, and I called him to come. He come from over there, and he hadn't had no supper. It was about night.

"Have you got anything to eat?"

"Yeah, we've got some beans."

He went in there and sat down and ate supper.

He had a run-about car. He said, "Will you do something for me?"

"What?"

"Get in my car and go over where I was and get me my needles while I eat supper." So I went and got the needles for him.

He was a goin' doctor. He sho was. I believe he really liked it. You've got to like anything to do it that much. He loved the people. He'd go to these log rollings. Then you cleared land and what you had was a log rolling. Had hand sticks, one on one side and one on the other. Now he was goin' to come if he could get off, and he'd go out there, and he'd take one of those sticks and somebody else over there, and I've seen him come up with a load! Somethin' he wanted for dinner—he liked 'em—this here grated sweet potato puddin', with nutmeg in it. He sho' goin' to want that. He'd eat dinner, and maybe he'd go on to somewhere else, but he was goin' to that log rolling for a little bit. You know they'd ask people in, neighbors, to come help roll the logs. He'd be there. It was hard work.

Verna: Some of 'em would be big logs. Ed said he had seen Dr. Rhines just come up with all he had.

Ed: My Daddy had a place about two miles down here. That's where I were born. Finally, I got aholt of this place. I went out in Smackover and worked for Southern Pipelines for about a year, then come back here and throwed up a hull of a house. We've fixed it up some, but we're satisfied with it because we're old folks and don't care nothin' about all this fine stuff. It don't appeal to us. We're comfortable. We've got water and a bath.

Verna: When Dr. Rhine first got the little run-about car, we had two telephones at our house. He paid the one on the Thornton line, and we had the one on the Fordyce line. The Davises down here, Will Davis, (Harvey was the one that was sick all the time) they would come and want us to call Dr. Rhines on the Thornton phone. Didn't have no long distance then. I'd call Dr. Rhines and tell him Mr. Davis wanted him to come down to see him. Well he'd kinda grumble a little bit. "I don't know whether I'll go or not." That left me in a pickle. But he'd finally say he'd come. Terectly, you'd see him pass, goin' down there. One day, he stopped, when he first got that car. He said, "Come on and ride down there with me. You never have rode in a car."

"No, I sure haven't."

We went down the road, and the Garrisons lived down there, and there was Nellie Maude and a bunch of them girls, they was comin' from down the road as we were goin'. They seen the car, and I don't know how them kids got over that fence.

He said, "What become of them girls?"

"Yonder they go, up through the field."

Ed: He had another car when him and Dr. Black had their office at the Stout Lumber Company Commissary. Several of us were standing out there, and he come out. It had a speedometer on it that registered miles. He said, "Do y'all want to go riding? I want to show you somethin' in this car." Of course, we wanted to ride. We got in and headed to what they called Mexican Town. It was a gravel road, no pavement. He said, "Now look-a-here. We're driving fifteen miles an hour!"

Verna: It would beat a horse or a buggy.

Ed: He had an old horse called Bill. I tell you he had a saddle that I don't know what it would cost now, and he'd get on that horse and in the wintertime, you'd think it was Santa Claus comin'. He'd have things over his head, you could just see his face. But one thing Dr. Rhine always done, he wore some good clothes. He'd come even it it would be snowin'—sittin' up on that big horse. Then he got a buggy with two ponies. Them things could might near keep up with an automobile. He'd jerk them reins up with a snap and down the road he'd go, waitin' on people, and he had a dickens of a territory. People liked him, and they used him. He'll never be a forgotten man here.

I've saw him and heard him tell it—"Man, that's a good pine stump out there." He kept a good sharp ax, and he'd take that and split off that stump and throw it in his car and take it home.

I never will forget one time I went by his house at noon. He said, "It's dinner time. C'mon in."

I said, "No."

"Yes you are. You're goin' to eat."

So I thought I had better eat. They always welcomed anybody, it didn't make no difference. We had a good dinner. Mrs. Rhine, I reckon, was always there.

Verna: I remember Dr. Rhine keeping hogs. He loved those dogs, too, and liked to hunt.

Ed: We had a sick cow one time, and I went to Thornton to see Gordon Newton, who was sort of a cow man. He didn't know what was the matter, so I said, "I'll go on to see Dr. Rhine."

"I don't know nothin' 'bout no cows. Can't hardly keep y'all straightened out," he said.

I told him what was the matter with the cow.

"Wait a minute."

He went in there and got a bottle of medicine.

"You give her that. That's what I give women folk." That's what he said. "You give her that, might near half a bottle, 'cause she's a cow. Then, I guess, get ready to drag her off in the morning."

I said, "O. K. Doc."

You know one thing, I give her that stuff, and the next morning that cow was a whole lot better. That cow got all right.

I went back up to Thornton, and I saw him out in his garden. I said, "Listen, Dr. Rhine, you are a good cow doctor."

"No, I'm not either."

"Well, you cured mine. That's all I know. That cow got all right."

He said he could doctor dogs and folks, but he didn't know nothin' about cows. But that tickled him.

If you had a dog you wanted vaccinated, all you had to do was drive up there. He kept vaccines for dogs.

Verna: He was just a good fellow.

Ed: I don't believe there was a lazy bone in that guy. He believed in doin' somethin', and he believed in *you* doin' somethin', too. I'm goin' to tell you somethin', he didn't have too much for a guy who wouldn't do nothin'.

He had a lot of friends, too. They named this park down here at Bearden after him.

Dr. Rhine delivered me, and I growed up with Dr. Rhine, and now we are the old folks.

Verna: He delivered Ed, he delivered me, and he delivered our son, Junior.

Ed: He had us to make a picture because of that.

A young doctor at Fordyce, Dr. Howard, told me this. He didn't know that Dr. Rhine was goin' to see this patient. They had called him, too. He knew Dr. Rhine and told him to go. Dr. Rhine said, "No. You go." So they both went. He thought Dr. Rhine would use a stethoscope, but he didn't. He listened with his ear. That was the first time he ever seen that.

Verna: You know how he would put his hands on your stomach or chest and beat with his fingers. That was the first time Dr. Howard had seen that.

Ed: Dr. Howard said to Dr. Rhine, when they come out, "Let's go get a cup of coffee." "No, boy. I'm goin' to tell you somethin'. You had better quit drinking it." He wouldn't eat much salt or pepper either.

Verna: I heard him say this. People would make this mulligan, and it would be made red hot with pepper. They'd say, "Doc, come on and eat some mulligan." We were all at a big supper, and he was waiting in line right along with us. He said, "No. I wouldn't eat that. That's just like a cuckleburr if you swallowed it going through your stomach."

Oh, he loved family dinners, church dinners. He'd always bring some kind of fruit—apples, oranges or somethin'. The kids loved him. He would always bring a sack of fruit for them. Folks would always think of him. "Be sure and call Dr. Rhines and invite him because he loves to come."

Ed: Mr. Bus Hearnsberger never had a better friend than Dr. Rhine. Neither did George Hearnsberger.

Verna: Talking about reunions, the Hearnsbergers always had them. That was a big day—the Hearnsberger Reunion. You couldn't stir 'em with a stick. They was a big family of them folks. It was always at Mr. Billy Hearnsberger's. He was the daddy of all these Hearnsbergers. I had three brothers who married Hearnsberger girls. I was a Gray.

Ed: Most of our sickness has been operations, but none of them too serious.

The first one I had was hemorrhoids. I just went and went, and Dr. Rhine would send me to a specialist. He'd tell me I'd need to have surgery, and I didn't quite have to have it, and I'd come home. It got so bad that finally I called him and said, "I can't go no further."

"I been telling you to go on up there."

The bus was running then, so we went to Little Rock to see Dr. Hoyt Allen.

"Well, I told you you'd come back."

"Dr. Rhine sent me up here."

"They are goin' to kill Dr. Rhine down there."

"What?"

"Working him to death."

The first operation Verna had was appendicitis. First he sent her to Little Rock to Dr. Fulmer—a stomach specialist. He said she had ulcerated stomach, and I don't know how much of this amphagel she took. I'd get ice and keep it on her stomach. You had to buy it. We didn't have no refrigerator. One day she went up here to a quilting and come back home and started cooking supper. I went in and she was all bent over.

"What's the matter?"

"My side's killing me."

That went on 'til after supper. I went up to see Dr. Rhine. He come out here.

"Get some ice and keep on her until tomorrow. See what she does."

It didn't get better. The next morning, I went up there again. "She's goin' to have to have an operation. Does she want to go to Little Rock?"

"I don't know."

"I tell you, Dr. Robbins at Camden can operate on her. It's not such a serious thing, I don't think. If she'll go down there, I'll go with her. But if she goes to Little Rock, I can't. You better find out what she wants to do.

"I'll go down there and ask her."

When he come back to see her, she said, "If you'll go with me, I'll go to Camden." Well she had that operation.

Verna: Dr. Robbins was a good surgeon, but it was good to me to know that Dr. Rhines was standing there by him.

Ed: When I had arthritis or something, they had to load me up in a truck, and I went to Little Rock to see Dr. Joe Shuffield. He found out I was from Thornton, and we got to talking about Dr. Rhine. He gave me some tablets, and in a week I could tell the difference.

This hospital in Fordyce, you know his picture is up there on the wall. He'd go up there, down the hall, "Howdy, Ugly," he'd say to the nurses. You could hear him comin', whistlin'.

Verna: He didn't see no strangers.

Ed: I heard this. There was a baby goin' to be born down in the Ouachita River bottoms. They got Dr. Rhine. They carried him so far in the car, and then, the water was high, they got in a boat and boated out to a house, and he delivered that baby.

My oldest brother, Will, told me this one. "Dr. Rhine woke me up last night." Some colored folks lived over across White Water and he had been over there in the night to see them. He had this surrey and the road was so narrow, he got his wheel hung up in some bushes. He got out and walked to our house, hollered around. My brother got up, found out it was Dr. Rhine, and he taken an ax and went down there and cut the limbs it was hung in, and got him out. That was way after midnight.

Verna: When we was children, and had two phones, we'd transfer messages between Dr. Rhine and his patients. He'd call our house in the morning to find out how his patients was getting along. We'd check, and if they was doin' all right, that would save him a trip. He never charged my mother anything when we had sickness. She was a widow.

My sister, Jean, had to have her tonsils out. We went to his office. He told Jean to get on the table and go to sleep. When he had taken them out, Mama tried to pay him. He said, "Miss Laura, you know I ain't goin' to take no pay from you." Some chloroform got on the dress Jean had on. We washed that dress, but she never would wear it again. She said that she could still smell it.

Ed: At his funeral, I never saw as many folks. They was people dressed up like somethin', and there was people dressed in overalls, all standin' out on the sidewalk. There was a public address and you could hear, but you couldn't see. One preacher that he liked was there, Brother Atchley. No one thought as much of Dr. Rhine as Brother Atchley. When Brother Atchley was at Thornton (Dr. Rhine came down to the office pretty early), he would go to Dr. Rhine's office, and Dr. Rhine would say, "Preacher, so and so's sick over yonder and so and so's sick. Are you going to see 'em?"

"Yes. I'll go."

I heard Dr. Rhine say one time at a church service (they had him to make a little talk), "When the doctor goes into a home, it's all tore up, not tidied up. But when the preacher comes——."

REVEREND CLINT ATCHLEY

TEMPERANCE HILL, ARKANSAS

I want to mention an experience I had with Dr. Rhine and one of his patients, Mrs. Bess Holmes. They called me one day, she lived just up above us, and said that she was real sick, so I rushed up to see about her. When I got there, Dr. Rhine, of course, was already there. He was out in the yard just wandering around looking down on the ground. I thought, "I wonder if he has lost his marbles." I went up to him, and said, "Dr. Rhine, what in the world are you doing?"

He said, "Oh, I'm looking for a stick to make a swab to swab Bessie's throat out. She's got diptheria."

I said, "Oh, my goodness! Is there anything that I can do?"

"Yes, there sure is. You take this prescription and go to Hunt's Drug Store in Fordyce and get it filled. Get back here just as quick as you can."

Well, I took the prescription and got it filled and came back. Dr. Rhine had used a stick right off the ground. He had whittled it off with his knife and rolled a big wad of cotton on the end of it. It looked like he was going to swab a cow's throat out with it. I never saw such a wad of cotton, but he got the job done. She was soon well again.

The most memorable experience was when our first little girl was born, Mary Theresa. We had come to Thornton from Arkadelphia and used a doctor there. (This was 1938, and it was my first pastorate.) He had a fancy office and came out with his white jacket on each time we went to see him. Of course, we had planned to go back there for the baby to be born. Well, we got up one morning and Kathryn was having pains. I called Nona Robertson, who was president of the Missionary Society, to come over and see about us, and she rushed over. Nona was very excitable anyway, and she was jumping up and down, not knowing what to do. She said, "Well, Brother Atchley, the only thing to do is to call Dr. Rhine."

"Mrs. Robertson, I had planned to carry Kathryn back to Arkadelphia to have the baby in the hospital."

"You do whatever you want to do, but Dr. Rhine's mighty good."

"We have never met Dr. Rhine because we have only been here three weeks. At least, maybe we ought to have him come and examine her before we go."

She called Dr. Rhine, and he stumbled in, he hadn't shaved in two or three days, and he asked, "What's going on here?"

"I think my wife is going to have a baby."

"Well, I'm not to blame for that!"

I looked over at Kathryn and two big tears were rolling down her cheeks. I said, "I want you to examine her, Dr. Rhine. See what you think about her. We plan to go back to Arkadelphia to our doctor there because he has been treating her all this time."

"I don't blame you. I'd take her to a good doctor, too. I don't know much about this stuff. I guess I've just delivered about two thousand babies, but I still don't know much about it. But if you want me to examine her, I'll do that."

He did, and said, "The baby is going to be here pretty soon. You can take her back to Arkadelphia if you want to, but the baby will be born on the way over there."

"Oh my goodness, Dr. Rhine, we can't afford to do that!"

"If you want to take a shot on me, I'll try it. We'll see what we can do. Nona, you go heat me some water."

Nona went to the kitchen. We had an old wood cookstove, and she took a white porcelain water bucket that held about two or three gallons of water and set it on the stove to heat. In a little bit, Dr. Rhine went in to get his hot water and there was this big bucket sitting on the stove. He called Nona,

"Come in here and pour me some water in a pan. This water wouldn't heat in a week in this big bucket on this stove." She came back, nervous and excited. In the meantime, she had called Mrs. Holmes and Mrs. Marks, and about that time they both came. Dr. Rhine got everything ready and in a little bit that little baby was here, and we were so proud of her.

About three years later, just before we left Thornton, when we were going to have our next baby, I asked Kathryn if she wanted to go to the hospital. She said she would rather have Dr. Rhine than any doctor in any hospital anywhere. So Jerry also was born in the parsonage at Thornton. The next day after he was born, he had some difficulty with his breathing. Dr. Rhine came and examined Jerry again, and said, "You've got to get this baby to Little Rock. I don't know what's the matter with him, but Dr. Charles Wallace will know."

"I'll have to have someone to go with me."

"Mrs. McDonald will go. She is trained to care for babies."

I borrowed a car from the coach; he had a new Ford car. My car wasn't very good. Mrs. McDonald and I started to Little Rock with the baby. On the way, she got car sick, but she wouldn't let me stop. She'd open the door, while I kept driving, all the way to Little Rock. She'd say, "We don't have time to stop."

When we got there, Dr. Wallace met us, and he examined the baby, and said that he had about a fifty-fifty chance. He had cerebral edema. I didn't know what that was. He put Jerry in an incubator and took care of him.

When I came back, Dr. Rhine met me and asked "What did Wallace say about him?"

"He said he had cerebral edema."

"Oh, that's not what's wrong with that baby!" So I thought to myself, I wonder why you sent me up there if you don't agree with what the doctor says. But whatever was wrong, he soon pulled through.

When we were leaving for Little Rock, Dr. Rhine stopped me and asked, "Preacher, do you have any money?"

"No, Dr. Rhine."

He reached into his pocket and pulled out a handful of wadded-up bills and gave them to me. It was probably $25.00. He said, "Take this. You may need it."

For any church dinner, he would bring large boxes of peppermint candy and hand out to grown folks and to children. He always came for dinner, he didn't have time to stay for anything else. He never missed a funeral, if it was anyone he had known even remotely. He would always make it by the church for a part of the service.

The day before we moved from Thornton, I went down to see Dr. Rhine at his office. Of course, it was just about full, like it always was.

When I went in, he said, "What are you down here for?"

"I just wanted to come see you and talk to you for a minute, Dr. Rhine. We are fixing to move."

"What are you moving for?"

"It's just one of those things. We are going to have to move."

"I don't see any sense in that."

"I don't either, but that's the way it is."

"Let me get some more of these folks in here and kill 'em, and then I'll talk to you."

He cleared his office out, and we went back into the examining room. I said, "I've just come to tell you how much I appreciate how much you have done for us, and how much you have meant to us."

"Preacher, there are three groups of people that I treat free of charge. That's preachers, school teachers and widow women. Of all the preachers that I have treated, them and their families, you are the first one that ever came by to thank me for it."

"Dr. Rhine, that's the least I could do. You wouldn't let me pay you for any of these services."

"Naw. Like I told you before, I don't charge preachers."

Then he said, "I want to tell you something now. You have meant something to me and to my family, especially to the girls. My daughters think the world of you, and you have meant a great deal to them. I want to thank you for that."*

After we had been gone from Thornton for several years, I was asked to speak at the graduation exercises. Dr. and Mrs. Rhine invited us to spend the night with them. We did, and of course, gracious as they always were, and Mrs. Rhine with her wonderful ability to cook and to make you feel welcome in her home, it was such an enjoyable stay. The next morning, after breakfast, as we were ready to leave, Dr. Rhine did something that surprised me. I knew, deep down, that he was always a real good man, but this was something I didn't expect from him. He went into the bedroom and brought out the Bible and said, "Preacher, before you leave, I want you to read some scripture and have a prayer." Well, it took me a little bit by surprise, but of course, I was so glad that he had said that. We had our scripture, the twenty-third Psalm, and our prayer together. Dr. Rhine, at that time, was not a member of the church, but I'd always admired him and respected him as a deeply religious person, but this experience just capped it for me, and I never shall forget that.

KATHRYN ATCHLEY

TEMPERANCE HILL, ARKANSAS

Mrs. Rhine was so wonderful for Dr. Rhine. She was a natural for a

---

*In 1948, Brother Atchley was the minister who married Susan Rhine to Milton Stark. He also was the minister who conducted the funerals of both my father and mother. PRB

doctor's wife. They tell about her doing some of his reading, research, for him. When he would have a baffling sickness and didn't have time, she would do the research for it, and then tell him what she had found out.*

*She knew what to do in emergencies, and she provided a lot of comfort to people who came, distraught and worried. PRB

"I don't care what you call me, just so you do what I ask you."

ANNA   TATUM   CROSBY

THORNTON, ARKANSAS

Oh Lord. Well, girl, you know, what year was it? I stayed sick, stayed in the bed for one year! Dr. Rhines, he come to see me every day, and at the last he come and I was setting on the porch. I had gotten so I could set up, and he come, and he says, "Anna, are you out of your pills?" and I says, "I'm just about out. I've got about two more doses." He says, "Well, I'll go bring you some." So I got up and walked out to the car with him.

He says, "Anna, you can't walk out here!"

I said, "Yes, I can, too, Dr. Rhines, I'm feeling purty good."

He says, "Well, well. Is you goin' to walk out here?"

"I sure is," and I walked to the car and he give me my medicine and then he talked to me. He says, "Anna," he says, "I have said that you and Cheetie Sanders" (me and Cheetie Sanders was sick at the same time). "I have told everybody that I had two patients that I know they wasn't goin' to live and that was Anna Tatum and Cheetie Sanders." Well, Cheetie did pass, but I'm still here, living.

After I got so I could walk a pretty good piece, well, he said to me "Anna," he says, "you come down to the office tomorrow. Can you come up there?"

"Well sho I can come up there."

As I crossed the railroad, there where the depot was, going up to the office, he started out of his office and he looked and saw me and he went back and sat down. He stayed there at the office until I got there. I walked in. He's setting down there like he always do, reading the paper. He sat there a good while, reading, didn't look at me at all. Finally, he look around. He always called me "Ole Ugly." He said, "What do you want, Ugly?"

I said, "Didn't you tell me to come up here? I feel purty good, Dr. Rhines."

157

He says, "Well, I want to examine you."

I had a knot in my side and I thought it was—you know, I ate dirt all the time. I'd just eat clay dirt. I'd go over there on the railroad, by Aunt Jo Smith's, and I'd get that clay off the railroad track and, oh, hit was purty. I'd get a gallon bucket full and I'd come home and I'd just set and I'd eat dirt, just eat dirt. Mama kept a-telling me, "Sis, you eating too much dirt." I'd say, "Mama, hit's *so* good. I just can't keep from eating it." I thought that knot was from some of that dirt I was eating.

After he examined me, he said, "Ugly, that knot's gone! Hit's done gone! You done quit eating dirt, ain't cha?"

"Yessir. I haven't ate any dirt now in a good while."

"Don't you never eat any more."

And I haven't ate any more dirt. I never have.

After that, after he got me up where I could travel and go, I said, "Dr. Rhines, I ain't got no money to pay you." I was washing for him and he was giving me two dollars a washing. You know, I'd wash this week, I'd get two dollars, next week, I'd get two. So he says, "I'll tell you what I'll do."

I said, "What?"

He says, "I'll give you a dollar and I'll keep a dollar."

"That will be all right, Dr. Rhines."

I went on then. I wanted me a house. I went down on the old Council farm and found this ole house. It wasn't painted or had stuff on it like wall covering. It was just straight planks, just nailed up. Dud Crosby, he come by and I says, "Dud, do you know where I can find an ole house? I want me an ole house. I'm just tired of me and Mama moving from place to place."

He said, "I know Mr. Johnny Hornsberger done bought that ole house down on the Council farm. We'll walk down there and look at it and see how it is. Maybe, if you like it," he says, "me and Mr. Hornsberger is just friends, and I know you can get it cheap."

We went down there and looked at it, walked all around down there. It had a kitchen built off from the ole house and some other buildings. We come back and Dud said to me, "Anna, I'm on my way to Fordyce. I'm going to stop at Mr. Hornsberger's and talk to him. l think you can get that ole house at your own price. I'll send you word this evening by Vernie Lee." Vernie was living in front of us.

I say, "All right, Dud, don't fool me."

He says, "I ain't."

That evening at six (Vernie was working at Fordyce) he come on in. He just waved at me and Mama. I told Mama, "Mama, old Dud Crosby done tole me a lie." Mama says, "Well, maybe not."

So the next evening when Vernie come from work, me and Mama was setting out on the gallery. He bust out in a laugh. He says, "Anna?"

Mama says, "Now you gonna get the ole house."

I says, "What you want, liar?"

He says, "Anna, forgive me. Dud Crosby told me yesterday evening to tell you what you and him was talking about. Tell you to go on down there and go to tearing it down, and he says you'll get it at your own price. You'll get all of them little ole houses around for ten dollars."

I says, "What?"

And so me and Mama went down there, you know how women are, we didn't know how to tear the house down. We was getting the side off it and Uncle Charlie Royston, he was down in there hunting and he heard us knocking and he come by.

He says, "How are y'all?" and Mama says, "We doin' purty good, Mr. Royston. How are you?"

"All right," he says. "Sister Johnson, y'all started wrong. You have to get the top off the house before you get the sides off."

Mama says, "Well, we didn't know."

So Mr. Royston, he laid his gun down and he went up on top of that house and he took all the top of it off. You know the top wadn't no count no how—just ole pieces of shingles and things. He got all the top off and he says, "Now y'all can get the sides." Me and Mama thanked him for it.

He says, "Now Sister Johnson, don't y'all work too hard. You be careful."

I says, "All right," and so me and Mama worked that day. We worked hard.

The next day, John Pickett and Ebenezer Rankins promised me and Mama, "Tomorrow, we are goin' to come and help y'all." So me and Mama fixed dinner, carried a big basket of food down there. Nobody show up, John Pickett nor Ebenezer Rankins either one.

I said, "Mama, the best thing for us to do is not depend on nobody but ourselves."

Mama says, "Yes, I can see that's right."

We went on working and Charlie Jones, he come and says, "Cousin Molly, I ain't got no job. I'm going to help you and Cousin Anna 'til we get it tore down."

I told him, "All right."

Every day Charlie, me and Mama would work.

After we got it tore down, Mose Johnson and Madison Oliver told us, "When you get it tore down, just let us know. We'll haul it for you."

They brought it right up here and laid it on this ground. "We won't charge you a penny." They brought all the scraps, too.

I said, "Mose there ain't no need on you bringing that."

He says, "Yes. Don't you have to have wash wood?"

I say, "Yes, that's so."

After that, Bob Jacobs, he told me and Mama, he says, "I'm goin' to help y'all. I'm goin' to get Buckeye to lay the foundation and frame the house up and cut the rooms all off and put the top on. Y'all can see me later" [pay him].

I told him, "Yes. Go ahead."

When we got where we could move in it, I had to have a roof. He had done put the top on it, and the ceiling—what you put the paper on. We was setting out on the gallery and Mama said, "What you thinking about?"

I said, "I'm goin' to see Dr. Rhines."

Mama said, "What you gonna see Dr. Rhines for?"

I said, "Just wait and see."

I went down to Dr. Rhine's office. I spoke to him and he said, "Now what do you want, Ugly?" I looked him right in the face, and I wadn't laughing either. I said, "Dr. Rhines, I want you to put a roof on my house."

He say, "What?"

I say, "I want you to put a roof on my house."

He says, "Well, you never see me you don't want something."

I says, "Dr. Rhines, listen," I says. "You know you never have come after me that I didn't go. Whatever you wanted me to do, I come up there[to his home] and done it."

He sat there a few minutes. "Well, Anna, I tell you. A tin roof would be better."

I said, "Dr. Rhines, I know it, but I'm not able to put a tin roof on it right now. I'm already in debt, and I ain't got nothing much to pay for it."

He says, "How many rolls will it take?" They wasn't using shingles then; they used tar paper.

"I'll tell you what you do. You go over to Lionel's store and you tell Lionel that I said to let you have enough paper to put a good roof on your house."

I said, "Thank you, Dr. Rhines."

I went to Mr. Lionel's and Mr. Lionel says, "Anna, what you want?"

"Dr. Rhines tole me to tell you to let me have enough paper to put a top on my house."

He says, "Well Anna, how many rolls will it take?"

"I don't know."

"I've got six rolls here. I'll tell you what I'll do. I'll send six rolls and you get Wes Barrett to put it on the house and then you'll know how many more rolls you'll have to have."

So he give me them six rolls. I went and got Uncle Wes, and Uncle Wes put them six rolls on, and it went nearly to the corner.

I says, "Uncle Wes, how many more rolls you reckon it will take?"

He says, "About seven more rolls."

Mr. Lionel had told me he had already ordered some more, and he would have them the next day. I went back and said, "Mr. Lionel, Uncle Wes says it will take seven more rolls."

"All right. I'll send them right on out."

Jabo Braswell was the delivery boy and he put them rolls on the wagon and brought them here. We put a roof on this ole house and me and Mama and her Mama moved in here. We didn't have a window and an ole piece of a door that wadn't no good, but we put it up. We stayed here that winter and, you know, we didn't have a cold! It was a bad, cold winter, but we didn't have a bad cold or nothing.

John Green, after it turned cold, I seen him, and I said, "John, I want you to build me a flue."

He says, "Anna, I'm busy. My hands are full. I just can't build you nary flue."

I says, "Looka here, John. I got to have a flue. My grandma's old, and she's got to have a fire."

I was looking at him so hard. (John told me after he built the flue, he says, "Anna, I couldn't turn you down. You talked so pitiful and you were looking at me right in the eye and I couldn't deny you.")

He told me, "I'm working every day, but I'll come every night and work on that flue, 'til I get it built."

He built me a double flue—one in my kitchen and one in the living room.

I said, "Well, thank you, John."

He says, "I know you ain't got no money, so I'll charge you six dollars for building the flue."

I says, "All right. I thank you. I can't pay all of it at once."

"I know you can't, but whatever you can pay me, you do it."

I kept giving him one and two dollars 'til I got him paid.

Them bricks for the flue, me and Ellen Arnold, Claud Arnold's mother, that ole lady, oh, she laid with me. They had a stack of brick, down at the ole mill, that was clean, but they had done sold them all. When I went and asked the man, he told me, "Girl, like times is now and you trying to build! I tell you what I'll do. If you can get somebody to help you to tear these brick down, I'll give them to you."

I come back home and I told Miz Ellen Arnold about it. You know she cussed all the time. She says, "Hell, I'll go with ya. We'll get them bricks."

So we went down there and we got four hundred. Mr. Trammel's boy, Gordon, he hauled them brick up here and put them out there and me and Miz Arnold set there all day and scraped and cleaned them brick. She really laid with me until we got it done.

I said, "Miz Arnold, I sho do love you."

She said, "Aw hell, I'll help you. Don't worry."

John had told me he had to have some sand and cement. So I got my wheelborrow and went to the road. There wasn't no highway through here, just a dirt road. I got me some sand. I hauled two loads of sand in my wheelborrow and John had a-plenty of sand, and I got a sack of cement. He fixed it and put that flue up and a heater. I had worked and worked.

Dud Crosby come by and said, "Anna, I see you got it up."

"Yes, I have," and I says, "Dud, I sho do thank you. Boy, you been good to me."

"Well, I try to help everybody I can. I been knowing you and your mama for years and years."

You see, we was all raised down close to Hampton. I'd see him nearly every Sunday, 'cause the girl that he married, she and I were school girls together, and whenever he'd come down, they would always come around to see us. After him and Connie got married, I didn't see Dud for a long time.

I went to somebody's funeral and he and Connie was there at the funeral. I was so glad to see him and Connie. I said, "Why don't y'all come to see me? You got a way to come. I can't walk down here."

He said, "I know. I been telling Connie we was coming up there to see you, but we ain't done it yet."

"Well, that's all right. I'll be looking for you."

He never did come, him and Connie, but sometimes I'd go to Fordyce, and I'd run up on him and we'd talk and have fun.

After Connie died, Dud come to me and Mama's house and he says, "Anna, I been in love with you ever since I've seen you. You are my first love. I still love you. I'm a widower now and y'all will be bothered with me."

I said, "Aw, shut up," and just laughed it off. I wadn't thinking that he meant it.

We got to going together and the first thing you know, we was married. We was married! He moved in here with me. His house was a little three room shotgun house and he says, "What you got, my little house wouldn't hold." So we lived together and got along good 'til he passed.

He was keeping Dr. Rhine's dogs and his own down in the country. He'd go down there every day or every other day and see about them. When time come to farm, he was down there every day.

They called him "Sheriff." He was a Deputy Sheriff. Everybody that knowed him, when they wanted to know something, they'd go see "Sheriff." He was a pretty good advisor. He was a great friend of Dr. Rhine's.

After we moved in here, my grandma got sick, and I sent for Dr. Rhines. We wasn't able to hire folks to bring us wood already cut. Aunt Margaret Green told me and Leona Edwards, she said, "Y'all go up in the woods, and there are plenty of trees fallen down. All the wood that y'all want, you can get it and I won't charge you nothing for it, if y'all get somebody to haul it for you."

So me and Leona and her children, we'd go up there and pile up wood, limbs and some trees. Madison Oliver, he'd haul it for us. I had a great big pile of wood out in the yard.

That evening when Dr. Rhines come to see Grandma, he come in, treated Grandma, give her some medicine and told me how to continue giving it to her. He looked around. I didn't have no wood cut on the gallery. Dr. Rhines put down his medicine bag. Willie Green had made me some sawhorses where I could put the logs in and saw them. Dr. Rhines, that evening, wooo, he sawed up a great big pile of wood. I sawed 'til I got tired.

"Dr. Rhines, I'm tired. I can't saw no more wood."

"Oh, yes. Come on."

OH—Dr. Rhines just worked me like everything. It was a crosscut saw. I was on one end, and he was on the other end. Shoot! Dr. Rhines cut enough wood to last us two or three days. Yessir! Dr. Rhines was good!

And I know when I was sick, the time when he said I wouldn't live, he'd bring me more stuff to eat every day when he'd come. He'd bring lots of food out here. I liked syrup. He'd bring syrup and meat, milk and bread. Selma Polk was cooking for him, and he'd make Selma to fix me up a big plate of food and bring it every day. He'd tell me, "Now you can eat. Get up from there." Yessir!

Everybody here miss Dr. Rhines. Everytime I go to the hospital in Fordyce I have to go in there and look at Dr. Rhine's picture hanging on the wall. Dr. Rhines, he was so good to everybody. I believe if anybody has gone to heaven, Dr. Rhines has gone 'cause it made no difference how bad the weather was, how it rained, how it snowed or nothing, Dr. Rhines would come. When he was riding hosses, he would come. When he got a car, he would drive his car as far as the road would let him, then he'd get out and walk to the house. Yes, he would. Dr. Rhines was wonderful! I sho do miss him. Mama did, too. He hoped me and Mama out so much, so much. He always called me "Ole Ugly" and I'd say, "I don't care what you call me, just so you do what I ask you."

(Anna, who is 80 years old, built her house in 1944.) PRB

*"A very strong aspect of his character, which was an intense loyalty
to people who he felt deserved his loyalty."*

DR. HUGH FIROR

CLEVELAND, OHIO

I spent that summer fairly close to Dr. Rhine, perhaps in a relationship which no one had been in previously, that is, a beginning medical student who virtually attended patients with him around the clock for a time and saw him in interaction with a number of people, both medically, socially and politically. Of necessity, some aspects of him probably were seen by me more vividly than to many other people. As my sister, Anne [Firor Scott] said, when interviewed for some publication, you must describe the warts as well as the halos, and I guess that's what I'm saying. I will not deliberately censor out aspects of Dr. Rhine which I remember. Any comments which others might take amiss are simply trying to resurrect impressions of a young student, looking at a very senior and rather unique figure in American medicine.

This was the summer of 1950, during which I spent a period of time with Dr. Rhine, perhaps eight weeks, plus or minus. I had finished one year of medical school at that time. At that time, I was very much convinced that I would do family practice, and had been intrigued by the idea of spending some time with a long-time family practitioner. I probably got more than I bargained for, as Dr. Rhine's background reached way back, actually, preceeding medical practice as I had known it in any way, shape or form. So that it was an interesting experience from the standpoint of historical perspective—the evolution of medical care, and, I suppose, a graphic illustration that in 1950 in a small, fairly rural area of America, medical practice was not the same as it might be in a large metropolitan area with a big medical center.

I was quite compulsive in those days and attempted to keep up with Dr. Rhine's schedule and fairly well succeeded. Eating early breakfast with him and Mrs. Rhine, who chronically tried to overfeed me, with breakfast, as I remember, of huge stacks of pancakes, fresh strawberries, eggs, ham, et cetera. It's a wonder I didn't weigh 300 pounds after that summer was over. Then making early morning rounds to see patients from six miles away in Fordyce, and usually two or three patients that would require some travel out into the countryside. These might be seen in the morning or some other time during the day. Then we would see patients there in the office in Thornton. Go home for another meal, which was again sumptious. At that period Dr. Rhine did take a little siesta after lunch, but it never seemed to last very long, and even at the age of twenty-one, his schedule for me was rather rigorous. We would see patients in the office in the afternoon and make further house calls as needed. Then usually came back to home base where he would spend some time looking after his July fox hounds. He had a litter of puppies that summer, and they were very highly sought after by various friends around the area. He spent a moderate amount of time taking care of those puppies. Dinner would be again too much to eat as I look back, but enjoyable. Although by that time he and Mrs. Rhine had gotten into the habit of eating out with what I perceived was more frequency for them. That usually consisted of going down to Allen's place. He and his wife ran a barbecue place a short distance down the road. So we ate there with some frequency that summer.

Evenings were not really a time for much swinging, and it was an early bedtime around the Rhine household. It was an uncommon night that we slept all night as house calls were frequent and many of these were home deliveries, anywhere from two miles away to twenty miles away. I was intrigued by the fairly common custom still extant at that time of people coming to get the doctor, either not having access to telephones or for some reason adherring to a practice of an earlier time. That is about an accurate description of the day's activities.

Social life was not very exhuberant in the context of what most people would consider social life. I went with Dr. and Mrs. Rhine out to dinner several times in the homes of friends. Usually we were surrounded by a large family with many branches and most of them had been delivered by Dr. Rhine. One night, and it was in Allen's [Lightfoot] household, I remember we went for supper. There was grandmother and her children and Lord knows how many grandchildren present. With the exception of one of the grown children and the grandmother, he had delivered everyone in the house, a measure of his years in that community.

He and I went to a fox hunt one night, which consisted, as far as I could tell, mainly of folks getting together and having a big feed, which was fun and contained, to other people, all the exotics of Southern rural eating, squirrel stew, et cetera. We did not stay for the festivities, which would apparently have involved sitting up all night and listening to the fox hounds as they hunted.

I remember Dr. Pat Murphey from Little Rock, an old friend of the family, visiting on one occasion and spending a couple of days. Dr. and Mrs.

Rhine went to Little Rock for a day, but they did not stir far from home outside of the day's activities, as a rule.

There were several neighbors who dropped in occasionally. A lady next door [Mattie Jackson], who had a grown-up son, who was close to the family and dropped by to see Mrs. Rhine fairly often, and some other people from the community.

The surroundings of the office were fascinating, and I remember vividly he had two rooms right next to the post office. About two hundred or two hundred and fifty yards from his back door, up a little alley and then a street. The office really looked the part of a 1900's doctor as he had a huge old desk with stacks of papers on it. He had a number of books, many of which dated back a long time, but he fairly often bought new textbooks, which amazed me. I recall that summer, he very pointedly bought a new edition of De Lee's textbook of obstetrics. In all honestly, it had virtually no application to the type of obstetrics he was doing, and I waited all summer to see him open the book and read it. I only saw him open it once and that was to show me something, but I think psychologically it meant something to have an up-to-date textbook.

He did not take many journals, but he took the AMA [American Medical Association] Journal, which I got acquainted with that summer and read quite a bit. I do not recall that he received any other journals regularly, although perhaps he received an obstetrical journal.

The office was really an antique piece. I understood from Mrs. Rhine that periodcally she had attempted to bring him into the modern era by suggesting or trying revisions of the office, none of which made any difference to him, apparently. The smaller room, which was the universal room for examinations, minor surgery, treatment, injections, and dispensing medicine, certainly was a period piece. Upon the shelf and sitting on the floor were many, many jugs and bottles of preparations, the majority of which I had never heard of before and have never heard of since. One must stop and remember that he graduated from a school which at the time subscribed to the homeopathic school of medicine in which many medications were mixed in small amounts to create medications. His use of these medications was fascinating to me. His ancient examining table-chair, which would convert from a table into a chair, was an antique which I suspect had not been even available on the market for thirty years or more. On the table under the window would be a pile of returned bottles, some of which had been returned when they were empty in case they were needed again for medication, and interestingly, intermixed with them were bottles in which urine specimens had been brought in. The casual way in which these bottles were stacked together gave me some cause for concern as the summer wore on.

Dr. Rhine practiced a type of family practice which is unknown today, and which to a 'modern' medical student of 1950 was almost unknown at that time as far as therapeutics were concerned. His forte medically was that he had the family histories available, in most instances instantly, as he had known these people all of their lives, and in most instances their parents and often their grandparents. Many of the patients we saw he had delivered, and many of them he had also delivered other members of the family and treated the parents, uncles, aunts and cousins.

Whatever the difference in his basic training, and as I recall, he did not have four years of medical school, probably had two or three, over the years he had observed thousands of patients, and his forte certainly was in diagnosis and in the nice decisions which had to be made in a rural practice as to when a patient's condition demanded transferral to a hospital or to the University Medical Center in Little Rock. I recall some cases in which his diagnosis was erroneous, but the corollary is that when these patients were referred to the Medical Center in Little Rock, they rarely improved much on what he had done, which, I think, has been a frequent observation of family practitioners throughout the country.

Case in point was a man we saw on a number of occasions who had been disabled after a logging accident in which he twisted his back and ever since had had sciatica, this to a disabling degree. He would periodically get periods of abdominal trouble with distention of his abdomen, inability to eat, vomiting, et cetera, had been sent to Little Rock where apparently they had treated him by putting a tube in his stomach and putting his intestinal tract at rest until he recovered, but had never pursued him beyond that point. At the time, this was an interesting phenomenon. In retrospect, the man almost certainly had a major ruptured intervertible disc. Whereas, Dr. Rhine termed it sciatica, the experts at the Medical Center had done nothing any more definitive. That caused me to sit and think a number of times in subsequent years.

He made diagnosis based on what you come to learn as years go by, the patient 'looking like that's what he had' rather than being able to list one, two, three, four, five, six—these are the reasons why this patient has a given condition. This looked like an impossible task to me at the time. I subsequently came to observe the same approach among the high class people who taught me and those I have worked with over the years.

He rarely used a stethoscope, saying those instruments could create sounds that weren't there, and he would put his ear on a patient's chest and listen very briefly. As a youngster of twenty-one, when invited to listen to the patients with him, I at least had discretion enough at that age to use a stethoscope. Some of the ladies we saw would not particularly, I think, have appreciated a young medical student putting his ear on their breast to listen to their heart. It was standard procedure for Dr. Rhine, and I never saw any patient act as if it was anything out of the ordinary.

Dr. Rhine introduced me to some conditions which I first saw with him and even remember today. An ancient lady in her seventies with extreme pain in the side of her face produced by chewing food, and he pointed out to me that she had tic douloureux, known more commonly as neuralgia of the trigeminal nerve or tri-facial neuralgia. A very disabling condition which occurs in older people producing severe pain in the distribution of the trigeminal nerve in the side of their face. It would require morphine to relieve her pain. At that time definitive treatment for this condition was being sought. In major centers, surgical attack on the trigeminal nerve had been carried out since the time of Harvey Cushing. I think that practice had not gravitated to the University Medical Center in the 1950's, or it was rarely done, so when she got that attack she would call Dr. Rhine and get a shot of morphine. I went back to school as perhaps the only student in the class who knew what tic douloureux was.

I remember seeing an ancient gentleman in his upper seventies. He was ancient physiologically, although seventies is young today. When we went in and saw him, the striking thing to me was he was about the color of a pumpkin. Dr. Rhine sat with him a few minutes and told me he had a cancer in his pancreas. I thought it was nothing short of remarkable. The old gentleman was sent to University Hospital where he had an exploratory operation, which showed a cancer of the pancreas. I came to regard that type of confirmation of his diagnosis as fairly standard that summer.

He sent a woman with a hemorrhage late in pregnancy to the University Hospital. They called next day and said that only a pumps transfer had avoided losing her child. His judgment as to when to do these things was really quite remarkable.

I saw the first appendectomy I had ever seen. A young woman with one or two children (he had delivered her), and we saw her one evening with some abdominal pain. We went back to see her the next morning, and he transferred her down to Camden and to Dr. Robbins, who at that time was politically prominent in the AMA [American Medical Association]. Dr. Robbins called and said, "Would you come down?" and he and I went down. Dr. Robbins removed her bad appendix, Dr. Rhine assisted and I watched, thinking this was really a marvelous proceeding.

As always, when we traveled around and saw patients, he introduced me in a semi-comical fashion, saying, "This is one of them there medical students come down to watch a country doctor at work." That introduction was repeated ad infinitum that summer.

The obstetrics we did was a revelation to a young medical student. We traveled all over the countryside and delivered babies in small homes, shacks, you name it. I was quite fascinated as we would arrive, and he would fill a basin with green soap and put on gloves and examine the patient, always doing vaginal examinations, which I had been taught were dangerous, rather than rectal examinations which were the standard for that time. Then he would give the patient a hypodermic and say, when I asked what this was for, that was to relax them so they would be more comfortable. In about fifteen minutes to forty-five minutes the baby would arrive, and be delivered. This pattern was repeated over and over almost without variation. I knew enough about the drugs he was giving to know that it was a pituitary extract which, once again, I had been lead to believe in pharmacology was a dangerous drug to use in obstetrics.

I talked to a young doctor who was down in Hampton, a Dr. Wendell

White, who was in practice right out of medical school a couple of years, and told him about Dr. Rhine's practice of giving this drug, and he said, "Well, he will produce a lot of ruptures of the uterus using that dangerous drug." Well, apparently, he never did, and I think this was once again a matter of observation and judgment. He knew when to use it and when not to was the simple answer. In looking back at this in later years and thinking about it, I realize that most of the deliveries were women who were having their third, fourth, fifth, sixth or tenth child. They had proven that they could deliver babies without difficulties, and they were far enough along in labor that this simply speeded it up. Certainly used without judgment, this would have been a dangerous practice. We delivered an average of three to five infants a week while I was there. I do not recall a single untoward event in any of those deliveries.

Dr. Rhine had given up surgery some years before I went with him. At the time he had a stroke some twenty-five years previously, he stopped doing surgery. The surgery that he had done was the kitchen table variety of "let's get it done as quickly as possible, because we don't have a lot of time," and certainly his forte was not surgical. He would sew up lacerations, did not bother to use any local anesthetic, and my main function was to hold the patient still, somewhat reminiscent of a much earlier era in surgery, when anesthetics were not available. I never saw him use a local anesthetic under these circumstances.

He understood something, which he had better left alone. An example was a youngster who fell and broke his arm and came in the office. He told me this was a simple greenstick fracture and looking at the youngster's arm I sincerely doubted that, not from the basis of any experience, but from the basis of inexperience. He put the arm in a cast and pronounced it all right and sent the child up to Fordyce where an x-ray was available. The x-ray showed both bones of the forearm were broken and rather severely displaced. The doctors there put the youngster to sleep and manipulated the bones and couldn't achieve a good reduction, and he ended up in the hospital in Camden being put under general anesthesia and cared for by one of the surgeons down there. At the time, Dr. Rhine insisted to me that the fracture had been properly reduced, but had slipped and recurred.

Perhaps the most mystifying thing about his practice involved the use of his homeopathic drugs. People came in with all kinds of complaints. His first approach appeared to be for treating things such as headaches and backaches, which required purely symptomatic relief. He kept two different colors of simple analgesic tablets, the same medication in two different colors. He would ask the patient what was the color of the medication they got the previous time and if they said pink, he would say, "We need to switch to something stronger" and give them the green or vice versa. This was a daily occurence. Or he would mix up in a bottle samples from three, four, five, sometimes seven or eight different liquid preparations and shake it up, telling the patient that this was extremely bad tasting medicine, but would take care of the problem. I'm sure this was just an attempt to reinforce and reassure people about things which were basically psychosomatic complaints in most instances. He certainly treated a diversity of complaints with this type of approach.

Women who were past about thirty-five and had non-specific complaints, he regularly whispered to me that they were very neurotic and gave them hormone shots rather indiscriminately, which I thought was terrible, and I looked at the drugs which he used and could see no rationale in selecting one over the other, and he used several varieties of hormone preparations rather interchangably and indiscriminately. I suspect this also was more of a supportive reassurance than it was any real attempt at therapeutic results.

Dr. Rhine's one concession to aseptisis was an old-fashioned boiler type sterilizer. Syringes, needles, et cetera, went into this. Other more gross instruments were simply rinsed off and put back on the shelf. He used hypodermic needles repeatedly with simply sterilizing them in-between times. I recall finding in the cabinet a box of unused hypodermic needles, and at least twice during the summer, in his absence, throwing away needles which had become hopelessly dull, and replacing in the sterilizer new needles, as I felt this was a very uncomfortable practice to be giving hypodermics with a very dull needle. He never noticed this or commented about it. In light of 1983, this was certainly a dangerous practice and in a metropolitan area would have spread hepatitis around en masse. I suspect there was very little harm produced by the manner of use, and in 1950 this was very close to the norm in many places.

He showed some characteristics in treatment which many people would decry, I suppose, but considering the era, considering his background, I certainly cannot be judgmental. White boys with gonorrhea got penicillin shots and black boys with gonorrhea got sulfa tablets to take by mouth. I noticed this on a number of occasions and remember it today. The difference in quality of treatment in his hands probably was not significant. One could make a big case that the sulfa treatment was becoming outdated. Once again, I suspect that it was in big cities, and I doubt that it was in the neighborhood of Thornton, Arkansas. But certainly, he was a product of his time and his paternalistic attitude towards the black patients was certainly there. The pleasant corollary is that I never saw him neglect a black patient. I never saw him refuse to go see a black patient, and I recall one fairly chronically ill black woman that we would go by and see regularly even when the family did not call us. When the family didn't call us and the congestive heart failure underwent deterioration, he vigorously reprimanded the whole family for neglecting their grandmother. Certainly he accepted all comers. He, to my knowledge, never refused to see a patient, and in the context of the way he practiced medicine, he did what he thought was acceptable practice for all the people who came to see him.

The financial side of his practice was an absolute mystery. Some people paid him in cash. He kept a sort of non-descript book on the table and would sometimes put down charges and sometimes not. I once talked about this with him, and apparently he listed charges of patients that he thought would come in and pay sooner or later, so he would have a record. Those that he felt strongly would not pay their bill in any event, he didn't bother to list charges, feeling that that was a waste of time, I guess. The only record I ever saw him actively keep was he kept a record of how many postage stamps he bought. He pointed out to me that that was necessary at income tax time because that was a deductible expense. I frankly wondered for years how he ever made an income tax return. He regularly had a roll of bills in his pocket, not in a wallet, but in his pocket. His whole financial structure to me was a total mystery and remains so today. Mrs. Rhine's pantry was kept filled with things which patients brought in, and we daily ate fresh vegetables, pork chops, ham, bacon, you name it, things which were brought in to the doctor by patients. I don't say any of these comments about his financial structure judgmentally. Matter of fact, I envy the opportunity he had to practice in a simpler day when our lives were not so circumscribed by the rulings of the IRS [Internal Revenue Service].

Our traveling around the area deserves comment. Rarely had Dr. Rhine ever allowed anyone to drive his car for him. I think the girls used to drive it for him sometimes, and Mrs. Rhine had told me about someone who drove for him occasionally. Apparently, I was the only person who ever drove for him regularly over a period of time. This may have been related to the fact that he was then seventy-four or so. It really was a relief to me when he didn't choose to drive, because he would concentrate on other things when he was driving, and it was a little bit hair-raising. He usually jumped in and drove on a night call, I think perhaps, from impatience, perhaps from habit. Whereas I did most of the rest of his driving, at least half of the time at night, he would drive. Perhaps it was because he knew where he was going, and he didn't have to tell me. One night, returning from a house call, I was compelled to reach over and grab the steering wheel and jerk it rather abruptly to avoid an oncoming car, which gave my nervous system fairly good exercise in panic reaction. He didn't comment particularly, and we went on home. That was the only near miss during the summer that I can recall.

I learned a good many other things about doctors of his era that summer, which certainly are related to his position as a practicing physician, but which range considerably outside the strict practice of medicine in the implications. First, he was a significant political power in that part of the country. That summer there was a very hot campaign for the governor of Arkansas between a fellow named Sid McMath and one named Ben Laney, and perhaps a third candidate. During the campaign, I met all of the major contenders, not because we went to political rallies, but because they came to Thornton to discuss with Dr. Rhine their campaigns, recognizing, I'm sure, that as he voted so would a lot of people in that area. It was common for local citizens to inquire of him as to who was the man for this particular race, and he would tell them fairly candidly that he was not supporting this one or was supporting the other one.

He was called upon almost as a chief of arbitration in some civic disagreements and some considerations about various activities around the area. Even in a very small and backwater town, which Thornton had become by the time I was there, he was probably the leading patriarch of the community. One of the other patriarchs was the postmaster, who was ill, and his wife was acting postmaster. His name was Roy Wise. Dr. Rhine basically appeared to be the single dominant figure of that part of Arkansas, politically and in these other aspects. He was looked up to and he was pampered by the whole community, starting with Mrs. Rhine, who really looked after him meticulously and with little consideration for her own convenience or preferences as far as I could tell.

The local barber, who was a little dried up old man, didn't seem to do much except give an occasional haircut and a shave and worked in the store down the street from the barber shop, would open the barber shop on certain nights to give Dr. Rhine a shave, which was about once a week on the average. The remainder of the time, he went without a daily shave, preferring to have it done at the barber shop, properly, when he had it done. Quite often, he would heat water on the stove and take a kettle of hot water to the barber shop with him for his weekly shave. I had a haircut or two there in that shop. I didn't indulge in having a shave, as I thought the little old gentleman was a little shaky, and I might have needed a plastic surgeon when he got through, but apparently he never produced this untoward effect on Dr. Rhine. The little barber was a remnant of the past and talked about the days when the mill was functioning and Thornton was a viable town.

Dr. Rhine apparently had had a significant involvement in medical societies over the years, but with increasing time and becoming a very senior physician, he had gradually dropped out of many of these activities. Certainly, there was no real medical brotherhood in that immediate region, that one could relate to very well without going some distance. He was a kindly father figure to young Dr. White in Hampton. I spent two or three days with him down there to see his practice. The contrast was really quite striking. Dr. White was a product of a 1949 graduating class, used only 'modern' drugs, techniques of minor surgery and even used an x-ray machine. He expressed mixed emotions about Dr. Rhine. He appreciated his kindness, but he regarded him as belonging to an obsolete era when it came to the practice of medicine, and yet would call him in consultation. Although, the times we went to see patients in consultation, it turned out that the patients had been patients of Dr. Rhine's earlier, but that meant traveling twenty or thirty miles to see Dr. Rhine.

It was a very intense exposure to me that summer to around the clock practice of medicine. Dr. Rhine took very little time off. Although I think the pace of his practice was diminishing, he wasn't keen on letting you know that. I was not constituted by nature to say to him, "The hours are too long, and I need some recreation," so I stuck with him.

I have been trying to put in a capsule my impressions of Dr. Rhine overall, remain factual as well as subjective. He is not easily put into a capsule. Some of my impressions were not those of that summer, I'm sure, but were those that developed in retrospect as I developed in medical training and looked back at what I had seen in Arkansas. He represented a previous era in the practice of medicine and one which today is all but gone from the scene. He took all patients, as I have commented, without turning one down. He treated them in the context of how he understood the practice of medicine. For the type of practice and the time in which he practiced, I suspect he did a good job.

The curious thing to a medical student, the admixture of using penicillin, digitoxin, diuretics and other newer drugs along with the mixture of all the homeopathic preparations, was quite a revelation. He used specific more modern drugs when there were clear indications for using them, and when there was no particular indication for anything, he fell back on the homeopathic preparations. He did not change quickly or easily. He used penicillin in beeswax for its long effect quite some years after it had gone out of general use because the beeswax was producing undesirable reactions. He was not therapeutically up to date. I recall him treating a young woman who was married with several children, for congenital syphilis because she had a positive blood test. Yet no one in her family had any signs of the disease. He had treated her vigorously with penicillin and when two or three courses of penicillin did not reverse her blood test, he went back and treated her with some of the rather severe medications of an earlier day—the arsynicals—in an attempt to reverse her blood test. It was three or four years later that I became acquainted with the false-positive STS [serologic test for syphilis]. I think that was what we were dealing with. Here was a patient being therapeutically abused by virtue of him not being up to date on the management of the problem—syphilis.

However, in the main, I think diseases for which there were specific medications, he treated very well. He used his homeopathic medications sometimes without clear-cut perception of what was being done. We saw a patient in consultation with Dr. White in Hampton, who had some congestive heart failure, and Dr. White already had him on a digitalis preparation. Dr. Rhine mixed up a bottle of his homeopathic drugs and added it to his medication, and within three days, the gentleman was in clear-cut digitalis intoxication. It turned out that the preparation was syrup of squill, which is a cardiotonic glycoside. When I tried to discuss this with him, he became quite defensive and pointed out that this was not digitalis. The gentleman's symptoms and difficulties disappeared when the one medication was discontinued and his digitalis level was brought back to normal. These are the ups and downs of that type of practice in that era, and I think are interesting history rather than very severe criticisms of the way he practiced medicine.

Dr. Rhine was an interesting study from many angles. He was a patriarch and quite autocratic, not accustomed, too often, to people disagreeing with the way he wanted to do things, accustomed to his patients

173

as well as other people doing what he said without question. He represented the old school where you accepted the doctor's advice and didn't question it. He didn't do a lot explaining to patients as to what, when and where, but his patients didn't ask for much explanation, having, I guess, been raised in the same atmosphere, so that appeared to be a symbiosis between people of similar thought, rather than a one-sided thing.

He was not very demonstrative of his feelings to anyone that I ever saw, and yet I think he had some very deep feelings of pride in his family. I think he even developed a certain regard for me, because this was conveyed in rather subtle ways, and when, five or six years later, I came through Thornton on my way back from the Navy, he really had, according to Mrs. Rhine, talked for several days about how pleased he would be to show me around. There was then a new hospital in Hampton.

He had an ego as big as all outdoors—no question about it. He had significant sensitivity and jealousy of his reputation as the 'iron man' doctor, who worked all the time and never took any time off. To some degree, I think, in later years of practice, he felt compelled to maintain an image of working twenty-four hours a day when practice had dropped off and he was not working at that pace anymore. He, noncommonly, would spend part of the afternoon in his examining room, propped up on the table taking a nap. I would sit in the outside room and read and diplomatically let him know when a patient came in. That wasn't an every day affair, but it certainly occurred fairly often throughout the summer. I understood it and thought nothing of it, but I think he felt that this was somehow not in keeping with his image. He was not terribly keen that people knew that this was what the schedule was.

Like so many solo practitioners of that era, he was fairly comfortable and related well to doctors at some distance. Dr. Robbins was his surgical friend in Camden. Dr. White he related to pretty well. He consulted younger doctors with a moderate amount of condescension, but attempted to give them support, and I think treated them very decently. He had rather puritanical views of such activities as smoking cigarettes, drinking whiskey and playing around with women who weren't your wife.

I've always thought that he was pleased that I came and spent the time with him, although he never said so. I never was really sure that he knew what my last name was. He had some difficulty pronouncing it, which has been fairly common. When I questioned him about things, he certainly, I think, was flattered that I asked his opinion. He went out of his way to detail to me what a given condition was and why things were done as they were.

He really wasn't bashful about letting you know that he was a pillar of the medical community. My first introduction to him was in Washington, D.C. when he was in the running for General Practitioner of the Year. It was a little bit of a jolt. The scrapbook, which Mrs. Rhine and the girls put together, would have been much more effective if someone else had shown it off, instead of Dr. Rhine because he really was not overweeningly modest when he discussed the many accomplishments which were recorded in the scrapbook. But once again, against the background from which he came and the position which he occupied in that community, I suspect this was normal, and I didn't think much about it.

He had a deep-seated, genuine, persisting and long-standing love and regard for Mrs. Rhine, although if one had waited to see him express it, it would never have happened. He was more likely to say something like, "Well, Ma is a real good ole gal," or something of that nature, rather than anything which would have appealed to the feminine mind as being a proper expression of affection.

Pat was a little bit of a problem for him, as I perceived it, because she didn't regard him as infallible, as her two older sisters apparently were raised to do. Her rather ebullient personality and effervescence thoroughly delighted him, but he was somewhat nonplussed by his youngest daughter, who just didn't fit the mold of 'being seen but not heard,' which was the context in which he was raised, and how he expected his children also to behave.

He wrote me a few times, and I corresponded with him some over the years after I was there. I wish that I had kept his letters. They were really classic but unfortunately I have moved too much and files get lost, and I do not have them. He never failed to assure me that he was still working twenty-four hours a day and showing those young doctors, who didn't work like he did, how it was done.

Interestingly, he used to tell me fairly often that we didn't work hard in medical school like he did, and I listened to this for the first part of the summer, and then one day, I made so bold as to ask him how it was that he worked so much harder in medical school than we ever worked, when eighty-five percent of what we were learning wasn't even known when he went to medical school. That eliminated that little dialogue from our subsequent conversations.

We got along well, and I don't recall us ever having a disagreement or quarrelsome words during the long hours of that summer. He expressed his approval in subtle ways. I recall the night Pat and I were going off to El Dorado with some friends from Fordyce to see the bright lights of the big city. He took me aside and slipped me five dollars and said that I had been working hard and was an awfully good boy and he thought we should go and have some fun. That was about the closest to a breakthrough into the modern era that happened that summer.

Looking back from a distance of some years, that was a good summer, and I learned a lot. Probably more about other things than I did about medicine, as it turned out. I didn't pursue my initial inclination to family practice, but I have thought many a time about experiences of that summer, and interestingly, most of the identifiable problems I saw that summer, I fitted into the context of my medical education as the years wore on, when it became an appropriate time. I was perhaps clinically somewhat ahead of my classmates because of the time I spent with him.

As to the question of could he have been a more effective doctor, I think the question is no different than what we would ask in 1983 about family practitioners in smaller cities and perhaps in larger cities. He would have benefited from regular, well done continuing medical education, which is no different than it is today, and which in some instances, we are doing better, but I'm not sure universally. When I, in 1961, went into practice in Idaho, I was in a small group, and there was a doctor in the group who could have learned a lot from Dr. Rhine about family practice. I think the quality was not as good as Dr. Rhine's and his personal attributes were not steady and of good quality either. In the context of both his era and the next decade or two during which I was in the practice of medicine, he stacked up very well.

Certainly the personal qualities, which he took into the practice of medicine, his devotion to looking after people, his willingness to see all comers and, although psychologically he discriminated significantly, as did most Southerners, against the blacks, he never discriminated against them in medical care. I think that is important. He was a very loyal individual. I don't remember the name, but he told me the story at least five or six times of a gentleman that he knew, when he came out of medical school, he went to this individual and said that he was going down to Thornton and open a practice, but he didn't have any money. This gentleman lent him, I believe, three hundred dollars. Maybe it was two hundred. He paid the money back, but for the next sixty years he looked after that man's family and refused to ever charge them for care, because he said that send-off into practice was the greatest accommodation anyone ever gave him. This illustrates a very strong aspect of his character, which was an intense loyalty to people who he felt deserved his loyalty.*

I don't think he built up more or less of a facade than many of us do. We all have our sensitivities in areas that we are defensive about. His, as years went by, was that he could outwork all the young doctors, and he persisted with that image, I'm sure, until the day he stopped practice. But that is a very benign type of facade.

Dr. Rhine's favorite comment, when a woman with a backache came in, was "God A'mighty should have made women without backs," because backaches were very prevalent and are very difficult to handle satisfactorily. It was sort of part of his stock in trade. He was, to some degree, an actor. He put on a different affect for different types of patients. Patients regularly laughed at his antics and commented to me that he was 'sort of a caution'—something we don't usually encourage today or feel that is particularly desirable. But it was his practice style. He had developed it over a long period of time. He was very gentle with little folks, but his gentleness was manifested mainly in trying to spoil the dickens out of them. We did not see a lot of pediatric patients, but when we did, he tended to take them over to the side and give them a quarter or a dime or occasionally a

*The gentleman was Mr. John Dedman of Fordyce, Arkansas, and the amount was forty dollars. PRB

fifty cent piece, if they had had something unpleasant done to them. He had a side to him which was fairly well concealed from the average observer, who might have thought him rather immune to such emotions. I don't think he was at all.

(In 1957, Dr. Firor named his first son Thomas for Dr. Rhine. He is presently at the Cleveland Clinic, on the staff in the Department of General Surgery and the head of the Section of Pediatric Surgery.) PRB

"He did more for more people for more years than any person in America. I believe that."

REESE PARHAM

FORDYCE, ARKANSAS

If he came to our house in the middle of the night when somebody was sick, he didn't hurry away. A lot of the times he spent the rest of the night to see how that patient was going to do. He knew that he was not going to get paid everytime he went somewhere, but it didn't matter. Years later, when I was in the Dallas County clerk's office, he was audited by the Internal Revenue Service two successive years. Now, the agent who had to make the audit came to me, and he said, "I know you are a good friend of Dr. Rhine's, and I know why he is being audited. He has bought an excessive amount of drugs, and he doesn't show that he sold it all. I know what the reason is. He doesn't get paid. I would like for you to make up a bunch of affadavits, in the office here, and get a lot of your friends, who use Dr. Rhine, to sign them, stating that, 'Dr. Rhine gave me medicine for my child or my wife or some member of my family certain times during the year and that he didn't charge more than a dollar or a dollar and a half for it.' That's why he didn't make any profit." We got together a lot of those affadavits and as people came in, and I made some trips out into the communities around Thornton, and I expect that we got sixty or eighty affadavits from people. After that the IRS didn't bother Dr. Rhine.

In the early days, I'm seventy-seven now, so I remember, he had three good saddle horses and two saddles. He lived with his mother. He called her "Mammy." She kept a fresh horse saddled, and so many times he would come in our home, and if we were sitting on the porch, he would speak, but he didn't say, "I want to use the telephone," but went straight into the house, and rang the old telephone, and this is the conversation you would hear every time. "Mammy, any calls? Saddle up old Bald (or old Buck). I'll be there in fifteen minutes. I'm at Hunter Parham's." And away he would

178

go, galloping the horse across the woods, back to Thornton. The next call might be to Tinsman, but he would go on horseback. That would be fifteen to eighteen miles.

This happened lots of times. Some black neighbor would come in and ask my daddy to call Doctor X in Fordyce. He would call, and then he would turn around and ask, "Do you have any money?"

"No."

"Well, he won't come."

And he would try another doctor, and it always, I mean always, wound up like this— "Dr. Rhine will come. Do you want me to call him?"

I think the reason they didn't get Dr. Rhine in the first place was because they already owed him a lot. But Dr. Rhine never failed to come, whatever time of the day it was, for any of those people. I'm talking about the black people who came there, and he, among black and white, I'd say there wasn't one percent of them who was not a close friend. Dr. Rhine never saw a person that he didn't like, and I know he never mistreated one. It's true that he talked a little rough sometimes— "Come on in to this office, and I'll kill you next." Well, I knew when I walked in he wasn't going to kill me because this was a friendly visit as well as professional.

The undertaker here for a lot of years was Carlton Mays, and he also was a close, close friend of Dr. Rhine. Dr. Rhine was always in a hurry, and the undertaker, a lot of times, would send the death certificate to the attending physician to sign. He showed me, one day, a death certificate that he had sent to Dr. Rhine. At the bottom of it, instead of signing it, he had just marked a little note, "I didn't kill this one," which was typical, because just a few words usually was sufficient for Dr. Rhine.

I went to see Dr. Rhine a few times with some problems with my legs. A red spot would come on my leg, never higher than my knee. It was so painful, I couldn't walk. It didn't swell up much, it was just red. He prescribed cortisone. This was in 1954, and cortisone was new. I didn't respond like he thought I ought to, and he sent me to a doctor in Little Rock, an older doctor who was his friend, and he knew him well. I went up there, and he looked me over, and he, too, prescribed cortisone. I told him what Dr. Rhine had said. He answered, "Why didn't you tell me that when you first came in here? If Ed Rhine said that's right, it's right."

I went home and took this cortisone for several days. Dr. Rhine came by every day, but I was not responding, so he suggested that I go to the hospital in Camden. I stayed most of the summer, and they did exploratory surgery, and I took all of the new medications that they could find. Incidentally, Dr. Rhine was down there every day or night— twenty-three miles one way. Finally, they flew in a specialist, and he looked me over for half an hour, and all the doctors were in the room, because I guess the case was unusual. They didn't ever diagnose it. Later, Dr. Robbins wrote an article for a medical journal about it. The Doctor said to me. "Mr. Par-ham, I'm going to take away all of your medicine. How does that sound?"

"That's great!"

"I want you to take just one little cortisone tablet each day."

Dr. Rhine was standing at the foot of my bed, and I said, "Dr. Rhine we ought to have stayed with it. That's what you started with." He smiled.

He didn't leave when the other doctors left. He said, "I sorta thought that to start with, and don't you buy that stuff. It's expensive. I'll get you a bottle of 200 at wholesale price." The day after I got home, he came out and brought the 200 tablets.

That just shows you, like the doctor I went to in Little Rock and four dozen others we might name in the state, who believed, like I did, in Dr. Rhine's diagnosis.

I said that he came down to the hospital to see me every day or night and sometimes twice. Dr. Robbins was my doctor because that was who Dr. Rhine sent me to. After I got out of the hospital (I had spent all the money I had and some of my brothers), my brothers gave me some money. "You go pay Dr. Rhine." I go down there to pay him, and when I got there, the office was full.

When I came in, it was not a surprise to him to see me, but he was glad to see his patient walking around again, and he said, "Come on in here. I'll kill you next." I motioned to all of the people. "Come on in here."

After a little visit, I said, "Dr. Rhine, I came to pay you."

"What for?"

"Well, you came to the hospital once or twice a day while I was down there."

"I wasn't your doctor. I sent you to Dr. Robbins. I came because I wanted to, and Graydon, your brother, drove me a whole lot of the times."

"That doesn't make any difference. I was glad to see you every time. More than Dr. Robbins or anybody else." He just insisted that I not pay him. My brothers had given me some money to give him, so I laid it down and started to walk out. He grabbed my arm, "Now, just one minute." He did keep a small amount of it. I don't recall how much. But he never charged anybody for anything very much.

And along this same line, he was one of the most patriotic men I ever saw. He volunteered during World War I and did a tour in the army. I was in the army in World War II for a couple of years. I think my kids had everything but hog cholera. They had childhood diseases, pneumonia, yellow jaundice, and my wife said to me when I got home, "You had better go pay Dr. Rhine. He was out here a whole lot, and he gave these kids medicine—a lot of medicine."

The same story again—"Dr. Rhine, I've come to pay you."

"For what?"

"You have been out to my house dozens of times while I was gone."

"You don't owe me anything. I don't charge men while they are in the service."

I didn't have a real fight with him over this, but I didn't win the fight, either, because he wouldn't let me pay him. He was like that. Dr. Rhine had principles that he lived by-high standards.

He was an enthusiastic Mason. The Masonic Lodge is not a church organization. It is similar, I'd say, and Dr. Rhine believed it was sacred. I recall one occasion when initiating ceremonies were going on, all grown men, of course, having some fun and some horseplay. He would sound that gavel, and say, "Just one minute here. We'll have no horse-play in this room." Dr. Rhine had real order when he attended Masonic Lodge. When you get away from the Blue Lodge, he was a Shriner, and the Shrine is a playhouse for the Masons. He really had fun going to a Shrine meeting. When my brother, Ray, and I were initiated into the Shrine, I recall that Dr. Rhine yelled out above everybody else, when I came on the stage, "Now that's my boy. I've known him ever since the night he was born. He can take it. He's in good physical health." And I got it.

I told him later, "Dr. Rhine, I thought you were my friend."

"I am. I wanted you to have the works."

What he believed in, he believed in strongly, and it rubbed off on others. They believed it, too. Everything he did he had a system to it. There was a reason for it, and he did it. He was also an excellent judge of human nature. I think he knew if you were telling him the truth, when he talked to you.

Not only was Dr. Rhine the greatest doctor in this part of the country for a lot of years, he meant that much to the Thornton school. He was on that board for so many years, but even when he was not, there were people on the school board, and my daddy was one of them, who went to him for advice.

During my high school years, he would come to school quite often and he would always be asked to speak in Assembly. Maybe all the kids didn't listen to him, but so many of them in later years, I have heard make remarks about "Dr. Rhine said that in assembly one time." What he did and what he said, though it may not have been so noticeable at the time, it has lived on and had some rewarding effects.

Everywhere he went, people always asked him to talk, because people liked to hear him.

Talking about the medals school children won, I think it is safe to say that those kids, most of them he delivered, were proud of their medal for two reasons. To excel in their class was one, but more than that, it was Dr. Rhine's medal, and it was quite an incentive to those kids. It had the effect that he wanted it to have. Incidentally, I never won one.

After he had been practicing a few years, he developed a habit of talking real short, sometimes, I'd say, gruff. He explained it to my daddy. I understood it then and I understand it more as I get older. He said, "Someday, I realize that some of my friends are going to die, and I've got to fortify myself against too much emotion. So I have created or cultivated this habit of being gruff to avoid emotions."

He had tears in his eyes at my daddy's funeral. When I saw tears in his eyes, I remembered what he had said to Papa way back yonder—fifty years ago. But he had emotions as much as anybody. He never let anybody do something for him that he didn't return it some other way. He always did more for others than they did for him.

He used to come to our family reunions. He did as long as he lived. Mrs. Rhine, too. As busy as he was and as she was, our family did not want them to bring any food. We wanted to do that ourselves for them. But no! He never did that! He would bring enough fruit or something else for the whole community.

In 1935 our home burned, and of course, we had to rebuild. Nobody had any money, but we had a lot of help rebuilding. People would come out there, to Temperance Hill, and say, "Dr. Rhine sent me out here." What he had done, people that came to him and said, "I'll pay you when I can. I just don't have any money now," and he would send them out to our place, saying, "I'll give you credit for x number of dollars if you want to go work on Hunter Parham's house."

"Sure."

So many people came out there every day. Papa or some of the rest of us would ask, "Did Dr. Rhine send you out here?" He sent dozens of people out there to work—a lot of man hours. He had a way of getting things done for others.

Here is an incident that happened at the old hospital at Camden. Dr. Rhine worked twenty-five hours a day, and sometimes it might be two or three days, before he shaved. Mrs. McCloud and Mrs. Snow operated the hospital. Dr. Rhine always had a patient down there. One morning, he came bursting in early, before visiting hours, before other doctors got up, to see his patient. He just walked on in the room. He hadn't shaved in two or three days, and this young nurse on duty tried to run him out, but he wouldn't leave. He said, "Oh, I just want to see old fuss-box" or something like that.

She went and got Mrs. Snow, saying, "There's a bum down here. I can't make him leave." She came rushing back with the young nurse. When she got to the door, she said, "That's Dr. Rhine!"

Later he told me, "The young lady was so embarassed. I tried to make her feel better, but every time I went down there after that, she was always embarassed when I came around." Even though he didn't always shave, he went like he was, he was welcome when he got there.

This was one of the highlights I remember when I was a small boy. Papa had called him for some black person over there, and maybe he hadn't been to that place. (There were a lot of black people who lived near us.) Papa tried to tell him how to get there. It wasn't too far, and Papa said, "Reese, can go with you." Well he was riding a horse, and he started leading that horse, it was not more than half a mile. He asked me, "Do you want to ride?" Shoot! I just lived to ride one of Dr. Rhine's horses. He had some good ones. So he let me ride his horse, and I stayed outside and held his horse while he went in the house to see the patient. I told everybody the next day at school about it. That was a small thing, but little things like that are what you remember the most.

It used to be, during his real fox hunting days, and for a few years thereafter, you might find a fox hound anywhere in this countryside. If you called the name on the collar, it was going to be Dr. Rhine, and he would know whether George Hearnsberger was keeping that dog or whether it was somebody near Tinsman. He bought dogs for many people, and he helped feed them, too. I've never been to Dr. Rhine's Park at Bearden for any function, but I pass by there a lot of times. I sort of feel like it is a sacred place. They are keeping fox hunting alive.

Even in his later years, he had the best memory of anyone I ever knew. People that were close to him, he could remember their birthday. He could read the label on a bottle, even fine print, without his glasses.

I would be curious to know how much money Dr. Rhine would have had if everybody would have paid him. It might have run into the millions. Dr. Rhine would come into the bank at Fordyce, saying, "I've got more money here than I want. I'll give you some of it." He didn't count it himself. He would pull out a handful of bills out of one coat pocket and lay it up there and Carmel Talbot, the bank president, would start counting. (Carmel always waited on him.) Then he'd empty another pocket, then his pants pocket, until he had a whole pile of money there, mostly ones, of course. While Carmel would count it out, he would be visiting with someone else. He completely trusted everyone. I have heard him say, "Everybody is honest, until they are proved otherwise," and I feel this is pretty good philosophy.

Dr. Rhine, he just did the unusual, the unheard of, the impossible. Like going to a man's house and on the front porch amputating a leg. He came to our house and took out my brother Lee's adenoids, sitting on the front porch. Another thing he did, as dentists weren't so common, he'd pull your teeth right on your front porch, and without anesthetic, too.

Wylie Parham was almost an invalid for a lot of years. He had asthma, and he had tuberculosis. Dr. Rhine gave him some shots for the asthma. His wife, Louise, could give him the shots. He got to the point where he just demanded it too often, and Dr. Rhine told Louise to give him warm water in place of the medicine. He could have been successful as a psychologist, too.

I'll never forget one time I had a big boil on my leg, real painful. I sat on his examining table and I said, "Doctor, can't you put something on that to kill it?"

"Oh, it doesn't hurt me."

I couldn't keep that leg still, so he sat on my knee where I couldn't see what he was doing. I almost threw him off though, when he cut it.

Another thing that Dr. Rhine was right about: I had bad teeth. Before I went to the hospital, he said, "I wish we had time to get your old teeth out." After I got home, and I had to stay at home from August 'til October, almost every day, in his rounds, and Mrs. Rhine was with him a lot of the times, they came out and sat on the porch with us to visit. More than once, he would say, "Why don't you get those teeth out?" Along about November, I decided he might be right, and I went to a dentist in Camden, Dr. Dietrich.

He did more for more people for more years than any person in America. I believe that. I just don't see how it could possibly be otherwise, because twenty-four hours was not enough hours in the day for him to get done the things that he had to do. And it was all unselfish.

When Dr. Rhine was gone, I thought, "What can I do now?" We knew for all of those years, until 1964, we knew that Dr. Rhine was there. He would be there.

RUBY MAE LYNN PARHAM

FORDYCE, ARKANSAS

When I was a child, our family lived beside Dr. Rhine in Thornton. I remember that every morning he would come out singing, "In The Good Old Summertime." The colder the morning, the louder he would sing, and he went about his chores singing that song.

One Sunday morning, we were awakened by the sound of horses in the grove in front of our house and beside his house. We looked out and people were milling all around. My Daddy got dressed to go out and see what the problem was—why so many people were out there. He learned that Dr. Rhine had had a stroke during the night, and the people were there to find out about it. There were few telephones then. They had to harness their horses and buggies to come in to find out about him.

He was not a person who very often showed his emotions. You knew that he felt things deeply, but he didn't often show it. One Saturday morning, his barn burned and some of the animals could not get out. That was one of the few times I ever saw tears running down his cheeks. It wasn't for the barn, it was for the animals that he was crying.

He came to the school often and talked in assembly. He nearly always came for Armistice Day. He would make a patriotic speech, and he would stir our enthusiasm to be good patriots. He was always interested in good citizenship. In the name of good citizenship, when I was in the fifth grade, he started giving a prize to the best citizen in each grade every year, and he did that for as long as he lived.* I got the prize the first year in the fifth grade, and I was so proud of it. I'm sure that every person that has ever gotten one, has treasured it.

His concern was not just for doctoring, it was also for human beings. If someone in the community was seriously ill, and he saw that the possibility of death was near, he never left the family alone. He would go somewhere

*The Dr. Rhine medals, as well as a Senior Scholarship, are still presented annually to the best students in each class at the Thornton school. PRB

184

else in the community to give them this word and see that someone was going to be with the family. I remember when Cora Harton's mother was sick, he came to my house and he said, "Mrs. Reynolds can't make it many more hours. Cora needs somebody with her. Will you see that somebody is with her all the time?" So we took turns staying with Cora as long as Mrs. Reynolds lived.

Another time, Judd Barner was seriously ill, and he needed to get to a hospital real fast. He had an obstruction. They did not have a car that Dr. Rhine thought would make the trip very fast, and so he drove down to our house and asked Reese if he would take Judd to the hospital. He made all such arrangements himself.

And pneumonia! This was in the days, regardless of what you did, you went through the crisis. The night that I was to go through the crisis, he spent the whole night at our house.

Mr. and Mrs. Parham both had March birthdays. One year, Dr. and Mrs. Rhine brought a cake that looked like a big open family Bible. Dr. Rhine gave the communion table at the Temperance Hill Methodist Church in memory of Mr. Parham.

As Reese said, "He had a way of getting things done for others." There was a meeting at the school in Thornton one Sunday afternoon to discuss the possibility of building a new school for the black children. This was long before the days of integration, and there was a need for a new school. Discussion was held, and most of the people (there were only white people present) who talked about it were definitely opposed. They felt that that money should be spent in their school, as they felt that they were paying most of the taxes. They were not interested in the other school. Finally, someone asked Dr. Rhine, "What do you think?" He got up and talked about five minutes, and the whole atmosphere of the meeting changed. Before we left the meeting, everybody was dedicated to seeing that a new black school was built.

Reese Parham: His opinion, and he had a real strong opinion, was accepted by everyone there, and we built the new school, and, at that time, it was more modern than the white school. He had a way with people. It all adds up to one thing—they believed in him and in what he stood for. I can also say that he was the most unselfish person I ever saw.

RALPH MORRISON

PANSY, ARKANSAS

Thinking of Dr. Rhine, who was my great-uncle, I want to tell you some of the things I remember about him.

In 1933, I had typhoid fever. Mother wanted him to see me. He came and told her I had typhoid. I was in a coma that lasted for five weeks.

Everyone said that I couldn't live. I was sixteen years old, six feet tall and weighed seventy pounds. I felt that with his interest and by the mercy of the Lord, my life was spared. In 1933 the roads from Pansy to Thornton were gravel. He would drive that thirty-eight miles, one way, every day for five weeks. He wouldn't take one dollar or even let Daddy put gas in his car. He put me on broth, two tablespoons every two hours for thirty-five days and nights. At that time they knew of no cure for typhoid fever. He told me later that now it would be no problem to cure.

At the time that he was waiting on me, Daddy asked him why he would feed 130 hound dogs, and he said, "I don't smoke, drink or have any hobby except for hunting." He farmed out the dogs to friends, then when he got an hour or two, he would meet them and turn the dogs loose. He had a new breed of dog, called 'July'. He found out we were hunting, and he sent me a pair of puppies from a gyp he had sent to Alabama to have bred. They were too fast for deer hunting. When he found out we were deer hunting, he sent me a pair of red-boned dogs.

He told me that when he was seven years old, he went to his first school one quarter of a mile from where I lived as a boy and where I live now.

When he was released from the Fordyce hospital the last time, May Dell, John and I went to see him. The doctors had told Aunt Nita not to let him have company. When we arrived, he heard us come in. He asked Aunt Nita who it was, and she told him it was me and my family. He told her he wanted to talk to me. When I went in, I knew his time was short. On our way home, I told my wife that he wouldn't last long. As we were leaving, Aunt Nita's sister and her husband came in, and they visited a while. Later, Aunt Nita went in to check on Uncle Ed, and he had gone into a coma. He passed away three days later. I was the last person to talk with him.

The name Ed Rhine will always stand out in my mind as one of the greatest men I have ever known.

"He was just—well, Dr. Rhine. That is all that can be said. He was Dr. Rhine."

SUE HEARNSBERGER HODNETT

THORNTON, ARKANSAS

I am one of Dr. Rhine's babies, and he was my doctor for as long as he lived. There is no way to even describe him—he was more than a doctor. Ever since I can remember, when my daddy would be sick, when Dr. Rhine would walk to the door, and Daddy would be real sick, just the minute Dr. Rhine walked in the door, a relief came over me. I thought, "Daddy's going to be all right, because Dr. Rhine's here." That's just the kind of faith I had in him, even then.

When both of the boys were born, Dr. Rhine was our doctor. They were just crazy about Dr. Rhine, from the time they were little. I remember when Kenny was going to have his tonsils out, they couldn't get them down, and every time he would see Dr. Rhine out in his garden or his yard, when we would be passing his house, Kenny would go up to him and say, "Dr. Rhine, look at my tonsils and see if they are down." He would just throw his mouth open.

When Dr. Rhine would come to see him when he would be sick (Kenny was a little bitty thing) he would reach over and kiss Dr. Rhine on the head and rub his head, when he would put his head down to listen to his breathing or heart.

We thought Kenny might have pneumonia, and Dr. Rhine was sick. Dr. Ellis from Fordyce was looking after his patients. One morning, real early (you know, Dr. Rhine got out real early) someone knocked on the door. (The night before, he had called Dr. Ellis and had him come down and check Kenny because he was afraid he had pneumonia, and Dr. Ellis came.) There was Dr. Rhine. He said, "I was just worrying about Kenny. I wanted to come check him myself." It was the first time he had been out anywhere. That's why I say that Dr. Rhine was more than a doctor. No wonder we loved him.

187

I used to tell him, when he would send us to Dr. Eubanks in Little Rock or others, "We go up there and pay those doctors big prices, we go in, and before they even ask us how we are, or what's wrong with us, we've got to talk about Dr. Rhine—how's he doing. Then they get around to us." You would go in there to his office, and Dr. Rhine would look at you, and he did not make an examination, he would tell you what was wrong with you by looking at you. I don't know how. Then he would send you to Little Rock, and it would be there. So many of those doctors, Dr. Eubanks, Dr. Armstrong and different ones we went to, said, "Very seldom, if ever, could you fool Dr. Rhine." He didn't make x-rays and all of that, but when he sent a patient up there and told them that he had a certain thing, you could just depend on it. Dr. Eubanks said that Dr. Rhine sent a patient up there and said he had a certain thing. Dr. Eubanks sent him back and said he didn't. And sure enough, he did.

I was in a room in a hospital in Little Rock across the hall from the nurses' desk, and I could hear the doctors and nurses talking. They made the same remarks about Dr. Rhine's diagnosis. They would take Dr. Rhine's patients when he would send them, because they knew that what he said was what it was.

He raised us; he knew our emotional problems and everything else we had. He knew our dispositions. He was just—well, Dr. Rhine. That is all that can be said. He was Dr. Rhine.

I worked at the post office for twenty-five years, and we used to tell him that we were supposed to know everywhere he went, what part of the country he was in, when he would be back. You see, the post office and the doctor's office was in the same building. People would come ask us in the post office for information about his whereabouts. And sometimes he did tell us, so that we could tell people.

So many times we would get in a mail sack, open it and whoooo— this is medicine! Maybe it would be a bottle of cough syrup—a jug, not a bottle— and it would be broken. You talk about a mess in a mail sack, or some of that female medicine. It all had the same taste. He would get jugs of medicine through the mail. And he would mail medicine to different people. He would mail pine splinters to Virginia or others. He mailed many hunting horns to people and doctors away off, and syrup, gallons of syrup, he would put in a box and mail to people.

Any way that he could help you, he did. He lived his religion every day, by helping people, and it didn't make any difference whether it was black or white or whether they had any money.

You know how his office was; it was just piled up all over his desk. I never would have found anything, but he knew exactly where everything was. One day, I was in there, and there was a drug salesman sitting by his desk. He picked up a doctor's book and said, "I wish you would look here at what he is reading." It was lying there open. "He keeps up with all the modern procedures in medicine, even though he's old."

He would always have an office full of people. Another time, this drug salesman was sitting there. Dr. Rhine came out and poured some medicine in a bottle, and gave it to a patient who said, "Now how much do I owe you?"

"Oh, give me about fifty cents."

The drug salesman said, "I know what that jug of medicine cost, and he is not even breaking even at that price."

So many stories like that, that is why I say he lived his religion every day, because he was interested in people, and we all loved him.

For his eighty-eighth birthday, it started out that we just wanted to remember him. Miss Gee Dedman called me from Fordyce, and she said, "We want to give one red rose for a family." Now, not just my family, but that would include Mama, my sisters and their families, too. Just one red rose from each family! "Would you tell the people in Thornton about it?" I said, "I certainly will." I started out. Some wanted to put six or seven or more. I said, "No, just one red rose." Soon, I didn't have to ask. People called me on the phone, and not just from here, from all around. The florist, Susie Campbell, said that when she was coming out to bring the roses, they were still coming in wanting to buy roses to put in the bouquets for Dr. Rhine. I believe there were 243 roses. It just skyrocketed. Susie just had to keep re-ordering red roses.

I don't suppose there is a person anywhere around that Dr. Rhine didn't help in some way. I mean more than dishing you out some pills. When Howell, my husband, had the heart attack and was going to the hospital in Camden, Dr. Rhine called down there and told them I would stay with him. When we checked in, by the time I got to the room, they were moving my bed in. There was not a thing in the world that Dr. Rhine could do, but he only missed one day coming to see him. I believe he was there for twelve days. As busy as he was, he missed just one day.

On Sunday, before Howell died, he got real, real bad, and we called Sadie to bring the kids down. He went by to tell Dr. Rhine that Howell was worse. Dr. Rhine had an office full of people, but it wasn't any time until Dr. Rhine came walking into that room. He didn't say anything. He just walked in and stood there and stood there. He walked to the end of the bed and rubbed his hand across Howell's feet and said, "This is the hard part of doctoring." He said he was so busy, more than he could do almost, but the more he thought about it, he had to come to Camden. You think you can forget people like that? I knew and he knew that they could not do a thing in the world for Howell, but Dr. Rhine came. It always did something for me when I heard him. You could hear him talking before he got there. You learned his step. Things like that mean so much to you. They will always be engraved on my heart.

Another thing that meant a lot to me. As a little kid, maybe in the third grade, I got my first Dr. Rhine medal. (I finished high school in 1934. I still have them all.) Mama got me ready to go to graduation. I didn't particularly want to go. They insisted that I go. I had a brown organdy dress, and they put that brown organdy dress on me. Well, I didn't care about dressing up to go to school, but I went. When they called my name, to go up on the stage, and I got that medal, it liked to have thrilled me to death. I got several others after that, but I remember that one best.

When I was about four years old, we lived out from Fordyce, I had to have my tonsils out. Dr. Rhine, Dr. Black and Dr. Harrison from Fordyce took them out at home. Afterward, Dr. Rhine came to see me. It is the first time I ever remember seeing Hershey Bar candy. He brought me a bar of that candy, and it just thrilled me. I never will forget. Another time he came, he brought me fifty cents. I kept it for a long time. That was a lot of money.

He used to have lots of watermelons on his porch in the summer. He would take some out under the trees, cut them, and have all the little kids that came along to eat watermelon. Man, that was a thrill for us. People would pay him in stuff, sorghum, hams, watermelons, anything they had.

Mr. Ike Turner was my grandfather. My father was Emmett Hearnsberger. Dr. Rhine was their doctor, too. He had doctored on my grandfather's mother, too. He was with Mama when she had all five of us girls. One died. Then he delivered my boys. That's five generations in my family that he doctored on.

I had both of my children at home. People didn't go to the hospital then. When Kenny was born, he came down. I had already had my bath, was cleaned up, and I was reading the Fordyce paper. He said, "I thought you were sick."

"Well, I am something because my water has broken."

I was easy. I wasn't having any pain. It was time, too. He didn't miss it by two days with either one of my babies.

"I'll check you and see." He gave me a shot.

That was at eleven o'clock, and at five minutes after twelve, Kenny was born. He helped Mama get the bed ready. You know something? Dr. Rhine would talk real gruff like, but he was the most kind, gentle person I have ever seen. He got out the little clothes, because I didn't know the baby was going to be born right then. I just got along fine. Not a problem in the world.

My sister Ruth's second baby was so deformed when it was born, and Dr. Rhine, it nearly killed him when he saw that baby, Ruth and Mama said. That baby lived ten days. Mrs. Rhine said that when Dr. Rhine came home, he just walked the floor. He hurt. He suffered with them. Naturally, when we all started having our babies, the first thing we thought about was, "Is it going to be all right?" Dr. Rhine had told them that it wasn't anything they did, they may never have another like that. It just happened. They did have two more. When Kenny was born, by the time his head was born, I was asking, "Is it all right? Is it all right?" Just as soon as he was born, Dr. Rhine picked him up and showed him to me, because he knew what I was thinking.

One time John Emmett, he was in the second grade, had two front teeth coming out. The others were coming in behind those. I couldn't pull them because they weren't loose. Jessie and me carried him to the dentist in Fordyce. We had gotten him out of school to go. He screamed bloody murder when we took him in, he screamed bloody murder when we put him in the chair, and then he gave him a shot, and he cried that much more, and then he cried when the dentist pulled the tooth. You could have heard him all over town. We started home; John Emmett was in the back seat by himself. When we got to the intersection, he said, "Mama, I'm going up!" and he fainted. We pulled into the service station and got water and bathed his face off and brought him on home. He had a time with it.

When the other one had to be pulled, I said, "Now Johnny, I carried you to the dentist, and you cried the whole time. It might hurt for a few minutes, but that will be all. Dr. Rhine is not going to hurt you. He won't even give you a shot." We went to Dr. Rhine's office, and he took him to the examining room, reached in his mouth and pulled the tooth. Johnny hollered a time or two, but by the time he got to the waiting room, he was laughing. He never had a minute's trouble. I don't know why we didn't go to Dr. Rhine in the first place.

When Dr. Rhine would be walking to the office, if he saw a piece of paper or whatever, he picked it up. Not very long ago, I was walking to the post office, I looked down and there was some trash. I reached down and picked it up, and when I did, do you know who I thought about? Dr. Rhine. That's exactly what Dr. Rhine used to do.

That's what makes life, is all the little memories, everyday things, not the big things. That makes life pleasant, and you have all those happy memories to make your life better.

There is no doctor like Dr. Rhine because Dr. Rhine just knew it. He would tell you, and you could just believe it. He might come by four times a day—just stop in to see how the patient was doing. You didn't have to call him. It would just make you feel so much better. He was just—Dr. Rhine.

We loved Mrs. Rhine, too, because she was a part of Dr. Rhine. She was there. I don't think I have ever seen a wife any more dedicated to her husband and her husband's job than Mrs. Rhine was. They were a part of each other. It took them both, and we loved her, too.

One morning, Ethel McDonald called me. "Sue, can you come? Get the doctor!" I thought it was Bob, her husband, that was sick because we was expecting something to happen to him any time. I called Mrs. Rhine. Dr. Rhine wasn't there. He was at the hospital at Fordyce. I told her that Ethel had called me to get the doctor. I said, "I imagine it's Bob." I went on down there, but it was Ethel. She was in there on the bed. I went in and said, "Ethel, what's wrong?" She said whatever it was hit her when she got to the door. Dr. Rhine left the hospital and came. He checked her and gave her something. He had to go back to the hospital. I stayed there with Ethel. She had her dinner cooking. Bob was sitting on the front porch. She said, "Don't tell Bob because I don't want him to get upset." So, we didn't tell him.

We was talking. You know she had pretty white hair. I was telling her how pretty her hair was. I turned around to go see about something in the kitchen. She made a funny little noise, and she was dead. I went running to the phone to call Mrs. Rhine and told her that Ethel was dead. "No," she said, "You mean Bob." "No, Ethel. Ethel is dead." In just a little bit, Dr. Rhine was back. Bob started into the room. I said, "Bob, wait out on the front porch." Ethel was lying there dead. He went back and sat down. When Dr. Rhine got there, he asked me, "Have you told Bob?" "No, I was waiting for you." We went out on the porch and I squatted down on one side of Bob, and Dr. Rhine on the other, and he told him. Bob lived fourteen days after that.

Dr. Rhine was so much a part of our lives.

LOIS MORRISON HENRY

THORNTON, ARKANSAS

I remember when he would go to feed the stock, his barn was right behind our property, and my mother, Pearl Morrison, got the biggest thrill out of hearing him, on a cold morning, singing "In The Good Old Summertime."

My children felt free to go to Dr. Rhine without their parents, if anything happened to them. Mary Margaret had a fingernail that was just hanging, and instead of coming home and getting me, she went to the office and let Dr. Rhine pull it off. The children remember the homemade candy that was waiting for them when they would finish their piano lessons with Mrs. Rhine.

When Mrs. Rhine was our study leader in the Missionary Society, we met at her home in the evening because she was the answering service and doorbell service. She couldn't leave to come to the church or other people's homes.

I'll never forget the Open House celebration for his sixtieth year of practice in Thornton in May of 1959. Green Punch! Mrs. Cook and I made the punch the entire afternoon. We started about one o'clock, and we didn't leave until six—making punch. And getting cakes out of the deep freeze. There were more people who came than they had planned on. People were coming in the back way and the front way.

At his fifty-fifth anniversary party in 1953, my son Pat was invited, but another son, Morrison, had to clean up the yard. He and Pat both worked on the highway with their dad, and he cleaned up that yard after work the day before the party. At that time, he had not decided that he wanted to be a doctor, so he was not invited, but Pat was, because he was already in medical school. The women in the community would make pies and cakes and come serve the meal.

192

The time we gave him the roses on his 88th birthday, he invited everybody to come by to see them that evening, and we all did.

He was the kindest man. The way that was proven to my daughter, Gin, was this—her dog killed one of his chickens, and he just said, "That's all right." She thought sure that she was going to have to kill her dog; she was a little tot. I expect the boys had told her that.

He got a lot of his medicine through the mail. Our mail was delivered by truck, and sometimes, there would be broken bottles—gallon jugs of cough syrup spilled. We always looked forward to our Christmas rush with him. At the post office everybody in town and far and near received a Christmas card from him. You should have seen the mail! He didn't mail it all in one day, thank goodness! [He always addressed and signed the cards himself.] We had a hard time trying to figure out where he was sending them. Doctor's handwriting was bad. I wasn't working at the post office at the time, but I heard Mr. Wise tell about the time Dr. Rhine had mailed some medicine to go out on the rural route. No one in the post office could figure out where it was to go. Finally, they took it back to Dr. Rhine, and he studied and studied and he couldn't read it either. He had to go back to his mail to see who had ordered it.

When I worked in the post office in Bearden, I carried medicine to different patients down there for him. They would give me a note to give to Dr. Rhine. When the medicine would come in, he would call and I would go by, pick it up and take it to them.

He was the doctor for my grandfather, Mr. Joe Orr, for my mother, for me and for my children—four generations. A few years after my grandfather died, the children sold the home place. My mother took some of what she received and had me go down to pay Dr. Rhine on my grandfather's bill. You know what he said to me? "I don't want to take this."

"Well, Mama wants you to have it."

"She will feel better about it, won't she?"

"Yes."

"I would have done anything for your granddaddy that I could because I hunted with him all those years."

I went back home and told Mama that he didn't want to take it, and she said, "I wanted him to have it." She felt that was her part, and she owed it to him.

I thought of him as someone who would be here always. I knew that he was sick, but I didn't give up on him until the day they came to take the telephone out of the office. That just shocked me. I hadn't realized that this was going to be it. I was an old woman, but I couldn't believe it. When they took the telephone out, it was a sad day to me. I knew that if he had ordered that telephone out, that he had decided to quit practicing medicine. Mrs. Rhine said that he did talk about what he might do at home about seeing patients.*

*He was recovering from pneumonia when he had a massive stroke and died three days later. He was eighty-eight and a half years old. PRB

Frank: Dr. Rhine had started to Harrell. He got between Hampton and Harrell and went to sleep, along there about Buddy Newton's. There was a bridge across there. He hit the bridge, went on and hit a fence. He called my brother, Earl, and me, and we went down there, looked it over and got it out, drove it home. We had to keep it four or five days. New fenders on it, new engine, transmission was busted and we took that out.

One morning about two o'clock, someone was banging at the door. It was Dr. Rhine. He said, "I got a flat." So I fixed the flat for him. Most any part of the night, when he had trouble, he would want me to fix his car. But he went any part of the night that he was called, too.

Before there was any kind of heater in an automobile, Dr. Rhine used a lantern. We fixed a place on the dashboard to hang the lantern, and that kept Dr. Rhine warm in the car. Defrosters on the windshields—there wasn't any such thing. We found upon a little electric thing that fit on the windshield with suction cups and had wires in it that would heat and defrost the ice, but you had to look through the gadget. It was about 6 by 8 inches.

Our son, Johnny, was his pride and joy. Connie Lee was expecting the baby most any time, so when Dr. Rhine would leave town, he would come by here and check, and when he come back into town, he would come by and check.

Connie Lee: So one morning about five o'clock, I got up sick. It was Frank's birthday, and I said, "Oh my goodness! We're going to have our child on your birthday." Dr. Rhine came down here and says, "No." Everything went away, and I got up and milked the cow. The next morning, Dr. Rhine came to see how I was feeling. "Feeling fine." I milked the cow and did what I was supposed to do. This went on several days. On Thursday morning when I woke up, I was in a puddle of blood. "Get up Frank, and go get Dr. Rhine."

"He'll think I'm crazy coming after him if you are not hurting."

"Well, I'm not hurting, but you'd better go on."

Dr. Rhine came, and he didn't examine me or nothing. He said, "I'm going to give you a shot to clot your blood. Then another one to relax you."

"Dr. Rhine, I don't need that. I'm all right."

"All right, but I'm going to call a doctor in Camden, and I'm going to take you to the hospital."

Here we went. When we got there, they examined me and said, "The baby is awfully high. Prepare for an operation." But it wasn't any time 'til Johnny was there.

It was such an unusual case (the afterbirth came first) that everyone came in to watch. Dr. Rhine said, "In my fifty years of practice, this is the only baby I have saved. I haven't lost a mother, but I haven't saved a baby 'til now." He was so proud of Johnny. Those nurses just took over Johnny. They would carry him up and down the corridors, showing him to everybody.

Frank: When I would go to the office, Dr. Rhine never would charge me nothing or Connie Lee either. He babied her. I went down there after Johnny was born.

"Well, Dr. Rhine, I've come to pay you for Johnny." He'd hem and haw around a little bit.

"I'll tell you what. Give me $35.00. If that's too much, that's all right. If it's not enough, it's all right."

Connie Lee: We paid Dr. Dalton $100.00 and the hospital $300.00. I was there a week.

Frank: One time he was sick. I used to drive Dr. Rhine to Little Rock a lot. He was in the hospital in Little Rock. I went in to see him. He was sitting on the side of the bed, and when I went in, he just cried, and I did too. He was so glad to see me, he just hugged me. I'll remember that 'til I'm an old, old man.

Connie Lee: Dr. Rhine didn't only doctor on people, he doctored on dogs, too. When Tommy's little dog, Rusty, got caught in a fence nearly every bit of the skin had been torn loose. He took the dog down to Dr. Rhine's office, and he fixed him up.

Frank: Doctor Rhine Day! Lands, there were lots of people there that day. We started to barbeque on the pork, and they had different ones barbequeing the pork, goat and beef. It come a rain, and they let all the pork spoil. We went and got another truck load of hogs. We had a hog-killing over beside the school garage that night. We started barbequeing again, but it didn't get done. So Larry Warren and myself was finishing cooking the barbeque during the afternoon. We didn't get to hear the speakers and the program because we were in the school kitchen all day long.

People was coming through, and I had saved me back a little bowl of that mulligan. They had a wash pot full of mulligan made up. One man says, "I'll give you two dollars for that bowl of mulligan."

I said, "No sir! If you want it that bad, I'll just give it to you."

We didn't get to eat any of the meat. We just cooked it and put it out on the table. Man, it was cleaned out! I've never seen such a crowd of people. There were people everywhere! That was a big day for Thornton.

Dr. Rhine was going one day down the Hampton highway to the Talbots. He was going down the road, you know how he'd drive, down the shoulder of the road. A policeman come along and stopped him. He come over to see if he was drunk. When Dr. Rhine got through with him, he was glad to let him go.

He told me one time about a black man, who lived just up the road from here, whose leg got all messed up. "That night, I knew I was going to have to take his leg off. We used a coal oil lamp for a light and a hand saw to take the leg off."

Connie Lee: When Dr. Rhine was sick and he was nervous, he didn't do nothing but work jigsaw puzzles. I had a tooth that abscessed in the springtime, and I just begged Dr. Rhine to lance it, but he wouldn't do it. It finally burst on the front side. I didn't know it, but it went down. That fall, I happened to see a hole in my gums. I could mash it with my tongue and see something come out of it. I was sick all the summer through. My heart got to running away. I had to stay in bed.

There wasn't no use of beating around the bush with him. I went down to him. He said, "I ought to get a board and whip you for not telling me about this."

"I didn't know about it either." He sent me to a dentist, and I had to have it pulled. It took me a long time to get over it. OOOOH, I was nervous. He said, "You just got to do it yourself. Nobody else can do it." So I thought, "Well, I know what you did." So I got me some jigsaw puzzles, and I worked on them, and I could calm myself down with them.

Dr. Rhine would give you some nasty tasting medicine that was the best nerve medicine there ever was. Doctors now don't know what it is.

When our second boy was born, Dr. Rhine came every day to see me. (I didn't have any trouble when he was born. He was born at home and weighed ten pounds and four ounces.) Dr. Rhine asked, "What's his name?"

I said, "His name is Thomas Earl Scott. Do you know who he's named after?" He laughed. I said, "You and my daddy and Earl Scott.

MAELEEN CLAYE ARRANT

PINE BLUFF, ARKANSAS

My parents were Thomas W. H. Claye and Carrie Lydia Storey Claye. My mother was born in Louisiana, and my father was born at Chambersville in Calhoun County. His parents owned a lot of land there. When my parents married, they lived in Fordyce. They had eleven children. Dr. Rhine delivered the last two children. Old Doctor March delivered the older ones, including me. I was the fourth child. My grandfather had five tenants on his big farm in Calhoun County—not too far from Hampton. The tenants worked the land, and my grandfather got one-fourth of the produce, such as corn and one-half of the cotton. He lived in Fordyce. He would go out to the farm in a buggy or sometimes a wagon. They had a good orchard—plums, peaches and one great big apple tree—which supplied the family and all the tenants with apples.

Oh, Dr. Rhine was my family's doctor after Dr. March died. That included my father and mother and the younger children. I had already left home. I've heard them say that he was like no other doctor. There wasn't but *one* Dr. Rhine. They would always say he was so human, he was personable, and all of his patients were important to him. Any hour you could go to him, in his home or in his office. If you called him, he would come. It didn't make any difference what time—two a.m. or two p.m.

When my father died at home—he just got up to go to the bathroom—my sister said he was walking kind of fast and she felt a little funny and went back there. She called Dr. Rhine, and he was there from Thornton in about ten minutes.

All of them say he was such a fine doctor, so human, no pretense, he didn't put on, just real. He was just Dr. Rhine.

He just loved people. I'd hear them say that often he would entertain for everybody-fried fish, squirrel mulligan stew—all cooked in a big pot in his backyard.

He felt like his patients were his family. When he would go to your house, he would make himself at home. He'd go to the kitchen himself to get a glass of water or a spoon to give the patient the first dose of medicine, or to wash the thermometer. Back in the early years, a lot of people didn't have plumbing, but it didn't bother him. He knew how to get water from the bucket that sat out on the back porch. He was never lost in anybody's house. If a patient was dirty and needed a bath, Dr. Rhine would tell them to clean themselves up. And no house was too bad for him to go there.

A person was a person to him. The nearest doctor I have seen to him is Dr. R. D. Dickens. When my husband was sick, he would come every day to see him. Half of the battle is a good doctor with a positive attitude and his acceptance of you as a person, and your belief in him that he will do all he can for you.

ANNE BRADLEY CLAYE

HOUSTON, TEXAS

Dr. Rhine discovered polio in one of my twins. He recommended that we get her to the hospital at once. We had to wait until the next day. We took her to Little Rock. She was fourteen months old at the time, but she's walking now and doing fine, thanks to him. This was in 1942, about the time polio was just beginning to be recognized. There were nurses at the hospital from Minneapolis who were trained. And he sent her *immediately*.

The reason for it was that Papa was reading the paper that morning about a child with polio, and he said, "I wonder if that baby has what is going around." I heard him, and something just struck me. In a few minutes Cliff walked in and said, "Did you hear what Daddy said?"

"Yes. Do you suppose she might have that?" She was ill at that time with high fever, not ever having tried to walk. "Let's call Dr. Rhine."

We took her right on to Dr. Rhine, and he made that discovery right then. I know that is why she didn't come out of it badly crippled. We were living in Fordyce at that time. I grew up in Pine Bluff, but Cliff, my husband, grew up in Fordyce. I will be eternally grateful to Dr. Rhine for that—eternally grateful.

Claye's cousin, Lucille Brantley Coleman, it was time for her to deliver, so they called for Dr. Rhine. Several of us were in the room after the baby came. Dr. Rhine came in with the baby and asked, "Who in here has had children?"

I said, "I've had twins."

"Here, take this baby and clean it up for me."

"Oh, my God!" I had the oil and a cotton swab, and I was wiping the baby gently.

In the meantime, Dr. Rhine had gotten the mother comfortable, come back in, and I wasn't through wiping the baby, scared I would hurt the baby. He saw me. "Hand it here." He took the oil and put some in his hand, rubbed it all over that baby, wiped it off, wrapped it up and laid that baby by the mother. I said, "Oh, I'll never tell anyone else I had twins again."

He was a wonderful doctor, wonderful. I'll never forget him. You could feel how Dr. Rhine felt about people. Call it vibes!

IRA AND FLOSSIE FILES

KINGSLAND, ARKANSAS

Ira: When I was two years old, living at the same place I live now, north of Kingsland, I was seriously ill. Dr. Johnson was our doctor, but my dad requested that Dr. Rhine give a second opinion. They finally located Dr. Rhine way up in northwest Dallas County, and he rode his horse from there to our house. When he arrived, he advised my brothers to take care of his horse, and he didn't need too much water. He was about burnt out. He had rode him 36 miles in three hours. He was faggin', but he was getting there just the same. By his and Dr. Johnson's doctoring, I pulled through. That was in 1920.

Flossie: We thought Dr. Rhine was something special. He delivered me and both of my children. I grew up out at Hopeville. Mr. Joe Gardner was my daddy. S. T. was born at Fordyce in 1941, and Johnny in 1948 [was born] over in Cleveland County. We didn't go to the hospital. When we called Dr. Rhine (Ira had to go get him, we didn't have a phone) everything was iced over, and he just come a slidin' right on over there. He said, "I mean this has got to happen. I can't come again with the weather like this." There was no nurse. Ira assisted. Well, and Mama Files was there. I didn't have any fear because I knew that Dr. Rhine was there. He was great. I thought I had two of the prettiest babies. I got along fine. There was one thing that he told me when my oldest son was born. I had toxeme poison before he was born, and Dr. Rhine said, "You lay down and don't you get up." Well, I got up. I'm not going to say what I done. He told me, "You will have that the rest of your life." I have told several doctors about that, and they won't open their mouth. But Dr. Rhine was right. I have it just every once in a while.

Ira: When my mother was sick, he diagnosed her trouble and sent her to Little Rock to Dr. Eubanks for an operation. When we took mother to Dr. Eubank's office, he had already received a call from Dr. Rhine, and he said, "There's not much use in me examining her, because Dr. Rhine has never been wrong when he sent me a patient." But he did examine her, and operated, and she recovered fine. She had a tumor, and Dr. Rhine had diagnosed it.

In the early forties, I had an attack of appendicitis. We were living north of Kingsland where I live at this time. Dr. Rhine came to see me, being our doctor. He waited until Flossie got me ready, put me in his car and took me to Camden to the hospital. He stopped along the way to call ahead for Dr. Robbins to be ready when we got there. My appendix had already ruptured. They took me immediately into the operating room, and he and Dr. Robbins operated on me. He didn't wait for the ambulance. He just put me in his car and took me direct on to Camden himself. And he split wood out in the yard, until she got me ready. I had stove wood, and he got his ax and split wood. That was twenty miles east of Thornton to my house, and then another twenty-three miles west of Thornton to Camden.

I've got a hunting horn that he gave me. I did a lot of coon hunting but no fox hunting.

Flossie: When Dr. Rhine died, they didn't have his obituary on television, and that just got me, as important a person as he was!

I'll tell you another thing about him. When someone called him to come see them when they was sick, you could always tell when they were bad. He never said a word. He got out of his car and come right on in. But if they was just puny, he would come in laughing and cutting up. But if they was serious, he was serious.

We were there for Dr. Rhine Day. There was a large crowd there, and we just had a wonderful time with friends of ours and his that we met and got to talk to. It was to honor him and his years of practice.

Ira: It was always amusing to me to go into his office with all of those bottles of medicine. He would just go—he knew right where every one was. When he would diagnose your trouble, he'd reach right over and pull out the correct jar every time. He didn't have to look around to find it. He knew where it was.

Flossie: Pick up that gallon, pour it into a little bottle and never miss a drop. I can just see it.

One time Ira got bit by a spider, and he came over and saw Dr. Rhine. Dr. Rhine told him, "When this hits you, you're going to feel like you're going up in flames." But he killed that poison. He come three times.

Ira: It was a black widow spider. We didn't know it at the time, but we went back and killed it.

Flossie: He lost ten pounds in two hours time. He was just tearing hisself to pieces. When he got home, he got in the house before I did. He had pulled the sheets off the bed, slips off the pillows and was just pulling at hisself, he hurt so bad.

Ira: Dr. Rhine told us, that spider was as poisonous as a rattlesnake, but it didn't put as much poison in me.

Pat Brown: Where on your body did the spider bite you? (Laughter.) Oh, did you sit down on him?

Ira: Yeah, in the outdoor toilet! When we got back home, we went out there and looked, and the spider was still there.

Flossie: Our oldest son had appendicitis, too. It was in the night, and Dr. Rhine come. Do you know how he found out it was appendicitis? He took his fist and hit him on his heel. It would jar him, and he would holler from the pain. "You've got appendicitis." I'll tell you another thing. If people would have paid him, he would have been a rich man. But he wouldn't turn anyone down, money or no money.

I'll tell you something else he told me: if you would eat cooked onions every day, it would help your nerves.

PAT GRESHAM TRAMMEL

THORNTON, ARKANSAS

It was a hard backed bug with lots of legs on it that you would see around lights at night. My sister and her husband were leaving, and I walked out on the porch, and the porch light was on. This bug flew straight into my ear and went out of sight. It sounded like a freight train in my head. I started screaming, and they put sweet oil in my ear to stop the legs from wiggling. They brought me to Dr. Rhine, and he had to take tweezers and dig that bug out piece by piece, and I never had any trouble. They didn't wash it out or anything. It wasn't pain, it was a roar. I was about twenty years old—married.

When you would go into the office to see him for treatment and ask him how much, he would look at you and say, "You owe me fifty cents" or a dollar, just whatever he thought you could pay.

The day they took Mrs. Trammel to Little Rock, Dr. Rhine came up and gave her a shot for pain. He called up there and told them what he thought it was. They ran all kinds of tests and said it was something else. He said, "I think it was a gallstone, and she passed it." She got over that spell.

Dr. Rhine always gave citizenship awards to the school children. Mrs. Rhine continued those after he died, and they are still giving them in his name. He would always say, "Now, this doesn't mean the straight A student. This means a student that participates and a good student that will make a good citizen." There was one for each class in the elementary grades. Then one boy and one girl from the High School would receive the awards.

"My, that's the purtiest music I ever heard in my life."

ALLEN LIGHTFOOT

HOPEVILLE, ARKANSAS

Dr. Rhine was something else to me all of my life. Way back, I can remember, he used to have some of the purtiest horses he rode, and he had those dogs trained to where he would turn them out there at home, in Thornton, and those dogs would follow him to where he was goin' to hunt. When he would get to where he was goin' to hunt, he would holler to them, and they would go huntin' and they'd jump a fox, and he would stay with 'em, maybe thirty minutes. He'd come back and if he was in the buggy, he'd go on. If he was on the horse, he'd go. (He had some of the longest-legged horses I ever saw in my life. I was so small I could walk under the horse's stomach.) He'd go see his sick folks, and he'd come back wherever the dogs was runnin'. He'd stop and listen a few minutes longer, then he'd come on and go see some more sick folks. Maybe, sometimes, he'd get to go back for awhile, but most times, he'd just work on, and when the dogs got through runnin' they come home, and they'd be layin' around the gate when he'd get ready to feed 'em.

He raised so many puppies, it's unbelievable! I saw him with those females with as high as sixteen puppies. He'd fix 'em a round bed. (You know he always had a world of split wood). He'd put that wood around that dog bed there. He'd teach those puppies to come up and hang their head over that wood, and he'd give 'em, one at a time, that bottle all the way around. He'd have to help Mama feed 'em. If you went up there after any medicine while he was feeding them puppies, why you'd have to wait 'cause he wouldn't quit feedin' those puppies.

He'd raise those puppies and don't *ever* try to buy a dog from him, 'cause that hurt his feelings. Just go to braggin' on one—how purty that dog was there—how you'd love to have it. Before you left there, he'd have it in your car.

"Would you like to have that thing?"

"I sure would. That's the purtiest dog I ever seen."

"I'm just gonna let you have that."

But don't ever try to buy one, 'cause that really hurt his feelings.

He'd order dogs and give 'em to his huntin' friends like Mr. Hearnsberger, George Pennington, and Daddy. OOOOOh, they hunted, and I've heard him set and talk about those old people. One morning, they was runnin' a red fox, and he come right up in Thornton there. Daddy had a store up there at that time, and that fox run under that store. They said all the people come out to see that red fox runnin' through people's yards and under houses.

As time went on, he got tired, and he carried his dogs in the back seat and under the turtle hull of his car. I remember, he had a '41 Ford that he really hauled lots of dogs in. I saw him with so many dogs in that car, it would just almost rare up. They was all in the back seat and under the turtle hull. But he enjoyed that. While those dogs was runnin' out there, he never was still. He'd be out there pickin' up pine knots and pilin' 'em up. When he wasn't huntin', he'd go back out by there and pick up his pile of pine knots and put 'em under the turtle hull. I've actually saw him fill up the back of the car.

The Dr. Rhine Fox and Wolf Hunting Association was called that 'cause everybody thought so much of Dr. Rhine. We got to talkin' about it, and one of the boys was instigator of organizin' it. Irving Colvert was the main boy. He went to see Mrs. Rhine and asked her if it would be all right if we named the Club after Dr. Rhine. Of course, she said "Yes." That's when it started, Dr. Rhine's Park, and that's been about eighteen years ago. The crowd has grown. We have had as high as five or six hundred people at one time. For these big suppers we fix for the hunts, we cook around five hundred to six hundred pounds of pork hams, potato salad, baked beans, slaw. We have all kinds of cake and pie, and we fix Kool-Aid and tea. We have the hunts in March for two days and in the fall on Labor Day weekend.

After supper, there is a Bench Show, and we will start with puppies from zero to six months old, show the dog and the female puppies. Then we step up from six months old to a year old, and we show the dog. By showin', I mean there is a bench about two feet high, and we put the dog up on the bench and the one that is perfect, wins. That is, about eight inches between the front legs, straight legs, tail straight and arched. They stand nice and straight, ears standing up straight. Each one of 'em counts ten points, and the one that gets the most points gets first place. We show the four classes of puppies, then we show the first place puppy in each class and pick out the best puppy in the show. Then the best female.

After they pass a year old, they are called 'derby' until two years old. We show the derby dog, then the female. Then we step up to the 'all-age' dog. That's a dog from two years old on as long as they live. We show those four dogs and pick out the best one in that class and the best of the opposite sex. That is a dog show.

We have what we call a 'natural carriage.' A dog carries hisself real nice and straight with a walk just like a gentleman would down the road, just straight and all. He wins a first place trophy. We have the best pair—a dog and a female—we show them together. We have what we call the best pack, three dogs or more, shown together. Each first class gets a trophy.

Most of my trophies have been won in the field, runnin'. [Allen has won several hundred trophies.] I hardly ever had any show dogs. Last year I run in seven or eight field trials, like we have here, in the state. At a field trial, in the morning we get up at four o'clock, eat breakfast and drive to where we are goin' to turn our dogs aloose. Sometimes, it's fifteen miles from the Park. Everybody gets his dog out, and it has a number on it from one to sometimes 700. You run those dogs through there, and the judges have a score sheet with each dog's number on it. When they call that number out, he marks it, that the dog has answered the roll. You stand until everybody gets through the line. The judge will say, "It's so and so time. We will call the hunt off in five hours." They blow a whistle, and we turn those dogs aloose. They let 'em run five hours with eight or ten men out there judgin' 'em. Each one of those numbers when they cross the road will score. If there are two all-age dogs runnin' together, they will get thirty-five points apiece, but if it is an all-age dog and a derby dog runnin' together, they only give 'em twenty-five points. (They claim they don't have any competition, but I don't understand that.) You have to have two dogs of a kind to get the full thirty-five points. They run for five hours and then they call the hunt off, and everybody goes to huntin' for dogs. The head scoreman is called 'Master of the Hounds.' The judges all come into camp and sit down and figure those scores out.

When they start out, the dogs are runnin'. They are judged on speed and drive, which is really runnin'. When they are huntin', they give 'em so much for huntin', and they are judged on trailin'. If you have a dog that has huntin' and trailin' and runnin', all three, he gets more points than the dog does for just runnin' or just huntin' or trailin'. A lot of times, they just get one item scored on. Sometimes, they will lose a fox after they jump it. They might run it for two hours, then lose it. They might get some score for huntin'. If the dogs are turned aloose before daylight, the judges can't see those dogs for about an hour. They won't likely get any huntin' scores. It will be mostly speed and drive.

At this show, here at Dr. Rhine Park, we'll have fifty hunters with dogs and have seventy-five hunters who don't bring any dogs. They either have to work, or they are scared they'll lose their dogs. It is a good size hunt.

The state hunt lasts a week. In 1982, it was at Mayflower. At the state hunt, they run for four days. They have hunts all over Arkansas, Texas, Louisiana. You look at a huntin' magazine, there are hunts scheduled all over the South.

In 1982, I went to the United States Open for the first time. It was in Louisiana. It had never been this side of the Mississippi before. This is a real show-down hunt. You carry your choice dog. Everybody has from one to four dogs from their pack. They turned aloose four hundred and eighty-six dogs that morning. There were people from more states than you would believe. Almost every state in the Union. Some were from Canada. We had two men one time from Canada to come to our county hunt. Believe me, they taken the trophies back with 'em. too.

It's something that gets in your blood. I've been huntin' now since I was seven years old. I'm seventy now. My Daddy give me a pair of puppies. After I got good sized, twelve or fourteen, Dr. Rhine began givin' me some of the purty puppies he raised. At times, I've had as high as sixty-seven hounds. I had three pens full out in the back. Now, I have nine runnin' dogs and six puppies.

Dr. Rhine's special dog was a July. He just thought a July hound was the only kind there were. But he had some good Walkers.

The first fox race I ever heard in my life, Dr. Rhine, Zell Hearnsberger, George Hearnsberger come down over here to what we call Little Bay. (It used to be a sawmill town, had a depot and a hotel.) They come down the power line and turned those dogs aloose this away, and I heard those dogs runnin' and I thought, "My, that's the purtiest music I ever heard in my life." I went to the back door, and it was cold. I stood there about half naked in that back door, listenin'. I asked Daddy, "What is that?"

He said, "That's fox dogs. That's Dr. Rhine and Zell and George and them over there huntin'."

Dr. Rhine had an outstanding dog he called 'Penny.' One he called 'Speed.' I never heard a dog bark like him in my life. He was the only dog who could bark both ways when he breathed—in and out. He could run all night barkin' like that and always carryin' the front end. [Leading the pack.] Penny, she had a nice, little fine, high mouth. You could hear her so far. She would be the last dog you could hear when they would go out of here and the first one to hear comin' back here. You wouldn't believe a dog's voice could carry like that, but some of 'em has a real carryin' mouth. At times, when the air is right, you can hear those dogs seven or eight miles. Everything has to be in harmony.

One night Daddy heard my brother John's dog. He had gone down to my cousin's to hunt at Eagle Mills about twelve miles away. It was up number nine [the highway to Princeton], and the dog jumped a fox. Daddy heard those dogs, and he thought they were up here about a mile, and he started walking. He walked up the road about a mile and they still sounded like they was about a mile away, and he walked on over to Moss Cemetery, which is three miles or more, and he could still hear 'em near. "My gracious! I've walked this far. I better not go any further." So he turned around and come home.

The next day when my brother got home, he asked him, "Where was you runnin' last night?"

"We were runnin' in an old field up number nine from Eagle Mills."

"I thought those dogs were right up here at Bethel."

"Daddy, you didn't hear those dogs that far."

"Yes I did. I heard old so and so just carryin' on and old so and so—"

"Well, I guess you did hear 'em then."

It's been a long, long life. It's been an enjoyable life—that fox huntin'. I've spent many, many dollars on my dogs, and there's no tellin' how much Dr. Rhine spent on dogs, 'cause he had money, and he'd order dogs in a minute. He'd sit down and order one out of *The Hunter's Horn* magazine, and back then dogs wasn't very high.

Back when I was young, things was so cheap. There wasn't any money much. He'd give twenty-five dollars for a dog, and we thought that was a terrible price. But now, a good dog cost you five hundred dollars. They want dogs that won't run a deer, and some people can train 'em not to run those deers. If they find one like that, they will buy it, I don't care what price they put on it-if it's a thousand dollars, they'll still buy it. Today, an ordinary twenty-five dollar dog sells for two hundred and fifty dollars.

In 1982, after our hunt at Dr. Rhine Park, I had two purty 'blanket-back' dogs. They looked like pictures.

An ole boy said, "Would you sell those dogs?"

"Well, I guess so." I never thought about anybody wantin' to buy 'em.

"What would you take for this one here?"

"If I wuz to tell you what I really wanted for 'em, you'd think I wuz a smart aleck." So I said, "Two hundred and fifty dollars."

"I'm just gonna take this one."

Another boy over there said, "Would you take that for this other one?"

"Well, I sure would."

"I'm goin' to take that one then."

They lifted me of my purty 'blanket-back' dogs right there.

Several years ago, I had one that was outstandin'. It was sick when I traded for it, but that dog come out of it, and it was so fast that I didn't have anything else could run with it. So I let my brother John out in Texas have it where they run a lot in the open country. And they didn't have anything to run with it, either.

I was out at the Texas State Hunt, and a boy got after me for that dog. I said, "I don't want to sell that dog."

"Well, I want to buy it."

"I don't want to sell it."

My brother said, "Why don't you sell that dog?"

"You want me to sell him 'cause you ain't got nothin' to run with him."

"Aaaaw, he ain't that fast."

"You know the other morning when they wuz goin' down that fence line runnin' the coyote, there wasn't a dog between him and the coyote. It wuz two hundred yards back to the first dog. Why?"

"That was just an accident."

"He done it ever time I've ever seen him."

I finally made that boy a price and that was back when dogs were still cheap—fifty dollars was a purty good dog. I thought I'd bluff him out. I said, "Two hundred and fifty dollars." Lord, he grabbed his purse, like to have tore his pants off gettin' it out, paid me for that dog.

They said, "That fellow would pay you five hundred dollars for that dog quick as he would have paid you two hundred and fifty." So he got my good dog.

I had another outstandin' one that they wanted out there, and I wouldn't let 'em have it, and they stole it.

I was fixin' to cast my dog [turn them loose.] I had done went through the line waitin' for 'em to blow the whistle. A fellow walked up to me and said, "Are you Allen Lightfoot?"

"Yes, I am."

"I found one of your dogs and three more way somewhere a while ago, and I put it in the 'catch' pen." We always have some place to put the dogs around where we cast, so people can go back and get 'em.

"As soon as I turn these dogs aloose, I'll go back and get her."

It was about a mile over there to where we had cast the morning before. They had 'em in one of those big cattle trailers. I went back over there as soon as I turned my dogs out, and she was gone, but the other three was still in there. I never have seen my dog since.

They were supposed to call the hunt off at eleven o'clock. One of the judges said, "You want to get your dog so she will be able to run tomorrow?"

"I'd like to."

"I'll carry you and show you right where they are runnin'."

We went over there at four o'clock in the afternoon and she was still runnin', and she was about as far as from here to the road out there ahead of every dog. They was goin' across a clearin', there wasn't a thing in the world there, and she was just castin' on that fox trail. Backwards and forwards across that field, flyin'. She done that two days in a row, and the third day, it was rainin' so hard it looked like it was foggy that morning when we cast down. She was purty well knocked out. She went off to hunt, but in about an hour, she come back. It was raining so hard, and she was so knocked out! I didn't win the hunt, but I had it won even if she had gone and crawled in a holler log. I'd have still won the hunt. She had more score than any dog there.

When they return to where you cast 'em, they scratch 'em. They don't get any score then. If they catch 'em barkin' out of place (they call that babblin'), they scratch 'em for that. A lot of young dogs will get kinda lost, and they'll stop and go to howlin', and they'll scratch 'em for that. There's lot of things in the runnin' they scratch 'em for. They have to be perfect. Down at the Texas Open the spring of 1983, they didn't have a dog to finish a hunt. They scratched every dog they had. They had eleven the last morning, and it wasn't an hour 'til every one of those was scratched. That makes you feel bad when you get your dog scratched.

You know there are all kinds of people in the world, but there are people that will pay those judges to score their dog to get a first place dog. In *The Hunter's Horn* there are a lot of dogs in there ran for stud. They get high scorin' dogs and put 'em in there and get a big price for breedin'.

To train a dog, you take 'em about eight months old and start carryin' 'em on hunts, and some are easy started and some are hard. Three years ago, I raised eight puppies, and I taken 'em down in the Navy area, where there wasn't any traffic. Wasn't anybody in the way, and I turned those puppies out, and I just walked and played and fooled with 'em for about two hours. I went back to the truck and laid down and went to sleep and just left 'em out. When I woke up, there wasn't a puppy there. They had all gone huntin'. They are born with the instinct. They already know what to do. It is just in 'em.

The next day after I got 'em back and brought 'em home, I put 'em in the truck with all my old dogs. There is a boy down at Eagle Mills, he's a big cattle buyer. He ships lots of cows, and he has lots of cows to die. He drags those dead cows out of the lot and up that power line 'bout a quarter [mile] and in the winter time, you just go there, turn them dogs aloose, and the race is on. These coyotes are right there eatin' before sundown. I went there and turned those puppies out with my grown dogs, just opened the end gate and let 'em all go together. I never did have a bit of trouble with them puppies. I started runnin' 'em in field trials the next week, and I never did have one of 'em scratched, for comin' back to the cast or babbling or howlin'. I run those puppies all that year, and in the fall, I run 'em durin' deer season for seven days, and had bad luck with one of 'em. She got her head hung in a plastic jug and smothered to death. That was the nicest bunch of puppies that I have ever trained in my life—the easiest startin'. They were trained from the time to go. Just turn 'em aloose, that's all you had to do.

But a lot of 'em you fool with. I bought a registered puppy up at the Arkansas State in the fall of '82, and it was hard to train. I turned that dog loose ten or fifteen times, before it ever did go, and it never has got trained yet. It would still come back while the dogs were runnin' even when it was over a year old. It ought to have done top job.

My mother was small and knotty lookin', but she was strong. She always loved to milk a lot of cows, and Daddy would try to keep her from milkin' those cows, takin' all the milk away from the calves. Daddy called 'em 'knock 'em in the head with a churn dasher.' She would pull those great big old calves off—weighed four hundred pounds—and tie 'em. After they'd nurse that milk 'til they'd get it comin' down good, she'd tie 'em off, and she'd get that milk that she wanted, before she'd let 'em go back.

She was sick a lot, but at the last, we was at Thornton in a cafe up there, and I had Mother out here, and I had a lady hired to stay with her. This lady called me and said, "Allen, your mother wants you to come out. She's sick." I come out every day anyway, 'cause I had some cows out here, and I'd come out to feed 'em and see about Mother and the lady. So I come on out.

Mother said, "I'm not goin' to live to be seventy years old. If I could live to twelve o'clock tonight, I'd be seventy years old."

"Mother, you are not sick."

"That's all right, but I'm goin' home tonight. I'm not goin' to live to be seventy years old."

Dr. Rhine had already been out to see her twice, but she wanted to see Dr. Rhine one more time. I said, "Dr. Rhine is worked to death, Mama, and you are not sick."

"You don't know. I want to see Dr. Rhine one more time." Dr. Rhine had already told me he didn't know what was the matter with her. She didn't act all that sick.

Anyhow, I called him, and Dr. Rhine come back, worked to death. He come in a whistlin', with his satchel in one hand and his hat in another. He sat down by the bed and felt of her pulse, punched around on her a little bit and talked to her. He said, "You don't seem like you are much sick."

"I may not be much sick, but I'm not goin' to live to be seventy years old."

He didn't think she was sick, and I didn't either, but she wouldn't let go of me. She just held on to my pants. Dr. Rhine visited awhile. He called me to the door and said, "I don't find much wrong with her. Her pulse is all right. Her heart is beating all right. I don't know what's ailin' her."

"I imagine she has just got a notion in her head." When she got her head set, you didn't change it.

That night, she kept talkin' about goin' and all. I called some of her friends, and they come down. At eleven o'clock, I was sittin' right there, right by the bed, she still had holt of my pants. She looked at me with one eye, and one eye looked straight up. She just stuck her hands up and said, "Come, Lord Jesus," and quit breathin'. I guess she was wore out and just ready to go home.

But she was mistaken. We got to figurin' up from the time she was born 'til then, and she was already seventy years old. She left us in 1950.

I got into trouble once with Dr. Rhine in all them years. He sent me and Pat to Conway [to Hendrix College] after Virginia and Susan. He sent us in that '41 Ford, and that was the runnin'est car I ever saw in my life. We left Thornton, and in an hour and thirty minutes we was in Conway. We oughtened to have told Dr. Rhine that. Boy, he ate us up when we got back, and the roads then went 'all the way by Laura's house'. Comin' back, we had the back seat piled all the way to the top with trunks, suitcases, clothes. The turtle hull wouldn't even fasten down but we got 'em home.

I drove the school bus from 1936 or '37 to '44, and I was up there with Dr. Rhine every day. When I would get off the school bus, I'd go to his office. If he had any long trips to make, like twenty miles up that away, he'd let me drive. When his oldest grandson, Tommy Brown, was a year old, they let me drive 'em to Pine Bluff for his first birthday. I'll never forget it if I live to be a thousand years old.

He was somebody that everybody loved. For Dr. Rhine Day, there were so many people in Thornton, they was parkin' plumb over on the highway and walkin' across town to the school house where the program was. There wasn't a place to park nowhere. The school ground was just solid people.*

I helped butcher the meat that we barbequed for that night. We had a hundred and fifty head of goats, forty some-odd head of hogs, sixteen head of beef (part of 'em we went to Arkadelphia and bought at the sale—big white faced steers that dressed out about seven hundred pounds).

We got all that meat on the pits. We had holes dug as long as from here to that house over yonder. We had wire on it and had that meat on it. We had people burnin' wood and puttin' coals under it. That night it come a storm and water run in those pits and put the fire out, and we lost every bit of that beef. Didn't save a bit of it. It just stormed and rained so that everybody left, but I stayed. The next morning by the time we could get a fire built back under it, it had spoiled. We hauled it off by the truckloads.

Now, all the goat was done. We had boys that boiled that goat in wash pots, so it was done when we put it on the pit, and it had been smokin' for six or eight hours when that rain come up, and it didn't ruin. That made me so sick. I'll tell you the truth. All those hogs and goats were donated, and a lot of the people who gave 'em come to help dress it. There were just crowds of people, gettin' into one another's way, tryin' to dress that meat. There were several cows donated. People donated a lot of money and bought those big white-faced steers that weighed seven hundred pounds. There's no tellin' how much money was turned in to that.**

I also did the barbeque for the celebration at the house, his 50th year of practice, when they announced that he would be nominated for Doctor of the Year in Arkansas. There were several hundred people there for that. For his 55th year, another big barbeque at the house.

I'll tell you what, you could get sick and call Dr. Rhine, and whenever you'd hear his voice at the front door, you was better. He didn't have to come give you no pills, he'd just come to the door and start talkin', and you was better right then. He was a wonderful doctor, a wonderful man. You could recognize the sound of his car. He'd get out of his car fussin'—didn't mean a thing in the world about it, it was just his way of doin'. "Aw, what are you gripin' about" and all that kind of stuff. He didn't make anybody mad 'cause they knew that was his way.

Our families were always close, 'cause Mother and Daddy thought so much of Dr. and Mrs. Rhine. When Pat was a baby, Dr. Rhine come to see a

*The registration book has over 3,300 entries listed. Many are signed Mr. and Mrs. So and So and children.

** Mr. Roy Wise, postmaster at Thornton, was the main instigator and Chairman of Dr. Rhine Day on May 17, 1946. Mr. T. G. Newton was secretary-treasurer. The record shows that $1,722.31 was donated. $157.34 was not spent, and in 1953, it was given to the Calhoun County Clinic to be used. There were 224 one dollar donations. 51 donations were less that one dollar. There were two donations of $50.00 each-from Bill Parker and O. E. McGugan. Four persons gave $25.00 each—Gurt James, Carlton Smith, W. E. Summers and Woodrow Manning.

lady that was waitin' on Grandma, and they come over here through the woods. Lee Payne lived back over there between here and the highway. Dr. Rhine got stuck, and I don't remember if it was Susan or Virginia pulled the keys out and throwed 'em out the window, and they couldn't find 'em. When they come in, Mrs. Rhine was totin' Pat, and Dr. Rhine had both the other girls in his arms and he was just a-sweatin', tho' it was purty cold weather. He was really exhausted and kinda miffed, too, 'cause he had to walk.

We drove cars in places then that horses don't hardly go now—old T-model Fords. The first car I saw was a '17 model comin' up that road. I run in the house and told Daddy, "There's a buggy comin' up the road that doesn't even have a horse hooked to it."

All those Anthonys bought Chevrolet cars. Mr. Oliver, Mr. Garland, Mr. Frank and Mr. Will Anthony was all raised right up the road, just two miles. They had a sawmill, a cotton gin and a general store. You could buy anything in there that was made. Those boys lived up there 'til long after they got married, and they turned into money. They just all had money. When Mr. Garland died, he had close to 100,000 acres of land all over Arkansas, Louisiana, Oklahoma and Texas.

I never will forget, Daddy would go to the cotton gin to bale cotton, and he would let me out at the general store and give me a nickel, and I would buy me a sack of candy that would be so huge that I would still be eatin' on it when he come back. They had a bench on the front porch, and I'd go out and sit on it to wait.

After I married Lillian and Jimmy was born, I worked at the big mill across the road. It was classy. It had a 'steam-nigger' on it, and it would cut lots of logs. It was the last sawmill the Anthonys had in Hopeville. I worked twelve hours for seventy-five cents. That was along in 1934, '35. Six days a week, twelve hours a day. There was always four or five men there on Monday morning wantin' a job, and if you didn't show up or wadn't a good worker, Brother, they'd just turn you off and get somebody else. It was work then. Now it's all done by machinery.

JOHN LIGHTFOOT

NACOGDOCHES, TEXAS

Our mother, Ludie Lightfoot, lived for several years after our father died, Robert Lightfoot. Dr. Rhine had cared for her for over a year before she died. The boys, Bill, Cobie, Allen and myself got together $200.00 to pay him for looking after Mother. Dr. Rhine refused to take the money, saying, "I promised your father that I would take care of Mrs. Lightfoot. That is our business and none of yours." He broke down as he told this to us.

I was the baby girl of Rufus and Mandy Jones of Little Bay. It was seven girls and three boys of us.

I remember one night that Daddy, Dr. Rhines and Mr. Lee Payne went to fox huntin'. Papa had an ole dog named Blue. He loved the ole dog better than he did us, 'cause when we come home ever evenin' from work, he be sure my mother would feed that dog. If we didn't have no bread, Mama had to turn around and cook the dog some bread.

Well, awright. Dr. Rhines and Mr. Payne, I think there was three or four of them, went to fox huntin' one night. It looked like it was gonna rain, and Mama said, "Y'all better not go down in them big woods huntin' them foxes tonight."

Papa, "Aw, now, we goin'. Dr. Rhines and them say it's a good night to fox hunt."

We had an ole horse named Fred. He was just like a human bein'. We would ride him and go out in the woods, and when he'd get tired of us pickin' blackberries and things, he'd go to snortin' and buckin' and we'd have to get on him and come outta the woods 'cause ole Fred he'd walk off and leave us. He'd go apiece and stop til we'd come outta the woods—them blackberries and huckleberries, whatever we was a-pickin'.

That night, Papa carried ole Blue. He was really crazy about ole Blue. Mama said, "Y'all not goin' to catch nothin'."

"Oh yes, we is. Dr. Rhines and all us got good dogs. We gonna put 'em in together." They wuz goin' way down there about Woodberry—in them big woods.

It come up a big rain. Dr. Rhines and Papa and all the rest of 'em wandered around down in there. Ten o'clock the next day befo' they got out. They couldn't find their way out. They was so far down in the woods, and they didn't have no compass. They made a fire down in the woods that night, after the storm was over, and dried theyself off some. But it was ten o'clock the next morning befo' they got home.

Mrs. Rhines and Mama, "Where in the world did they go? How come they stayin' so late?" Mama knowed Papa go to work in the morning to the mill up in Thornton—at the sawmill.

Mama said, "There's som'in' done happened."

When they come walkin' up, Papa had ole Blue laid up across the hoss's back. Ole Blue had run his legs off. They had killed three or four foxes. Dr. Rhines had two in his sack.

Papa said, "I didn't go for no fox. I went with 'em 'cause I had a good huntin' dog."

They sho' was lookin' bad when they come back. They were wet; they were scratched up.

Papa said, "Trees were just fallin' down in our faces. I know my hoss gonna lead us outta here."

Papa said he got on ole Fred, and said, "Fred, carry us home."

Dr. Rhines said, "I'll foller. I'll foller you, Rufus," and they come out. Ole Fred brought 'em out—about ten o'clock the next day.

My mother and Mrs. Rhines said, "The next time that Doctor and the rest of 'em go in the woods a-huntin', they better carry somebody that knows where they was a-goin'."

Mama said, "They didn't have no business goin' that fur. What in the world did y'all—."

"Well, that's where the foxes wuz."

Dr. Rhines had some people at the office waitin' for him, and there he wuz, scarred up, wet, bent up.

Mrs. Rhines said, "Lord, Mandy, what is we gonna do wit our husbands? When they get ready to go to a-huntin', that's just it! We just at home by ourselves!"

What he tell you, you better do it! He'd come to yo' house and tell you, say, "So and so, y'all take good care of him, 'cause I don't think he gonna last very long." And he wouldn't last very long.

He'd come there and say, "Aaaah, ain't nothin' but old age. You just need a rest. Take this medicine, and you'll be awright." That's what he'd tell 'em.

That's what he said 'bout my daddy. My daddy worked for him down there at his garden; he helped him raise a garden. Dr. Rhines would go down in the country, all 'round, gather up chickens, eggs. Mrs. Rhines would say, "Why in the world do you bring all this food here? Give some of it away."

Dr. Rhines would say, "Rufus, don't you want some of these here eggs I got?"

"My hens is layin', but give me some of 'em."

Papa come walkin' in wit a sack full of stuff. Dr. Rhines would give him shoulders of meat, ham meat, just anything. Mrs. Rhines wanted to get it out of her house. She didn't want all that stuff in her house. We would laugh about that. I went at home once, after I was married. I said, "Mama, where y'all get all this ham meat from?"

"Dr. Rhines give it to your daddy."

"I'm gonna carry some of it home wit me." So I brought some home wit me, cooked it and eat it.

When Dr. Rhines was livin', he would come, and if he thought he could do you any good, he'd tell you. And he'd tell you what to do. If you didn't do it, now he'd get kinda aggravated at ya. He'd tell you, "If you don't do what I said do, don't come after me, 'cause I've got other patients that will do what I say do."

I 'member one time down there, a man had to have his leg amputated. He went out in the dew and got mildew in it. Dr. Rhines told him, "You fool around now, Pledg, you gonna have to get that leg cut off. You better stay outta the field."

"Naw," Uncle Pledg say, "I won't. I wrap it up. Put some coal oil on it."

I think he got it cut with a saw. Sho' nuf he had to take that leg off. Uncle Pledg Jacobs died with one leg.

We always would do what he said do. The morning Mama had the last stroke, my sister, Lola, was workin' for Mrs. Rhines then, he said, "I'm goin' to tell y'all. You can just keep her comfortable. Give her some water, if she'll drink it. It's nothin' else I can do. Her time is out." That's the way he wuz about my daddy, too. He say, "Rufus is old. He got nothin' to build from. His time is out. Just make him comfortable—cool and comfortable."

Lola worked for Mrs. Rhines ten or fifteen years. Mrs. Rhines would ask her, "Lola, is this your mission meetin'?"

"Yessum, I'm got to go to mission meetin'."

"When you get through your mission meetin', you come by here and do such and so." Lola would do it, too. Lola was gonna stick with Mrs. Rhines.

I come here to Pine Bluff when Miz Ruth [Jones Roberts] come here in 1938, from Fordyce. I started workin' for her in Tinsman, when they had the mill down at Tinsman. I was goin' to school and workin' part time, on Saturday mostly. After they moved to Fordyce, I quit goin' to school and went to workin' regular, 'cause she wuz at the store, the Anthony-Jones Lumber Company store. They built me a house over the garage. After Mr. Fred [Jones] sold the mill there, he started one at Pine Bluff. They moved here and built me a house here, in 1938. I'm still workin' for her yet. I tell you what. We always have gotten along.

I laughed and tole Miz Ruth the other day, "My Mama sold me to you."

"She didn't do no such thing."

I had to work durin' the Depression to help my folks. They wuz gettin' old and sickly. I been workin' *all* my life. I'm seventy years old now.

When we wuz in the Depression, we had plenty of meat, plenty of lard, plenty of food. We had fruit, too. When we didn't have enough jars to can it in, we cut the fruit off and dried it and put it in sacks, and we'd go out and get chinaberry leaves and put in them sacks to keep the worms from gettin' in them peaches and apples. The meat, we mostly let it cure. Salt it down for a time, then wash it off and smoke it with hickory or oak in the smokehouse. Then we'd paint it with molasses and brown sugar and wrap it in cheesecloth or an old pillowcase and hang it up and smoke it, if you wanted to keep it for awhile. That would keep the flies off. If the flies go to the bone that would ruin it. Oh brother, you could smell that ham way *down* the road. I'm tellin' you could.

In later years, the Home Demonstration Agent come down through there, and she showed us how to can beef. That was a good idea. We'd meet at the school house at Little Bay, that's where we lived. They had put a kitchen on the school. A lot of people couldn't eat a lot of fat meat like pork. They would kill yearlings in the fall, and we'd cut it up and can it. It would keep all winter.

I know the time my daddy used to kill so many rabbits until we just—I don't like rabbits to this day. We'd kill rabbits and Mama would kill two or three chickens, and we'd grind it up together and make rabbit sausage. That's what we'd have for Sunday morning breakfast. Good ole rice, hot biscuits, jelly. We had plenty of jelly and syrup. We'd put pepper, salt and sage in it, and honey, that was good eatin'! Make some gravy—um, um.

We'd work in the field. We'd go out in the mornings. We'd get up at five o'clock, and we'd get them hoe handles, and Papa would sharpen the hoes. He'd say, "Listen, when I make a round, I want y'all to make a round." We'd grab them hoes and he be dirtin' up that cotton behind us. We'd be gettin' out the grass. They'd be four or five of us. Mama would help for awhile. She would always go back and cook dinner for us about eleven o'clock, after the mailman run, and he run about eleven o'clock. When evenin' come, we'd be done cut that ten or fifteen acres of cotton out, and be dirted up the middle.

A lot of times, if it rained a lot and it would be hot, you couldn't see the cotton for the grass. We'd have to get that grass out. If we chopped for someone else, we'd get paid a dollar a day and dinner. Sometimes you would look up at the sun, and it looked like that sun done hung there— about two o'clock. That sun wasn't goin' to go down. We stayed in the field, too, 'til that sun went down, tryin' to get through. We'd laugh and talk, and a lot of times, it was cooler out in the field than around the house. Only thing, the sun just hurt your feelin's—wadn't hurtin' your back.

All day Sunday, we'd be at church—one church or the other. You'd be at the Baptist Church or the Methodist Church, come back to the Sanctified Church on Sunday Night. The Sanctified folks have their church most on Sunday night. They'd be shoutin' and jumpin' and talkin' in tongues. We enjoyed that, we didn't want to leave. Papa said, "You better come on from there 'fore twelve o'clock. You got to go to the field tomorrow." We'd leave about ten o'clock with our little boyfriends, swingin' along. They'd say, "Get in front of me." You and your boyfriend went in front of your mama and daddy.

On Sunday, after three o'clock service, they'd say, "We'd better go on. Y'all girls get in the road now. Let's go home now."

If you wanted to do any kissin', you had to get behind a pine tree, and it wasn't no love-makin'. You just kissed and go on, quick. If a girl come home with a baby, she done 'broke her leg.' Lord have mercy! That was just too bad, too bad.

We'd carry our silk stockin's and our new shoes. We'd wear old ones. We'd take our bath on Saturday night, wash our feet on Sunday and grease our legs good with Vaseline. Our hair would be fixed, and we'd wear our nice little starched, ironed white or blue colored dresses we'd have. We'd get in the road and walk. Near about to Bethel Church, there was a great big log up there. We'd always stop on that log, spread some papers down and sit on the log and put on our good shoes and stockin's. Stick our old shoes up under the log in a paper sack.

When we come back, we pick 'em up. If we was with our boyfriends, we would keep our shoes on. If we wadn't with no boyfriends, we'd put our old tennis shoes back on and walk on home. Save our good shoes and stockin's, cause we didn't get 'em often. If it come a run in your stockin, you'd sit down and take a needle and sew it up, and you couldn't hardly tell it was a run in 'em. They wadn't high, but you couldn't get none—silk stockin's. That's just the way we had to do.

Everybody, it look like, got along in the country well. If anybody was sick or anything, everybody knew about it, because they'd all be at the church. "So and so died. We goin' to set up with him tonight."

I never will forget this as long as I live. Cousin Bruce Stell lived over in the country. He lived out from us, and he had a house full of children—girls and boys. They all wanted to be school teachers and things. Cousin Bruce would sell everything that wasn't nailed down and would carry it to Thornton up to the mill. He would sell everything he had in the field. His wife was a good friend of Mama's, they kinda grew up together. When she needed anything, she'd come over.

"Sister Mandy?"

"What say?"

"Could you lend me a little few peas?" or "Give me buttermilk?"

When she got through gatherin' up the stuff she needed, she'd have a whole supper for 'em.

"What do you let your husband sell all your cabbage and things out the garden for? Sell all the food for your children? Y'all got to eat."

"You know how it is."

The women at that time, they obeyed their husbands; they didn't argue with 'em. Whatever they said went. My mother and daddy wasn't thataway.

Cousin Bruce Stell died one *cold* winter day. I never see'd the likes of freeze in my life. Mama and us went to church that Sunday, and it commence to rainin' and sleetin'. When we got back from church, Mama said, "Bob Jacobs" (he didn't live too far from us) "come to church and said he passed about one o'clock."

Papa say, "I'll go over there to help 'em lay him out."

The next day, the ice was so bad, mules couldn't stand up on it. The ground was slick as glass and trees was poppin' in the woods. About Tuesday or Wednesday, it had let up some, but the ground was still slick. Papa said, "You young people ought to go over there and sit with the family." They couldn't get to the cemetery. No way to get to the cemetery. Be 'bout a week before they could bury him.

Awright, we got together about seven of us and went over there to Cousin Bruce Stells. They didn't have no wood. They had a heater and a fireplace. They had him laid out there where they had the fireplace. That's where we oughta been. I never got so cold in my life! We got up that night about twelve o'clock, moon shinin' purty and bright. Went out there and went to tearin' out the bottom of the barn to get wood. Them lazy boys wouldn't even snake up no wood.

Papa said, "I would take a load of wood over there, but my mule can't stand up."

Cousin Bob, he had done snaked up some wood, limbs and trees along. They sawed that up. Those boys wouldn't try to do nothin'. The girls, none of 'em had married, five of 'em, 'cause their daddy thought they was too good to marry. They didn't want to marry nothin' but a preacher or som'in like that—some big shot. Big shot folks didn't want them.

My feet felt like I was walkin' on sticks when we left there the next morning.

"I don't care who die, Papa, if you die, I ain't goin' to let my feet get cold again." My feet stayed frost-bit the whole spring. Tryin' to be nice to 'em and they didn't even have enough to make a place for us to be. They oughta a had the body in the hall, and we could have sat in the front room. They didn't have half enough to eat. Mama and them got together, and Papa would take 'em some food.

Cousin Bruce died of malisnutrition. He didn't half eat. Dr. Rhines said he did—died of malisnutrition. He wouldn't eat enough. Them girls was slim as sticks.

A A R O N   B R A N D O N

THORNTON, ARKANSAS

First time I got with Doc about the dog business was up at the deer camp in 1942. Dr. Rhine never carried a gun, he just listened to the dogs run. He liked to hear them run. Every year then from 1942 until he passed away, we had many a dog story.

If I ever found a dog that was sick, I took it to him. Especially one year, 1957, we had a lot of sickness in dogs. Me and Fred Tomlinson had five dogs together. They got sick. Dr. Rhine come up to see them, and he said, "Now you bring those dogs by every other day about four o'clock, and I'll give them a shot."

One day, I dropped by there, and, my goodness, there were fifteen or twenty people in the office. I stuck my head in the door. He said, "Come on in."

"Dr. Rhine, I'll come back later."

"You won't come back later either. You come on in here."

He gave them three shots, but I thought they were getting weaker. He said to just bring them on back anyway, but they died in a few weeks. I believe they call the sickness hepatitis.

I was working in the post office, right by his office. Every morning he would come in, talking about dogs. Once or twice a month, he would get hunting horns in for different people. He said, "Now Aaron, when you get time, you come over to the office."

Asbury Thornton come back in, so I said, "Doc wants me to blow some horns, so let me go before he leaves."

I went in there, and I would blow the horns several times for him. That morning, he had two horns, one about fourteen inches long, the other about twelve inches long. They come off the same cow—matching horns. I blowed the little one. Man, you could hear it clear out yonder. I blowed it about four times. Then I blowed the other one.

He said, "Blow the other one again." I did. "Which one do you think is the best?"

"Doc, I believe the keenest horn is the little horn."

"You are right. I'm going to give that to a doctor in Little Rock. That other horn is yours." That was in 1957. I've got his name on it.

I said, "Let me pay you for it." Man, he like to have eat me up, I'm telling you.

He took care of my dogs all the way through. I remember one day, I was feeding my dogs. I had about twenty. I was running a cafe, and he come down by one day to get some barbeque for the American Legion.

"What are you doing with all those cracklings here?"

"I'm mixing them with this corn meal, cooking it, feeding my dogs. Make them tough."

Well, he fed everybody's dog in the country.

He come back about a week later and said, "Will you order me some of those cracklings?"

"How many do you want, Doc?"

"About a thousand pounds."

"A thousand pounds?—

"Yep."

I got them in, called him and said, "Dr. Rhine, I've got your cracklings in here."

He said, "Now, Bill Parker is goin' to come by and get some, and Allen Lightfoot is goin' to come by and get some, and Dud Crosby is going to come by for some. I'll take Claud Arnold's to him." And he took the rest to his house.

When you gave dogs this to eat, they would really talk to you, I'll guarantee you. It made them long winded, too. It was a lot better than that dog food was. That meat put a lot of grease in there. The corn meal was just yellow corn meal like you make cornbread with. You put it all in a pot, like a wash pot. It was like a mush.

He got two dogs in. Two Julys, down there through the post office. The freight truck brought them. I said, "Boy, them shore are purty puppies." He gave a high price for them dogs, too. He was going to let Claud Arnold have one and Bill Parker the other. He was a July dog man! I like red-boned, black and tans and Walkers, but I mean he liked them Julys, I guarantee. Allen Lightfoot kept a few Julys, but he liked Walkers. But way back then, in the 40's you know, you didn't have many Julys and Walkers. You had blue ticks and black and tans and red-boned dogs. Mr. Johnny Davidson, he kept a few dogs for Doc, too, back then.

I never did get no puppies from him. I had a lot of dogs. I didn't need any more. He asked me several times if I wanted any. "I got more dogs than I can feed now." I had twenty-seven one time. Mr. Pemberton had sixty some odd.

We went deer hunting in 1956. We usually had about twenty-five to thirty dogs. We got up there, and we had sixty-eight hounds! They all scratched under the fence and got out. You talk about a race!

Each deer season, Dr. Rhine would bring a case of apples and a case of oranges for the kids. We had to keep sweet milk or chocolate drink for Dr. Rhine when he came. He didn't drink Coca Cola or coffee, only milk or chocolate drink.

William Henry Brandon, Sr. was my Grandpa and one of Doc's early patients. My uncle, Henry Brandon, Jr. was his first white patient. My father, Harvey, called 'Kitchen', had a toothache. "I'll pull it for you. Come on in here and sit in this chair." He just got his 'pullers' and went to pulling. No pain medicine or nothing, unless you took some before you got in there.

I went to him when I come out of service in 1955. "Doc, I've got a hurting in here in my chest. I have a horror of a heart attack." I smoked a lot of cigarettes and drank a lot of coffee.

"Well," he said, "You got a little ole hernia in there."

I didn't know what he was talking about. I went on awhile, and I said I was goin' up to see Dr. Harry Atkinson.

"Go on up. He's a good doctor."

I went to the hospital, and he told me I had a hiatal hernia.

"Well", I said, "Send me to Little Rock. I want one more chance." I went to the VA hospital, and they said it was a big one, too. I quit coughing when I gave up cigarettes, but cornbread! It'll fix you up good.

I have Dr. Rhine's name on a deep freeze at my barbeque place. I had just got that deep freeze the day he died, so I stuck his birthdate on it and that day, with his name. It's been on there ever since.

We have his picture framed for the Lodge. His caps and working tools that he had for the Lodge and the Consistory we are putting in a box frame to keep there.

TOMMY TRAMMEL

THORNTON, ARKANSAS

I had a squirrel bone caught in my throat. It had gotten where I couldn't swallow. I went on down to Dr. Rhine's house. He got a straight back chair, turned it over on the floor and told me to lay down on the floor with my back on the back of the chair. He got down and straddled me. He had a long teaspoon in his hand. He put his knees on my arms and went to punching with that spoon and punched that squirrel bone loose and on down. I didn't even have a sore throat from it. It was cross-wise in my throat. I just bucked, trying to get up, but he held me. I was a grown man, already married, when it happened.

My parents, Buck and Ruth Trammel moved to Thornton around 1931. Dr. Rhine delivered me fifty-two years ago, and my younger brother, Jimmy, later.

The Deer Club we have now is part of the same bunch that started out at Princeton years ago. When they opened the reserve there, folks moved in all around us, so we moved our camp to Chambersville. It's still called the Thornton Hunting Club. Dr. Rhine used to have a big, big part in that. He did up until the end of his life. Every year he'd send a box of apples and oranges to the camp.

Dr. Rhine used to keep fox hounds all the time. He would give them to Allen Lightfoot, the Hearnsbergers, Bill Parker, Dud Crosby. There are a lot of 'em that has horns that Dr. Rhine had given 'em.

Bill Parker was the one who got me started deer hunting. I was about a junior in high school, and then when I got out of the Army, me and him would go hunting.

Connie Lee Scott, the cook at our camp, gets up at 4:30 in the morning and starts breakfast. We usually get up about five and eat. Then we decide where we are going to 'stand' that day, so we'll know which way to run the dogs. We usually get to the stand before daylight. Me or Bunny Steelman turns the dogs aloose. The dogs are mine. There are twelve, and we turn the whole pack aloose. We usually stay on the stand 'til ten or eleven o'clock. We have dinner, play a game of Rook, and then go back 'til it gets dark.

The first two days of the hunt last year, we had fifteen hunters. The rest of the week, we had eight or nine. No one rides horses anymore because the woods have gotten so thickety, you can't get through them. When I first got in the camp, Allen Lightfoot and Sidney Holmes were the two who rode horses to keep up with the dogs, so they wouldn't get lost or get too far away. Back then, there wasn't any Jeeps or four-wheel drive vehicles, and if you killed a deer way back in the middle of the woods, they would load it on a horse and bring it out. Now, you can just about get to them anywhere in a Jeep and bring them out.

I'll tell you a good one on Fred Tomlinson. Year before last him and John Evan Tomlinson, me and Jesse Brandon, Paul Cayce and Bunny Steelman were hunting. Fred was on the stand, and we ran a big eight point deer right by Fred, less than thirty steps. Fred jumped out of his truck, shot the deer—shot him twice. That was all the shells he had!

"I could have shot that deer two or three more times."

Jesse said, "Yeh, if you'd a bought some more shells."

We tracked that deer for about two miles, before we lost it. Can you imagine anybody going deer hunting with just two shells? He'll never hear the last of that one. We told him we knew he wasn't goin' to carry any cigarettes, but we thought he would buy some shells.

He denies it, but he shot on the hunt again that same year. He was afraid we was goin' to cut his shirt tail off. It is customary, if you shoot at a deer and miss it, they cut your shirt tail off. O. D. Cathey was close to Fred and heard him shoot, but Fred just denies it up and down. When O. D. started to leave, he pulled out four shells and gave them to Fred. "I know you don't have any shells. You'd better take these."

There are fifteen members of the Club now. We stay in the old Hugh Gresham house. We have three bedrooms and eight beds. Some of them have camp trailers out there. We hunt one week in November, one week in December and two days after Thanksgiving. You can't run dogs then. You have to 'still' hunt. We built platforms up in trees [stands]. It is not near as dangerous, a person getting shot. Deer don't look up. They will come out right under there. They can't smell you up in the air like that, and you can see better, too.

Dr. Rhine never charged you over a dollar for medicine—pour you some in a little old bottle. Never spill a drop out of them gallon jugs.

I had asked my sister, Pat, to do something for me, and she said she wasn't going to do it. I had a rubber gun in my hand, and I hauled off and shot her with it. She grabbed that thing out of my hand, hit me upside of the head and split my head down through there. Mother carried me down to Dr. Rhine's office. He looked at it and said, "I'm going to have to put a clamp in it." When he turned around to get that clamp, I left. I cut out. It just healed up without a clamp.

I sprung my ankle playing basketball. I went up there, and he taped it right over all them hairs. He told me when to come back. I went back. He grabbed that tape and jerked. All those hairs pulled off. The next time I sprung that ankle, I shaved that leg before I went down there.

I broke a rib one time, and he taped me up for that. He taped me so tight I couldn't hardly breath, but it got well.

Mother was in Little Rock in the hospital and one of her doctors, Dr. Hollenberg, was asking Daddy about Dr. Rhine. He asked Daddy if he had ever gotten any diagnostic equipment. Daddy said, "He's got all that he needs. He's got those things he sticks in his ears."

Dr. Hollenberg said, "Dr. Rhine is the best in the country at diagnosing, without anything to do it with."

Right after World War II was over with, ('42 cars was the last you could get) and the '46's first started coming, the first one that come in up at Everett Ford in Fordyce was Dr. Rhine's. He really needed it, too. He had hauled too much pine and scrap iron in the back of his old car. He had driven it day and night, too. Mr. Everett told 'em that the first one to come in was Dr. Rhine's.

The office desk piled high ... and the 1903 Oliver typewriter equipped with a purple ribbon.

This is typical of the kind of rest which sustained him during those long, busy years—the telephone is within reach.

The "collapsible" examining chair and the medicines.

His car contained jacks, pumps, axes, spades, chains, lanterns, and boots as well as bottles of medicines.

The famous gallon medicine jugs from which he dispensed tonics and syrups.

The laboratory—a centrifugal instrument, water buckets and pan. He also had a microscope.

A part of the crowd at Dr. Rhine Day, May 17, 1946, in Thornton.

Ham Moses, president of Arkansas Power and Light
Company at that time, was a speaker at Dr. Rhine Day.
Rep. Oren Harris is at the right, laughing.

Dr. Rhine speaking to his friends,
several thousand of whom came to
honor him that day.

Receiving the Charter of the Thornton American Legion Post, which later was to be called Dr. T. E. Rhine American Legion Post.

THE WHITE HOUSE
WASHINGTON

January 23, 1950

Dear Dr. Rhine.

I want to thank you very much for the fine sugar cane syrup which you sent me through John Steelman. I am sure that I shall enjoy it.

After we returned from Florida I learned from John that you had paid us a visit, and that you came to the White House and visited my office. I am sorry we were not here at that time.

With all good wishes,

Very sincerely yours,

Harry Truman

Dr. T. E. Rhine
Thornton,
Arkansas

Letter from President Harry Truman to Dr. Rhine after his visit to Washington.

Arkansas Fox Hunter of the Year, 1956. Looking at the plaque are (from left): Dr. Perry Dalton, Camden; Dr. Rhine; Dr. Henry Hearnsberger, Jr., Stephens (now lives in Little Rock); and Dr. Joe Shuffield, Little Rock.

An avid fox hunter, he loved to present horns to his many friends.

Dr. Rhine's grandson, Tommy Brown, and a cherished fox hound with one of the famous piles of pine knots in the rear.

Distinguished Arkansans honored at a cocktail party at the AMA convention in 1949. They are from the left: Dr. and Mrs. Hunt, president of the Arkansas Medical Society; Dr. and Mrs. Rhine, Arkansas Doctor of the Year, 1949; John Snyder, Secretary of the Treasury; Governor Sid McMath of Arkansas; Mrs. Emma Steelman, wife of Dr. John R. Steelman, advisor to President Truman; Miss Frances Greer, Metropolitan Opera star; Mr. and Mrs. Frank Pace, Under-Secretary of the Navy; Representative and Mrs. Oren Harris; Ike Murry, Attorney General of Arkansas; and B. T. Fooks, Grapette bottler of Camden and a co-host with the Arkansas Medical Society of this affair.

Dr. Rhine, with daughters, Virginia and Pat, shows Governor Sid McMath souvenir Razorback hogs, given by Dr. Rhine to the guests at the party for Distinguished Arkansans.

"He was a legend in his own time."

DR. RAYMOND IRWIN, JR.

PINE BLUFF, ARKANSAS

I first heard of Dr. Rhine when I was a freshman in medical school—really, before I ever heard of the town of Thornton—because he was a legend in his own time. A small town doctor who had delivered over 5,000 babies and really had a reputation for being a very astute physician, who, on his referrals to the clinics at the University Hospital, and also to the private practicing physicians in Little Rock, usually was very shrewd at knowing just what was wrong with the patient, in which area continued treatment needed to be carried on. I never will forget him sending in patients with a little note,"I believe this patient needs a tracheolight examination" which he had no facilities for in Fordyce or Thornton. We didn't call it a tracheolight. We called it a bronscoscopy. Still, he had the right idea.

I have heard it said by some of the physicians to whom he referred patients, that he was possibly the only doctor in the state that they never questioned his diagnoses. At least, my experience with the way he referred patients, he didn't actually give you a diagnosis, he would give you an area in which he thought the patient was having trouble. And he was very shrewd, very astute in this.

As years went on, some of the younger fellows participated in the general practice program, which they called a preceptorship. At that time, several, whom I knew quite well, in their senior year of internship, got to spend some time with Dr. Rhine. One of these was Jim Bethel, who lived in Benton, but who practices at the out-patient facility at the Veterans' Hospital. He used to be in general practice in Benton. Every time he got back to Little Rock, he had to come tell me some more Dr. Rhine stories. Chiefly of these were the great respect and regard that people in that area held for him. Most people would not make a decision, certainly not a medical decision, and sometimes not a business decision, without talking to him first. Seated in his office in turn would be people seeking business, as well as medical advice, dogs, cats and other pets that needed treatment, who took their turn. Jim really enjoyed the time that he spent with Dr. Rhine.

Another thing that he mentioned was that he dispensed his own medicine from large jugs, and he handled these jugs in the crook of his arm, and poured the medicines into a small bottle and not a drop would hit the floor. Then he would wink at Jim, and say, "I'll bet that you can't do that." Of course, none of us could have.

Basically, I think the regard that Dr. Rhine built for himself during his practice years dealt around his loyalty to his patient clientele in a very small town and the fact that he stayed there for his whole practice.

I did hear him mention one time that early in his practice years he had a stroke and was in St. Vincent's Hospital in Little Rock. The consulting doctors around his bed all told him that he wouldn't practice again, if he lived. At the time he related the story to us, he was the only one of the group surviving. All of the consultants were dead.

He was quite a remarkable man, both in the service he rendered to people and in the reputation he enjoyed with his fellow physicians.

When Dr. Rhine was selected Arkansas Doctor of the Year in 1949, there was an article in the newspaper stating that he had delivered over 5,000 babies. I was in medical school at the time, and our attention was called to this. He went any time of the day or night. That is remarkable that he could stand up to that many years of practice doing that.*

Then, the people relied on him for everything. What is happening now in the small towns (people wonder why they can't get doctors in small towns) is that people want to drop by the doctor's office on the way home from work and get something for a cold, or someone to come give them a shot in the night for nausea or vomiting, but if something is really wrong with them, they go to the city to a specialist.

(Dr. Irwin is a general surgeon and has been practicing in Pine Bluff for twenty-six years.)

D R .   R O B E R T   W A T S O N

LITTLE ROCK, ARKANSAS

I first met Dr. Rhine at a dinner meeting of the Ouachita County Medical Society in Camden in 1942. He had just returned from making a

*He gave up obstetrics and night calls in January of 1964, the year in which he died at the age of 88.) PRB

house call in the country, having traveled part of the way by wagon, and was wearing knee length black rubber boots, as commonly worn by him during the winter.

Later, when I would receive a letter addressed with a purple typewriter ribbon, I knew immediately who it was from, and furthermore, I knew that whatever diagnosis he made inside that envelope, it would be accurate. The typewriter that Dr. Rhine used was an Oliver #5 that was manufactured before World War I.

(Dr. Watson is a retired neurosurgeon, who practiced in Little Rock.) PRB

DR. ALAN G. CAZORT

LITTLE ROCK, ARKANSAS

(In a letter to his daughter, Cecile Zorach, in the spring of 1983)

I remember Dr. Rhine very well. He was my ideal of the best family doctors. Maybe because he sent me so many patients. He was one of the first out-of-towners to do this and continued as long as he was active. His patients were *people*, friends. He knew them, as well as their complaints.

(Dr. Cazort founded the Arkansas Allergy Clinic and practiced until about 1974.) PRB

DR. PATRICK HENRY

ST. LOUIS, MISSOURI

We had made several calls that morning in Fordyce and Temperance Hill so Dr. Rhine thought we should stop and see Mr. Wheeler. We parked in front of the large, unpainted house, but Dr. Rhine paused before leaving the car to tell about the man we were about to see. He said, "You are going to see what to me is one of the saddest parts of practicing medicine—a man once vigorous in body and mind who has lost all his mental abilities. He just lies there day after day, not knowing who or where he is. His wife, children and neighbors must do everything for him."

As we looked toward the house, Dr. Rhine lowered his head, and said, "There is nothing I fear for myself and my family, except this. I hope I die before being reduced to this." We left the car, climbed the steps and knocked. Mrs. Wheeler let us in, Dr. Rhine explained my presence, and then he went to the bedside, pulled up a chair, sat down and took Mr.

230

Wheeler's hand in his, told him who he was, but there was no recognition from Mr. Wheeler.

Dr. Rhine, head bowed, was silent for a few moments as he stroked the patients hand and arm, and then be began talking with Mrs. Wheeler about her observations of the past week. We took no instruments inside, wrote no prescriptions, handed out no pills, yet Mrs. Wheeler seemed visibly improved by Dr. Rhine's fifteen minute visit. As we left, he promised to visit again next week. In the car, he commented again on the sadness of such an existance for a man he had known for many years. As I drove us toward Thornton, he was quieter than usual.

In August of 1957, I had just completed my preceptorship in Camden the previous day and stopped in Thornton for a visit before returning to begin my fourth year in medical school. The following morning we made several house calls, spent some time in the office, had lunch at the Rhine's and then came a call for help from a family in Bearden. A woman was having a baby, and the doctor in Bearden was off for the afternoon. The directions to the house were confusing, so we stopped twice to be certain we were on the right track. We were, but the track ended at the edge of a large field, and the house was a small two-room cabin about a half-mile away. When we arrived on foot carrying the obstetrical equipment, the temperature outside was about 102 degrees. Inside, a wood-burning stove was being used to heat water, so the temperature seemed like 110 degrees, and there wasn't a tree in sight. The patient was in bed with several quilts over her, so Dr. Rhine and I washed up in preparation for the delivery. A cry was heard, and the mother said her baby had already been born and was wrapped in a quilt on the floor. We tied and cut the umbilical cord, and Dr. Rhine asked for some baby oil, but there was none. "What about butter, margarine, lard?" he asked. Some lard was found by the woman helper, and she was told to give it to me. Dr. Rhine explained that I was to rub a thin film of grease over the entire baby's body, so I went outside, sat down in a porch swing and greased that baby. After completing his work with the mother, he ascertained that there were no supplies in the house for the baby. So, on our return trip through that part of Bearden, he made certain that some of the churchwomen know of the new baby and its need for diapers, baby oil, food, etc. I don't recall ever having been as hot as I was that day in the little house with its wood-burning stove.

Much of the office was occupied by a large amount of quart, gallon or two gallon containers of medications (tonics, cough syrup, antihistamines, antispasmodics, etc.) which had to be transferred to other bottles as small as one or two ounces for an individual patient. I marveled at how he could accomplish this, seldom spilling a drop on the floor. Sometimes he asked me to do the honors. Gradually, with time and a few spills, I managed to become reliable with the bottles of four ounces or greater—the smaller ones I left for him to do even though that resulted in his teasing me most every time. An obvious advantage for the patient of this bulk purchase by Dr. Rhine was that the cost was much less than that at the drugstore in Fordyce or Bearden.

Occasionally one of the more persistant salesmen would find Dr. Rhine in his office. They always had a 'new' discovery for him to consider. He spent very little time with them, but did accept their samples for later distribution to patients without funds. One day a particularly eager saleman appeared with a new treatment for rheumatoid arthritis. The conversation went something like this:

Dr. Rhine: "Is your new pill better than aspirin?"

Salesman: "Some doctors find that it is, others are not so sure. It is being compared with aspirin at the present time, but remember it is the newest thing for your patients."

Dr. Rhine: "Unless it is better than aspirin I don't want to be bothered. Let me know when it has been proven. In the meantime, I'll stick with aspirin."

What a joy it was for me to see him insist on some evidence before he accepted the newest drug as being automatically superior.

Dr. Rhine had several stethoscopes, but often did not use them for listening to the heart or lungs of his patients. Instead, he placed his ear against the chest and listened carefully. If the patient was a woman he always placed a clean handkerchief or a sheet between his ear and the patient's breasts when listening to the anterior lung fields or the heart. This was the way he learned to auscultate in medical school. I used his method several times, but settled on my stethoscope since that was the method I had learned in school. I never saw anyone use this method until the movie version of William Faulkner's *The Reivers* showed an elderly, inebriated doctor place his handkerchief and then his ear against the breasts of Boon's woman friend in a very amusing scene.

I don't recall that we ever had significantly different findings with our different techniques.

The last time I visited with him in his home, he was reading in his recliner chair. I greeted him and asked how he was doing. He said, "Well, thank you. I'm reading my new edition of Cecil's *Textbook of Medicine* which just arrived this week. I hope to find something useful in here for some of my patients."

The impression of him sitting there, in his eighty-seventh year, still reading and learning, his mind still alert and active, remains quite vivid today. When I received the call about his death, I felt great sadness about the loss from my life, but I also felt joy that he had not had to endure a gradual decline in his mental functions—that his greatest fear had not been realized.

(Dr. Henry is head of the Department of Medicine at St. John's Mercy Hospital in St. Louis, Missouri.) PRB

DREW STURGIS

LITTLE ROCK, ARKANSAS

When I was a child, I was often sick, and my parents, Floyd and Rita Sturgis of Fordyce had taken me to Ochsner's Clinic in New Orleans and other large medical clinics for a diagnosis. None of them really helped me to overcome the malady. One day, Dr. Rhine came to our house for some other reason. He walked in the door, and all the way across the room, he looked at me and said, "Why that boy has asthma!" Dr. Rhine spotted the problem immediately. That was indeed what was wrong with me.

EDITH WILLIAMS HOLMES

THORNTON, ARKANSAS

He wasn't always right! Archie and I had been married for about eight years, and we wanted a baby so bad. I went to Dr. Rhine and talked to him. He looked at me real mean and real sour and said, "No, you aren't ever goin' to have any young'uns." I went home crying. I really was pregnant, but I didn't know it. After a while, I went to a doctor in Camden, Dr. Robbins. I wanted to find out what was wrong with me. Dr. Robbins told me I was three months pregnant. I came back home all aglow, happy and grinning from ear to ear. It wasn't but a few months 'til I was as big as a barrel. I went in the post office and met up with Dr. Rhine. He looked at me real mean and sour and didn't say a word. He wouldn't even speak to me. It wasn't but a few months later that I was in the post office and met up with Dr. Rhine again. I had a big, bouncing baby girl on my shoulder. He looked at me real mean, sure enough then. He didn't speak to me. I felt bad about not using him because he had always been our doctor, but I was thirty-one years old, and thought I needed to be in a hospital, so I went to Camden, the nearest hospital at that time, to have my baby. I got a big kick out of the way he acted. He wasn't really mean to me, he was just upset with me because I had used another doctor. He was pretty mad at me, I'm sure. It wasn't often that he was proven wrong, but this time he was dead wrong and the expression on his face was something!

EDWARD AND MARTIEL WOMBLE

THORNTON, ARKANSAS

Martiel: One of the first things I remember about Dr. Rhine at the Dallas County Hospital was after he made his rounds, he would always come by

A-wing desk and call Mrs. Rhine and ask if there were any more calls that he needed to make. Every time I would see him coming down the hall with his particular rolling gait, I would dial the number, so that it would be ringing when he got there. Mrs. Rhine would answer. He'd say, "Nita, any stops I gotta make?" She would tell him if he did or didn't. He'd say, "All right. I'm on my way home." He always called home before he left the hospital. That was the last thing he did.

Another incident I remember at the hospital. Soon after some young doctors came (just passed the State Boards), they thought they knew everything and could make no mistakes. Everything was right by the book, no question about anything. One of them had gotten a little gruff with Dr. Rhine, accusing him of being behind the times and not up on the new medicines. He stopped by the nurses' desk and said, "You know, people that claim they never make a mistake, have already made their first mistake."

One young woman here in town, Colleen Simpson, had poured hot grease over her hand. She told me this and remembers it well. She said that she wet a wash rag with ice water and ran up there to Dr. Rhine's office. He gave her a big jar—she says she remembers how big it was—of Yellow Gold. That's what they called it. It was Furacin ointment. "He gave it to me and told me to keep it all wrapped up with that ointment on it and to keep it cold." The skin had already turned white by the time she got to the office. She just knew that she was going to have a terrible hand, but it didn't even blister. She added, "And do you know, he just gave me that big old jar of ointment."

I remember with my own kids, Edward being there at the post office next to his office, when they would get up in the morning, puny and with an elevated temp and sore throat, I would send a pint fruit jar with Edward, and he would fill it up with his tonsillitis medicine. I don't know what it was, but let me tell you, it was the best I ever used.

Edward: It was out of a big, brown bottle about sixteen inches high. In fact, everything almost was. He bought it in bulk.

Martiel: He would send me that pint fruit jar out on the route, when Edward came by, and he would always say, "Now let me know how they do, but they'll be all right." He had already told me how to give it, and he said, "Give it to all of them. If one of 'em has it, they all are going to have it. So give it to all four of them at the same time."

Edward: I'd say, "Doc, how much do I owe you?" "Aw, a coupla dollars."

Martiel: He would always warn me of any hypochondriacs that came in town. "You stay away from them, Martiel. They'll be wanting you to give them shots and this, that and the other. You leave them alone." I always appreciated that. If he had an active TB case in town, he would always warn me of that.

Edward: I was a grown boy, and he fixed me up a bottle of that same sore throat medicine. There was a skull and cross bones on it. Poison! I said, "Doc, that bottle says poison." "Why sure. You're full of poison. You know you have to fight fire with fire." I'll admit I was a little hesitant to take it, but he told me what it was supposed to do, so I did.

He was a great one for dogs. Several years before he died, I started keeping dogs—beagle hunting dogs. First one thing and another required a vet, and we didn't have a vet in this part of the country. Something happened to one of the dogs, and I asked him if he knew what was good for it, because I knew he kept fox hounds. Mine were beagles, but dogs are dogs. But I found out there is more to it than that. He said, "Yeah, I think I've got something here that will help." He reached for one of his stock of medicines. Poured me a bottle. I said, "Doc, that's human medicine, isn't it?"

"They are built just like dogs. Medicine for the same infection for one will work for the other." It cured my dog.

Several times after that, I got medicine and maybe even some shots were involved in it for my dogs. Everytime I would ask him how much I owed him, he would emphatically reply, "Nothing. As long as we are doctoring those dogs, it's all on the house. We charge for humans, but the dogs are our pets." He never charged me a dime for anything I poked down those dogs.

Martiel: Back when he was delivering babies at the hospital in Fordyce, I worked nights quite a bit then. When he had one to come in, we'd call him and tell him the patient was there, and he'd show up in just a little bit, and he would sit right there with them. He did not depend on us to examine them and check them. He'd stay right with them. He was always real gentle with his patients. He was firm, but he was gentle, and they knew what he meant to do, what he wanted them to do.

Edward: Talk about him being gruff! I used to wait every once in a while in his waiting room for something. I always got tickled. Old women went to the office and waited, lined up around the wall. Little bitty dried-up women. He'd drive up. He would look at one, probably in the hypochondriac class, and the first thing he'd say in the gruffest voice, "What's the matter with you now?"

"Oh Doc, I've got so and so."

He'd give her a little bottle of something. "Run on, run on." He'd walk in the door saying, "Looks like I got a big mess in here to clean out." They really loved it.

Martiel: If Dr. Rhine said it, it was really so. When he would deliver premature babies, even if it was only seven months' gestation, if it was a girl, he would tell us she was going to live. If it was a boy, he would tell us not to work too hard with him, because he wouldn't make it. We have a law that requires putting silver nitrate in newborn babies' eyes. He would say to us, "Don't you put that in my babies' eyes. You squirt it on the floor." I always did what he said. The purpose of that was to protect the baby from infection in case the mother had gonorrhea and the baby came out over the infection. It was so strong, it often irritated the babies' eyes.

Edward: There was a very thin wall between my office in the post office and his examining room. One morning, a black boy came into his office, and this is the conversation I overheard. "Doc, I've got something wrong with me."

"O.K. Let me see what your problem is. Well, have you been messing around?"

"Messing around, Doc?"

"With girls, with girls."

"Yessir, yessir."

"It shows, too. You sure have."

"What's the matter, Doc?"

"Didn't you see them little rattlesnakes all around there? One of 'em bit you."

That was the only explanation he gave to the patient, but it was graphic and understandable.

Martiel: I was helping Dr. Rhine on a home case in which an elderly, white male was in the process of dying. In this case, it took about a week for him to die, and the family was wanting something to be done for him. This was before we had the hospital in Fordyce. I said to Dr. Rhine, "Don't you want me to take his blood pressure?" because the family insisted that he be given a bottle of glucose.

"What's the use, Martiel? That's not going to save him."

Dr. Rhine would come two or three times a day to check on him and the family expected it.*

Edward: When I was a kid, we lived back door to back door to Dr. Rhine. On cold winter days, I would be out bringing in wood. Dr. Rhine, early in the morning, would go out to warm up his car. He would pull out the choke and start the engine. It would just roar. He'd walk back into the house and let it sit there and roar for five or ten minutes. I don't know why it didn't blow up.

(Edward is Post Master at Fordyce and Martiel has been a nurse since 1947. She graduated from Baylor School of Nursing in 1951, and has been on the nursing staff of the Dallas County Hospital since it opened in 1958. She also has been the school nurse at the Thornton Schools, and gave many immunizations with Dr. Rhine before he died.) PRB

N E L L   W E L L S   R I C H A R D S O N

FORDYCE, ARKANSAS

I first met Dr. Rhine when I moved to Fordyce and went to work as a public health nurse in Dallas County in 1935. He was one of my very

---

*Daddy believed there was a big difference in prolonging life and prolonging death. PRB

special doctors because he always co-operated in the school work up in the country where he practiced, and helped me in any way that he could, and I needed him for that. I helped him, too. He used to call me and say, "I have a patient here that needs to go to the hospital." Then times were real bad, and I would take them to the hospitals in Little Rock—University, Baptist, St. Vincent's and a lot of them to the Children's Hospital. I remember one case—a Hudson boy—that he called me about, saying he needed to go to the hospital. I said, "Dr. Rhine, can I wait until in the morning?" It was ten o'clock at night. He said, "No, this boy needs immediate attention, and I believe you had better get him to Little Rock if we are going to save him." I took him, and he had a ruptured spleen. They operated on him immediately, and he wouldn't have lasted until the next morning.

Another time, he called me that he had a patient up in the country. I went up there and got that patient, took them to St. Vincent's. They operated, and it was appendicitis. Dr. Rhine was real grateful for all I did, and he showed it in many ways.

I was a Public Health nurse in Nashville, Arkansas from 1930 to 1935, during the real bad Depression. Terrible times! Children who were sick, needed tonsillectomies, had sore throats and such, there was no way to get them taken care of, because small towns didn't have hospitals. The only hospital was Children's in Little Rock.

During the War, I was surgical nurse at the old Ouachita County Hospital in Camden. The doctors in Camden had the most respect for Dr. Rhine and his opinions. When he called in saying he had a patient coming in with appendicitis, the doctors didn't wait for the patient to get there, and the nurses didn't either, they got ready in surgery to operate on that patient, because they knew Dr. Rhine would be right in his diagnosis, and he always was. He didn't do the surgery, but he always scrubbed out and was in the operating room and observed. A few times, he did assist when no assistant was available, but he didn't like to. But he always scrubbed out if it was his patient, and he always wanted to see if the trouble was what he thought it was.

I helped open the hospital in Dallas County in 1958. I was in charge of surgery. Dr. Rhine was always available if the patients needed him. He supported the hospital and the nurses. He was easy for me to get along with. He was never gruff to the nurses or to his patients who were sick in the hospital. I never knew him to speak a cross word with nurses, patients or doctors, but I think he could have, if things weren't as he thought they ought to be. He would observe surgery and be with his patients, and would visit them twice a day, just like the other doctors.

During his illnesses, I did nurse him through all of them. One of the most amusing things I found out about Dr. Rhine was that you had to give him a dose of medicine and *then* tell him what it was. If you didn't, he would say, "I don't need that." I usually was able to say, "Here, take this," and get it down him before he had time to ask me what it was and why I was giving it to him. I nursed him three different times through serious illnesses, one

237

time in Little Rock. I was always there when he needed me. [He wouldn't have anyone else nurse him.]

Once, I went to his home every day to bath him and take care of him, and I nursed Mrs. Rhine through an illness at home.

One of the times, I was on the three-to-eleven duty. He was slated to have an enema that morning. The young nurse came in to administer it, and Dr. Rhine refused to let her do it. When I came on at three, I said to him, "You were supposed to have had an enema this morning. Why didn't you?"

He replied, "That nurse couldn't even take a temperature, so I certainly wasn't going to let her give me an enema. You are here now, so I'll have it."

I retired from nursing in 1968. Dr. Rhine was always on my side, when he thought I was right.

One time I wished for a cherry tree outside my kitchen window. The next morning, there was a cherry tree outside my kitchen window that Dr. Rhine had sent. I always got sorghum molasses from him. He always sent sorghum molasses to the doctors in Little Rock, in Camden, in Fordyce, and I got mine, too, in the fall. He didn't know how much I appreciated that because I was raised on sorghum. My grandfather made it, and I would visit him for a week before school started, and I would cook apples in the syrup, eat cane and always have hot biscuits for breakfast with syrup.

J U D I E   W H E E L E R   S M I T H

FORDYCE, ARKANSAS

The first thing I remember about Dr. Rhine was when my sister, Jessie, and I were both sick. John Wheeler was my father and my mother was Mattie McDonald. Her daddy was Dr. James Henry McDonald, a country doctor at Ramsey. I was three years older than Jessie. One morning here come Dr. Rhine. They had called him. Cora Reynolds was sick, too. He had been to see her, and then come on up to see us. I was a little backward or something. I didn't talk like Jessie did. She had pretty brown eyes and pretty curly hair. I had straight pigtails. She goes to talking to Dr. Rhine and I don't say a word. He examined her real good, and she did everything he asked her to let him do. Then he come to me. I shut my eyes and wouldn't say a word to him. I don't know why. I remember it just as well. Finally, he said, "John, this child [Jessie] has pneumonia. I'll have to guess at the other one, but I guess she has it, too."

He dished out the medicine and told how to give it. Then he said, "Be sure and give them a little toddy." I had heard about whiskey and how awful it was, and I thought, "No! I won't have it." He come for four or five days, every day. The day he decided we would be all right, he brought Jessie a sleeping doll. She would really go to sleep. He didn't bring me one, and I found out he brought Cora Reynolds one, too.

The next time I remember about him was when my youngest sister, Juanita, was born. One morning, Papa woke us up before daylight and said we were going to Anna's. She lived at Ramsey at Grandpa's. It was cold, but he put us in the wagon and made the horses run all the way. He put us out, and we spent the day and night there. I didn't know why. The next morning, he come after us and told us we had a little sister at our house. They told us that Dr. Rhine had been there.

Later on, we moved to Ramsey and lived with Grandpa. Every time Grandpa McDonald would get sick, Dr. Rhine would come to see him, but he would never charge him anything. I was a little kid, but I remember that. Dr. Rhine was so good to come see about him. A lot of times, he would be passing by and stop in to see Grandpa.

Dr. Rhine had the first car that we ever saw in Ramsey. In the summertime, he would have the top down. We would run out to the road to smell the gasoline after he passed. We'd just smell and think about Dr. Rhine and his car. Several times he had a woman with him, and she had a pretty hat on. We all just had a spell about Dr. Rhine and the woman with the pretty hat on passing by. We could hear the car coming, and we would know that it was Dr. Rhine's car. It was a one seated car. I can just see it now. We had summer school at Ramsey at that one room schoolhouse. We were a little bit jealous of that woman [it was Miss Nanita Raines] because we claimed Dr. Rhine—just kids.

James, my son, was sick. He was eight years old. We didn't know what was wrong. We waited a day or two, and he lost the use of his legs. We felt like then that something was bad. We called Dr. Rhine, and he come and examined him. He said, "I hope I'm wrong, but I'm afraid he has infantile paralysis." He called Dr. Atkinson from Fordyce and waited for him to come out there. They decided that he did have polio. He couldn't use his legs for some time, but finally he did get the use of them back.

I started working as a nurse's aide the first day the hospital opened here at Fordyce in 1958. I worked fourteen months and Mr. Stewart said he wanted me to go to nurse's school. I thought I was too old. He said I had to have a nurse's license, that I was making everyone like the new hospital. So I went to Pine Bluff and took a course in practical nursing. I worked four months there after I finished my training, and then come back to the Dallas County Hospital and worked there until 1981.

Dr. Rhine had so many patients at that hospital, and they were so glad to see him. Any time he hit the front door, you would always hear his voice. He was always in such a good mood. He'd say, "I'm all right, but sometimes I'm mean, mean, mean, thinking about the folks I have to deal with." He'd make all those patients feel good. He'd joke with them to really see how sick they were. They all looked forward to him coming.

"Dr. Rhine was generous to a fault—always ready to take someone in."

MARY SUE RAINES MOSELEY

EL PASO, TEXAS

Dr. Rhine, who was married to my sister, Nanita, was generous to a fault—always ready to take someone in. The George Moseley family spent time there on two different occasions. The first time was in the 1920's. George was traveling, and instead of going with him from place to place, or staying alone in a rented apartment, Dr. Rhine and Nanita insisted that I stay with them in Thornton. Nanita had a hard time with her back when she was carrying Pat, and could only walk with that low chair pushed ahead of her. Years later, Dr. Rhine thanked me again and again for staying with them and taking care of her during that time. I had to remind him that it worked both ways. I had no place to go, and staying there was a God-send.

The other time was during the Depression when they took us all in. George was without a job. Dr. Rhine insisted that George more than paid our way with the work he did around the place, making a garden, tarring the roof and such. Nanita would always laugh and say that this was the only time their garden was laid out by an engineer, complete with strings to mark the rows. I taught the girls expression, as well as an expression class at the school and one day a week at Hampton. He even trusted me once to drive the car to Bearden for repairs. The two days or so when Dr. Rhine had the flu, and was in bed, when everyone else had it, George 'made house calls' for him—that is, he delivered medicine to the sick folks.

He and Nanita never let us feel that we were imposing on them by staying there, which made us feel better about it, of course. We had just built our home in Camden, and we rented it in order to make the payments on it.

Mrs. Carrie McDonald served as nurse for Thornton and around. On

240

the morning when Pat was born, Nanita had only gotten her stockings on, when she realized that this was the time. Selma Polk, the Rhine's cook, called Mrs. McDonald to come. In the meantime, Dr. Rhine gave me orders to get Nanita ready, first by removing her stockings. I was so excited that I ripped them off and flung them right into the sterile water that was sitting there ready. Dr. Rhine dismissed me from the case right then. Shortly, Mrs. McDonald arrived and took charge, cleaning up the baby.

He had many good friends among the doctors in Little Rock. Several times, one or more came to visit, and he'd take them on his rounds, getting their opinions on special cases. He made no claim to being a surgeon, but there were times when he had to set a broken leg or arm in his office—or on someone's kitchen table.

Dr. Rhine loved to dance. He didn't get the chance often in later years, but anytime he found a few square feet of empty floor, and someone was plunking a guitar or strumming a fiddle, he'd grab a partner—a young girl or a middle-aged woman, no matter—and start swinging. He and Nanita were seldom partners, though, because she was more often at the piano.

This is the story of how Pat became Pat. She was named for Dr. Pat Murphey of Little Rock, who had been the neurologist for Dr. Rhine when he had his stroke in 1924. They had become fast friends. Hoping that she would be a 'lady,' the family called her Patricia, which as she grew older she objected to very much. Dr. Rhine had a custom of calling all black men 'Preacher' because most of them did preach at their churches. One day at lunch, a black man came to the back door and knocked. Dr. Rhine called out, "Come on in, Preacher." With that, Pat jumped up in her chair and announced, "See, I no Pricher, I Pat." So from that day, she has been Pat.

KATHRYN MCNEIL CONDRAY

CAMDEN, ARKANSAS

What I remember most about Dr. Rhine was his pine knots. He had piles of pine knots that he had collected over the countryside. People would ask him, "What are you going to do with all these pine knots?" He would then tell them, "I'm saving them for Nita's second husband."

Another thing was: when he was working on a jig-saw puzzle in his living room, regardless of how many were standing in line on the back porch, waiting to see him, he kept at it. Aunt Nita would come in there and tell him that someone was out there to see him. He would continue to work that jig-saw puzzle for thirty minutes, it seemed, before he would ever go to see his patient.

He was very close to my husband, Rhine Condray, who was his nephew, and whose family lived with Dr. Rhine at one time, when he was a little child. It really was like a father-son relationship because he looked up to him so and wanted his approval. When he said "Uncle" he said it in the tone others would use for "Father." It is hard to describe the closeness between them. When Rhine was in bed for all those years with rheumatism, Uncle took such good care of him, and finally did get him back on his feet. In later years, when he would go to visit them in Thornton, it was like going "home."

When Rhine died of a heart attack in January of 1964, it truly affected Dr. Rhine, and he didn't last long after that, either.

We stopped by to see him on our way to Little Rock when Rhine was having rectal problems. We said that we were to see Dr. Bill Stewart, and he replied, "You have a skilled surgeon. A slip of the knife in that area can ruin you for life." In this, as in all other things, whatever Uncle said, was it.

MAXIE STRAIT JOHNSON

WARREN, ARKANSAS

I have such pleasant memories of the Christmas visits that our family used to make to Uncle Ed and Aunt Nita's: the crackling fireplace, Aunt Nita's jam cake and all the other goodies that we only had at Christmas during those days. I also remember that our parents, mine and Dorothy's, would take us every year to a 'graveyard working' over at Prosperity Cemetery in Cleveland County. My dad was Hugh Edwin Strait, a nephew of Uncle Ed.* I remember how the people would be waiting for Dr. Rhine to make his appearance. There were so many ailments that they would want him to see about. These visits were just like work for him, and it was all free. He always brought ice, which was not common in that vicinity and had cold drinks for people to drink. I really would like to know just how many he did bring because so many people would be seen drinking a soda.

Eugenia Hearnsberger Smith told me this story when they lived in front of us at one place we lived in Warren. She had a brother called 'Red' Hearnsberger who was sick, and Uncle Ed told him to bring him a specimen of his urine. 'Red' brought him a specimen in a bottle, and when Uncle Ed finished with the urine, he rinsed the bottle out and put some medicine in the bottle for 'Red' to take. Eugenia told me that 'Red' had a difficult time swallowing that medicine. They lived at Fordyce at that time.

*His brother, John Strait, lived with his Uncle Ed when he was young and went to school in Thornton. PRB

"He was one who practiced friendship as well as medicine."

JACK GRESHAM

FORDYCE, ARKANSAS

My earliest memories of Dr. Rhine deal with the time when he was our family doctor. In fact, he was the doctor who delivered me. I can recall with fondness when he visited in our home, when members of our family were sick. His characteristic greetings were always "Good morning, Mr. Ugly. Good morning, Miss Ugly," or "You aren't really sick are you? Or is that mean stuff coming out of you?" To one encountering this type of greeting for the first time, I'm sure he appeared to be a gruff old man. But underlying that initial impression was a kindly mannered man with a twinkle in his eye and a warm, friendly handshake. Those who knew him, learned to love him and not be frightened by the seemingly gruff manner that he had when he approached you.

I can remember my mother, Nell Harris Gresham, telling about him as a young man. She knew him when he came to Thornton to begin the practice of medicine in May, 1899, which he did for a long time by horseback and by buggy. She said that he was, indeed, a great sport, but he wasn't any great shakes as a dancing partner. He couldn't keep his feet off of hers. I know that he did love to dance, however, because anything he participated in he did with a flair and with enthusiasm.

Another era of my life in which I recall many wonderful things about Dr. Rhine were the school years and his interest in the school. He was a member of the local school board for thirty-five years, and he took it upon himself to check on the school from time to time. Frequently between his medical calls, he stopped off in the mornings at the high school. Usually he came during the assembly time (we called it chapel), and he took his accustomed place by the piano on the main floor just to the right of the stage. I can still see him now with his arm propped on the top of the piano as he viewed the proceedings of the assembly. More often than not, the

243

superintendent would close the chapel by saying, "Dr. Rhine, would you like to say a word?" and Dr. Rhine always was prepared to give words of wisdom and encouragement to the pupils assembled there. I know that he for many years, provided medals for students for excellence at the close of the school year. It was always a highlight of the closing assembly to see who got the Dr. Rhine medals.

In my last years of high school and during my years of college, I came to know Dr. Rhine on a little different plane because at that time I was interested in seeking for myself a way of life outside the home, preparing myself for college and future employment. I found him to be one who was always interested in discussing with me the little problems that I had and the situations that I would come upon that I needed some counsel about. You see, I had no father. My father died when I was eight years of age, and so often I found men of his stature a comfort to me in giving me counsel. Many a time, I stopped by his office to discuss personal experiences and to seek his guidance. He was never too busy to stop and spend some time with me. I didn't have to have an appointment. I simply walked in to his office, and in a few minutes he would say, "Jack, what's on your mind?"

I remember the big hogs that Dr. Rhine raised. He had a pasture back of the house that many of us who lived in that area cut through going to school. It would cut off about a third of the distance to school, rather than going around by the Baptist Church. We would always be sure that big hog was not out of his pen before we climbed the fence to the pasture. He was huge! At the time, he seemed as big as an elephant.

He also raised fox hunting dogs. I only went fox hunting one time, with the Hearnsbergers. They ran me through the woods all one night, and I got into briars and got scratched every way a person could be scratched trying to keep up with those dogs and that fox. That was my first and last time to go fox hunting. But I always knew Dr. Rhine was an avid fox hunter, as evidenced by the fact that they call it Dr. Rhine Park.

My mother's brothers owned and operated Harris Brothers store in Thornton, and I got preferential treatment there. Sometimes, I could go behind the counter and get a handful of candy without being admonished. It was an all-purpose store. We children loved to play hide-and-seek in the casket room. They had a room that had caskets of all kinds—a lot more caskets than they have on display at Benton's. You could name anything and they sold it. They had wagons and buggies and all of the equipment for them, plows, as well as the usual dry goods, food, clothes, and shoes. The brothers were Will, Charlie and John Harris. John was also a Primitive Baptist preacher and was a great friend of Dr. Rhine.

Dr. Rhine had a real fast walk. He walked real spiritedly, just like he had to be there right away, and he'd just be whistling up a storm.

Another thing that I recall about him was a day in May, 1946, when I had just returned from a tour of duty with the Navy during World War II. They had set aside a day of recognition for Dr. Rhine in appreciation for his many years of service to the community. The local postmaster, Roy Wise, persuaded me to make the welcome address to the assembled group, which I did with much pride. Dr. Rhine Day was held on the school grounds—the playground area. There was a platform, a stage, where the people who participated in the program sat. The attendance was excellent. I never saw so many people. People from all over the state and outside the state came back in tribute to his service to them.*

After I left Thornton and came to Fordyce, my friendship with Dr. Rhine did not end. My mother lived in Thornton, and, of course, I visited her with frequency, and on many of my visits to Thornton, I dropped by the old office and chatted with Dr. Rhine to bring him up to date on the affairs of my life. Certainly, he was one who practiced friendship as well as medicine.

The role of the medical doctor today is a far cry from that of the country doctor, which characterized the practice of Dr. Rhine. He was unacquainted with the nine to four working day, with weekends off. Had he operated under such a schedule, he would probably have lived to be a hundred, but then, he wouldn't have been Dr. Rhine. Thinking back, I can appreciate him more now for his dedication, his genuine concern for all of his patients—black or white, rich or poor. He truly was one of a kind.

(Mr. Gresham was superintendent of the Fordyce Public Schools for 28 years.) PRB

RUTH HARPER JONES

THORNTON, ARKANSAS

I was thirty-five years old, and I thought I was past going to school. I'd always wanted to go to college, but the opportunity had never come up for me to go. It came, but I didn't decide to go until I could talk to Dr. Rhine about it.

"What do you think about it? Do you think that I should go?"

"Girl, go get it."

Daddy thought that when a girl finished high school, if she finished, her only opportunity was marriage and a family. I wanted to go to college, but I couldn't. I went to college, and I graduated. Dr. Rhine lived to see that. (I had taught for two years when he died.)

Mrs. Rhine told me that the week before he died, when he had pneumonia and was in the hospital, he told her, "I've got to get up from here. I've got to go see Ruth Jones. She won't take care of herself." I had just had a hysterectomy and didn't even get to go to his funeral. Mrs. Rhine told me, "I wanted you to know that he was thinking about you, rather than

*There were people there from Louisiana, New Mexico, Alabama, Washington, D. C., Texas, Florida, Illinois, Tennessee, California, Oklahoma and New York. PRB

himself." Just before I had the hysterectomy, I had a D & C [Dilatation and Curettage] operation. They let me come home, and I ran some clothes in the washer and was hanging them out. I heard someone calling, "Ruth, Ruth!" I got in the back door, and it was Dr. Rhine. What he told me was a pretty plenty. "You get in here. You are not one of these modern day women. You get in here and go to bed until you get over this."

My son, Jimmy, thought that if his dog got hurt or sick, he could take it to Dr. Rhine, and never one time did Dr. Rhine say, "Jimmy, I'm not a vet." He doctored that dog and sent Jimmy home happy as a bug in a rug.

When Dr. Rhine would walk to the office, he would stoop down and pick up all the big rocks, and when he would come to a hole in the road, he would drop the big rocks in the hole. He would get out in his pasture and pull up thistle and weeds. "I'm doing this for exercise, but also, to get rid of it."

One time he was back in his examining room stretched out on his old chair, taking a nap. He heard someone in the outer office. They thought they were there by themselves. Oh, they were making fun of his office. "Just look at that!"

He told me, "I never did let them know I was back there."

"I would have told them."

"I didn't, because their birth wasn't even paid for. They could afford now to go off and come back and make fun of my little office, and yet my services hadn't been paid for."

Dr. Rhine really wanted honesty from people. One day I was sitting on my porch, and this man and Dr. Rhine met. Dr. Rhine told him what he thought of him right there. I heard it. In a few days, Dr. Rhine saw me and explained, "Ruth, I just want people to be honest with me. He had promised me over and over that he was going to pay me, and he hadn't done it. I told him, when the time comes when you can't pay me, come and tell me. That's what it was all about." He wanted the truth.

At the time Jimmy was born, women had babies at home. When I got sick, we didn't have a car. Herbert, my husband, walked down and told Dr. Rhine. He said, "I'll be right there." He came at ten o'clock at night and he stayed until 5:30 the next morning, when Jimmy was born. It was so personal. I felt that he was interested in me and what happened to me and to my family.

He would talk about his 'special children.' Those were the ones he had delivered. He would tell Jimmy, "You are just one of my special kids."

The love that he had from his family all through his life is one reason he had so much love to give others.

I felt free to go to him with any problem or discuss any subject other than aches and pains with him. Herbert had an afflicted sister. Before I had any children, I went to Dr. Rhine and talked to him about that. "I wouldn't want Herbert to know anything about it, but before I start a family, I want to know if it is inherited." I felt free to talk to him. "Have your family." he said. I miscarried after I had Jimmy, and he didn't encourage me to have any more. "Just enjoy the child you have."

The whole time I was carrying Jimmy, I'd tell Dr. Rhine I couldn't get around because there was a possibility I would lose him. Dr. Rhine would say, "Ruth, I know so and so who had to stay in the bed like you are, and they had twins."

"You're a great comfort to me."

I went to him and talked to him about things that you don't discuss with just anybody, and it never went out of the office. He was my friend. He really was as much a friend to me as he was a doctor. Several times he would tell me, "Ruth, I see potential in you." He had faith in me, and he encouraged me to do things that I would do. I lacked that self-confidence, and he would give it to me. He would say, "It's there. The potential is there." He saw something in me that I didn't see in myself and nobody else saw.

When I went to college, Jimmy was in high school. I didn't want to do anything that would be a detriment to my family. "Go right ahead," Dr. Rhine advised me. Every once in a while, when he would see me, he'd say, "How are you doing in school?" So many times I wondered why I was there. But I enjoyed it! I went to Henderson State Teachers College. I went to school for three and one-half years, and I only was there one fall semester. I got it in the summer, on Saturdays and Mrs. Patterson in Fordyce was teaching courses at night. In the summer, I stayed on the campus. I'd leave early Monday morning and come home about 2 o'clock Saturday. I'd cook and wash clothes, that's when we had to iron. I'd get all the clothes ironed and cook my family enough food to last 'til Thursday. I don't know how I did it, but I did and I enjoyed every minute. It was a happy time. My family didn't suffer from it. I would have to buy the groceries, too, on Saturday afternoon when I got home. I taught a Sunday School Class full-time, and every one who was absent, I would write them a card when I would get back to school Sunday afternoon. I would sit out under the pine trees on those concrete benches and get it in the mail that day. I couldn't possibly do it today. The good thing is that Dr. Rhine lived to see me finish.

DOSHIA WILSON

THORNTON, ARKANSAS

For many reasons, I'll never forget Dr. Rhine. He was our neighbor, our friend and our family doctor. He delivered two of my three daughters, Mary Nell and Pat.

I recall one winter night. Bobbie Jo waked up late in the night with a rigor and fever. Snow was everywhere. I just didn't like calling him out at night, especially with snow on the ground. I did call him to ask if giving her aspirin and wrapping her up good wasn't about all I could do for her for the time being. He said it was. I turned the light out and sat down by the fire, hoping she would soon get better and go to sleep. In a few minutes, Dr. Rhine's feet hit my front porch. He had walked through the snow. He said, "When I talked to you, I wasn't good awake. Then I got to thinking that sounded mighty like pneumonia to me." There won't be any more Dr. Rhines. We also loved Mrs. Rhine and miss both of them.

One day a friend and I went down to a cafe for lunch. I ate coconut pie, one of the no-no's in summer, so I learned. That afternoon, about the time I was starting supper, I began to feel sick. I'd feel better, and here it would come again. It was pretty thick, and I realized that I had something bad. I said to one of my children to run tell Reba, my friend, and to bring Dr. Rhine. They came quick. I was about gone. He gave me a shot. He came back that night and came the next morning without being called. He really looked after his patients, if he though they were *really* sick.

Late in the afternoon, when everybody else had gone home to rest, a few people would come to his office, and call him back to the office. Sometimes, he would walk over there. Along the way, you could see him bending over, picking up something. It was rocks. He would drop them in the pot holes.

His land joined our land right behind my house. Lots of late afternoons, he would be out there along the fencerow picking up something. I learned it was ragweed and goldenrod that he was pulling up. He said that it caused hay fever. It wasn't unusual to see him stop his car along the streets and pull up a bunch of goldenrod or ragweed.

SCOTT WASSON

PINE BLUFF, ARKANSAS

My dad, who was also Scott Wasson, was a drug salesman for Lederle Pharmaceutical Company. On one of his trips to Thornton to call on Dr. Rhine, he found the office full of patients, but the doctor wasn't around. Upon inquiring as to the whereabouts of the doctor, someone remarked that they thought he might be down the street. Dad went out in search of the doctor and found him several blocks away—down in a ditch cutting down the goldenrod, which was in full flower. Astonished at this unusual activity with the office full of sick folks, he asked the doctor why he was engaged in this task. The doctor replied, "I have had so many people coming in with hay fever that I thought it would be good to get rid of the source. You know that I believe in preventive medicine, too." With that, Dad got out of his car and began pulling up weeds to help Dr. Rhine eliminate the irritant.

FORDYCE, ARKANSAS

Dr. Rhine was one of the most influential people in my life in that the things I thought he stood for, I wanted to, too. Such as honesty, integrity, getting an education, making something of your life (I always felt that he was proud that my sister and I went to college), strong family ties, and mostly, I felt like he loved me and cared about me. My daddy, Henry Brandon, Jr., was his first white patient when he started practicing medicine at Thornton. He was about two years old. The first patient was a black baby.

He was our family doctor all through those years, delivering my sister and me. When he was eighty-four years old, I was expecting my first baby, and I wanted him to deliver it. I talked with him about it. Childbirth was more or less natural, and Dr. Rhine knew how to deliver babies. He took real good care of me, gave me vitamins, checked my urine, and had me x-rayed before the delivery to see the size of my pelvis. I had a small pelvis and the baby was going to be large, so I had another x-ray just before delivery. He made arrangements with Dr. Harry Atkinson to help him should he need him or if the weather was bad. It was February. Dr. Harry did come. Lisa was born in an ice storm, and Dr. Rhine came on the ice to the hospital, and he and Dr. Harry delivered Lisa. He was caring for me with my second baby in 1962 when he was eighty-six. The same arrangement was made that time, and she was also born in a snow storm, so he didn't come to the hospital that night. Dr. Harry did the delivery. My doctor bill for the care beforehand and the delivery for Lisa was $35.00. If I had to have any medicine, that was extra, but it wasn't but a dollar or two.

After Lisa was born, I felt like we had so underpaid him. I went to him and offered to pay him more, and he didn't want to take it.

"Dr. Rhine, I can afford to pay you more, and I want to."

"No, I believe in letting the other fellow live, too." Money didn't mean that much to him. The majority of the people that he cared for could not afford high doctor fees, but the ones who could pay more, he didn't want them to pay more.

He took care of them as little children, too. We lived with O. D.'s grandmother, Mrs. Oliver Anthony. O. D. promised Mr. Oliver that he would live with her as long as she lived. O. D.'s mother was there most of the time, too. Both worried about the children and would try to tell me how to raise them and what to do. The baby just loved carrots and would eat a lot. They thought she would get yellow jaundice if she ate carrots.

Dr. Rhine was someone I could confide in. I asked him. "Will carrots hurt my baby?"

"It's your baby, and you do what you think is best for her. If you do everything that people tell you to, you'll kill your baby." He helped me through those times.

Some people thought Dr. Rhine was a little gruff. I guess his voice was deep and loud. But even as a little girl, we talked about things together, and I never felt like he talked harsh to me.

O.D. went to him one time for a cold, and Dr. Rhine gave him a handful of pills for fifty cents. O. D. tried to pay him more. He said, "If I had wanted more, I'd have asked for it."

He was special to our family. When I would come home from college, on weekends, I would go see my grandfather Brandon in Thornton, and I would go by his office and see him. I knew that he wanted to see me.

O.D. kinda holds it against him that he named him Oliver Daniel because he thought it was a bit of a long name. He was named for his two grandfathers. Dr. Rhine had an influence on O. D.'s life, too, and his Grandfather Anthony really did, and to be his namesake is fine. There again, he knew the family so well and choose the grandfathers' names for him.

FLORIDA CAYCE WISHARD

LITTLE ROCK, ARKANSAS

I can remember as a young girl, Dr. Rhine would call Mother and ask her if she could help with deliveries. I wish I knew how she got started helping him, because we didn't move to Thornton until 1929. It was about that winter that I had pneumonia and some new serum had been introduced which he wanted to give me. I don't know how long I had been sick, but I remember 'coming to' as he was giving me an injection in the chest above one breast. That was the second or third injection that I had. I began to get better, and, of course, everyone was so thankful that he knew about the serum. That was *years* before any antibiotics were on the market.

When I began to get interested in medical technology, Dr. Rhine talked to me about the profession and loaned me several of his books. I enjoyed learning about different tests, even though I didn't understand a lot of the chemistry and theory involved at the time.

A few times after I was in medical school and at home, he would discuss how things were when he went to school. My! what a difference then, and these students now would hardly believe the inconvenience, hardships and difficulties the medical students had when he attended school.

One time he told about having to go to the basement to get his 'stiff' (the cadaver he dissected), snow was about a foot thick, and the only way to the second floor laboratory was via outside stairs. He put his stiff over his shoulder and trudged up the stairs. After the session, he had to reload and go back down to the basement.

I can remember a few of the deliveries Mother helped him with. One family had already had five or six children, and some remark was made about money. He said he had delivered every one of them and had not been paid for even the first. When one of the Hodnett (Howell and Sue) boys were born, he was real concerned, because the baby was jaundiced. He made several extra trips to observe and check the baby until he was certain it was going to clear up.

The only time he criticized negatively was when they delivered a baby for 'Nub' Ethridge. The filth and dirt was so bad, they used several bottles of alcohol trying to clean a little. That is the only time I remember Mother coming in and leaving her shoes outside and taking a bath immediately.

When the last Southall baby was born, Dr. Rhine was out on another call and this was about ten at night. My telephone rang, and Mr. Southall was really upset. Dr. Rhine was out, and he had called a nurse who told him to get Mrs. Southall in the car and take her to the hospital. He told me the baby was partly here, and he needed help now. Naturally, not being a nurse, I wondered what I would do. I went, and just as I went in, the baby arrived. All the other children had gone to a ball game. I had Mr. Southall get me some string from a flour sack and scissors. I managed to get the baby sorta cleaned up before Dr. Rhine came. I told him that Mrs. Southall had not delivered the afterbirth. He gave her some medicine and proceeded to deliver the placenta. This was during the time his right hand was so swollen, and I know it was painful. He wrapped the cord around this sore hand and pulled, and the placenta released and came out. He took a large pan I had in there, cupped his hands together, and dipped blood from the bed into the pan. In just a few minutes the flow of blood stopped. We changed her bed, and she rested.

I worked in Camden before working at the hospital in Fordyce. Especially when I was at Fordyce, he would come by early in the morning and take me out in the country—way in the backwoods—and I would draw blood for laboratory tests on some patients. He would do this for them rather than have them come in themselves. He could easily have lost me out in the woods. He knew every little trail though. Some of the people didn't have telephones, so he would make a trip back out to give them the report and give diet directions. He had several diabetic patients at one time.

Dr. Rhine did support all the churches in Thornton. I know deep down he must have been very religious. Every time they had an 'association' or several days of meetings when a crowd was expected, he would bring syrup, potatoes, butter or anything else that could be used. I'm sure he had been paid in produce. He was sharing and helping.

All high school seniors looked forward to being entertained with a dinner in the Rhine home before graduation. That was really a highlight and one everyone remembers.

Mrs. Rhine was certainly a devoted companion and helped him in many ways. When my children were in school in Thornton, she taught music. I know she gave many hours of her time, and many children would have known no music, had it not been for her. She also taught private lessons which both of mine took. They both loved her dearly and would do anything for her.

Everybody Has A Story

KELSEY CAPLINGER, JR.

FORDYCE, ARKANSAS

We had always used the doctors in Fordyce, but during the war [World War II] my wife, Ethel, got really sick, and there was not any doctor around. I called Mrs. Rhine in Thornton, and she said that Dr. Rhine was on his way to Fordyce. She would contact him and have him stop by. When he knocked on the door, my sons, Kelsey, who was six and Tommy Ray, who was four, went to let him in. He was always so great with children. He said, "Who's boss at this house?" One of them answered, "Mama is, and she's right back here." Dr. Rhine examined her very calmly and got out some medicine to give her.

I asked, "Won't she need a prescription?"

"What for?" You know, he always had his medicines with him in his car.

He took care of her and straightened her out, coming several times a day at first and then once each day for a couple of weeks. I gave him ten dollars on my bill, and he said that was okay. I was working for my Dad at Caplinger's Home Shoe and Clothing Company for $200.00 a month. Later on I gave Dr. Rhine another ten dollar bill and asked him how much more I owed him. He answered, "I'll have to ask my bookkeeper." The next month, I ran into him at the bank. He was making a deposit, and he had a pile of folded up money on the counter. (He folded each bill a certain way in order to help him remember who paid him.) I gave him another ten dollar bill, and he handed me five dollars back, saying, "My bookkeeper says that's all you owe me." Can you believe $25.00 for at least fifteen or twenty visits?

For years, he had bought clothes at our store. He came in one day (this was several years later) with his old hat sittin' crossways, as usual, on his head, with a hole in the top of the crease where he pinched it when he took it

252

off. I said to him, "Doctor, I have a hat back here just about your size."

"I've been thinking about getting a new one."

He tried it on and as he reached into his pocket for some money, I said, "*My* bookkeeper told me that hat was already paid for."

So, for the rest of his life, whenever I could catch him, and he needed one, I would give him a new hat.

JOE COLVERT

LITTLE ROCK, ARKANSAS

When I was a boy, I had a little black dog whose name was 'Nigger.' He loved to chase rabbits. Once in the summertime while he was chasing rabbits, he ran into a thorn bush and run a thorn down in the corner of his eye. I was a little ole dirty barefooted kid in the country, and I had nothing to treat that dog with. I was worried to death about him. I was down at my uncle's house. He was a bachelor, and he kept track of every car that went by, and he was talking about Dr. Rhine's car just gone by. (Everybody knew Dr. Rhine's car.) I didn't know if he was going to come by his house going home or go another way, so I took Nigger and went up to the church house. The road forked there. I sat there and waited and in a little while I saw Dr. Rhine's car coming. I got up and flagged him down. I told Dr. Rhine, "My dog has a thorn in his eye, and I want you to do something for him." He got out of the car, and got his little satchel, went over in the churchyard and sat down under a tree. He put that dog's head in his lap and took some tweezers and pulled that thorn out. He put some medicine on it, and I asked him if I owed him anything. He said, "Not a thing." I never have forgotten that. I was about fourteen years old, and that black dog, 'Nigger,' was the only friend I had.

GEORGIE GRAY

FORDYCE, ARKANSAS

I worked as a clerk for Arkansas Louisiana Gas Company from 1958 to 1965. We had an elderly, infirm black woman, a customer, who lived alone. She had no family in Fordyce. She always walked to the office to pay her monthly bill. After a long absence, she came back and told us that she had been very ill, and she looked it! She said that 'Dr. Rhines' had taken care of her. After he had prescribed her medicine, he found out that she had no one to see that she took it, nor did she have a clock to be able to tell that it was time for her medicine. Dr. Rhine went to her neighbor's houses and asked them to look in on her regularly. He then went to town and bought her an alarm clock. He wrote down the times that she was to take the medicine on a piece of paper for her, telling her how to mark off each time she took a dose of medicine, and how to set the alarm for the next dose.

JAMES LYNN

FORDYCE, ARKANSAS

When I was a senior in high school, I got injured playing basketball. They carried me to a doctor here in Fordyce. He said that it was pretty bad. That I had a fifty-fifty chance of recovering. That upset my mother. I was too young to worry about it. To make sure that everything would be all right, she called in Dr. Rhine. He came to our house to check me over. He didn't use any instrument, stethoscope or anything. He used his natural ear. He prescribed some medicine, and I'm still walking around today. He came by to see me twice a day, morning and afternoon for about two weeks, just to make sure that I was all right. The injury was from the chest bone being knocked over on my heart muscle. My mother thought he was everything, and whatever he said, went.

MABLE DEDMAN BUTT

CAMDEN, ARKANSAS

My father was Reverend J. L. Dedman, and he was the pastor of the Methodist church in Thornton in 1917.

I was born in Thornton, and Dr. Rhine delivered me. I have an empty bottle of his, with powdered medicine still clinging to it. It hasn't ever been washed. It's a pretty bottle with a handsome glass stopper. Mrs. Rhine's sister, Mrs. George Moseley, procured this for me when my mother told her I would love to have a medicine bottle of Dr. Rhine's.

Eight or ten years ago, passing through Thornton, my mother, younger daughter, Mary, and I tried to find the old Methodist Church and the parsonage. Since fifty years had passed, mother was unsure about the two buildings. About a year ago, Mary and I drove through Dr. Rhine Park. We were sad to see it had been neglected.

I never drive through Thornton that I don't think of Dr. Rhine.

VIRGINIA MCGUFFEY CLEMONS

THORNTON, ARKANSAS

My first husband was John Stowe. When he was a boy, his father, not feeling too well, sent him over to Dr. Rhine's office with the instructions for Dr. Rhine to send him the meanest, nastiest tasting medicine that he could fix up for him, which the doctor proceeded to do. Two or three days went by, and Dad Stowe was not feeling any better. He walked over to the doctor's office.

"Dr. Rhine, that medicine you sent me is not doing me one bit of good."

"It wasn't supposed to. That's what you asked for. You sent John over here for the nastiest, meanest tasting medicine I could fix, and that's what I sent you. Now, I don't come over there and tell you how to shoe horses. Don't you send over here and tell me how to make up medicine." Then he proceeded to examine him and gave him the correct medicine.

John and I came from California in 1949 on a visit to Thornton. Naturally, we wanted to see everyone that we could, including Dr. Rhine. Our daughter was nine years old at that time, and she had heard about Dr. Rhine all of her life, but never having been to Arkansas, she had never seen him. We went down to the Rhine family home to see Dr. and Mrs. Rhine. Our daughter, being nine years old and rambunctious, darted in the front door and said "hello" to everybody as Dr. Rhine was coming in the back door. She headed on back, saw him, and his favorite greeting to all girls was, "Hello there, Miss Ugly." We had neglected to tell her that. She was always considered to be a beautiful child. She was taken aback by that greeting. She stood there and said, "Who are you? I thought you would be Dr. Rhine." We had to explain to her that that was a compliment to be called 'Miss Ugly.' We laugh about it to this day.

EDITH FEASTER MAY

ELLISVILLE, ARKANSAS

On the night of the 6th of February, 1923, William David May decided it was time to be born, although the ground was covered with ice and snow. The ice had formed from copious rains freezing on the ground, then about two-and-a-half to three inches of snow falling on the ice, making a treacherous surface to walk on, let alone drive a car over.

It was about nine o'clock p.m. when Pete and Edie, David's parents, got the notification of David's intended arrival.

The question of a doctor to call: arrangements had been made with Dr. Fowler, the only doctor who could 'born' a May baby, *but* Dr. Fowler lived across Moro Creek. And Moro Creek was in flood after a week of heavy rains, the sloughs all full from hill to hill, and now a frozen slush.

So, David's granddad, Will May, got on the old crank telephone to Thornton to Dr. T. E. Rhine. The good doctor was taken completely by surprise, and asked, "Will, why are you calling me when I have had no previous contact on the case? And you have never used me before?" But granddad insisted, and said, "Well, I'm using you now. You come, we need a doctor." The doctor brought up the subject of the frozen, slick roads, but finally said, "I'll start—maybe I can make it."

Well, David wasn't in too big a hurry, and the dear doctor made it in time. But he had to stop every few miles and take an ax to chop the balls of ice and snow off his tires.

After that, Dr. T. E. Rhine was the May family doctor and saw Will through his last illness.

L O I S   S P E E R   N A N C E

HOPEVILLE, ARKANSAS

It was the nineteen twenties and there was a baby boom. Oliver, my husband, and I were born with Dr. Rhine delivering us. We carried all our childhood, and later adult, ailments to Dr. Rhine and took many a bottle of his *bad* medicine. Then came our years for child bearing and we weren't having much luck, for I was an habitual aborter. Then came the nineteen fifties—the men were home from the war—and there was another baby boom. But of course, there was always a boom for Dr. Rhine, because he never failed to answer a call, with no discrimination, whatever. After nine months confined to bed, we finally had Beth born to us.

Dr. Rhine knew we wanted a son, too, so he watched us closely as I carried a normal pregnancy. Then came time for John to be born, but Dr. Rhine was in the hospital, sick and worn out. Dr. Rhine had always maintained a 'gruff' attitude toward people, but it was really just a cover-up for a very big and tender heart. We will never forget his tears because he couldn't deliver John. Dr. Harry Atkinson, a dear friend of Dr. Rhine's, tried to use the tactics of gruffness to cause Dr. Rhine to control himself, but I think Dr. Rhine saw right through it.

Seven months later, we almost lost John. We called Dr. Rhine. He administered something that caused a very well known pediatrician to remark about the knowledge and wisdom of Dr. Rhine. You see, Dr. Rhine kept up with the latest in medicine and practice. How and when he did with his busy life remains a mystery. Small wonder that we all wept when he passed away.

ROBERT   CLIFFORD   BIGGERS

NEW BRAUNFELS, TEXAS

Dr. Rhine, anytime he would make a trip down the Hampton highway, (we lived about ten miles south of Thornton toward Hampton) would stop at our house. We had a well that was high in sulphur. He would stop and ask my mother to draw him a drink of water from that well. He would drink one or two big peanut butter glasses of this sulphur water for health purposes.

He was our family doctor, and we trusted him in all respects. I came from New Braunfels to Thornton for Dr. Rhine Day. We drove 500 miles to be here. He delivered my younger brothers and sisters. He was one of the greatest men I ever knew.

My mother held our family together. We were the poorest people in nine counties, because we lost our father, and our home burned twice. I was the oldest of five children, thirteen years old when our father died, during the Depression.

Dr. Rhine didn't only practice medicine; he practiced psychology and love. But he would come into the room, and you were sick enough to die, and do you know the first thing he would start doing? Fussin' at you! He would make you so mad, you wanted to get up and fight before he would even start to examine you. But everybody knew him and loved him. Unbelievable!

BILL   ROTHWELL

CHAMBERSVILLE, ARKANSAS

My wife and I named our baby after Dr. T. E. Rhine—Thomas Edwin Rothwell. They have the same initials. He delivered him at the Dallas County Hospital. He delivered our first two sons at our home. We thought so much of Doc, that's why we named him for him. He was so pleased, he gave him a blowing horn as a gift. Before my house burned, he had given my oldest two sons and me a horn, but they all burned up. He come right around and gave us all another horn.

FLOSSIE   MCPHAIL   OLIPHANT

LITTLE ROCK, ARKANSAS

I remember particularly, after I was grown and lived here in Little Rock, that Virginia stayed at our house a great deal. I went home with her one weekend to Thornton. We were having lunch and right at noon Dr.

Rhine came in, like he always did, right at meal time. He sat down and hadn't eaten very long and the phone rang. He answered the phone, and in his gruff voice, he sounded like he didn't have time to fool with anyone. He'd come to the office when he got ready; there probably wasn't anything wrong with them. He called everyone, all women, young and old alike, "Miss Ugly." I was sitting there thinking if I called a doctor and he answered the phone like that, what would I do. All the time he was finishing eating, grabbing his hat and out the door, to take care of his patient.

During the night, there was a "Hello, hello!" at the back door. Dr. Rhine would call out, "Who's there?", go to the door and take the patient to the bathroom, to be doctored on for whatever was wrong.

When I was a little girl and the Rhine family would come to visit us sometimes in Kingsland, I remember Nanita saying that she never knew if they would get to come or not. If a call came before they got off, they couldn't come. So she would always have a wet washcloth ready and clean the children in the car, after they were on their way.

When I was in college, Dr. Rhine gave me some medicine—an envelope full of green pills. Another time they would be pink or white. Those pills got me through college. They would cure anything. I don't know what they were called.

There were certain favorite doctors in Little Rock that got gifts of honey from Dr. Rhine. One of them was Dr. Eubanks, and I can't remember the others. My mother, Allie McPhail, also got a gift of honey from him.

When we used to have the Marks Family Reunion at Poole on the Saline River, I was a little girl. It was understood by everyone, even us children, that the blessing would not be said and the lunch begun until Dr. Rhine got there.

At his funeral, I was struck by the several generations there. I particularly remember one family, there had to be at least ten people in that group, who came down to view the body. They even had a child in arms. You could tell there were three or four generations of that family that came to pay their last respects. The grandfather was in overalls. It was so touching. I can still see that scene of the entire group of people. That had to have been a lot of love.

SUE RUSSELL HILLMAN

FORDYCE, ARKANSAS

The memory of Dr. Rhine that stands out the most in my mind is that when I was a child, and we would go to the Marks Family Reunion, it would always be Dr. Rhine who would have a huge, new galvanized wash tub that would have a big chunk of ice in it, and he would make lemonade, a tub full of lemonade for all of us to enjoy.

DORIS ATTWOOD WALKER

RISON, ARKANSAS

Once, at the Marks Family Reunion, I remember that he had the only car, and he would take all of the children riding up the road, but Charlie Marks sat in the front seat with him, and Charlie would throw his tie out so the wind would blow it. Another time, he brought a stalk of bananas for the children. He brought something every time for the children. I hated to grow up. He loved it, or put a lot into it, not to have loved it.

WILLIE FREY

FORDYCE, ARKANSAS

He was the most wonderful when he was handing out peppermint candy to the children at the Marks Reunion, and they looked forward to it. He first took care of my son, Evan. He would come to see him [almost to New Edinburg, about twelve miles], and when my husband, Bruce Frey, was sick, he came. My brother-in-law, Marks Frey, he did everything he could to help him. He had rheumatism since he was twenty years old, paralyzed in a sitting position. He lived to be sixty. On through the years, Dr. Rhine and Nanita were my greatest friends. I just loved them.

RUTH TALBOT BRANDON

FORDYCE, ARKANSAS

My husband, Henry Brandon, Jr. was Dr. Rhine's first white patient when he came to Thornton. He was just a baby and he had the colic. Dr. Rhine cured him.

When I was a girl, he used to come by our house on the Hampton road going on calls down below us, and we would get in the car and go with him. We would stay in the car or around the car while he went in to see the patient. We always had to ride in the back seat with a dog, but it was a thrill to ride in a car. We enjoyed it. It had a little rumble seat that we sat in. It was a little Ford.

THORNTON, ARKANSAS

I guess he brought me into the world. I was born in 1904. I was born between here and Little Bay, beside the railroad. I remember when he would go down to see peoples on an old horse. Then he got a buggy, then a car. He hadn't married when I first knowed him. He kept us all livin'. My parents were Will Braswell and Armetta. My brother was Ed, and he died in '57. Dr. Rhines was doctoring on him. His heart was bad. He had done overstrained it. He told me, "Sometime, some night, he might slip away from ya", and he did. I thought he was resting, but he was dead. I ran up to get Dr. Rhines, (we just lived down the road a bit). "Dr. Rhines, Dr. Rhines, come down and see Ed." He said, "I'll be there as soon as I get a little breakfast." He come in a while, and said, "I told you."

He was so good to doctor on the people. He was the cause of old people getting things, groceries and things. My mother was a widow woman, and she didn't have but one boy, and he couldn't do much work, so he helped her out. He doctored on her free and Ed, too. We didn't have anything, and he took care of us free.

My health is purty good except for—they call it arth-a-ri-tis. Folks used to call it ole rheumatism, but they all got it named now—arth-a-ri-tis.

M A R I E C A S H

FORDYCE, ARKANSAS

My father was Dave Cash, a native of Cleveland County. He was Sheriff of Cleveland County for two terms and then was County Judge for two terms. He moved to Fordyce in 1942, and that was when Dr. Rhine became his doctor. He discovered that my father had a heart condition, so he would frequently drop by to see about him when he would be making other calls in Fordyce, even though he had not been called to come. My father had more faith in him than in any other doctor. My brother took him to Little Rock to see some doctors, but they said he did not have any heart problems. Dr. Rhine looked after him until he died—of heart disease. He meant a lot to my father.

EARNESTENE BRASWELL

THORNTON, ARKANSAS

Yes, you call Dr. Rhine anytime, he was there. He would come to my house when my daughter was taking diptheria. He rode day and night for her. He come every day, sometimes twice a day. Sometimes he'd come in the morning before seven o'clock. He'd come in the house. She'd say, "Mama, I don't want him to look at my mouth." He come for about fifteen days, and she got all right when her fever got clear. He was so nice. He really rode day and night. She was about three years old then. She is sixty-two years old now. He delivered every child I had, but one, at home. I had seven. The first one Dr. Black delivered. Every one at home. Out on the road, anywhere he at, he would stop. You call him, he'd see about you. He'd take care of you.

FRANCES SPEAR WILLIAMS

BEARDEN, ARKANSAS

When my son was seven, he had strep throat. We lived in Hopeville, and Dr. Rhine came three or four times to see him. I was so glad for him to come, and I told him, "Dr. Rhine, I appreciate your coming very much." He looked at me and said, "You didn't expect me not to come, did you?"

ALMIRA SHOOK WATSON

THORNTON, ARKANSAS

When Aaron Brandon was a little boy, his mother was in the hospital, and he was staying with us. We all had the flu, and his nose bled and bled, and we couldn't get it to stop. He was just about to bleed to death, we thought, because it just kept on. So finally, we called Dr. Rhine. He had to give him a shot, and it was in the rear end—and I'm telling you, Aaron come up from there fighting. We thought he was about dead. "Don't do that. I'll kill you!"

It like to have tickled Dr. Rhine to death. He laughed.

Mama got on to Aaron. "Don't say such a thing as that to Dr. Rhine."

"Well, that hurt."

I heard Dr. Rhine tell one time about a very young black girl who was having a baby. They couldn't get her to stay in the bed, and she would run round and around the house. Her mother would run and try to get her back, but she would run around just hollering. Finally, Dr. Rhine just wore his patience out, and he walked to the door and picked up a piece of wood and as she came by, he told her, "You see this? You get in that bed, and you stay there or I'm going to use this on you." She got in the bed and had that baby.

RHINE CONDRAY, JR.

CAMDEN, ARKANSAS

When I was a boy, I remember him telling me about one guy who fell off the top of the railroad station. He busted his scull wide open to the brains. Dr. Rhine took grass out from around his scull and inside his scull and sewed him up. He told the guy that he might not live—but he lived.

Another guy that was working at the sawmill, cut some fingers off. After Dr. Rhine fixed him up, the guy said, "I gotta go back to work. I might lose my job."

TOMMY NEVELS

THORNTON, ARKANSAS

I have lived next door to Dr. Rhine's home place the past seven years. Stories that people still talk about are his pine pile, the Scott's daughter going across the road and Dr. Rhine giving her candy, people going to take piano lessons from Mrs. Rhine, a little bit of everything. It is kinda interesting to sit back and listen to what people tell. His picture is hanging in the hospital up in Fordyce, and I have seen a picture of him on some doctor's desk in Fordyce, or maybe it was Little Rock. Every once in a while, someone comes up and says something about Dr. Rhine, and because I live next to where he lived, I listen. I can remember Mrs. Rhine, just barely, out there walking on the concrete driveway.

"In the arena of dealing with people, I have no doubt but that Dr. Rhine taught me more in a short time than any other person, any formal course I have taken, plus all the reading I have done."

CLYDE T. ROSS

MONTICELLO, ARKANSAS

While I was at Thornton, from 1936 to 1941, Dr. Rhine was aware that I was young, inexperienced and my interests were toward schoolwork and learning to deal with people rather than medicine. Consequently, most of our discussions were in the area of education, geared toward dealing with people and community problems, at which I still consider him to have been a past master.

When Dr. Rhine had something he wanted to talk with me about, he would call late in the afternoon, asking what I was doing that night. Knowing there wasn't anything much to do in Thornton, and before I had time to answer, he would say, "I'll be by in a few minutes," and would drive by, (at first in an old green Chevy), would move from under the wheel, and tell me where to go. On most of these trips, he would appear to be asleep, but once in a while he would whistle "Silver Threads Among The Gold." I believe he never realized he was whistling. Not even once do I remember discussing any problems on the way to see a patient. On the way home, however, and after getting back, we usually had a very thoughtful talk on some specific problem.

On one such occasion, he seemed in a hurry, telling me to drive as fast as I felt was safe. Upon arriving at the home, he was out of the car by the time it stopped and went into the house at a rapid pace. I walked up to the porch. At about this time, the lady of the house started to scream and cry, saying over and over again, "Why did the Good Lord take my baby?" As they came out on the porch, Dr. Rhine turned to her and said, "Lady, the Good Lord did not take your baby. She died of diptheria, and if you had had her vaccinated she would be alive." Then turning to me, he said, "Come on,

263

Ross. We are going home."

Dr. Rhine had an abiding faith in the medical profession. At times, he would express his thoughts that some day young, bright doctors would develop simple to complex sure-fire tests of the blood, urine, fecal material, etc. to isolate and identify the germs causing a given illness. Then they would develop medicine to cure, or better yet, a vaccine to stamp out that particular disease. He usually ended saying, in effect, "I wish I had the time, money and equipment to study just one disease and come up with medication to destroy the germs, or better still, something to establish body immunity." Then he would grin and say, "You know, germs are just like any other living thing. They can be destroyed."

In the arena of dealing with people, I have no doubt but that Dr. Rhine taught me more in a short time than any other person, any formal course I have taken, plus all the reading I have done.

He would advise that when a parent, parents, or a group came in and were quiet, respectful, and wanted answers, you had better have good answers, show reasons for what you did, and take the lead in the discussion. However, if a parent or parents came in fussing, storming, and using uncalled-for language, just sit tight, listen, and let them have their say without trying to explain anything for (I think I can quote), "They are giving vent to their frustrations, showing inability to cope with their child or children, and just have to blame somebody for their failures. You have been elected the 'goat.' Keep cool and hold your temper, for they are very much in need of understanding and kindness."

Not long after this discussion, an incident came up wherein I decided to see if it would work. As I drove up to the school early one morning, a gentleman yanked open the car door and lambasted me in a lusty voice from 'here to yon.' After he got that out of his system, he asked, maybe stated, "You whopped my boy yesterday, didn't you?"

My reply was, "I am not sure who you are, but I did spank a couple of boys yesterday."

He shot back, "You get out of that car for I am gonna whip your butt." (Not the exact word.)

As I sat there, all 130 pounds of me, looking at a husky well-built man that I guessed to be around six feet tall and weighing 180 to 200 pounds, I grinned at him and remarked, "Well sir, you certainly look big enough to do what you say you are going to do."

He backed away from the car saying, "Aw, get out, and we will talk this over."

I've had many such encounters with different overtones since, and the technique most usually works.

What brought up the above counsel was: I had a 'rhubarb' with a high school senior. Both of us lost our tempers, and all I could think of was to rough him up a bit before he slaughtered me, which I proceeded to try to do. Afterwards, Dr. Rhine supported me publicly and in school board meetings. However, privately (person to person) he dubbed me, "Our fighting superintendent: one who prefers to get his experience the hard way rather than seeking advice and counsel. You will learn, but it may cost you some self-respect."

Another incident that I still appreciate, developed about as follows: We were in the last week of school when I was umpire for a soft ball game. Somehow the bat got away from the batter and struck 'Shinney' Green in the forehead. Dr. Rhine put two or three stitches to close the gap. After 'Shinney' left the office, Dr. Rhine turned to me with a stern face and said, "I guess you had better lock up the balls and bats for the rest of the week before some child gets killed."

I thought about that for a few seconds, and replied, "I totally disagree. I'd rather take the chance of someone getting hurt than have to discipline no telling how many fights or near fights if the students do not have something to occupy their time during recess and noon."

Dr. Rhine looked at me with a grin, saying, "I just wanted to find out if I had taught you to stand up to any and everyone when you thought you were right. I'll give you a passing grade for this term. Maybe, a low 'C', but you passed."

Also, since there was not much to do around Thornton and young folk had little or no money, I agreed to open the gym on Sunday afternoons about one p.m. and close at four p.m. provided they (the young people) would help keep the gym clean and help limit participants to students only. Things went along nicely until one Sunday morning, I was not only surprised, but very ruffled, when the Methodist minister really let the hammer down on me. "Remember the Sabbath and Keep it Holy" was his theme—that Ross was leading the young folk to Hell and Damnation by his Sunday afternoon unholy activities.

I was furious, as you might guess.

Anyway, I called Dr. Rhine late that afternoon, and he invited me over for a chat.

I almost got angry with him for he grinned and chuckled as I reviewed what had been said, and how I felt about it. After I had growled and probably snorted, too, Dr. Rhine asked if I wanted his advice. "Of course", I said. That was what I was there for.

He stunned me at first by saying, "Lock the confounded gym up next Sunday afternoon, but be sure the boys know tomorrow and the reason why."

I'll never forget how amused he was when I started objecting. He turned his head sideways to me looking out through his eyebrows, so to speak. He said—this may not be an exact quote—"Now, young fellow, hold your horses. You lock up the gym next Sunday, and I will bet you a good fox hound, the mothers will have you to open it the next Sunday, and the preacher will never say another word."

It worked out exactly as he predicted it would. I always had a feeling that he had something to do with the community reaction.

Once, when politics were rather hot, it was mentioned that I should take part, but for some reason, I felt I should not. Privately I told Dr. Rhine my reasons. After thinking it over, he came up with a jewel of an idea, asking how long it had been since I had visited with Mother and Dad. As I recall, it had been about a year. His reply will always stick in my mind. "Your Mother and Dad deserve better than that from you. Don't you think this would be a good time to visit with them?"

That I did, and never heard another word about politics.

An official of the Fordyce Lumber Company (also a member of the Thornton School Board) approached me, saying the lumber company had been trying to purchase some timber from Dr. Rhine without success, and if I could influence him to sell, I'd get a commission.

The next time Dr. Rhine and I were together, I told him exactly what had been said. He looked at me for a few seconds and in substance, replied, "You tell Mr. So and So that purchase is not likely to be made, for that is part of my insurance that my daughters will get as good an education as I can provide or that they will take, and you can tell him not to bother himself about my timber any more."

Several years later, after one, maybe both of my children had been born, I stopped by for a short visit. As I was about to leave, with a grin he asked, "Do you own any virgin timberland?" His way of counseling—provide for your family.

Just a wee bit on fox hunting. I only went once.

We never wasted time on discussing the weather or other trivial matters, but fox hunting stories were as big and important as a blast from a volcano. When he got a twinkle in his eyes and started on a fox hunt story, you just might as well relax and enjoy the colorful description, for you were going to listen whether you liked it or not. After I had married, he offered to pick out and give me a fox hound puppy for, as he put it, "A man has not become a real man until he owns a good fox hound." I declined the offer.

Among his first counseling sessions with me, he commented that the Thornton School Board had a policy to employ only unmarried ladies as teachers, adding, he didn't know why and possibly would have to change the policy sooner or later. "At any rate, the ladies are all single—you are single. Now, when you get the urge to go courting, be sure to take your itch as far away as Hampton, maybe Camden, and better still, go to El Dorado."

Dr. Rhine had a high regard for education and the people who went into the public schools. Tangible evidence of this was that, in so far as I ever knew, he never charged a teacher for an office visit when he or she was ill.

In the years after I left Thornton, I would stop by as often as I could for short visits. I never knew if he had pressing obligations or not, for he was relaxed and took a keen interest in what I was doing, plugged for continuing education, and was most interested in reports on the family.

Dr. Rhine, from the outside, was a rugged, gruff, rustic individual, but in reality, he was a very sensitive person who took a decided personal interest in the people around him. I think he was incapable of being critical without proven reasons. I doubt if he ever indulged in wishful thinking, but took life and conditions as they really were without trying to change the world—only trying to give leadership in the community where he lived. He was, in my estimation, a *most remarkable man.*

ROBERT OLIPHANT

LITTLE ROCK, ARKANSAS

I taught junior high school science in Thornton around 1952 or 1953. He gave all teachers free service. I went down there to his office, sat in that old dentist chair. There was medicine all over the floor. He poured some out. It was for an upset stomach. It was that pink medicine.

MARVIN KAUFFMAN

SHERIDAN, ARKANSAS

I first learned of Dr. Rhine in 1932, when he attended a patient in Dallas County about a mile from where I grew up, which was about five miles east of Princeton. He took over the patient that Dr. Harry Atkinson, Sr. left in his care just two days before Dr. Atkinson's death. Dr. Rhine was my mother's doctor in her last years.

My own personal association with the fabled doctor started in 1938. I had made application for a teaching position at Thornton High School upon my graduation from the University of Arkansas at Monticello (then Arkansas A. & M. College). I received the position as mathematics teacher of grades seven through twelve and given the additional assignment of coach and high school principal.

Before leaving to begin the school year at Thornton High School, I ran into Waymon McDaniel. 'Mac,' as we knew him in those days, wanted to give me a little advice, since he grew up in that area and knew Dr. Rhine well. "Now Marvin," Mac said, "let me give you some advice. You are going into an area and school system where Dr. Rhine is well respected and the most influential person in the county. First thing you should do is get acquainted with him and be very sure you never do anything that would displease him. He isn't on the school board now, but Thornton High School is something special to him, and he carries the weight when there are any decisions to be made. And don't you ever forget that."

I should have told initially that when I heard of the vacancy at Thornton, I was told that when I got there to stop and see Dr. Rhine first, that he would advise me which board member I should see in making my application. I never did see a board member. Dr. Rhine took care of my application for me, and I suppose had me selected as a teacher.

Well, everything went rather smoothly, I thought, during the school year. I remember I stayed very busy teaching five math subjects, plus business arithmetic one semester and a course in physiology, along with coaching, that required daily practice and games twice a week. Then, since I was principal, and schools in those days had no office staff, I had to make out the monthly, quarterly and annual reports to the State Board of Education. I summarize all this as a part in the criticism I was to receive at the end of the school year.

As I stated above, I thought the school year went off rather well until the last week or so when notices began coming out advising several teachers that their services would not be required the next year. In short, they were being fired. This included the superintendent. At this time, it looked as though most of the faculty for the school year 1938–39 would be replaced. This led up to my first and only confrontation with the legendary Dr. T. E. Rhine. I thought that if I was to be fired I was due an audience and explanation as to why. Therefore, I went to Dr. Rhine's office and stated to him that I would like to discuss with him my future at the school. It didn't take long for the doctor to give me a pretty good idea that I had some ground to suspect that my job was on the line. I will relate two things that Dr. Rhine brought up to suggest that I was in trouble. First, I was reminded that during the year, there was one problem in an algebra course (lesson assignment) and one in geometry that I never solved to the class's satisfaction. As I remember, I must have explained that in my heavy daily load, I let them slip by and forgot to get back to them. He next brought up our losing out in the District Basketball Tournament in our second game after winning the first game by a score of ninety-two to thirty-eight. In Dr. Rhine's comment, I felt that I, the coach, was to blame for the loss. I guess I was so shocked that I asked the doctor if he was there. (I knew he was not.) He dropped the subject. This seemed to put the interview on maybe even terms, and Dr. Rhine's next statement was, "Well, we will see what we can do."

A couple of days later, I got a letter from the school board advising me that I was rehired for another year, and I was given a $5.00 per month raise. It's needless to say that I was most appreciative to the good doctor. It became necessary for me to tender my resignation in a couple of weeks, as I received a better offer elsewhere. In fact, that ended my planned teaching career, as I went on active duty in the military that summer.

I believe that my experience with Dr. T. E. Rhine emphasizes the stature and influence that he possessed as a leader in community affairs, the advice that others sought from him, and the mark he left on all that came into contact with him. He served his fellow man well as a doctor, leader, and humanitarian. He was a statesman among men, and he left many long lasting memories. To me they are fond memories.

DR. LEVENIS PENIX

THORNTON, ARKANSAS

I was raised in Thornton. I came back in 1958, after school and the service, to the Thornton school system. I became principal of the high school in 1970 at the time of the integration of the system.

When I first remember him, he was driving a 1939 blue Ford, and everytime I would see that Ford coming down the road, I knew that it was Dr. Rhine. Somehow I perceived him as being the last of a breed of doctors who truly were committed, dedicated to the profession of medicine and to health care because I saw him traveling throughout the countryside, up and down the dusty roads in summer, up and down the muddy roads in the wintertime, going over the snow, carrying shovels and picks in case he got stuck. He definitely had his patients' care at heart. He wanted to serve the people with the best medical care that he could possibly find. He was our doctor.

Dr. Rhine was truly committed to education. He appeared always to be a promoter of education. He wanted to see boys and girls in school. He wanted to make sure that the boys and girls were healthy, in order to go to school. He encouraged parents to see that their children went to school. I'm sure that he had a big hand in seeing that the black school survived. Had it not been for the medical care, for the type of doctor that he was, going over the countryside, I feel there would have been many children unable to go to school, because of health problems.

DR. JAMES O'DELL

THORNTON, ARKANSAS

I'm starting my twenty-seventh year as superintendent here, and I have been mayor for eighteen years.

The first time I met Dr. Rhine, I was at Tinsman, and I had a couple of children that broke out in red spots, and I had no idea what they had. He was the county health officer, so I called him down. I thought they had scarlet fever. He looked them over and said they didn't, but that they could, but he didn't think they did. I asked him if I should shut down and quarantine the school. He gave me a little chewing out and told me that he was the county health officer. He'd make those decisions. I told him I was just asking.

I came to Thornton about six years later. Dr. Rhine had been on the school board for years, and Mrs. Rhine was teaching piano at the school. Soon after I got here, he came over to me, told me about his being on the board, he was familiar with everything that went on, and that if I ever needed any help to come over to see him. So many things in schools are traditional, or they were back then (there weren't many policies written on various things), so regularly, I went over and asked him how things had been handled in the past, and what the people would accept in certain areas, etc. He always had the information that I needed. Of course, some things I didn't ask him about, new things. If he didn't like them, or if he heard criticism of them, he would call me or send me word that he needed to see me. I would go over, and he would discuss them with me. Usually, we were able to make the changes necessary to be acceptable to the community. Some people might have resented this, but I didn't, because my philosophy as school administrator is that the people in the school district are paying me, and I should do things as near like they want them done as is educationally sound.

After two or three years, Dr. Rhine became a strong supporter of mine, and if anybody started giving me a problem in the community, he straightened them out, many times, with my not knowing about it until later. With the experience that he had in the community, there wasn't anyone going to buck him. Of course, he listened to people even if they had a petty complaint. But when he got through listening to them, he set them straight, and that would be the last you ever heard of it.

As soon as I came here, we went to work on a new building. The second year I was here, we got it finished, and in 1960 we had him over and had a dedication ceremony with practically the entire countryside turned out for it. The cafetorium wouldn't hold all of them. He was really proud of the fact that the school was dedicated to him. He had spent all of those years [thirty-five] on the school board. He was very active in seeing that the bond issue passed. It passed with a large majority. One of the reasons being that he put out the word. There was virtually no opposition to the bond issue.

All during this time, he acted as the unofficial school physician. Any time a child got hurt and he was in his office, he was over here immediately. I had one boy who was working in the shop who fell off a ladder. The boy had a bad concussion, was throwing up. He was a big boy, and I was trying to turn him over to keep him from choking. The principal ran out to tell Dr. Rhine to hurry—hurry. Dr. Rhine said, "I'm going as fast as I can." When he got there he realized the symptoms, gave him a shot, and told us how to handle him. The boy was out for three days, but when he came to, he was all right.

One other time, I had a little girl who had some kind of seizures. She would scream, fight, claw her face, and I would have to hold her down until Dr. Rhine could get here to give her a shot. He never did charge for these services. He didn't hardly charge anybody for anything.

I had a boy break his ankle down in the gym one day. He made me promise that I wouldn't let anyone give him a shot. It was a greenstick break. It was a dandy.

"I'll call Dr. Rhine, and I'm sure that he won't give you a shot unless you want it." It was one of the Lightfoot boys. I called Dr. Rhine and the boys mama, and we carried him to the hospital.

I kept telling everybody, "Now don't give him a shot." I stayed in there with him. It was such a bad break that Dr. Rhine wanted to look at a book to see the proper alignment of the bone, and he was always singing a little song and humming to himself while he was doing it. He got his stuff on, and Dr. Harry Atkinson came along down the hall, and he hollered for him to come in and help him. Well, he got it all like he wanted it, and he told Dr. Harry, "Now, when I pull over on the toe, you push on the heel."

The boy, by then, had a hold on my arm and had buried his fingers to the bone. It was about to kill me. He still hadn't had a shot. Dr. Harry pushed the heel in the wrong direction. The boy nearly came unglued, and Dr. Rhine gave him a cracker-jack chewing out. The next time they did it, they did it right. The boy went home and after about three days, he finally let Dr. Rhine give him a pain shot. He wasn't out of school long. It knitted back, and he started playing ball. It was a good set. He never did limp.

Everyone knows that Dr. Rhine was extremely fond of animals, especially dogs. Since I kept a large pack of dogs—beagles for rabbit hunting—he kept me posted on what to do for my dogs and how to keep them alive. He checked on them regularly.

It was common knowledge that one of Dr. Rhine's least worries was his fees. One of my kids had a low grade fever that none of the medicine he was prescribing was doing any good. He had some new medicine come in, so I went over, and he gave it to me. He couldn't find the bill of lading, he wasn't interested in that anyway, so he charged me two dollars. He told me how to give it, and in about three days it broke the fever. In about three weeks, one of my other kids started very similar symptoms. He felt it probably was the same thing, and he gave me the same new medicine again. That time, he told me it was six dollars. I said, "I'll have to write you a check. I don't have that much money. Last time you charged me two."

"I found the bill on it. It's six dollars."

"I'll write the check to include the four dollars I owe you from the other."

He got all upset. "If I told you two dollars, that's all I wanted. I know what I want for my medicine."

So I paid him two dollars one time and six the next.

I used to go over and watch him mix medicines. He could pick up a jug that looked to me like it had five gallons in it and pour it in a two ounce bottle and not spill a drop. He was at least in his eighties then. He could mix two or three medicines out of those big jugs, proper amounts, and never spill a drop.

He was the first doctor I ever saw who had an integrated waiting room. Everybody waited in the same room if they wanted to see him, and no one ever seemed to think anything about it. I mean, nobody ever mentioned it. [It had always been that way since 1899.]

One day at his office there were two or three black ladies there together. It came their turn. They told him, "Dr. Rhine, we don't have any money.

We want to charge this." He ate them out good. He said, "Yes, when you have the money you go to see those other doctors. When you want to charge it, you come to me." He went ahead and took care of them, but they had to endure a chewing out, which he could do pretty well when he wanted to.

One day I was over at his house, and he had this big array of hunting horns on the back porch. He wasn't there, and while I waited I told Mrs. Rhine that I had picked out one I wanted and would she tell Dr. Rhine to leave it to me in his will. It had a mouthpiece on the side—very unusual design. She said she thought he had already promised all of them. I said if he had, I still would like some old horn of his for a keepsake. I didn't hear anything from him. But one day, he called and told me to come over to his office, he had something to talk to me about. I couldn't figure out anything that I had done wrong, so I went over. He had several patients waiting, so when he got through, he said, "Let's go outside." We went out, and I thought, "I don't know what we are going to do." He reached over in his car and got a black, carved goat horn that he had gotten somewhere. It had the holders for the carrying string carved into it. It had a brass mouthpiece. He gave it to me. I never did carry it hunting. I was afraid I might lose it. I just put it in my gun case, and it is still in there. You really hadn't arrived in the Thornton area until you got a gift of a horn from Dr. Rhine. If you did something outstanding or took care of his dogs, or did a favor for him, sooner or later, he gave you a horn.

Dr. Rhine's driving always cracked me up. He had a Falcon, and his idea of getting a car to go was that you had to wind the motor up first. And he always wound it up [revved it], and let his clutch out, so it wouldn't stall on him. When he left, he left in a hurry. Anybody else would have worn the clutch out in a week, but he had the process down pat.

He liked to fold up dollar bills real small and stick them around in his various pockets. When he would have to make change, he'd pull out a whole handful of folded up bills. He always had them on him. I guess he folded them small to keep them from being so bulky.*

He kept on going so long, it seemed like there would be no end to it. It was a great loss to the community when he died. It seemed like another era started then.

*He didn't carry a billfold because in his hip pocket he carried a syringe case with small ampules of narcotics. PRB

"The town was his town. We all lived in it, but it was his town."

VERA MAE HARPER

THORNTON, ARKANSAS

Dr. Rhine was our family doctor all those years. My grandfather was Tom Turner. Dr. Rhine saw his mother the night she died. She had cancer in the eye. My parents were Fell and Mae Harper. He delivered all of Mama and Papa's children in the home—all girls—Alma, Marie, me and Dorothy. He delivered all of Alma's children and one of her grandchildren. I know he delivered Donnie. That's six generations of doctoring in our family.

One of Alma's children came early, that was Donna; and Dot, Dr. Rhine and Mama delivered it. They finally got Mrs. McAllister over there to help, but she fainted. Dr. Rhine told Dot, "This baby is almost here. You are going to have to help."

She said, "I can't, Dr. Rhine. I've never done anything like this."

"Well, you will," and she did.

They were all delivered at Mama's home. Alma always said, "It just made you feel better when you heard his feet walking across the floor." I often wonder how he would cope with Medicare and Medicaid.

When Mother and Daddy married, they lived out in the country, and Daddy said, "We are going to use both Dr. Rhine and Dr. Black." Mama said that Daddy got sick first, and he said, "When I get sick, I get real sick, so I better have Dr. Rhine come out and see me." So they did.

Marie was the next one to get sick. "Marie is bad to have pneumonia. We better get Dr. Rhine to come out to see her."

Mama said, "I was the next one to get sick. I looked up the road coming, and it was Dr. Black." Dr. Rhine was our doctor always, and he also was our advisor. We certainly loved him.

If we were off somewhere and got sick, we came home to Dr. Rhine. I came home every week-end, and I went to see him whether I was sick or not. I went to the office—we all did—and we didn't pay a dime, we just went in.

273

We were always scared to death at night to call him. You know, Dr. Rhine was an important person to us, and we didn't want to disturb him. But he could give you that gruff voice! He was different when he came in, he was a doctor, and he didn't have that gruffness in his voice when he came in to treat you. Even if I saw a doctor somewhere else, I wasn't satisfied until I got home and went to see Dr. Rhine.

He kept his medicine on ice at Jordan's store. Me and Daddy took cold shots every year. You took five shots altogether, one a week. He'd go over to the store and get enough serum in one needle for both of us. I always wanted to be first, because I didn't want to have him stick that needle in Daddy, then me. Course, he always used lots of alcohol. I never had anything from it, never caught a staph infection, but you often wondered why you didn't. We are all still living. Mama never wanted to take the flu shots. She would always stay in the car. He came back with his medicine one day and saw her outside. He said, "Mae, come on in. You need this shot, too." She answered, "Well, I never heard of anybody dying on account of it."

A lot of the bottles we carried up there, he just rinsed them out and used them again.

I had empyema when I was eight years old. I was the third person in the United States to live over it. Dr. Rhine had it diagnosed right down to what it was, but he couldn't reach it with a needle. It was abscesses formed after pneumonia. I wore a tube for two years inside for drainage from the abscesses. I had gotten so full of it that I couldn't drink any water. It would make me too full. They finally got me to Little Rock about a week before I was about dead, and they gave me three days to live.

Later, I said to Mama, "Why didn't you take me to Little Rock sooner?"

She said, "There was no car in the family, and there was no heat in any car." I came back by train. Someone met me in Fordyce. I stayed in the hospital three weeks. My doctor was Dr. Anderson Watkins. Every doctor's office that I ever went into all had Dr. Rhine's picture on their desk. It was a serious thing that empyema. Dr. Rhine used to have doctors come down here to see me, when they would come bird hunting. He would bring them around so he could tell my story and let them see me. I'm sure that he is the one that pulled me through. The doctors said he had it pin-pointed. All he had to do was look at you, maybe stick out your tongue, and he would know what was wrong with you.

I'll never forget his green 'aching tablets.' He had them in a big jug, and then all that little envelope would hold, he could lick it and stamp it down. You got that many for fifty cents. You paid at the end of the month or at the end of an illness. He'd add it all up in his head, never used an adding machine, but he could type on that typewriter—maybe two fingers, but he could do very well with it. When we started trying to find green 'aching tablets' from Dr. Harry Atkinson, he said, "Mine are pink." They could really cure headaches—it just took one. It took us fifteen years after he died to find out that they had those in the drug store—APC's.

A doctor in Hot Springs told me one time that I was in critical condition, and I might just as well get a Sunday School Class and raise some chickens. I would never be able to work. I was real despondent. I came home, went to see Dr. Rhine, and he said, "That is just a matter of opinion. You just take a few more weeks to gain a little strength, then get you a light job," and that's what I've been doing ever since.

He would say, "It won't take long to kick 'em all out of here." He'd have about twenty people in the office. When he'd answer the phone he would say that.

I was as scared of him as a bat when I was young. When I was sick, and would get out, I would hide so he wouldn't know I was back in school.

Mama will be ninety-one in December. She's blind and she can't hear, but she takes her own bath and comes to the table to eat her meals. She is in her own home, and Dot and I live with her. It is a case of elderly people being accepted, and she never feels shunted aside. When she is in the bed sick, she kinda gives in to us, but the minute she gets back up on her feet, we know who's boss.

This town was built around Dr. Rhine. He was this town. Really, you associate the town with him. He not only was the boss of the town, he was head of the school. He told them who to hire. He always came to the school opening and the graduation exercises. There wasn't a thing in this town that got by Dr. Rhine. Things were done to suit him, because they knew that was the way things were going to be. I don't know of any school superintendent or official that ever wanted to displease him. A lot of people would like to give Mrs. Rhine credit for things, but you know there was so much to talk about Dr. Rhine that she never got the gratitude that she should have. I imagine our family saw him more than his children did. But this was a good town, a really good town. We had a great doctor and great people. I will really have to say the town was his town. We all lived in it, but it was his town.

REV. FLOYD O. AND MATTIE JONES

THORNTON, ARKANSAS

Floyd: I've lived all my life in Thornton. I was born in 1912, and he was the doctor who delivered me. Mary Jones and Reverend Steve Jones were my parents. I'm pastor of Mt. Olivet church in Bearden, and I have been there for thirty years and Harmony church in Sparkman. I've been there for thirty-two years. I've been moderator of the Association for twenty-six years.

I can remember when he rode horseback. I was a little fellow. He was our family doctor for sixty-two years. One thing we always learned about him. You know we didn't have cars. We didn't even have telephones 'way back then. We always had to go get the doctor. In the day time, we knew to go to the office. After night, we knew to go to the back gate, turn the back gate, knock on the door. He would holler, "Who is it?"

"This is Floyd Jones."

"Whatcha want, Floyd?"

"Need you to come see the children."

"Which one?" He knew them so well. We had three at that time.

"I'll be out there in a while."

At the time when our babies were born, I'd walk down to get him. "Let me know." When he come, if it wasn't right at the time, he didn't go back home, he stayed right there.

They had Dr. Rhine Day here and they gave all the babies that he delivered a button with an 'R' on it. That was a big day in Thornton. People came from all directions. It was amazing how *old* some of those babies were.

We always laughed about it. He bought the medicine in those big brown jugs, and he had all those jugs on the tables and the floor. "You want some cough syrup?" He'd just reach over and get that jug. Sometimes it looked like he hardly looked at it. He never used like a funnel or anything, he just pick up a jug, pour it into a bottle, and nothing dripped.

For the older folks, he was a doctor and a dentist, too. He'd meet my ma on the street. "Mary, what is it?"

"I'm started to the office, Doctor."

"Whatcha want done?"

"My ole tooth."

"Where is it, Mary? Let me see it." And he'd pull it out, right on the street.

When anything went wrong in the community, a health problem or anything, I never did think about going to Hampton. I'd go to Dr. Rhine. "Dr. Rhine, such and such a thing happened."

"We'll see what we can do." That's as far as I had to go. Dr. Rhine took care of it.

As he grew older, he used to tell us all the time, "Well, I won't be around here much longer. You'll have to go to those hospital doctors. They gonna treat you right." But we miss him. I go to the hospital in Fordyce where his picture is, and it looks like he's looking right at me. "That's Dr. Rhine, from Thornton." We knew that he loved us and cared about us.

Mattie: What was so funny to me, when he would come in, he didn't care how sick you was, he would dance a jig. If it was night, he would say, "Good morning. Morning, morning." Anytime, it was 'good morning.' "What's your trouble?" He'd just jump around and dance. "Can you do that?"

Floyd: The most humorous thing I remember about him was I was sitting there in the waiting room. He had a lady back in the back. She said, "Doctor, what's this here in my stomach? It just feels like" "I don't know. It may be pigs or something." And we laughed. We laughed so.

He never denied any of us, money or no money. Now, if a man had a

276

family, and the man was trifling, he was gonna catch it from Dr. Rhine, but his wife and children, he never denied them. He would often send a donation to the church, and he would come by the church on a special occasion and speak.

I can remember when we were children, we didn't know anything about toothpaste and stuff like that. He had a committee to come just as school was turning out, and they gave us little tubes of toothpaste. Most of the kids ate it up, before they got home. He pioneered all of that. Dr. Rhine would come to the school, and William Stout. As long as he lived, he would come, he and Dr. Rhine.

Back then we had a Christmas tree at the school. Every little baby even, if it was old enough to have a name, got a bag from the tree. We didn't have commodities that come through the federal government, but somehow or another, Dr. Rhine would get hold of things and funnel it to the school. We had a lunch program out here years and years before others. Dr. Rhine was responsible for that. He was just a father to all of us.

Elsie Johnson was principal of our school. William Stout, you know he had black hair, (we learned to know him) would say, "Elsie, what do the kids need to make them happy?" At that time, we had eighth grade testing there—a state examination. We had manual training. We started manual training in the fourth grade for boys. In our agriculture department, we had everything we needed—chickens, hogs, horses. All of us had a plot of ground. Somehow or other, Dr. Rhine would secure them. All of us got those seeds, plant those plots. No rural school anywhere had that back then.

Elsie Johnson was educated in Virginia. All of our teachers were good, too. Up through my high school years, other than a music teacher, I didn't have a teacher from Arkansas. I had a native Hungarian for a Latin teacher. Three years of Latin was what we had. My mother always told me, the morning I was born, Miss Elsie was there, and she would tell me later, "I know every bone in you." During those days, the church, the school and the home were of one accord. They were close, and everything was lovely, too. The child, the whole child.

On rainy days or stormy, many didn't get to school. Miss Elsie had a girls' sewing class, and we boys were in the back. She was trying to teach them how to make a knot in the thread. She didn't teach all of them, but I learned how to make a knot. Miss Elsie was somebody.

We didn't have a gymnasium then. We didn't have anything but a big hall. But in the hall each morning, the children assembled and one of the teachers or Dr. Rhine or somebody would be responsible to talk to the children. Elsie's husband, we called him Mr. Johnson, would remind us on Friday to go to church on Sunday, and on Monday, "How many went to church and Sunday School?" He was superintendent of the Sunday School of this church across the street from the school. After he would get the teachers started, he would get in his old Ford and go see if the children were in Sunday School. And at night, you'd see a flashlight flashing—ooh the

277

boys would go. They knew who it was—Mr. Johnson. "Get off the street." That's just the way it was.

I started to farming after the war was over. Dr. Rhine liked white peas. "Be sure and plant some peas," he'd say. "That's fine. That's fine." Folks would bring him peas, some would bring him molasses, whatever he liked.

You know, he loved his dogs. They used to claim that Dr. Rhine had so many dogs, he couldn't keep up with them. "Hey, Doc, here's one of your dogs." "Just throw him over there in the dog yard." He was gonna feed him and take care of him. He was known as one of the great dog raisers in America—fox hounds. Dud Crosby and Judge Montgomery, they'd keep his dogs. Mr. Claud Green said that Judge Montgomery would hunt every night in the year, by himself. Dr. Rhine furnished the dogs and would feed them.

Whatever program that had to get over, it had to come from the church. That was the only public meeting place we had. "Dr. Rhine's on the outside." "Dr. Rhine's coming." He never did walk with a drag. He stepped.

Mattie: He didn't believe in sending you to the hospital unless you just had to go.

Floyd: That was a day when the news came about Dr. Rhine's death. We had heard in the evening that Dr. Rhine was low. I don't know why I went to the hospital, but I did, and all the doctors, Dr. Harry Atkinson and them, was in the corridor there. We all went to the funeral. On the outside, there was hardly any room to stand. I heard the men around me, Tom Campbell, Jimmy Campbell, Munch Chiles they all were talking about Dr. Rhine— Dr. Rhine. His influence reached so far. And you just had one doctor for whatever was wrong.

Mattie: And he examine you and tell you *exactly* what was wrong. I've known the time he would say, "Now you can go to so and so." One time we went and checked, and it was exactly the same as he said, and he didn't have all the machinery they put on you.

Floyd: The day of his funeral, one of the young doctors was outside talking about one day at the Universal hospital. Dr. Rhine come to see somebody. They were talking about the patient, and he asked them, "Have you tried such and such a thing?" The young doctor hadn't heard about it. They thought it was amazing that a man of his age kept abreast of what was new. There will never be another one like him.

FRED NICHOLS

THORNTON, ARKANSAS

Dr. Rhine caught my first baby in 1915. Dr. Rhine was our doctor for as long as he lived. His picture is up in the hospital now at Fordyce. We lived down in the country, and he used to ride a blaze-faced horse. I'm eighty-nine years old, and my wife, Bit, is eighty-six. Bit worked for Mrs. Trammel for sixteen years. He doctored on my mother, Louise Nichols, the whole family. Henry Baker was my wife's daddy. He doctored on all their family. He and Dr. Black were the doctors in Thornton then. The mill was here then. This used to be a big place here.

I worked at the mill for years, and I worked on the Cotton Belt Railroad for eighteen years. I'm living off the retirement from the railroad. Dr. Rhine was a good doctor. We miss him. I started working for the railroad when I was sixteen years old—totin' cross ties, puttin' them ties on the railroad, workin' like a mule.

You know, in this whole territory, everybody did what Dr. Rhine said. Once our boy, Butch, was sick, and he come up to see him. He got on the telephone, called the sheriff in Hampton, and told Sheriff Parker, "Turn Fred out and let him come on home. Buck Trammel is comin' down to go his bond. His son's sick, and his wife needs him here." I had been fightin', I had stobbed a man—like to have killed him. And Buck come one mornin' and I come on home. When Dr. Rhine would speak, that was it! I was glad to get out of jail. I had been in there three weeks. I'm lucky to be livin'. I used to be so mean. Dr. Rhine used to fuss at me a good bit.

Sheriff Benton Ritchie wanted me to go out on the county farm and plow. I was raised on a farm. I told him, "Man, I don't know nothin' about no mule or horse."

"You'll feel better. You'll get stiff layin' up in this jail."

"Let me get stiff. I ain't goin' out there and plow." And I didn't go.

In 1958, I had to have an operation. Dr. Rhine told Dr. Atkinson, said, "Take your time with him. He's a mighty mean nigger." That's what he said, "He's a mighty mean nigger." I never will forget that.

"And then he had a whole lot of that Dr. Rhine Masonry that he had put in there, too, which was real good."

J. B. TILLER

THORNTON, ARKANSAS

I came to Thornton in 1933. I worked for the Cotton Belt Railroad as a maintenance way foreman for thirty-nine years. I retired in 1967 when I became sixty-five years old. They say don't ever retire, because you won't last long, especially if you just sit down after leading an active life. I've had a garden, a big lawn, a hedge to trim, teach an adult Sunday School class, Masonic work, Eastern Star and Amaranth. It all keeps my brain active.

Dr. Rhine was very active in the Lodge. If it hadn't been for him, there wouldn't be a Lodge here. He was the hub of this Lodge before I went in, and he was the hub of it as long as he was able to go. He kept this thing going. It's the George Washington Lodge #231. It was begun in 1859 at Chambersville, one of the oldest Lodges in the state. When the Cotton Belt came through here in 1882, they moved the Lodge here. It originally sat on what is now Highway 79, just west of where it is located today. It was moved to a building on Main Street that burned. They had to start over from scratch after that.

Dr. Rhine was very active, and he was very proficient in his lectures and in the work as a whole. When I first went in, not every Lodge had the same wording in the lectures. I learned it the old way. The Board of Custodians came out with a uniform lecture that was to be used all over Arkansas. That was about 1947 or '48. Dr. Rhine had it the old way, and he didn't change his, because he was set. And then he had a whole lot of that Dr. Rhine Masonry that he put in there, too, which was real good.

The year that I was Worshipful Master, we would be putting on degree work, and he would come down to the Hall. While I was performing my part, I would see him counting on his fingers. When it was over, he would say, "You did a good job, but you made two or three mistakes."

280

I tried to go the certified way, and he didn't like that. He wanted it back the old way. "Did I do that, Doc?"

"You sure did."

"I'll try to do better next time," just pass it off like that, knowing all the time that I was going to keep on the new way.

He was a grand character. He knew his Masonry, and, as I said, if it hadn't been for Dr. Rhine, there wouldn't be a Lodge here today, because he kept it going.

The Lodge bought the old bank building about 1948 or '49. When the mill was here, it was the Bank Building. The Post Office moved in when the bank failed in 1931. There was an apartment on the south end of the building. That was Dr. Rhine's office. He paid $10.00 a month rent for those rooms. He had a dentist chair in the back room, and he would pull your teeth if you would let him.

Before we acquired that building, after the other one burned, we just had to meet where we could. After they built the new gym at the school, we met in one of the front office rooms, if there wasn't a ball game going on. We carried the paraphenalia around in an old basket. Dr. Rhine took care of that for a long, long while. Mr. C. Scott owned the post office building. We bought it from him for $2,600.00. We took up donations and raised about half of it and borrowed the rest from the bank to pay Scott. The post office stayed there for a long while, until they built the new one, in 1967.

When I went out as Master, they put me to pushing that pencil. That is normal procedure if the present one wants to quit. I did it for five years. When I came back to Thornton in 1958, they put me back on that pencil job, and I have had it ever since. I'm on my 27th year as a pencil pusher.

In Masonry, we go from the Blue Lodge-three degrees, which is what we have here. You can go on to 12th, 14th, 18th to the 32nd degree. There is a 33rd degree, but you have to earn it. You can buy the rest of these but you have to earn the 33rd—it is honorary. When I first went in the Lodge, there were only three, maybe five 33rd degree Masons in Arkansas. You had to do something outstanding to earn it. Dr. Rhine was a 33rd degree Mason. He was both a York Rite and a Scottish Rite Mason. He became a 32nd degree Mason in 1908. Remember that picture? [It hung over the fireplace in the middle bedroom and is one of my early memories.]

Dr. Rhine was a man of integrity, sincerity and an A-number-one citizen. That's how I would classify him. He was always willing to help in any way. I don't care how black you were, or how poor you were, or how ragged you were, he was ready to help.

We have a monitor in our Masonic work that is divided into three sections for the three degrees. He had the same attitude that I have. The smartest men in office today read their speeches. Preachers are reading off their sermons. Dr. Rhine said, "If you want to impress somebody, learn it by heart and look them right in the eye when you give it to them. They will remember it that way. If you are holding a book, reading it to them, they are going to wonder, 'Well, if it's all that good, why haven't you learned it?' "

Dr. Rhine has told me this time and time again when I'd go in his office and be talking with him. When he first started learning Masonry, he was using a horse and buggy. He'd go fifteen or twenty miles to see a sick patient. Going out, he wanted to get there and see about them, but coming back, he'd put his reins around the buggy whip, open his monitor and sit back to study, because that horse was coming home. That's how he learned his. He wanted everyone else to do it by memory, too.

Now we have too many ring wearing, card carrying, knife and fork Masons. They want to have a big Lodge, but when the Big Day comes, two or three carry it on, just like Dr. Rhine did here. Put on a feed, and those knife and fork Masons will be there.

"This was not to be just an ordinary American Legion Post."

GERALD HEARNSBERGER

ELLISVILLE, ARKANSAS

After World War II there was an intense interest in the Thornton area for an American Legion Post. According to the application for the permanent charter, there were about 150 ex-service men in the area to draw membership from. On this application which was dated April 3, 1948, there were ninety-seven paid-up members.

But this was not to be just an ordinary American Legion Post. Dr. T. E. Rhine was a veteran of World War I and was very instrumental in the organization of this post. Dr. Rhine had practiced medicine in this area for many years, so he was the practicing physician at the birth of many of the veterans. It was decided that the charter members would be only Dr. Rhine 'babies.' On the 7th day of November, 1947, a temporary charter was granted to the Thornton American Legion Post No. 281 with thirty-three charter members. These members were: Lamont Brandon, George R. Cathey, William O. Clemons, Lee Roy Cottrell, Clyde Easterling, Jr., Jim Reed Easterling, Thomas C. Ellis, John R. Emerson, Cecil C. Evans, Charles C. Evans, Howard L. Evans, James C. Evans, Thomas E. Evans, Watt R. Files, Ira B. Green, George R. Gresham, Max E. Gresham, George S. Harper, Derwood Hearnsberger, Dilmus Hearnsberger, Gerald L. Hearnsberger, Herman Hearnsberger, Jimmy L. Jackson, William L. Lucas, Robbie D. Marks, Royce H. Marks, Lawrence L. McDonald, Coby Steelman, J. R. Steelman, D. A. Thornton, Vollie Trucks, Bill Williams and B. Edward Womble.

Of course, when you organize, a name must be decided upon, and since this was a rather unique post, they wanted the name to be the Dr. T. E. Rhine Post. Since posts are not named for living persons, it was decided that the name would be 'Thornton' until Dr. Rhine's death, and it would then become the Dr. T. E. Rhine American Legion Post.

Meetings were held once each month with a potluck supper held at the Thornton School Cafeteria. Dr. and Mrs. Rhine always brought Aaron Brandon's barbecue.

The first officers of the post were: Gerald Hearnsberger, Commander; Coby Steelman, 1st Vice Commander; D. A. Thornton, Adjutant; Thomas E. Evans, Finance Officer; George R. Gresham, Service Officer; Royce H. Marks, Sgt.-at-Arms.

On April 8, 1948, the permanent charter was granted. The post became inactive in 1969–1970.

"Another thing about him was the way he loved old people."

JEWEL JAMES

THORNTON, ARKANSAS

When we first came to Thornton in 1939 from Holly Springs, Dr. and Mrs. Rhine were about the first people we knew. I certainly knew to holler for him for any problem. I don't guess there was anyone who had any more different kinds of experiences than I did, and I know there wasn't anybody that loved him any more than we all did. He was sure a wonderful person. We loved Mrs. Rhine the same. She was the one that kept everything going, but he was the one that had to do the doctoring and had the say of everything.

One day I was out on the front at the old store [at the intersection of highways 79 and 167]. I guess I had probably been to the ice house or was waiting on a car, when a car just whipped up and stopped. It was really going fast. Just as he whipped up, he held his purse out to me, and he fell over. I run up to see what he wanted, but he was just dead passed out in the seat. It scared me to death, and I hollered, "Run call Dr. Rhine, quick." I felt like maybe he had done had a heart attack. Dr. Rhine came right on. He would always drop everything when I called, because I had told him once that if I ever called him, he could know that I really needed him. One time he was in the store talking about how he had been up all night, something that wasn't really necessary. He said, "I'm going to quit this going out at night. People just call you for everything. I'm getting too old to be out all night every night and all day every day. I've got as much right to my rest and sleep as anybody has, and I'm just going to quit going at night when they call me that way. A lot of 'em feel bad all day and call me to come sit up with 'em all night."

"I'll tell you one thing, Dr. Rhine, if I ever call you, you come, because I'll be needing you."

So when this happened, and I had someone call him, he came right on over, and I gave him the purse. He opened it up and there was a paper inside that said, "Call ambulance service in El Dorado," and if you couldn't get them, there was another number to call. He ran in the store and called, and they said the man was a diabetic. He had gone into a coma. He told them to call the ambulance and send them. It wasn't too long before the ambulance came. In the meantime, Dr. Rhine gave the man some orange juice and a shot of some kind.

Just a day or two after that the boy came back, and he was driving his own car. He said, "I sure am thankful for a doctor like Dr. Rhine who would know what to do and how to do it and find out what was the matter with me. I also appreciate you seeing that it was all done."

So many things like that happened that I didn't know how to manage, what to do or how to do, but I'd always call on Dr. Rhine, because I knew he knew just exactly what to do.

Vissie Hopkins was a great big, heavy set woman, and her husband was a little bitty man. They had several children. She traded at our old store. She was in getting her bill of groceries one morning, and she was over behind the meat counter. She hollered for me. "Mrs. James, come here quick!"

I dropped everything and went to her. She says, "Hand me some big bath towels!" I reached up in the cabinet right around the kitchen door and got several big bath towels and gave them to her. She just put them up between her legs. She had on a dress or a housecoat. She had a premature baby right there behind my meat counter on those bath towels. I pushed a chair up to her and told her to sit down until I could get hold of Dr. Rhine. I called and told him to come, and he came right on, and, of course, took charge. Gurt and Dr. Rhine together carried her home. She just lived across the street.

He called me to come help him when my daughter-in-law's sister had her baby, and I did. And another time, I helped him with a baby, cleaning it up and such after he delivered it.

One night about two o'clock, a taxi came up to the store and wanted to see me. It was a driver that knew me, and he wanted to get hold of Dr. Rhine. He had a woman in there that was having problems, and she had a seven-month-old baby with her. She claimed that she and her husband were having trouble, that he had hurt her. I couldn't tell what the matter was, so I just got in the taxi and went with them to Dr. Rhine's.

When he came to the door, I told him, "I hated to come down here and wake you, but this woman is in a bad shape for some reason, and has this baby with her, and I don't know what to do, Dr. Rhine." He said, "Go on over to the office." The taxi driver and I went on to the office, and Dr. Rhine wasn't but a few minutes getting there. He let us in and Dr. Rhine and the taxi driver got her to the examining table. He said she was doped up and a nervous wreck.

I asked, "What am I doing to do with this baby?"

"Can you take care of it?"

"I'll do the best I can for it?"

Dr. Rhine then called the hospital in Fordyce to tell them he was sending a woman up and not to let her leave until some of her people came for her. The taxi driver took her to Fordyce to the hospital. When I got home with the baby, my youngest children, who were little things, Barbara Sue and Jimmy, were so excited. They both wanted the baby to sleep with them. She had brought the baby's formula and his clothes with her. She intended for me to have him. It was about two days after that that her parents, who lived in Sparkman, came for the baby.

John Brumbley was at our house the night that Barbara Sue was born. Dr. Rhine came in while John was there.

I said, "John, have you ever met Dr. Rhine?" John got up (he was very polite, had a world of money), stuck out his hand and began telling Dr. Rhine who he was. He lived in Texas then.

"I don't believe as much as I've been up here to Gurt and Jewel's I've ever met you."

"Yes, you did, son."

Dr. Rhine told what year it and said, "Out here across the creek, I was in my horse and buggy then. I got a call to come out there. Some lady was fixing to have a baby. I went out and delivered it, and it was you." He knew every one he delivered.

That's one thing he said he didn't do was name babies or weigh 'em. I got sick on Friday night and Barbara Sue was not born until Sunday night, and he wouldn't go out of town without checking me.

When she was born, Dr. Rhine was cleaning her up. I said "Dr. Rhine, hurry up. I'm hurting."

"I'll get to you when I take care of this baby."

He went on taking care of her, and when he turned around, he said, "No wonder you was hollering. You are trying to have another baby." We lost the little boy.

We couldn't make up our mind what to name the baby. When she was fourteen days old, Dr. Rhine came to the house and said, "Well, Mrs. James, we are going to have to name that baby today."

"Charles and Bill T. want to call her Sandra Sue and Jo Ann wants to name her Patricia Lynn."

Jo Ann cried out, "Oh goody, I'll get to name her. They aren't here, and I'll get to name her."

Dr. Rhine said, "No. We are not going to do Charles and Bill T. like that. We'll just call her Barbara Sue."

So he named her, and she is so proud of it. She just brags about it all of the time. She was his baby as long as he lived, and she was in college when he died, but she came home for his funeral. She came home often on weekends, and sometimes Dr. Rhine would be at the store waiting for his grandchildren, Tommy and Ann Brown, to come on the bus from Pine Bluff. When she would come in, she didn't know but what he had come to meet her, and she would go and hug his neck and push his hair back and kiss

287

him on the forehead. She still thinks there is nobody in the world like Dr. Rhine.

He didn't care that much about Jimmy. The weekend that Barbara Sue was born, we had a lot of family here visiting. Mrs. James lived with us, and all the family came here to visit with her. I told Dr. Rhine then that if I ever had another baby, I was going to leave home to have it, because you never heard so much door-slamming, kids hollering and cooking going on in your life.

So when I found out I was expecting, I went and talked to Dr. Rhine about it. I was thirty-nine years old at the time. When I told him that I wanted to go to the hospital, he said, "I can't wait on you then. I can't make those trips anymore from here to Camden to take care of you." He told me that, and I just took it that he meant that was final. He never did change it, anyway. So I went down and talked to Dr. Robbins, and he told me that when I got sick to come down there. Do you know that Dr. Rhine got mad at me about that for just a little bit? He pouted more at Gurt than he did at me. You know a doctor is the most jealous person about their patients and their babies than anybody. You see, my father-in-law was a doctor.

Just after Jimmy was born, Gurt got sick one night, and we called Dr. Rhine. He came up there. Gurt said to him, "Doc, I want you to take a look at my boy while you are here." (His navel wasn't going in like it should.) "I don't believe you have seen him."

"Take him back to your city doctor."

"Now wait a minute, Doc. You know Jewel and I talked to you about you taking care of her, and you said that you were getting too old to deliver babies and to go that far to take care of her. You know why she wanted to go to the hospital. That was the only reason in the world she went down there. There was no place here where she had any privacy or the baby could sleep. So many people here all the time, in and out, and Jewel's a nervous wreck. You know, she's not as young as she used to be and having three babies right along together." Dr. Rhine cried just a little bit, shed a few tears. That made me and Gurt both cry. We couldn't stand it hardly.

When Dr. Rhine died, I guess that he and Mrs. Rhine both thought as much of Jimmy as they did any child in the whole town, and the reason they did, Jimmy was determined that Dr. Rhine was going to love him. When he got big enough that he could walk, he would hold onto Dr. Rhine's hand and walk to the front door with him. We lived by where Dr. Rhine walked to the office from home at noon, and when Jimmy got older, he would see Dr. Rhine coming, and he would take off and go get Dr. Rhine by the hand and walk with him to the dog pen fence. Then he would hold onto the fence and watch the dogs. When he started to school, instead of going by the road, he would cut through by Dr. Rhine's pasture and tell him he wanted to help him gather the eggs and feed the chickens. When he got big enough that he could kill snakes, he always went to school through Dr. Rhine's pasture, and he would always help him do whatever he was doing if he was down there. Mrs. Rhine said if she was baking or making candy, Jimmy would always stop to see how she was getting along (he could smell the cooking), and she would fill him up with whatever she was cooking.

He couldn't even reach the pedals when he started driving a car. He was a good driver, careful. After he got more experience, Dr. Rhine would let him drive him on calls. Dr. Rhine had to love him, because he wouldn't take no for an answer. But I could take those kids down to the office to get a shot or something, and Dr. Rhine would always give Barbara Sue a piece of candy. Maybe Jimmy would get a piece and maybe he didn't. But he usually asked for it and got a piece. You could tell that Dr. Rhine was so partial to Barbara, and she loved him, too.

Mrs. Rhine had given us a picture of Dr. Rhine with two of his dogs, and Barbara always tells me not to ever give anyone that picture, because it is ours.

Many, many times he rode in the ambulance with Gurt to Little Rock or Hot Springs when he would have those bad heart attacks. Someone would follow in the car and bring him home.

In Fordyce then they just had a little clinic—Dr. Estes and Dr. Atkinson. Gurt had a bad spell on the street there one day, and they took him to the clinic, but he was hollering for Dr. Rhine. Right at that minute they couldn't get hold of him. Dr. Estes sent his car to Thornton to get me. When I called Mrs. Rhine and told her the situation, she got hold of him, and it wasn't too long before he got there. Dr. Harry Atkinson came in with Dr. Rhine, and Gurt was really bad. Dr. Atkinson told him, "Gurt, you can get all right now. Here comes your little tin Jesus." And Gurt did get better. He just got better right off.

Another time we went there and the clinic closed about nine, and Gurt was getting worse all the time, so we called the ambulance and took him home, but he kept getting worse. I always tried to keep a little money there at the house. You didn't have any insurance to amount to anything then. Dr. Rhine came in the kitchen and said, "Mrs. James, we've got to get Gurt to the hospital in Camden. You haven't got much time to get ready."

I said, "I'm ready."

Bill T. whispered, "Mama, do you have any money?"

"Yes. Go in the dining room and look over the door on the door facing. There is a box there and there's plenty to take with us." When you don't know what's going to happen, you have to make special arrangements.

Gurt always said he knew if he had Dr. Rhine doctoring on him and Roy Wise praying for him, he would pull through any spell. He had a lot of confidence in Roy Wise, too.

I went down to Dr. Rhine's office late one afternoon. Gurt was having a problem with his stomach. When I went in, I was kinda limping. Dr. Rhine was fixing Gurt's medicine for me to take back. "What are you limping about?"

"Somebody left the ice pick laying on top of the ice house door." (Then you chipped your own ice, whoever was buying it, from an ice house beside the store.) "When I opened the ice house door, that pick stuck plum up to the bone in my foot."

"Did you get a tetanus shot?"

"You know I didn't. I haven't been down here, have I?"

"No. You need one."

"I'll run down here in the morning and get you to give me one."

"No, you'll get it while you are here."

"All right."

He gave me a shot and about four o'clock the next morning, I woke up and I was so swollen! I was allergic to tetanus. I got up and almost fainted. Gurt grabbed me and got me back to bed and called Dr. Rhine. Dr. Rhine came. He was laughing when he came in and wanting to know what I was fussing about.

"And you are to blame for it!"

"I didn't know you was allergic to it."

"I didn't either." I don't guess that I had had one before. It took him about a week and a half to get me over that.

I told him, "I sure did disturb your sleep, didn't I?"

"If you hadn't, somebody else probably would have." I don't know how he stayed up at night and went like he did day and night.

The week before he passed away, he was in the hospital in Fordyce with pneumonia. I went up to stay one night with Mrs. Rhine. He was still practicing medicine even though he was out of his head. He'd say, "Nita, you'd better fix some more bandages."

"All right."

One time he woke up and said, "I've got to go down close to Tinsman to take care of old lady so and so."

Mrs. Rhine would answer, "Don't you think that she could wait until in the morning for you to come to see her?"

"She needs me to come tonight. I'll go on down there."

"I'll go with you," Mrs. Rhine would answer.

"O. K., but Nita don't you drive fast."

She'd shake the foot of his bed. "Nita, don't get too fast."

He lay there and he practiced medicine as long as he lived. As sick as he was, he was thinking about going down and taking care of that old lady. He had others at heart. He wasn't thinking about himself. There'll never be another Dr. Rhine.

Gurt was gone on a week's fishing trip, and one of his fox hounds got sick. It was hemorrhaging at the kidney. I didn't know what to do. It was just a little while before Barbara Sue was born, because I had an emergency number to get hold of Gurt in case she came a little early. I put a rope in the old dog's collar, and walked him down to Dr. Rhine's office. I'll bet there were fifteen or twenty people waiting to see him. Dr. Rhine came out of the little room into the waiting room, and he saw me standing outside the door.

He said, "What you fussin' about?"

"Gurt's not at home, Dr. Rhine, and one of his dogs is sick, and I thought maybe you could tell me what to do for him or give me some medicine for him."

290

"Bring him on in."

"I'm not in any hurry. I'll just wait 'til you get through."

"I said bring him on in."

I lead him in front of all those people, took him in the office, and Dr. Rhine gave him a shot and gave me some medicine to give him, and he was all right the next day. Gurt said, "Dogs get sick just like people." Dr. Rhine thought so much of his dogs, and he knew Gurt did, too, so he took the dog right in.

I saw a side of Dr. Rhine that many people did not see. He was just as gentle and kind and sweet and fair as a person could ever be. On his birthday, one time, I baked him a lemon pie. It was his favorite kind. I called Mrs. Rhine and she said he was at home. I said, "Tell him not to run off. I want to see him a few minutes."

I went down and carried this lemon pie. I went over and hugged Mrs. Rhine first, then I went over and hugged his neck, and I said, "Dr. Rhine, I just want you to know that I haven't forgotten your birthday. I haven't got money enough to buy something that you haven't already got or that you would use if you had it, but I do want you to know that I love you, and I never will forget your birthday."

He kinda choked up a little bit for just a minute, and then he said, "Sit down there and stay a little while. I want to tell you something. I never have done anything for you."

"What are you talking about, Dr. Rhine? Why I even come talk to you about how to vote."

"There are people here who I have practiced for for four and five generations, and some of them have paid me and some of them never did even say, 'thank you.' They don't remember my birthday. I appreciate you coming down."

I knew that he did. That lemon pie meant more to him than if I had gone to town and paid fifty dollars for something (which I couldn't have, even if I wanted to). Back in those days, nobody made any money.

Another thing about him was the way he loved old people. My mother was walking to the post office, and she had a little dog who bumped her in the bend of the leg, and she fell over backwards and hit her head on the brick sidewalk. Somebody called me, and I went right straight and got her and carried her home and called Dr. Rhine. He said that she didn't need to be in a hospital. She was so restless and loved to be at home so much. I stayed with her every night and part of the time in the daytime. Dr. Rhine went every morning, and sometimes two and three times during the day he'd go by there and see how she was doing. If she needed any medicine or anything, he would take care of it. He knew that I would be there or have somebody there with her.

After about three or four weeks, she got to where she could get around and walk. She went to his office one day. I don't know if anybody was in there—probably one or two, there nearly always was.

He says, "What you fussin' about?"

"I came by to pay you."

He turned around and looked at her. "I didn't know you owed me anything."

"You mean to tell me that you have been to my house once or twice a day and took care of me like you did and that you didn't know I owed you anything?"

"You get on out of here! I carry sticks for folks like you!"

She didn't know how to take him, but later on I told her that was his way of showing her that he loved her. "Mama, I don't guess he charged an old person in his life for a dose of medicine or a trip to see how they were."

Every two or three days, Mama would go out and there would be a little pile of pine splinters out in her yard. One day, she saw Dr. Rhine out there unloading some pine that he had gathered up on his rounds. He would pick up rich lighter pine and split it up into kindling, and he would leave it in a box or sack for her.

Later, she had hardening of the arteries, and her mind got so bad. For about three years, she didn't know she was in the world. About every week or two, I'd go get her a pot of flowers. She loved flowers and always worked on them. She had a green thumb, and she would have flowers when nobody else would have flowers. When she would have a restless spell and her mind would get to wandering, she would want to transplant 'em. I would have Calvin Marshall go out and get a five gallon can full of good, loose, rich dirt and take in her room. I had linoleum on the floor. She'd sit there and move those flowers from one pot to another and water them, and then she'd be so tired, she'd go to bed and sleep for four or five hours. But she would be satisfied. She had done something she wanted to do. She would be happy and content then.

Dr. Rhine came over one day and said, "Mrs. James, you've got to get out of here. You haven't been out of this house in six months."

"Well, I used to have Lillian Parker come half a day for me to get my hair fixed and to give Mama a break, too. The last time I went, Mama tried to get up and it scared Lillian, and I never did leave Mama after that."

"I want you to get Ruth Jacobs (Ruth was always so dependable) to come down and stay with your mother one day this week, and I want you to catch that early bus and go to Little Rock or somewhere. I don't care if you don't even get off of it, but I want you to go somewhere just to get away and relax a little bit."

"What if she gets sick?"

"I promise you I'll be over here three or four times and check on her."

"I would enjoy it and I need to."

"You go on and don't you worry about a thing. Me and Ruth will take care of Granny." (He called her Granny, too.) So he did. Ruth said he came by four or five times and walked through and talked to her. Asked her if she needed any water, if there was anything she wanted. Ruth had fed her and changed her and all. He did that several times before she passed away.

I talked with Dr. Rhine about dying with a heart attack—to be snatched away without a minute to think or talk to God. He said, "Mrs. James, that's a good way to go. In fact, that is the easiest and the best way to go." Then he winked at me and said, "If you are prepared."

Bill T. had broken his arm, and we had him at the clinic at Fordyce. Dr. Rhine, Dr. Estes and Dr. Harry was in there setting it. He came out in the hall where I was sitting, crying. He said, "What are you bawling about?"

"You can hardly stand to see one of your children suffer. I wish that it was me that had broken my arm instead of Bill T."

"Mrs. James, I'm going to tell you something. The Lord knew that. He knew that a woman would do all the suffering if she could, so he made it impossible for her to do all the suffering. If he hadn't, she would have been the only one who ever suffered. She would have done the suffering for everybody and everything."

He told me one night about Gurt. Gurt was having a spell. He had gotten it into his head that he was going to die. That was twelve or fifteen years before he passed away. Dr. Rhine told me that he was going through the 'change.' He was kidding me, of course. I had worried with him and been up with him all night and taken care of him. I had taken him from one hospital to another, just anything that he wanted to do.

I said, "Dr. Rhine, what am I going to do?" I knew that I was having to call Dr. Rhine two or three times a day, and he was going to run me ragged.

"Well, Mrs. James. I'll tell you what he is going to do. He's going to run you crazy, but he ain't gonna take me with him."

"But I will. If he runs me crazy, I'm going to take you with me."

Typical expressions of Dr. Rhine as he listens to a drug salesman in his office, 1958. These pictures were taken by Milton Stark.

The Rhine home in Thornton as it looked from around 1921 to the present day.

STAFF PHOTO OF THE *HUNTERS HORN* MAGAZINE.

The cover picture of *The Hunter's Horn* magazine, June, 1953. l. to r. Milton Stark, Susan Rhine Stark holding Amy, Dr. Rhine, Mrs. Rhine and Virginia Rhine Stein.

ALEXANDER PHOTOGRAPH, FORDYCE, ARK.

Open House, May of 1959, to celebrate 60 years of practice in Thornton. Dr. and Mrs. Rhine greeted many guests all day and into the night.

Bamma Howie and Lou Ella Henderson, members of early families who continued to use Dr. Rhine, served cake and punch at the Open House.

Dr. and Mrs. Rhine with their grandchildren, Tommy, Ann and Richard Brown and their parents, Pat and Ed Brown at the Open House.

Some of the medical friends who came to honor Dr. Rhine were, l. to r.: Dr. H. Fay H. Jones, Little Rock; Dr. E. J. Byrd, Bearden; Dr. Rhine; Dr. Robert Eubanks, Little Rock; unknown; Dr. Joe Shuffield, Little Rock; and Dr. Allen G. Talbot, Lake Village.

Dr. and Mrs. Rhine in 1963 with all of their grandchildren except Virginia. They are (seated on the floor l. to r.) Amy Stark, Tommy Brown and Mary Stark, (seated on couch l. to r.) John Stark, Richard Brown, David Brown, Nita Stark and Ann Brown.

Dr. and Mrs. Rhine among the 243 red roses sent to Dr. Rhine on his 88th birthday by his loving and appreciative "families" on April 2, 1964.

FURNISHED BY FORDYCE NEWS-ADVOCATE, FORDYCE, ARK.

A portrait of Dr. Rhine was presented to the Dallas County Hospital in Fordyce after his death. l. to r. Wilton Stewart, Administrator of the hospital, Pat Rhine Brown, Ann Brown, Tommy Brown, Nanita Rhine and Carlton Mays, Chairman of the Hospital Board.

Virginia Brown, with her mother Pat, was only four months old when her grandfather, Dr. Rhine, died. The Rhine carport and sleeping porch are in the background.

PHOTO BY ROGER COLEY

Pat Rhine Brown

Thomas Edwin Rhine, M. D. 1876-1964

BRACKEN, CAMDEN, ARK.

"Lots of funny things happen, along. Lots of sad things—pitiful, pitiful, pitiful."

DR. THOMAS EDWIN RHINE

1876–1964

(From a tape made in April, 1960, when he came to Pine Bluff to become a charter member of the Fifty Year Club of the Arkansas Medical Society.)

In 1898, there were three doctors to examine me to certify me to practice medicine. Dr. Beck at Locust Bayou wanted me to come down to stay with him that summer, so I went down to see him for a week. I had to go back to school the next week to stand my examinations. I rode up to see old Dr. Jones, but couldn't see him. I went on to Thornton to see the doctor there. He asked me a big bunch of questions.

Going down the road, I ran into old Dr. Dunn. He was one of the three. He came from a side road into the road I was on. I had been once to his home. He asked me some questions as we went along the road. When I got to where I had to turn off, I did. I never heard any more from him. One day, I used Dr. Beck's buggy and drove to old Summerville to see Dr. Jones again. I got there about night, so they invited me to spend the night. He was gone. When he came in, I talked to him. He said, "Go on to bed. I'll see you in the morning." I said, "All right." He was a big fat fellow. In the night, he had to go out in the country on a case of obstetrics. He was still out there the next morning, so his son drove me out there. When I got out there, he said to his son, "Take the team back. I'll keep him here to help me deliver the baby, and then we'll come on." After a while the baby was born. He made me deliver the placenta. We got ready to go. We got in his buggy. We just drove along, he asking me questions. The buggy was tipping up on my side. I was very slight of build. The wheels were just jumping up, and I had to hold on. When we got back to his house he said, "Boy, go on back. You are practicing down there with Beck. He needs you. We'll see about getting you a license.

300

Don't worry about it." I said, "All right." That was in May. I got the license in September.

Two of Dr. Jones' sons became doctors. One, Dr. Sam Jones, was a dentist in Pine Bluff. The other one, Dr. Jack Jones, was the father of Dr. Erner Jones and Dr. Bob Jones in Little Rock.

One time a church group took up a collection to pay me for delivering a baby that I hadn't gotten anything for. It was around five dollars. The girl was a member of the congregation, and they sent a delegation to the office to give me the money.

I have delivered at least 7,000 babies. Recently, I delivered four babies in about twelve or thirteen hours. Course, there was a set of twins in that bunch.

Well, lots of funny things happen along. Lots of sad things—pitiful, pitiful, pitiful.

The only life I ever saved was a Negro they brought down from Fordyce with his throat cut. He was bleeding, and he was just barely gasping. He had no pulse at all. He had bled until that big vein was just bleeding a little bit. They brought him down to my office on a Sunday afternoon in a big ambulance. We got him in the back room, and I just reached in with forceps and got part of that vein that was cut, and then I got the other part. I didn't take time to clean him or nothing. Then I tied them together. Then, I tried to clean him up a little bit. I went to the telephone and called the University Hospital. I said, "I have a Negro man here with his throat cut. I've got the jugular vein tied. I've cleaned him up best I can, sewed him up, and dressed it. I'm sending him on up to you in the ambulance. They'll be there as quick as they can drive up there. Prepare to give him a blood transfusion, if he isn't dead. If he is dead, of course, don't give it to him." That was Sunday evening. They gave him a couple of blood transfusions, and he was back here the next Wednesday for me to dress his neck. [There were so many clamps that were used to close the cut it looked like a necklace around his neck.]

When they were putting him in the ambulance, he was jostled a bit, and I said, "Be careful of that man." One of the boys replied, "He carved his initials on me last year, so I don't care what happens to him." The Harlem Grill and the Blue Anchor Cafe in Fordyce were where most of the cuttings took place during those years—the 40's.

The first car I ever saw was a White Steamer. It had a gasoline burner on it and a tank of water on it. It belonged to Mr. Taylor, foreman of the shops at the mill. And so, I was going up in the country, and Mr. Taylor said, "Get in. I'll take you up there." I went with him, and we picked up John Harris. I don't recall just how far it was. Two sat in the front seat, and there was a little seat behind. No top. About halfway to Fordyce at Lansdale, he said, "I don't believe we have enough steam to pull that little hill. You and John had better get out." John and I got out. He got about halfway up that little hill, and the steam gave out on him. He commenced rolling backwards. He couldn't drive very good and the thing ran upside a bank and turned over. When it turned over, it broke the governors and that let the engine just run away. You never heard such a racket. John and I thought Mr. Taylor was pinned under there, so we ran down to pick the car up and let him out. When we got there, he was crawling out, and man! we left that thing. We went up the hill! He cut the gasoline off and stopped the engine. No foolishness! With the governors broken, it wouldn't run, and so we gave a boy, Ragus McClain, a dollar and a quarter to hitch his mule to that car and pull us to Thornton. We got in the car and he hitched his mule to it and got on his mule, pulled us back to Thornton.

I performed the only hip-joint operation I ever saw. I removed the little piece of leg that was left from the hip joint. A train had run over him and cut his leg off. Dr. Black gave him the anesthetic. It was in a hut down from the mill. When we got down there, they had him layin' out on a mattress on the front porch. It wasn't bleeding because it was mashed together. I said to him. "Man, you just about dead, ain't you?" He said, "No sir!"

There was a Negro man they found by the railroad track at Little Bay about three miles from Thornton. He was from Fordyce. His leg had been cut off, maybe an arm. They figured he fell off the train, and it ran over him. I kept examining around and found a hole in his head. I would push his head up and down and you could hear something rattling around. I brought his body back to the office, and sawed the top of his skull off and found a bullet. I got it out and gave it to the section foreman of the railroad. They could have sued the railroad if I hadn't found that bullet someone put in his head.

Pat Henry and I went down to deliver a baby around Bearden. She gave me five dollars. That is all she had. I didn't expect anything. Pat, he wasn't used to things like that. We got down to the old house, no steps to the porch. We had to pull ourselves on to the porch. The baby was already born. The mother and the baby were lying on a pallet on the floor—dirty. I said, "Pat, you can look after the baby, clean it up." He did the best he could.

I was president of the school board then. Mr. Johnson invited me to talk at the closing of the black school. The principal speaker was Lindsey Burrough, a Baptist preacher. He said, "Now, friends, I'll tell you. I have been pastor of this church for thirty-nine years, and I've been trying to tell you how to live, so that when you pass on, you'll go to a better place than this." When it came my time, I said, "Well, I'm just like Lindsey. I've been practicing for you for thirty-nine years, but I've been trying to keep you from going to the place that Lindsey has been trying to prepare you to go to." It tickled them to death. They just laughed and laughed.

The other night, I had my second set of triplets born. They were little Negro babies. They were born twelve miles up in the country. Cold! They didn't have enough clothes for them. Maybe for one, but not a thing for the others. It was way past midnight. This is the way we managed. We built a fire in the kitchen where they eat. We pulled the eating table by the heater, and put a quilt across that. It was folded six times. We wrapped them up in anything we could get hold of, had cleaned them up. Of course, the little things were cold. We heated some bricks. Laid one on the outside of one baby, and a brick on the other side. Put the second baby up beside it and then another hot brick. That made three bricks. We put the last baby and a hot brick on the outside of him, and covered them up. The next morning I went back up there, and the women had scoured the country over and had gotten them some clothes somehow or other. Their picture was in the paper when they were several months old.

NANNEITTA (NANITA) RAINES RHINE

1894–1979

(From a tape made in 1970)

When I was asked at the American Medical Association Convention in Washington, D.C., in 1949 what it was like to be the wife of a country doctor, I answered, "It is a very compensating life if you can live over it." I never did overcome my feeling of sympathy for the people who needed help.

When Doctor suffered a stroke in 1924, people would come. (When people 'took sick,' others came in droves to see about them. Doctor would often remark, "You must not crowd into a room around a sick person.") They came by droves to see what they could do to help Dr. Rhine. He would hear someone's voice out in the yard, and he would say, "Oh, I hear so and so. I want to see him." Mr. Jim Steelman sat himself under a tree outside, telling me. "If Doctor needs anything, be sure to call me." So, if I had to move him for some reason, I would call Mr. Steelman in to help. That satisfied them both.

We were going to Temperance Hill to a funeral. We were in a rush to get off—a little late, of course. Doctor grabbed his hat, and as we went out the door, I noticed that he had a hole in his pants. I said, "Now you can't go like this." Well, he didn't see any reason not to, but I insisted, and he went back to change his pants. We went on. That hat had a hole in the peak. When we got there, I stayed in the car because the funeral had already begun in the little church. He went on into the cemetery. Some fellow, sitting in his car, came over and spoke to me, and crawled into the car with me. I realized that he had been drinking, but there was nothing that I could do about it—so we sat and talked. He kept looking at Doctor's hat that was sitting on the seat. Finally, he reached into his pocket and pulled out a five dollar bill and said, "Here! Give this to Doc and tell him I said to buy himself a new hat." It embarassed me very much, but he insisted. When Doctor came back to the car, I said, "Well, here's five dollars to buy you a new hat. That fellow kept looking at the hole in your hat." Doctor replied, "If you had let me wear those pants, maybe he would have bought me a new suit of clothes." Reese

Parham, who was sitting in the next car, fell over laughing and said, "Doc, he could have bought you two or three suits and then still owed you."

One night a drunk man came up to the back door. He was cut up. He kept trying to explain to Doctor how it happened. Doctor would tell him, "Shut up! I don't care how you got cut." Just about the time we got back to sleep, he returned to the back door shouting, "Oh Doc! Doc! I'm ready to tell you the truth this time." "You get away from here or I'll bash in the other side of your head." They were always 'playing around' when these accidents occurred.

Another time, a girlfriend explained that she was just 'wrasslin' and threw her boyfriend down, and his head hit a telephone pole. The cut was smooth, like a knife would have made and was about four inches long.

His greatest dislike was drink. He had very little patience with people who drank. However, a journalistic classic involved a patient of his who would quite often go on a spree. He was the editor of a weekly paper in another town. Once, as a result of a spree that lasted several days, the paper arrived with large letters across the top, "At the request of the subscribers, we are reprinting last week's edition of the paper."

Mr. Dan McManus had a blacksmith shop across the street from Doctor's office. One day, a drug salesman came to see Doctor. He asked him how old he was. Doctor answered, "I'm seventy-three years old and can outrun any seventy-three-year-old man in Thornton." Dan put his hammer down, came over and challenged Doctor. "All right, Doc, let's try it out." They started running down that street, and Dan later told me, he thought, "If one of us falls down, can the other one pick him up?"

I remember one time when Pat was a baby, Doctor came in one morning. There was a safety pin lying on the floor. He stood and just looked at that safety pin and looked at it. I said, "Why are you looking so at that pin?"

"I'd have given a hundred dollars for that pin last night. I delivered twins. They had clothes only for one of them and very few at that. There wasn't any safety pins."

I got up all the clothes that I had and Doctor took them out there. The neighbors went to Fordyce the next morning and bought the twin babies some clothes.

One of his patients that he always got a lot of fun out of was Gurt James. One night, Doctor was taking him to the hospital in Little Rock in an ambulance, and Mr. James was scared to death. He had had a heart attack. He just knew that he was going to die. Every once in a while he would say, "Doc, I think I'm going to die. Do you reckon I'm going to die?" And Doctor would answer, "I don't know. You might." Later, Mr. James would tell this and laugh, but at the time, it wasn't funny.

Doctor was in the hospital a few times. One time he had had a light pneumonia—flu, anyway, and we took him to Fordyce. He got along well and in a few days we were to come home, or thought we were. Our bags were packed to go home on Monday morning. He called to me and said,

"Tell the nurse to come down." I got her, and he told her to call Dr. Atkinson and tell him to come back. He had already been there earlier. Dr. Rhine said, "I have a strangulated hernia and they are going to have to operate."

Dr. Atkinson came and said, "I can't believe this."

"It's true. I have already found it and you call Dr. Jamison and tell him to sharpen up his knives. He is going to have to operate."

He was then in the hospital for several days. It was quite strenuous, and there were many inquiries as to his condition from well-meaning patients. There were so many, in fact, that the hospital administrator, Mr. Wilton Stewart, would report his condition to the radio station twice a day for the news broadcast.

One afternoon, several days later, there was a knock at the door. I went to see who it was, and a woman was standing there. She said that she wanted to pay Doctor what she owed him. I told her that I didn't know how much it was. Could she wait until we got home? She answered, "I know how much I owe him, and I've owed him that for twenty years. When I heard on the radio that he was sick, I couldn't wait to come pay him. He came to see my child once, when we couldn't get another doctor. Please take this twenty dollars."

Though he drove many miles, he had very few accidents. However, one early evening, he had started to Bearden, and a big truck hit him in passing and bashed in the side of his car. It bummed him up a little—hurt his leg. He got out, and the truck had stopped. The driver came back to check on him. When the State Police arrived, Doctor explained that it wasn't the driver's fault, that the trailer had swung over. They let the truck driver go on. The policeman wanted to take Doctor to the hospital, but Doctor objected saying, "I've got a sick woman to go see." He went on in a neighbor's car to make his call, before returning and allowing the policeman to take him to the hospital to be checked for injuries. Nothing but a cut on his leg.

Another time on a call to Harrell, he must have gone to sleep and drove the car into a ditch. When he couldn't get it out, he walked about a mile or so to a house and got them to take him to see the patient in Harrell. He then called home to have me send someone to get the car out and come pick him up.

Then there was the time we were hit by the freight train. That was quite an accident, but we were fortunate that no one was injured very much. I had a little break in my ankle, and Doctor had one or two ribs broken.*

*They were coming home from the rehearsal dinner. Ed and I were getting married. Daddy stopped at the railroad crossing, but when he saw the signal man wave his light, he started across the tracks. The signal man was waving a train to come on, and it hit them, pushing the car about a hundred yards down the track. Mother's head was cut in the hairline and down her forehead, so we took her to the office to see about it. Daddy was so distressed, he was sobbing and trembling. I was standing by Mother, who was in the examining chair. I closed my eyes for just a moment, and when I opened them, the professional had taken over in Daddy, and he was now a calm, unemotional and able

At the end of his sixty years of practice in Thornton, in May of 1959, he decided that he would have a celebration of some kind, and so we planned an Open House. I went to Fordyce to see if I could get someone to bake a huge cake. I went to the bakery, but he didn't have any pans as large as I thought we would need. He didn't understand at all why I wanted a cake so large, but he said that he could get the large pans. So we had a four or five-tiered cake made, and it looked like it would feed an awful lot of folks. Even when he brought it, he said, "You are going to have half of this left." Even so, I had thought that might not be enough, so I had made some cakes earlier and put them in the deep freeze, in case we did need them.

The party was to start about one-thirty or two in the afternoon, but that morning people began to come in about ten o'clock. I know that I said that was one day that I never did get my hair combed. I just kept meeting people at the door and doing around. We had asked different members of families that were there when Doctor began practicing to help serve. They were all pleased to be included in the party.

But when we got up that morning, I went out on the front porch to pick up the paper, and there were signs all over the place—KKK [Ku Klux Klan] signs. I couldn't see any except in front of our house. We certainly wanted all of the people, black and white, to come and be part of it, because he served everyone and did the best he could for everyone. I called Doctor, and he called the sheriff's office. He did some investigating and found they were everywhere, so we went ahead with our plans. We had visitors all day and into the night, and there was no cake left, even in the freezer. Everyone had a good time together.

When Doctor was to be eighty-eight years old, April 2, 1964, some ladies in Fordyce decided they would give him a surprise for his birthday. The day before his birthday, Miss Gee Dedman called to say that they had asked each family of his patients to give him one red rose. He was very fond of red roses. They were going to bring them down around noon the next day and wanted me to have Doctor there. I thought that I had better bake a cake to have for anyone who came and make some punch, too. I urged him to go 'stretch out' for a little and rest. I heard the doorbell ring, but I let him go. Naturally, he thought that it was a patient. There were three women with huge baskets of roses—243 of them. They wished him a happy birthday, visited awhile, and had cake and punch. Then they went on. Doctor went back to the office. Some more friends came by. I called him back, and for the rest of the afternoon people came in to wish him a happy birthday. This went on until late in the night. The last to come were some people who had formerly lived in Thornton, but were now living in Texas. They had stopped at a filling station and learned about the birthday and came on

---

doctor. He proceeded to stitch up Mother's cut, as he would any other patient—very proficiently. That was an astonishing transformation. The next morning, after making his rounds to see sick folks, he took Mother to Fordyce to be x-rayed, as well as himself. Both had broken bones. PRB

down. That was one of the happiest days that he had because so much appreciation was shown him, and he had always said that he wanted his roses while he could smell them and not later.

Through the years quite often people would come and ask him for help in ways other than medicine. He always tried to give help whenever he could. I used to tease him by asking, "Are you also a lawyer, a farmer, an agriculturist, a livestock man, too?"

During the last few years of his life, he devoted much time to going around making talks promoting the building of a hospital in Fordyce, because he realized that the days of a country doctor going to a home many miles away and taking care of a patient was a thing of the past. He also worked for a clinic in Hampton. They did get a hospital in Fordyce in 1958. I feel that his practice was prolonged because of it. He could have his patients there instead of traveling many miles to see them.

His last illness—I drove him up to the hospital myself and he said that he would not recover from that illness. I told him, "Yes, you will." He had a kind of pneumonia and got along just fine. We returned home, and every day he improved just a little. He was even talking about seeing a few patients at home the next week. He knew that he had had a light stroke while he was in the hospital, and also one earlier in the year, around his birthday time. On Sunday, he had a massive stroke and only lived for three days. He had always told me when you have small strokes you might look out for the big one, and that proved to be true in his case.

Since then, so many wonderful things have been said about him and so many stories, people seem even not to realize that he is gone. He seems alive to his patients. They are constantly recalling different things that happened and telling funny stories that he told, things that he did for them, unbelievable things that he did in the practice of medicine.

VIRGINIA RHINE STEIN

ANN ARBOR, MICHIGAN

Our family life was conditioned and subordinated really, totally, to his supreme devotion to the practice of medicine. Daddy's day usually began as early as four-thirty or five in the morning when he got up to feed his dogs and take care of the livestock and milk the cow at the barn. Very often, he was off making calls by five o'clock, and Mother had to take over those chores. Usually, I, being the oldest child, was responsible for answering the telephone, and calls always began to come in by six o'clock or six-thirty. I can remember that, as early as five or six years old, I was already taking calls from people who were calling in for Daddy's services.

One of Mother's favorite stories was about how I took a call one day, and the lady said that her child was so terribly, terribly sick, and, in imitation of my father, said, "Oh well, all you do is give 'em half a gallon of castor oil and follow that with a gallon of epsom salts." This was Daddy's favorite way of telling people to purge themselves after taking calomel tablets, which was one of the great remedies in the practice of medicine during his day.

The telephone was a very important piece of technology in our house. Our telephone was in the kitchen on the wall, our first one, and it was hooked up to the telephone at the office, so that if anyone called the office number, the telephone automatically rang at home, and if we knew that Daddy was not at the office, we could answer the phone at home. Our telephone number, I still remember, was 2–4, and Miss Essie O'Keefe manned the little telephone board out of her house over near the jailhouse in Thornton. She was a very important adjunct to Daddy's practice of medicine, as were the telephone operators of the Fordyce exchange after the Thornton exchange was discontinued.*

These ladies, such as Miss Ellie McClain, would keep the calls for Daddy, acting as an answering service for him when he was away. One of our jobs, always, when we left the house to be gone any amount of time was to "tell Central" where we were going and how long we would be away. Daddy always called when we got back to see if any calls had been left, if there were any trips he would have to make.

Our leave-taking was always an excitement and a time of stress, because we never knew exactly when we were going to get away. If Daddy came running in from the office and said, "Let's go for a little visit" to somewhere, Mother was ready with a wet rag and clean clothes. She would grab us children, and clean us up in the car, so that we could get away ahead of any patients coming in who required Daddy's attentions or ahead of a call that would take him out in the country again. I well remember once when we were planning a nice trip, I don't recall where, but we had already gotten into the car and Daddy had the motor going when someone drive up and asked him to make a call in the country. We had to pile out of the car and give up our trip. This happened rather often, so when we were getting ready to go, we had a saying, "Run turn off the pump and tell Central." Those were the two obligatory functions that had to be performed before we left home.

Daddy had a little slate out at the back door. People who came while we were away could write a message on the slate. Mother often left a notice on that slate-board, too, of where we had gone and when we expected to be back.

You might say that our house functioned as hotel, emergency room, clinic, even hospital, because during the course of my childhood, we saw the house function in all these capacities. Daddy did surgery, minor surgery, a tonsillectomy on Alpha Barner. Daddy didn't very often do surgery in his office. Usually, he took patients, even for minor surgery, to Camden or to

*Our telephone number then was 521-J1. PRB

Little Rock. But in the case of Alpha Barner, her tonsils were taken out in Daddy's office, and then he brought her home and installed her in our front bedroom, so that he could watch over her the rest of the day after the operation and during the night. She stayed overnight, and the next day she was well enough that Daddy thought she could be taken home.

Another time, when a young couple from El Dorado, had gone to Pine Bluff to a dance and had imbibed too much, probably, and on the way back, in the wee hours of the morning, they failed to negotiate the ninety degree angle turn in Thornton onto the El Dorado highway and had an accident. We were all waked up and Daddy jumped in his car and ran over to the corner and brought the young girl back. She was in a state of shock. She wasn't injured too badly, I think, but she was put to bed, too.

So many people came to our house with cuts and broken bones. I remember one late fall evening when Mr. Lewis Simpson came in with his arm gashed almost from his shoulder to his elbow from a run-in with a wild hog. Daddy wasn't at home, so he had to wait on our back porch until Daddy came to tend to him.

An especially exciting time was early one morning. I was perhaps nine or ten, when a lady came with her child who was having convulsions. The grandmother was in the car. They brought the child onto the porch. Susan and I helped Mother get hot water and cold water. We ran from the kitchen to the porch with a pan of hot water, then a pan of cold water, to plunge the baby in, to try to control the convulsions. The mother was so distraught that she kept marching up and down the sidewalk, shouting, "Oh Lord, have mercy!" She was so distraught that she wasn't much help. The grandmother held the baby and helped Mother try to control the convulsions. Daddy came in after the baby had been brought out of the seizures.

Almost every Saturday night there was an invasion of people who had gotten into fights either at home or at some of the cafes over on the highway or in Fordyce. They would come driving up to the back of the house, stop in the grove, and shout for Daddy. Daddy knew they had been into some kind of mischief, so he would be terribly gruff. He'd say. "What do you mean waking me up in the middle of the night?" He would always crawl out of bed and either take them to the office to stitch them up or bandage them up, but very often he would bring them into the bathroom at home, so he wouldn't have to dress and go out.

One time, a bunch of people came down in two cars. One of the fellows had gotten pretty badly cut up with a razor blade, and he came in. While Daddy was fixing him up in the bathroom, the people out in the other car got into a fight, and he had to sew up a second one. That happened to be on Christmas Eve night, and the next morning when we got up, we found the steps covered with blood and blood all over the bathroom floor. We were expecting company that day for dinner. (Mother always had Daddy's family—sisters, nieces and nephews and their families—for Christmas dinner.) We had to get busy cleaning up that mess, scrubbing the floor and steps early that morning.

Once I remember getting terribly upset when Daddy had to remove the nail from an infected finger of little Sue Ann Thornton. She was brought over by her mother after supper one night, and Daddy proceeded to take the nail off. I remember how she screamed. I was in the bedroom with Mother, and I think that I was screaming right along with her. I got so upset that Daddy was hurting her so. I shouted to Mother, "Why doesn't he stop? Why doesn't he stop? He's hurting her so. He's hurting her so." I think he was hurting me as much as he was hurting her, in a way.

In those days, back in the late 20's and 30's, there was no hotel in Thornton, there were no restaurants, so our home was the place where any visiting "big-wigs" ended up for meals or even for overnight stays. We used to always have the Commencement speakers for the High School graduation in our home, when they came from another town, and they spent the night. One particular time, a professor from Hendrix College was the speaker. He was a very interesting person. He was a White Russian emigre from the Bolshevik Revolution and had a great deal to tell about his previous life in Russia. He didn't know all the Arkansas folkways, and Selma, our cook, was absolutely "laid out." She came early the next morning to make breakfast for the company. She had ham, biscuits and "red-eye" gravy. When she passed the gravy to this professor, he asked, "What do I do with that?" Selma let out a laugh and said, "Lawd-a-mercy, Sir, you puts that on your biscuits!"

Daddy never hesitated to bring people home for lunch or even for supper. We always had a lot of food, and he was extraordinarily hospitable. Mother never knew how many people she was going to have around the table for any given meal. I think the record though was the time Daddy brought home the entire State Game and Fish Commission. This story became part of the family lore.

Upon inviting people home for a meal, Daddy would always say, "I can't promise you anything good to eat, but I can give you a glass of cool water." The State Game and Fish Commission had come down to look into the affair of the draining of the pond, which I'll tell more about later. Daddy called from the office this time and said, "Nita, I'm bringing over the Game and Fish Commission members for dinner." That was the noon meal. That really turned us into a tailspin. Mother had already gotten dinner onto the table in the kitchen with a table cloth that had a hole in it. She sent us all scurrying around. We got the table re-set in the dining room with a clean cloth and had most of the food transferred to the dining room, when in came Daddy with twelve men! Fortunately, Mother and Selma had usually cooked up enough for the noon meal and supper, so there was plenty of turnip greens and mashed potatoes. The Chairman of the Commission, seeing what a stew we were in, walked to the swinging door between the dining room and the kitchen, poke his head in and asked, "Ladies, is there anything I can do to help?" Selma, without batting an eye, and handing him a dish, said, "Yessir, you can set these taters on the table." Mother was so embarassed that Selma had done that, but it became one of those lines that you repeat over and over.

Daddy always brought company in the back door, which bothered Mother a bit. Once, when he brought William Stout home for a meal and came in the back door, Mother asked him, "Why do you have to bring these important people to the back door? Can't you bring them in the front door?"

"Nita, they are all human beings. They all get sick. There's no difference between them and anyone else."

Because Daddy was on the school board for thirty-five years and president part of that time, we always knew when he was going to be interviewing prospective teachers. Very often, after he had given them his own brand of "going over," he would bring them home for a meal. We often knew who would be the new school teachers for the coming year well ahead of a public announcement.

Whenever the churches had a revival meeting in the summertime with guest preachers coming for a stay of a week or even ten days, Daddy always invited the visiting preacher and the local resident minister to have dinner with us. Although at table Daddy never said "grace," he always made sure that when we had a visiting minister or someone he knew was a faithful churchgoer, he would ask them to say grace at the table.

One of the things we learned very early on as children of T. E. Rhine, M. D. was how to exercise extreme discretion. We learned to be very discreet in what we talked about. We were never allowed to gossip. In the case of the school teachers, even though we might know, we were not allowed to talk about this. We often knew about the patients. We had to be mum when we heard talk about girls who were pregnant out of wedlock or when Daddy acted as marriage counselor (which he often did) to couples having trouble in their marriage. There were many things that we had to keep to ourselves. Not that they were divulged to us, but because we saw who came to the house, and overhead remarks that could not be talked about.

My own initiation into learning about being discreet was when I must have been eight or nine years old. It was close to Thanksgiving time and Mr. Zell Hearnsberger had brought a great big bird for our Thanksgiving dinner. Mother and I took a walk down the street to our Auntie Condray's, and on the way we met Mr. Peterson, and I piped up with my childish enthusiasm, "Oh Mr. Peterson, do you know what we are going to have for Thanksgiving? We are going to have a great big bird that Mr. Zell just brought in." Well, much to my astonishment, Mother whisked me away, brought me directly home, and it was the only time I ever recall being threatened with a spanking with a hair brush. I had no idea what the problem was. I broke into tears, where upon she told me that this big bird I had been so excitedly talking about was a wild turkey that Mr. Zell had shot out of season and under no circumstances was I to broadcast this because it might get Mr. Zell into trouble with the law. From then on, I never "talked out of school."*

*My recollection of later "big birds" being brought by Mr. Zell was that they were always referred to as "capons," and were especially delicious, the breast being sliced off, breaded and fried as you would a country fried steak. PRB

Daddy never talked about his childhood very much. I once asked him when he had decided to become a doctor. He told me that ever since he had been a little boy, picking cotton on the farm, that he had known that he wanted to be a doctor. I've often wondered since I grew up who must have been his role model. He never mentioned any old doctor who might have given him the inspiration to become a practitioner of medicine. Maybe it really was, like Mother used to say, he, like a minister, had had a calling to the practice of medicine.

He must have worked very hard on the farm, being the only boy of the family. Aunt May, his youngest sister, has told me that Daddy would take her out in the field with him when he was chopping or picking cotton, and she would stay all day long, playing at his side, while he worked the rows of cotton or corn. As a result, she was devoted to him, really looked up to him with adulation all her life.

Daddy had a great sense of loyalty and love for the neighborhood of Pansy, where he lived as a boy, and the people he knew there. He often talked about the Thomasson family. Even when we were growing up, he tried to go every summer to the Prosperity Cemetery graveyard working located in that vicinity. It was always in August, and it was terribly, terribly hot.

One particular one I remember, I must have been eight or nine years old, Daddy went to the store before we left, and instead of Mother making fried chicken and packing a picnic basket from the kitchen, he bought oranges and store "light" bread and bologna and took it over there. I remember yet, as Mother spread out the bologna, bread and oranges, those young farm children of that rural community gathering around. I'm sure they didn't have oranges very often or bologna either, so when they saw this on the picnic table, they grabbed it up quickly.

I felt sorry for and puzzled by those young people, because I saw the girls wearing long white stockings. In the heat of the summer, it seemed so hot to me. They were very conservative people and probably the parents felt the young girls' legs should not be exposed. I myself was in knee socks, so it seemed to me those long stockings must be most uncomfortable and old-fashioned for girls to be wearing.

Two things that Daddy used to recount about his years in medical school. One was the fact that he made ninety-nine percent, as he put it, on all of his exams. This record he held up for us to emulate. We used to kid him a bit and dubbed him "ninety-nine percent Rhine." For me, it was a very exacting and difficult standard to meet. I longed for my Father's approval, and I thought the only way I could get it was to do well in school. I really worked hard to win the medals that Daddy gave to the best students in each class in school, hoping that that would receive Daddy's approbation. I don't recall that he ever bragged on me though I won the first place medal every year except the year when I skipped from the fifth to the sixth grade. Daddy always expected me to do better than I had done. If I made a B+ in Deportment, he would say, "That can be improved." So he had very high and very exacting standards for us.

The second thing that Daddy talked about was the time of his graduation from medical school. He was to be given the second highest award in the class for scholarship. He wrote to his father asking for money to buy a new suit of clothes for the graduation ceremonies. His father refused, but his Mother sent him eleven dollars, money that she had saved from selling butter and eggs. With that money, he bought a new shirt, a new tie and a secondhand suit. We still have the shirt and the tie that he wore at his graduation.

Daddy was devoted to his mother, who came to live with him in Thornton several years after he came there and kept his house until her death, shortly after he and Mother were married in 1921.

The above anecdote perhaps explains why Daddy was always at pains to ask us (it was one of the ways he showed his love for us) when we were leaving home to go away to school, or for me to the East, or just away for a visit, if we had any money in our pocket. Whether we said yes or no, he always insisted on pulling a few dollar bills and some loose change out of his pocket and pressing the money on us to take "for a little good time" he would say.*

Of the period of his life during World War I, Daddy used to recall two stories over and over. He apparently got a tremendous kick out of the throngs of celebrants in London when the Armistice was signed in November of 1918. He was in Leicester Square and an old English lady grabbed him around the neck and gave him a kiss on either cheek.

The other story of his war time experiences was this. He was walking down a street in London when he spied, on a corner, a black American soldier. He called him, of course, in the parlance of the 30's, a "darkie." He walked up to him and said, "Boy, where are you from?" The soldier boy replied, "Boss, gimme a dime." Daddy then found that the soldier came from Eagle Mills, Arkansas, and those two American Yankee soldiers found some brotherly love there on a London street corner in the midst of World War I.

Mother and Daddy were married on September 28, 1921, and the plan was that they would go to Niagara Falls, on their honeymoon. They were married in the home of Aunt Sudie and Uncle Vasco Hinton in Little Rock and left immediately after by train for Memphis, where they stayed overnight in the Peabody Hotel. There, Daddy got sick, and he also learned that his Mother had had a spell. She apparently was very upset at the idea of her son getting married. Mother recalled that Daddy got a "sick stomach", and from then on, every time he had to leave home, he would get an upset stomach. We called it "the Rhine stomach," and I think I inherited it. At any rate, the honeymoon was cut short and they went back to Thornton

---

*One of the great satisfactions and pleasure for him, he later told me, was to be able to buy nice clothes for us during our teen-age and college years. During the Depression of the 30's, we all wore "hand-me-downs." I was fourth in line for hand-me-down clothes, so it is not strange that I can remember the first outfit bought expressly for me. I was eleven years old. PRB

from Memphis. Mother always claimed that Daddy owed her a trip to Niagara Falls, which she never collected.

The early days of their marriage must have been rather rough with "Mammy" Rhine in the house and Mother a new bride there. She never dwelled on the early days of her marriage except for this example of "assertiveness." Daddy was a typical man of his era, considering that the male was the head of the household and the provider. He must have carried the idea of authority into the early days of his marriage. One day when they were first married, Daddy was out in the garden planting some onions. He called her to come to the garden. She went out, and he said in a most imperious tone, "Go up to Mr. Edmondson's and get me some more onion slips!" It was characteristic of Mother, who was only four feet and eleven inches tall, that she replied to him, "Dr. Rhine, you may *ask* me to go to Mr. Edmondson's, but you will *never* order me to go."

I never heard any harsh words between Mother and Daddy. They never, at least before us, were disagreeable to each other. Daddy was never one to give people compliments. He could never really tell us that we looked pretty. I don't recall that he ever gave Mother many compliments. When he wanted to tell her that she looked well, when he happened to notice that she had a new dress on, he would say, "Well Boss, that dress certainly does come right at you!"

Among the bunch of letters Mother had saved was one of the few letters he had ever written to her. He ended it by saying how much he missed her music. His love of music was a tie between them. Often, as he would rest by the fire, he would request some of his favorites, such as "The Blue Danube" for Mother to play on the piano while we sang.*

They both had a sense of humor. In the terrible mid-years of the Depression when Daddy was seeing the whole community in such poor circumstances, people hungry without adequate clothes, children without shoes, he came in one day from his rounds. He was in a tremendous depression. Mother saw him come in the back door, and he had in his hand a little bunch of carrots. The tops had wilted over, and to her he looked about as wilted as the carrots. She looked at him and laughed and said, "Well Dr. Rhine, you can still bring home the bacon." He gave a sheepish grin and brightened up.

There are two times I recall when Daddy was deeply, profoundly affected by the death of one of his patients. One of these was the death of the first Mrs. Hugh Gresham, who was a young woman, I imagine in her thirties, and she had just given birth a few months before to a baby. She had pneumonia, which was untreatable in those days. It wasn't often that someone recovered from pneumonia, and Daddy had attended her day and night for a week. Daddy was so upset by his inability to save her, knowing

---

*Mother frequently played the piano on Sunday afternoons, and we would dance if she played waltzes or two-steps. I loved to waltz with Daddy, because he would do it with a great flourish and many twirls. PRB

314

that she had this young family, that he couldn't bring himself to go to the funeral.

The other incident was the death of the little blind girl down at Harlow that Daddy had helped get to the Arkansas Children's Hospital, where she had been treated, and with some glasses had gained some sight. Her mother had been doing a washing out in the yard with a fire under the pot, and this child had fallen into the fire and was burned so badly that she died. Daddy cried over that death. Daddy had taken Pat with him to see that little girl. She had come up to Pat, felt her face and said, "She's got eyes. She has a nose. She has a mouth." Daddy was so affected by the fact that his child was all right and that child was so handicapped.

Daddy was very concerned about helping the farmers to upgrade their crops and their livestock. One of the ways that he helped to do this was by giving settings of eggs to anybody that would come and ask for it. He had fine Leghorn chickens and Rhode Island Reds. He also saved the seed from the best watermelons, dried them and gave them out. He tried to introduce pheasants into the woods around Thornton for hunting. I remember a crate of pheasant eggs arriving—they were a different color. He had those eggs hatched and put the young pheasants out near the farms, but they didn't survive.

He raised hogs. I was about five years old. He had an enormous hog that had won first prize, the blue ribbon, at the State Fair. It was taken to the State Fair the following year, and we all were taken to Little Rock to see the hog and go to the Fair. We got up about three o'clock in the morning, and at Fordyce we took the route by the lumber mill (I recall the piles of sawdust burning) because we were going to Ramsey to pick up Mr. and Mrs. Naylor and their young daughter, about our age, who had fallen and dented in her scull. She was being taken to Little Rock to have a metal plate inserted in her head where her brain was being pressured.

When we got to Little Rock, we found out that the hog had been maimed in some way by some ill-intentioned person, and it had to be slaughtered when it was brought home. Mother always talked about the great amount of lard that they rendered from that one hog, probably thirty or forty gallons.

By rendering, I mean the procedure we went through every winter in the kitchen. People very often paid their bills with whole hogs that they had fattened up, slaughtered and brought in to our house. We had to cut the fat up into chunks, one or two inches square, and boil it in large pots, either on the kitchen stove or in black iron washpots outside, until the fat had been "rendered" out of those chunks of fat with the skin on the outside. That's the way we made the lard that we used the full year for cooking. The lard was stored in big earthenware crocks. The cracklings, which were the crisp outer skin with a bit of fat remaining on them were used in making 'cracklin' bread. That is, added to corn bread batter and cooked. We also ate brains and eggs scrambled together for breakfast the next morning after we had received a hog. Selma would make a liver and lights stew, and the best

315

part of the hog was the tenderloin. The hams were cured in our smokehouse and stored in a large wooden bin, salted down.

One of the greetings that Daddy had, particularly for older women, was, "Mornin, Miss Frisky. How are you this morning?" Pat, quite young, picked this up and while walking down the street with Mother, met one of Mother's friends, and Pat piped up, "Good morning, Miss Frisky. How are you today?" and Mother was mortified.

Daddy, on two occasions that I can remember, was under some danger from patients and others, from threats against his life. Mother and Daddy tried to keep things of this nature away from us—tried to protect us from the fears that were generated by his practice and also the sadnesses. A lot of that, however, filtered through to us, and because it was filtered, I don't know many of the details.

His life was threatened once by the father of a young man who had syphilis and who was treated by Daddy. The young man died subsequently as a result of the syphilis, and the father threatened him. There was concern for some time that he might do harm to Daddy.

The other threat was a result of the political ambitions of one "Turkey" Fultz from Bearden, who was running for sheriff of Ouachita County. In order to woo votes, he decided to have a big, big fish fry. He elected to get his fish supply by bringing some of his cronies up to Thornton one night and breaking the dam of the Little Pond and catching all of the fish, draining the pond dry. He had his fish fry, but as a result of that, Daddy got the State Game and Fish Commission on to the case, and "Turkey" Fultz was tried and sentenced to prison by the Prosecutor Oren Harris. "Turkey" Fultz vowed that when he got out of prison, he was heading to Thornton with a shotgun to get Dr. Rhine. He did get out, and the first encounter did not result in any harm to Daddy, but there was this concern, and I remember that when we knew that "Turkey" Fultz was going to be released, there was a good bit of tension around the house.

Daddy and Mother were determined that all of us should have a good education, and it was talked about in the home. That was really our goal. We were going to be given a chance to have a good education, and it was our responsibility to take whatever we got and do something with it. We also knew that the money for financing that education would come from the virgin timberland that Mother and Daddy owned. They would say, "If we have to sell the timber for your education, we will be glad to. That's what it is for." We also knew that it was in jeopardy from fires and that it was Mr. Vernon Jones who was the caretaker of it and our education.

Mr. Vernon Jones was a forest ranger with the State Forestry Service. He lived about halfway between Thornton and Hampton, and there was a fire lookout tower across from his house. That was a terrible catastrophe in those days, for fire to start in the forests, because there was no way to fight it, except perhaps starting a "back fire." That was one of the things the CCC [Civilian Conservation Corps] boys did in the 30's. They had a camp, again halfway between Thornton and Hampton, a few barracks. One of the jobs that they did was to clear roads through the forests to act as fire breaks.

I would say to Mr. Jones, "Take care of my education. Don't let any fire get into our timberland."

I suspect that the death of Daddy's mother some months after his marriage, my own birth, and the very fact that his whole life pattern changed so drastically, really quite late in life (he was 45 when he married, 46 when I was born) must have been contributing factors to make for a build-up of stress which did, two years after I was born, result in a stroke of paralysis.

Mother always said that she was absolutely terrified when he had the stroke that she was going to be left as a young mother with two tiny children—I was twenty months old and Susan was five months old—and an incapacitated, invalid husband. I don't remember when Daddy had his stroke, though I'm told I was extremely upset when I had to be taken away from his bed where I had been sleeping.

Daddy's doctors in Little Rock, Pat Murphey and Anderson Watkins, who remained long and steadfast friends throughout their lives, thought that he would never practice again. He had a tremendous willpower and a strong physical endowment, and it was less than a year after the stroke that he was able to go back to practicing medicine.

The event that really got him back on his feet was the fire that destroyed the barn and burned up some of his horses. The barn caught fire and in order to try to save his horses, Daddy got up, ran to the barn and tried to get the horses out. That was the turning point in his recovery. He always said that he practiced far harder after his stroke than he ever did before.

My first memory of Daddy was when I was three years old and I woke up in my crib one fall morning, a cloudy, dark morning. I heard strange noises in the front bedroom. Little noises that sounded like a little lamb, and all kinds of coming and going down the hall and into the bedroom. Daddy came into the room, came to my crib, lifted me up and took me to the front bedroom. I met for the first time my new, little cousin, Nita Raines Moseley. Aunt Mary Sue had come to our home in Thornton for her confinement, and Nita was born in the early hours of November 1. However for us children, it was Halloween night, so from then on, Nita was dubbed "Spooks," and we called her that for many, many years. She would always call Daddy "Uncle Doctor."

Thornton was a thriving town when Daddy came there in May of 1899 to begin his practice. * His office was at the back of the mill Commissary. The front of the Commissary also housed the drug store and pharmacy which Dr. C. T. Black ran. There was also an ice cream parlor there, and some of the old wire ice cream chairs and tables that Daddy had in his office years afterward were part of the equipment of that old pharmacy.

*His first office was in the Belk Hotel, where he lived, until he became a doctor for the Stout Lumber Company in 1900. PRB

I remember going with Mother and Daddy to a silent movie in a motion picture house that was located near the Commissary. I was so tiny, Mother sat me up on the arm of the seat, and I watched some clipped, white French poodles being put through their tricks. I recall being taken to a circus under a big tent that was pitched on the old tennis courts across the street from the Commissary. I was taken by Uncle Rogers, the old colored man who often did yard and garden work for Daddy. Uncle Rogers got so tickled at one of the performers who had a mustache that curled around in a nice little curl over each cheek. He described it as having "swallowed a pig and left the tail hanging out."

I was three years old when the mill burned, and I can remember that it was on a Christmas Eve and a Christmas morning. I remember coming out into our backyard and standing on the sidewalk and seeing the sky completely filled with dark, murky smoke and seeing red flames on the horizon in the direction of the mill and seeing the cinders from the burning mill falling into the yard around us.

This spelled the end of Thornton as a prosperous mill town. Within a year or so the head management had left and many of the inhabitants had left, too. Only those who were elderly or did not wish to make a new life for themselves remained. In a sense, Thornton became a kind of ghost town.

By then Daddy had expanded his practice to the countryside around Thornton and was not dependent solely on his position as mill doctor, so he elected to remain in Thornton. By then, he had been there more than a quarter of a century.

There was only one time when there was the possibility that he might leave Thornton. After Dr. Harry Atkinson, Sr. died and Dr. Wendell Ward left Fordyce, some of the city fathers, a delegation of them, came down and asked Daddy if he would consider moving to Fordyce and setting up his practice there. What a turmoil this created for Daddy, and the stress of the decision for him to make a change was indeed great. He went to Little Rock to talk with Dr. Murphey about whether he should make the move. His advice was, "I give you one year to live if you take on that big practice." Daddy was amused in later years, and I think proud of himself for it, too, that during World War II he virtually did assume the practice in Fordyce and added it to his own and at a very advanced age—late 60's and early 70's.

I can still feel the sense of relief that Daddy exuded when he walked into the living room and told Mother and we girls that he had decided not to go to Fordyce. I was too young to understand the decision at the time, and I was very resentful and disappointed that Daddy had chosen not to move us to Fordyce. I had many friends there already. I was a member of the Girl Scout Troop; we went to Fordyce to have dancing lessons; I had voice and piano lessons there. I was really eager to move to be with the new friends I had made and who shared many of the same interests that I had. I felt at the time that he really didn't take into account his children's interests and needs.

Indeed, my early memories of Daddy are of a very stern and authoritative parent. Susan and I were particularly affected by the paralysis that Daddy had and the aftermath. Mother always said that he was extremely nervous, and she had to keep us from crying around him. We really learned early on to repress our feelings and didn't have the freedom to be children that most children have.

We were especially afraid of Daddy when it came to having to take shots. Everybody in the neighborhood knew when we were going to have shots because we screamed to high heaven. We had to take lots of shots, and how I hated them! And how I still hate them! Daddy's manner of carrying on his practice subjected us to a lot of exposure to diseases. Very often people came to the house to wait for him, for fear they might miss him. The effect of this was that we were constantly exposed to childhood diseases, the parents not knowing what their children had. They came with whooping cough, diptheria, scarlet fever or whatever. Daddy had to give us immunizations if we got exposed. I can remember once he had to immunize us with horse serum because we had been exposed to scarlet fever. I screamed and cried. Mother always held us in her lap. She was the comforting, nurturing person in our lives. The needle looked as if it was long enough to go clear through my body. The shot had to be given in the chest, and when Daddy withdrew the syringe, the needle stayed in my chest. I shouted at him, "I hate you. I hate you." I could not then appreciate that he was protecting us from much worse illness and even perhaps, disabling kinds of sicknesses.

Today, it would be considered kind of unethical for a doctor to practice medicine on his own family. I don't think that it ever occurred to Daddy to send us to another doctor for the normal kinds of medical service that would be required. In the first place, the nearest doctor would have been in Fordyce, and in those days with roads that ran around everybody's front porch it took more than thirty minutes to drive to Fordyce on a not-always-good gravel road. I suspect, too, that Daddy's own confidence in his ability to practice medicine precluded his seeking other help for the family.*

He could look awfully stern at us out of those piercing blue eyes when we had misbehaved or when we were crying because of taking shots. One time at the supper table, it was in summer, and summer was always a time when we had to take typhoid shots. I always dreaded when people began coming in for their typhoid shots because that would remind Daddy that it was time for our series of shots, three of them. Susan was six and I was seven. Daddy stood up at the head of the table and announced that he was going to give us our shots. Susan got so upset that she began to cry, and he spoke to her so sternly, "Hush your crying!" that she vomited in her plate.

Other children got peppermint stick candy, which Daddy kept at his

---

*One time he had Dr. Ellis to come to see me. I was playing paperdolls on the bare floor in the sleeping porch. I had scooted along and picked up a lengthy splinter in my upper rear thigh. Dr. Ellis had to cut it out. PRB

office, when they had similar treatment at his hands. I don't remember that we got candy, though I think on occasion he may have given us a nickel or a dime when we had to undergo a particularly unpleasant medical treatment.

My first birthday party was a disaster! To be five years old, and Daddy, in his usual generous spirit, decided to invite all of the children in town from my age up to fourteen or fifteen. I was so excited the morning of my birthday, seeing Daddy drive up with his car full of watermelons on the back seat. The children started arriving about two o'clock. I stood alone on the sidewalk in front of our house, watching those children play. Many of them I didn't know too well, and the big boys looked really enormous to me. I was absolutely horrified and mortified as well, when the big boys discovered my graveyard in the corner of the yard where I had buried my pet canary and a Kewpie doll made of celluloid that had gotten smashed. The boys dug up my precious items, and laughing and shouting taunted me with my treasures. I burst into tears and ran into the house away from the party.

After that, Daddy took very little hand in celebrating any kind of anniversaries. I don't think he remembered, working as hard as he did, Mother's birthday or their wedding anniversary. She was the one who would remind him that these dates were on the calendar.

But when I was in school at Columbia University, in the late forties, Daddy asked me to get Mother a special present, and I haunted the antique shops on Madison Avenue and found a very lovely, old Italian cameo in a handsome setting. I bought that, and Daddy presented it to Mother at Christmas.

Daddy was always one to "jump in the fray" when there was a crisis in the community, such as a fire or a tornado. Once when I was about five years old, Daddy took a notion to drive over to see his old friends in the Pansy neighborhood and to visit Toledo, a community in Cleveland County near where he had grown up. We went in his T-model Ford. It was the kind of car that when it rained you had to get out and put up the side windows and button them on. We had gotten over beyond Rison when a terrible thunderstorm came up with a high, high wind. I remember it particularly because I had on a pair of new shoes and socks. I was sitting in Mother's lap with my feet propped up on the dashboard. Daddy got out to put up the sides, but the rain came in and wet my new socks which faded, and that was a catastrophe for me. The wind got so high and the trees began to fall around us. Daddy decided he couldn't go any further, so he turned around to go back home. As we made our way back, enormous trees had been blown down, and Daddy would have to get out and lift smaller trees off the road to make a passageway for us to get through.

I don't know if it was this time or another time, but word came that a tornado had struck Toledo, and a lot of people had been injured. Daddy immediately packed up a surgical kit, got all the bandaging and medicine together that he could and went over to help treat people who had been hurt

320

in the tornado. Two or three days later he took us with him to see the destruction that had been wrought on this little community. I remember seeing an old lady who was sitting in a rocking chair, rocking back and forth, and she had been sitting in that chair when the tornado had come through, and her entire house had been blown from around her, leaving her sitting in her rocking chair.

I remember, too, Daddy laughing about somebody who had been churning butter, and the churn had been whipped out from in front of them and had been up-ended on a fence post about a quarter of a mile away. He pointed out the churn, still on the fence post. It was an old blue tin one, and the wheel was turning idly in the wind as it sat perched on the upright post.

Whenever there was a fire in Thornton, we were alerted, particularly at night, by the firing of a shotgun. It was the standard alarm and understood by everyone when they heard it that somebody's house was on fire. Shortly after we heard the gun, we were alerted, too, by Miss Essie O'Keefe who ran the telephone switchboard, and she would tell where the fire was.

The night that Mr. Columbus Cathey's house burned down I well remember. It was just across the grove from us, and Susan and I were asleep in the sleeping porch. The alarm went off, and we got up and stood on the bed at the window and watched the house burn. Daddy, as was his usual wont, organized all the men into a "bucket brigade," passing buckets of water from our well and from Mr. Jim Thornton's well to try to put out the fire, but in the case of Columbus Cathey's house, the fire had gotten too far and the house couldn't be saved. I remember the darkness being lit up by those red flames and seeing all of the black figures of the volunteer firemen silhouetted against the red flames of the burning house as they hurried to pour water on it. I especially remember the enormous, heavy roar as the roof caved in and the sparks flying up to the sky.

The burning of the old Strong house (the Lionel Robertsons were living there) was memorable to me because it was directly across from our own house and the fire threatened our house as it burned. I was on the playground at the school, it was during the summertime, and someone shouted down the street that the Strong house was burning. I hot-footed it across our pasture and ran home. The house was then in full flame. Mother was trying to get blankets and quilts wetted down so that we could place them on the front of our house to keep it from catching on fire. Fortunately a fireman happened to be passing through, and he stopped and went into our house and placed his hands on the walls and felt to see how hot they were getting. He told Mother he felt that if she could damp down the walls on the front that were exposed to the burning house across the street, we could save our own house. So every quilt and blanket in the house was dumped in tubs of water and hung from the roof to protect it. It did work.

The refrigerator did run a close second to the telephone as the most important piece of equipment in our house. Daddy kept all of his serum in the refrigerator to keep it fresh, and we had to know what was there, because very often he sent over from the office for vaccines and serums to be given.

One Sunday afternoon Daddy and Mother had gone to a family reunion at Mr. Dick Harper's. That was one of Daddy's favorite pastimes. He was considered so much a part of the families among whom he practiced, that he was always included in the family reunions and big family dinners. He would try to make those if he possibly could, if only to get there for just a bite of dinner. On this particular occasion, I had not gone with them. I had stayed at home. Albert McGuffey came running in about two o'clock in the afternoon, saying that his mother was dying, he thought. I knew that the closest telephone to the Dick Harper's was at Mr. Will Zumbro's. So I called Mr. Zumbro and asked him to please go up to Mr. Harper's, which was only about a quarter of a mile away, and tell Daddy that he was needed at the McGuffey house. I felt such a sense of responsibility, and my heart was pounding, trying to figure out how to get a message to Daddy to come home promptly. Unfortunately he did not get back in time to tend to Mrs. McGuffey before she died.

I think that Daddy never got more than four or five hours of sleep at night. Of course, our sleep was disturbed as well with the calls that came from people who needed him to come. The telephone would ring. He would answer it in a gruffy, sleepy voice, usually berating the people who called. His litany usually ran like this: "What do you mean calling this time of night?" "Don't you know it's after midnight?" "He can't be that sick. He's just puttin' on!" "When did he get sick?" "You mean he's been sick since this morning and you wait a whole day before calling me, at this hour of the night?" And so he'd fuss and grumble and then agree to get out of bed and make the call. At that point, the light over his bedstead would go on and he would crawl out of bed. He would very often sleep in his BVD's or his winter underwear, so that he would be half dressed when he had to get out at night.

When he would be gone longer than Mother thought necessary for him to be away to make a particular call, she would sit up in bed each time a car light came by, waiting for him, watching for him. Sometimes a call would have come in for him to go someplace else while he had been away, and she would hop out of bed the minute he turned into the grove. She would run to the light switch on the back porch, turn it on and off, to signal to him not to put the car in the garage. He would know at that signal that he would have to make another call.

Daddy never sent a bill. Furthermore, he never charged preachers, teachers and widows. I would never have dared ask him, but once I asked Mother if she knew how much income Daddy made. Daddy managed all of the finances, he did all of the banking, and he paid all of the bills. It was his pleasure to go around at the end of each month to pay the bills and visit a bit with the merchants and telephone operators and other people whom he owed. He was absolutely meticulous about paying every bill he owed by the first of the month. Apparently, Mother never knew exactly what their financial status was. She told me, however, that she thought that probably Daddy had never earned more than five or six thousand dollars. He might have, in the peak years of his practice in the fifties, earned nine or ten thousand dollars. He charged so little for his services.

When we found his ledger books from his practice, back to 1899, there were entries that showed that he had been paid ten pounds of cotton seed for setting a broken limb. Another entry indicated that he had been paid half a bushel of potatoes for delivering a baby.* Indeed, a good deal of his income was in produce. As a consequence, we were never hungry.

My own involvement in the family finances came on the very day that the bank in Thornton closed. It was in 1931. Daddy was very upset. Shortly after he learned of that, he got a call from Fordyce that he had a new hound dog, which had just arrived at the freight office. The charges were collect and Daddy owed $3.50. At that point, Mother and Daddy realized they had no cash in the house. I went to the bedroom. I got my little piggy bank, in which I had been saving pennies for about a year. I brought it and handed it to Daddy. He took a hammer, broke the bank, and had enough money to get that puppy.

This incident may account for the fact that I have never had much love for dogs. On the other hand, there may be the factor, too, that I remember how much work it was for Mother and for Selma to cook the "dog bread" (a corn meal and water bread) every day to feed the hound dogs and bird dogs that he kept.

There was the crisis, too, in the family, precipitated by the necessary decision of whether or not Daddy should cash in his life insurance in order to buy gasoline and medicine to continue his practice in the early 30's. It was a tense time in the family. Mother finally said, "Dr. Rhine, it's your life and our life and without it you couldn't continue, so we must make this sacrifice."

Mother was really as dedicated to the community and to Daddy's practice as he was. She was on duty at home, taking calls, without interruption day and night. She rarely left home, and when she did, it was most often to go to Little Rock to take us to have our teeth straightened. Even then, the car was often used to send patients along to go to the hospital or to a specialist in Little Rock. She never begrudged the time that Daddy spent in his practice, and she was left alone a great deal of time just with us children. I never heard her complain about the fact that she couldn't have more clothes or finer things in the house.

Just before the Depression hit, Daddy had urged Mother to buy herself a new piano, and she had gone to Camden and looked at a grand piano. But she was very reluctant to spend the five hundred dollars that it would have cost on herself. So she had delayed making the decision. That delay cost her the piano because the bank closed, and from then on there was never a

---

*Other methods of payment during the early years included doing his washing and ironing, firewood, and hay for his horses. These ledgers, dating from 1899 to 1964, are in the library at the University of Arkansas School for Medical Sciences in Little Rock. PRB

question of having that kind of money to spend on a piano. She often referred to this incident and laughingly advised us never to delay making a decision when only money was involved.

The only time our straitened circumstances really got to her involved myself. I was going East to Washington and New York, and I needed a good, warm coat. Mother and I had gone to Little Rock and found a coat that looked very, very well on me. She always liked to have us buy things that were becoming to us. She never was very anxious about clothing for herself, but she enjoyed buying nice things for us. The coat we found was quite expensive for that time, 1943, and she thought we had better consult Daddy. When we got home, she told Daddy the price of the coat, and he said, "We don't have enough money to buy a coat that expensive." Mother was terribly upset. She said to Daddy, "Dr. Rhine, you and I both have worked so hard, and here we don't have even enough money to buy Virginia the coat she needs to go away in." She later told me that she had cried all night long. The next morning Daddy got up and said to her, "Nita, go buy the coat." I still have that coat, remodeled twice, but it reminds me of the sacrifice they must have made to get it for me.

Most of our outings when we were growing up in Thornton were keyed to Daddy's professional life. There were numerous reunions and dinners. I remember the gatherings of the Hearnsbergers, the Harpers, the Greens, the Evanses, the Ellises, the Steelmans, the Nutts, the Lightfoots, the Anthonys, the Parhams, the Easterlings, the Grays, the Brandons, the Hardmans, and, of course, the annual Marks family reunion, which was Mother's family.* That reunion was a highlight for us children, because it was held during the 30's over on the Saline River just above Kingsland. It was the one opportunity of the long, hot Arkansas summer when we had a chance to play in the water and to swim. Later on, Daddy joined the Country Club at Fordyce (during the summer months only) so that we had an opportunity to swim almost every day. Sometimes Daddy was able to slip away from his practice and drive us to the pool and take a swim himself. We sang all the way there and back, which he enjoyed. "The End of A Perfect Day" was one of his favorites.

Then there were the meetings of the Ouachita County Medical Society. Those were especially pleasant for us because they were in Camden, and we visited with Aunt Mary Sue and Uncle George Moseley. The bad thing about it was that when Daddy stayed for the entire meeting, we wouldn't get home until twelve or one o'clock, and after such a short night of sleep, it was awfully hard to get up early the next morning to go to school.

On two occasions Daddy invited the entire Ouachita County Medical Society, and other doctor friends, up to Thornton to have supper. Those were really festive occasions for us. The first time, Mother attempted to serve dinner inside the house. One of the menu items was corn on the cob.

*The July, 1985, gathering at the Marks Cemetery in Cleveland County, Arkansas, will mark the 108th consecutive reunion of this family. PRB

There were enormous pots of boiling water to cook the corn, I can remember. The professional highlight of that evening was a presentation by Daddy of some of his most bizarre and exotic patients. I was particularly touched by one, because it was of a young woman who had a rare case (at least for those doctors) of elephantisis.

The second great occasion at home was the time Dr. Robbins announced that Daddy was Ouachita County Medical Society Doctor of the Year, and was to be nominated for State and National Doctor of the Year. [This was in 1948, and it also marked the completion of Daddy's 50th year in the practice of medicine.] Mother had supper served on long trestle tables out in the side yard. The whole town took part in catering that affair. Mr. Roy Wise, Bill Parker and Claud Arnold made big wash pots of squirrel mulligan. There was bar-be-qued meat, and the ladies of the town prepared all the accompanying dishes.

Dr. Robbins came to us after he had made his speech of nomination, and told us, "Now it's up to you to get all the documentation together to make Dr. Rhine's nomination effective." During a two week period at the end of that year, I came home for Christmas vacation and spent the entire fourteen days getting together the material and putting the framework, the beginning of the scrapbook that accompanied Daddy's nomination to the State Medical Society and to Washington, for which Mother prepared the biographical sketch of Daddy's life. [It is the beginning section of this book.]

There were trips to Hot Springs and Pine Bluff to State American Legion meetings. Daddy was very active and supportive of the American Legion. At the time, the closest Legion Post was in Fordyce. Once we went to Little Rock for him to attend a State Masonic Lodge meeting. Daddy was a devoted Lodge member—a 33rd degree Mason.

His Masonic activities are strongly etched in my mind because I recall that he always had his little blue Masonic Lodge book on the car seat beside him whenever he took us on calls with him. (That was about the only time we got to be with Daddy. I usually sat in the front seat and Susan and Pat in back, playing games on the rough roads and having a good time.) He would oftentimes mumble to himself with the little blue book open beside him. I must have been eight or nine years old. I asked him what he was saying. He replied in his rather curt way when he was preoccupied, "I can't tell you about that. This is secret." I remember how rebuffed and closed out of Daddy's life I felt at that moment.

Indeed, it was with Mother, perhaps naturally as girls, that we exchanged our intimate thoughts and feelings, disclosed our ambitions and desires. Not to Daddy. As a grown woman, on reading a letter from a contemporary of ours in Thornton, telling us how much it had meant to her to have the advice and council of Daddy on her intimate, personal and family problems, I broke into tears because I had not had the privilege of knowing my father on that level.

During the late 20's and early 30's very often on a Sunday in the summertime, he would suggest that we go with him on his after-supper rounds in the country. Those outings I remember very vividly. He always drove by the office first to make sure there was no one waiting there to see him. We never got out of town without stopping to see a patient or two, often many more, at the office. To ride in the car was to cool off on those hot summer evenings. Once, Daddy simply couldn't get away from the office. Every time he would close the door behind him another patient would come up. We sat in the car for more than an hour, while he "kicked patients out of the office." I usually had a book to read, so I could pass the time pleasurably, but we certainly learned the virtue of patience, with those long waits. All the time we could hear him saying, "You been sick since this morning and wait all this time to come up and see me? I oughta let you go home without lookin' at you the way you treat me!" Of course, everybody knew that his bark was worse than his bite.

He would often get letters, brought in by children coming to school from the country areas, asking for medicines to be renewed. He also received many requests for medicine by mail. One of the most amusing letters that he got came from Mr. Davis who lived below Chambersville. He had been a World War I veteran, and he was constantly getting pains and aches in his body. [A sample of the frequent communications from him to Daddy will be found in the last section of the book.]

Daddy's income came under question once with the Internal Revenue Service that I recall. This was in the early 1950's, and he had been working so hard, what with the influx of people at the Naval Ordnance Plant east of Camden. The IRS checked his accounts and declared that he had falsely reported his income, and that he owed something like $1500.00 in back taxes. His deposits at the bank showed that his income was more than he had reported. This was a terrible ordeal for Daddy. He felt that he had correctly and honestly reported his income, but he couldn't prove it. He felt this very, very deeply. It was a challenge to his integrity and to his honesty, and it was something that really bore in on him for weeks. Mother said that he was in a deep depression. He wouldn't tell anyone what had happened. She couldn't find out what was going on, but she knew that he was terribly, terribly distressed.

Then one day, Dud Crosby, one of Daddy's good black friends, came up to the house, came into the kitchen and said to Mother, "Mrs. Rhine, something is going on with Dr. Rhine. I want to know what it is. I'm worried about him. I'm afraid he's going to do something to himself, he's so upset. I wanted you to know that he came to my house this morning and borrowed back his shotgun that I've been keeping for him."

When Daddy came in that evening, Mother said to him, "Now Doctor, I know something has been going on that has been disturbing you, and I've got to know what it is." Whereupon Daddy told her. He said, "Nita, I know that I reported my income tax correctly, and I cannot figure out how those deposits are higher than I reported."

He had already paid the $1500.00 amount which amounted to a sizeable percentage of his income that particular year. They thought and thought, but they simply couldn't puzzle the problem out.

Sometime later, someone came to the house and got some medical treatment. They said, "Doc, would you cash my pay check and take out what I owe you from it?" Daddy took out his part and gave the man the remainder from his pocket. Mother suddenly said, "Dr. Rhine, that is how your deposits exceeded your income! You were cashing paychecks, taking a few dollars out and returning the rest to them and then depositing their paycheck!" Daddy recovered his self respect.

Shortly after Pat was born, Daddy bought a second car. It was called "Mother's car," and it was a 1928 Chevrolet. We kept it until 1942 or so. It was a venerable car, and you might say, it was a community car. Victor Cone taught Mother to drive, but she was never an assured driver. She was nervous and even terrified behind the wheel. She had learned to drive with the two of us, small children, in the back seat, very often fussing and fighting, and she would have to turn around while driving to calm us down. So driving was a traumatic thing for her. She did manage to drive us to school every morning but to drive to Fordyce was a fearful prospect for her.

Daddy used Mother's car when his own had to be in the garage for repairs. It was more frequently used as an ambulance for taking his patients to the hospital. The car was also used by the community for funerals. Whenever one of his patients died, Daddy would offer his car to the family to drive to the church and to the cemetery. On one such occasion, a family had borrowed the car, and they had been taking on so with grief at the time they piled into the car to go to the cemetery, they forgot to close the doors and drove off through the pine saplings at the church and knocked the doors off the car. For at least a year after that, we had to climb over the front seat to get to the back seat, because the doors had been wired shut. Daddy hadn't been able to spare the car to get the doors properly fixed.

I was particularly embarassed by this, because I was in my mid-teens and becoming aware of the opposite sex, and I was driving the car up to the swimming pool, the car full of children. The Jackson boys went with the three of us, with often a friend or two, and I was embarassed to be driving a wired-up car in front of the young people I knew from Fordyce.

Daddy taught me how to drive a car, and he was not a very patient teacher. He was very impatient. At any rate, he undertook to teach Susan and me how to drive, but I was the first victim because I was a year older. He didn't teach us on the highways, because there was a bit of traffic. He would take us out to the worst backroads in Calhoun County. It was one of his virtues that he knew the roads that he drove on like the back of his hand. He knew every curve; he knew every hill; and he knew where every single mudhole was, and not only where it was, but he knew its contours. He knew which side to enter it and which side to avoid to keep from getting stuck. Unfortunately, to this day, I still can't tell my right hand from my left hand unless I face the way our piano was turned in our living room at Thornton.

Daddy took me one day on a road that was hardly more than a path, going through the piney woods from the Hampton highway over toward the Steelman residences. It was a road that was just about wide enough for the car. We came around a curve, and there was this big, wide mudhole straddling the entire road and probably longer than two car lengths. Daddy said, "Baby, you take the right hand of this mudhole." I absolutely headed for the left hand side, and before he could yell, we were mired up to the hubcaps. Oh, he was furious. He got out of the car, and cut some pine saplings to put under the back wheels and managed to get us out. He took over then and took the right hand side of the mudhole and got us through. Mother always said that he could dodge any pine sapling in Calhoun County, but when he got into city traffic in Camden, he was really uneasy.

Another problem was shifting the gear in order to get more power. Daddy would yell. "Shift into low!" and I would grind the gears, slow down to a stop, loose momentum and start off again lurching and jerking toward the fearsome mudhole, half in a panic. It didn't help to have Pat and Susan in the back, laughing at my predicament.

I don't recall who the visitor was at the time, but Daddy came in and announced to Mother that he had to make some calls. He was going to make a call in Shine, and then he was going to switch back over to Texas and from there he was going to run over to Mexico. He would be gone about an hour and a half. When he left, the visitor was absolutely bug-eyed, and said to Mother, "Mrs. Rhine, has he taken to an airplane to cover that amount of territory in an hour and a half?" Shine is an area on the north side of Thornton where a portion of the black community live. Texas is on the south side of Thornton where another part of the black community live. Mexico was a vestige left from the mill days, when the mill company had brought in and employed some Mexican labor and had built houses for them near the mill on the west side of town, near Punkin Hill.

I celebrated my forty-second birthday in August of 1964 at home. I got off the plane with Eric and saw Daddy standing at the airport gate. I was shocked to see how frail and pale he looked. His hair was cottony white, and he was walking almost with a stagger. He had asked Marshall Whitley to drive him and Mother up to meet us. It was one of the few times he ever came to Little Rock to meet me when I would fly in. I remember how courtly he was, gentlemanly, as he was introducing Eric to Mr. Whitley. We had lunch at the airport. I said to him, "Daddy, you look so pale."

"I'm just tired from the trip up. I'll be all right when I get a little food in me."

We went on home, and let Mr. Whitley out at his place. Daddy drove then. When he turned into the grove, he almost lost control of the car. I mentioned to Mother that I thought he had failed a great deal. She answered, "Oh no. He's all right."

That was a lovely week. On my birthday, which was the next to last day before I was to leave, Daddy made a little speech at the dinner table saying

328

how glad he was that I was spending my birthday with them.

In the evening, Daddy was napping in his reclining chair, when a telephone call came asking him to come see someone who had gotten sick in Bearden. Daddy didn't know the people, but they couldn't get a doctor, so he agreed to come. He asked for instructions about how to find their place. He got up to go get the car out of the garage. I asked if I could drive him, and he said that he'd appreciate that. So we drove together to Bearden. He directed me to a particular street, and we stopped in front of a house. He leaned over into the back seat to get out his medicine satchel. We were parked under some trees, which made that part of the street quite dark, although there was a full August moon shining above. Daddy had to negotiate a rather deep ditch to get to the front porch of the house, and he fell in the ditch. He picked himself up and got his bag off the ground. He knocked on the door, calling out, "This is the doctor." A man came to the door, and it turned out that we had stopped at the wrong house. He directed us to a house further down the street.

He got back in the car, and I drove down the street and parked so that the lights would light his way to the house.

The quality of the evening I can feel now. The air was warm, and there was the brilliant light of the full moon. I thought that Daddy seemed so sick and this might well be the last time I would see him alive.

I could hear him examining the woman in the bedroom through the open windows. He would ask her to move her hand, lift her fingers. Then when he got through, he asked the husband to step out on the porch with him. I heard him tell the man that his wife had had a slight stroke, and he gave him instructions as to what to do. He came, got in the car, and we started back on the trip to Thornton. I wanted to tell him that I loved him, but there wasn't an opportunity. He was regaling me all the way home, pointing out the spot where he had been side-swiped by a truck trailer. He had been knocked into the ditch.

The next morning we were to catch the bus around 6:30 or 7. Daddy was always ahead of time to catch trains or busses for fear that he would have a flat tire. We waited for the bus at Mr. Gurt James' cafe. It came on time. Daddy got the suitcase out of the car. As the bus driver stepped down, Daddy took me by the arm and introduced me to the bus man, saying, "This is our oldest daughter, and she is going home." It was almost as if he was confiding me to the safekeeping of this total stranger.

I climbed onto the bus, turned to wave goodbye to Mother and Daddy, the two of them there. Mother was standing with tears in her eyes, blowing kisses to me, but Daddy was already turned around and was rummaging around in his car for his little black pill bag. A patient had already accosted him there at the bus stop for some medicine. His white, cottony hair was sticking out from around the old, worn grey felt hat.

A few days later, I got a letter from Mother telling me of the school opening. She had, for the first time, realized that Daddy was getting frail, because at the school opening where he was to make his annual speech to the students to exhort them to do their best, to get a good education, he had had to have the assistance of Mr. O'Dell, the school superintendent, to get up the two or three little steps onto the stage.

Mother told me later that on Labor Day Sunday in September of 1964, Daddy had been at the office all morning, and about eleven o'clock, an old man drove up to the back of the house, came in and said to her, "Mrs. Rhine, I wish that you would get Doctor out of the office. Something's wrong with him. He's sick, and he's still got a whole lot of patients to see."

Mother answered, "You know there is nothing I can do to get him home if he has got any sick people at the office."

Later, around one o'clock, Daddy came in, and Mother saw that he was dragging his leg, the one that had been paralyzed. (Always, when he was very tired, he would drag that leg. She never had throw rugs in the house, because he might stumble on them.) He took his hat off, and said to her, "Nita, I've gone as far as I can go." He hung his hat up on the wall on the back porch. He went to the telephone and called the hospital in Fordyce, and said, "This is Dr. Rhine. I'm sick. I think I have pneumonia, and I'm coming up to enter the hospital."

That was one of the few times that Mother drove the car to Fordyce. She took him to the hospital. He admitted himself, and the nurse called Dr. Harry Atkinson, his doctor.

After about ten days, the pneumonia cleared up, and Daddy urged Dr. Harry to go on a hunting trip to Canada that he had planned to make, which he did. Daddy stayed another day or so, and having admitted himself, he discharged himself, and they went back home.

On the way home, he said to Mother, "Nita, I don't feel so well. I think I have had a little stroke. I haven't told you but I have had several light strokes during the last few months."

On Friday night, he called me, and from the tone of his voice, it was apparent that he was very distressed. I said to him, "Daddy, what is the matter?"

"Oh Baby" (he always called me Baby), "I've had to make a terribly hard decision. I've had to decide today to close my office after all these years and just practice from here at the house."

"Well," I said, "that's not such a big difference. You've been doing half of your practice out of the house all these years. I don't think that will be so different."

"I guess you are right." And I think he did take heart from that thought.

But on Sunday, two days later, I got the call from Mrs. Jackson that Daddy had had a massive stroke and was back in the hospital. I went home as soon as I could and spent the last hours of his life with Mother and Pat at the hospital with him.

Once in the middle of the night, when he was having a very bad time, in a coma, he opened his eyes. They were unseeing, of course, but they were still piercingly blue. I asked the nurse to call a doctor. She said there was nothing the doctor could do that she couldn't do at that point. I countered by saying, "So many people have called him out at night when it was not really necessary. This is one time that we will disturb a doctor for him."

During the last hour of his life, Mother held his hand, Pat, Aunt Mary Sue and I stood by his bed. Allen Lightfoot and Reese Parham were also there. How grateful we were for their presence. They represented the deep friendships that had grown up between Daddy and all of those people that he had practiced for and loved so much.

Graydon Parham drove us home from the hospital after Daddy died. As we entered the house, Mother cried out, "What am I going to do?" He represented activity in her life. Over her quiet sobs, we heard a man's voice, like a town crier, calling down the street, "Dr. Rhine is dead."

Today, twenty years after his death, in cleaning out the basement of my home, I have found, tucked away in a corner, a gallon of molasses, a big box of pine knots with some kindling that he had split, and an envelope containing two little pill envelopes on which is written, in his famous illegible handwriting, "White Althea seeds" and "Purple Althea seeds." Finally, a tiny little pill bottle stuffed with cotton containing seeds identified by a label on the outside, "Redbud seeds."

The most touching thing that he ever sent to me was in March, the year that he died. I received one of his tall boxes. Everything was always sent in big medicine boxes that the jugs of medicine came in. It was filled with layer upon layer of flowers—spring flowers from the garden—that he had wrapped very carefully with wet cotton and put into plastic sacks. There was japonica, forsythia, a few jonquils and hyacinths. Some of them had not survived the trip, but I did have a bouquet from it. I have always thought of that as a very dear thing for him to have done. He knew how much flowers would mean to me in snow-bound Michigan, and he knew I loved the spring garden flowers.

On that last visit home, when he already was sick, I recall him coming home from the office late one afternoon and standing outside, near the back door, lifting his legs up and down, and telling me that his legs didn't work like they used to, and he had to exercise them to keep them going. After a few leg lifts, he got a pail of water and went to the grove to water the redbud seedlings that had come up, volunteer. That was often his occupation late of an afternoon in the dry, hot summer months. He had a special system, I remember. He would take large tin cans, drive holes in the bottoms and sink them into the ground by the plants. The water would then seep slowly into the ground and not run off quickly.

I think I have saved those items—the molasses, the pine—all these years as a kind of personal shrine to my father. Certainly, the redbuds that grow on my place in Michigan are a living reminder to me of him—of all the good and caring things that he did and of the great, great love he bore for his fellow man. That was the underpinning of his whole life and medical practice.

LEONA VALLEY, CALIFORNIA

I remember going with my Daddy, as I frequently did as a child to see a sick patient, and after examining them and making a diagnosis, he would take a bottle out of his medicine bag, pour some in an empty bottle, cork the bottle and label it with handwritten instructions. Then he would ask for a teaspoon, pour a dose of the medicine in it and warm it by holding the spoon over the chimney of a kerosene lamp to give to the patient immediately. If the medicine was in powder form, he would take a piece of newspaper, fold it in three-inch squares and cut each piece of paper with his pocket knife. He would lay out as many pieces of paper on the kitchen table that he wanted as doses of medicine. Then he would use the blade of his knife to scoop up and measure the dose to be placed on each piece of paper. He carefully folded each paper and gave instructions to dissolve each dose of powder in water in a spoon, as needed and we'd be on our way.

Our home phone was used constantly to receive phone calls about where Daddy was needed to see a sick patient. He had no nurse or receptionist at his office and kept no regular office hours. Thus, one would have to take their chances on a long wait until he finished his home calls and returned to the office. When a call came in and we knew he was seeing a patient in that area, we then would phone someone along his route of travel to 'flag him down' and tell him to see the other patient in that area, to save him another trip. This saved him much travel time but this was quite a responsibility to place on us as children, who also 'took his calls.'

All envelopes which letters came in were saved for Daddy to dispense pills in—quite a savings. This was a bonus at Christmas time.

He wore a brown felt hat, quite worn, with holes where the creases met.

He had a very tender face so he only shaved about twice a week and that was done at the barber shop.

He never wore a wrist watch, but carried a pocket watch tied to a belt loop with a leather thong.

He never carried a billfold, but would fold each bill of money eight times, as small as it would fold, and just put it in his pants pocket as one would carry loose change.

He cashed patients paychecks out of his own pocket, though he was not a wealthy man, for he charged so little for his services. He'd say, "If I want to commit highway robbery, I'll get a gun and do it that way."

On each very cold morning in the wintertime, he could be heard singing very loudly "In the Good Old Summertime" as he walked to the barnyard to milk the cow at six a.m. or on his way to his office. Another favorite song of Daddy's was "Little Brown Jug" and a favorite saying was, "I am just a jack-legged country doctor."

When making a speech, and this he did in his community frequently, he always held a toothpick between his fingers, as others would a cigarette. He especially took great pride in presenting a gold engraved medal to the student in each class who received top honors scholastically. He furnished these medals for many, many years because he always encouraged high quality education for everyone.

Daddy raised White Leghorn chickens. He would order 100 baby chicks that would come in the mail, and they would be placed in a chicken house where he had a stove to keep them warm. This stove was an oil drum, half buried in the ground with chicken wire around it, so the chickens couldn't push each other against the stove and get burned. Wood was the fuel used in the stove, so it had to be stoked up several times a day. It was my job to feed and care for these chicks. As they got older and the weather warmer, they were allowed outside. Selma would wring the necks of the roosters when they were old enough to tell hens and roosters apart, and we ate those. The hens were allowed to mature and lay eggs. Daddy saved these eggs (unrefrigerated) to give to anyone who had a 'settin' hen'. He was always interested in improving the breeding stock of his chickens, hogs and dogs. He never believed in selling animals.

He loved his fox hounds, and he sent his female dogs as far as Alabama to breed to someone else's dog. This was done by train, and sometimes the dog would be half dead by the time the train arrived—a very cruel way to improve the breed. The station master at Fordyce would call our home to tell Daddy to come pick up a crated dog which had just arrived with no water or food for maybe five days. He meant well, and he always gave these puppies away to a child or adult who wanted a good dog to hunt with. We had as many as forty dogs in our 'dogyard' at one time. He also raised bird dogs, one named 'Reba' that slept under our house. That was before the house was closed in underneath, around the foundation. These dogs were used to hunt quail.

Daddy had a love of canary birds. He had several large specially made bird cages hanging from the ceiling on the back porch. In nesting season, Mother would make a nest for the birds by using a box that shotgun shells are sold in. In this box, she would sew cotton, then attach it in a corner of the cage to await the laying of eggs. Each day fresh newspaper would be placed in the bottom of the cage, after lowering the cage from its hook on the ceiling, and each night, the cages were covered with cloth covers.

During the Depression years, Daddy loaned the use of his second car to transport the family to the funeral of a loved one since most families had no car, and the funeral home did not provide this service, only the hearse to carry the casket. Also, our family car was frequently used to take an ill patient to Little Rock for more advanced medical examination. All too often, this was done when our family was making the trip and the ill patient would occupy the back seat of the car.

We three girls were raised in a home which also served ill people at all hours of the day and night. The living room couch served as a bed for a patient having her gall bladder drained—an all day procedure; our guest

333

room bed was used for a child just having had a tonsillectomy; or the bathroom served as a place to sew up a person cut in a fight on a Saturday night.

We children would frequently go with Daddy on his 'calls' in the country. As he drove along, he would greet people along the way, working in the fields or relaxing in a rocking chair on the front porch, by calling out, "Morning, old folks", no matter what time of day or night it was.

The favorite game we children played as we rode along with him over the dirt, rutted and often muddy, roads, was to 'stand' on our knees on the back seat, facing backwards and not holding on to anything with our hands. As the car would hit bumps, swerve to avoid a stump in the road or follow a rut, we would sway and fall over. The winner was the one who could stay upright the longest. Sometimes we bumped the window and got hurt, but we kept doing it.

Often as I went with Daddy in the country, he would tell me the names of the trees, and we would stop and get a leaf to add to my collection of various tree leaves. He didn't seem to know wildflowers.

Daddy never got involved in politics, though candidates frequently asked for his endorsement. He always refused, but in a quiet way gave them his support. As local citizens asked his advice on how to vote, he would say, "I can't tell you who to vote for, but I am voting for so and so." That was all that was needed, for his opinion was highly respected.

Daddy was accused or teased by us as having a "political machine." Each election time a local character named "Nub' Etheridge would find out how Daddy stood on certain issues, then he would go around town, telling everyone how he and Daddy were going to vote. 'Nub' a rather illiterate and neglected person, was the 'crank' for Daddy's political machine. *

Daddy also paid the poll tax for many who could not afford this fee but he never advised them how to vote. He just knew they had this right to vote.

Daddy was not a fast driver, and surely not a city driver. When he had to go to Little Rock, which was out of his familiar area, he had Victor Cone or someone to drive for him. Otherwise he drove many miles daily on his rounds. The roads were not paved, except for the through highways, and on these he was most cautious. When he would meet a car, he would drive as far to the right as possible. Yes, on the shoulder of the road, "to give the other car plenty of room." But on the dirt country roads, he felt very comfortable, and it was here that he taught two of his daughters to drive a car. I learned to dodge ruts and mudholes, high centers in the roads and trees along the roadsides, long before I learned to signal for a left turn or pass a car. Driving in traffic was frightening to me because the trees in the country did not move as I went by. Daddy carried a shovel and ax in the trunk of his car at all times in case he got stuck in a mudhole. Occasionally

* 'Nub' named his last child Irving Abbott (for the sheriff) Lindbergh Etheridge, Junior. PRB

334

no amount of digging or placing brush under the wheels would help free the car. In such a case, he'd walk to the next house and ask the owner there to bring his horse, mule or tractor to come to his aid. The ax also came in handy as he drove along the country roads in the forest area. If he wanted to relax or get some exercise, he'd stop, walk into the woods and chop at a rotted, fallen pine tree, returning to the car with pine knots or a straight piece for splinters to start wood fires. He'd toss these into the trunk of his car. At home, he had large piles of pine knots in reserve. Some of these piles were possibly eight to ten feet high.

Daddy *never* put the car in the garage for the night without first filling it with gas, in case he had calls to make during the night. He was compulsive about this.

He took pride in walking at a fast clip and erect for his age in the eighties. He was somewhat stooped from riding horseback for many years.

He enjoyed Will Rogers movies. On radio, he listened to 'Lum and Abner', 'Fibber McGee and Mollie' and 'The Grand Old Opry', as time permitted. Then on TV, he enjoyed 'Lawrence Welk.'

He loved to work jigsaw puzzles, sometimes finding it difficult to leave one to go make a call, saying, "Now just one more piece I'm looking for."

He wrote an occasional letter to his children after they left home. These were typed on his 1903 Oliver typewriter with a purple ribbon, and using only his index finger to 'peck' it out. These letters were short, usually only two or three sentences and never more than a paragraph, always ending with "Your Mother will write the news." His handwriting was unreadable, and he always used purple ink in his fountain pen.

He loved his friends and family, but found this difficult to demonstrate. He was generous, kind and gentle and easily hurt.

He was deft with his stubby fingers in surgery, but his mended fences were a sight to behold. His knowledge of anything mechanical was limited.

Daddy loved his country and its people and devoted his lifetime to serving both. He served in World War I as a doctor, so when World War II began, he contacted the Army to volunteer, even though he was far too old. [Sixty-five years old.] He received an answer from the Army saying his services were needed more by continuing to serve the people at home, thus keeping them healthy so the young men and women in the Service would not have to worry about relatives left behind. He worked very hard to meet this need. He also collected scrap iron to aid the war effort. As he drove along the country roads and visited the sick, if he saw a discarded tool, piece of equipment, etc. he'd ask permission to donate it to the cause. Into his car trunk it would go, and then he unloaded it at our home to await being picked up to be melted down to make tanks, guns, for the Army.

If a soldier became ill or was hurt in an accident, as a troop caravan went through our town (and there were several), Daddy treated them with no charge.

During World War II, a young man who lived in Oregon came back to pay Daddy for his birth, because he knew his parents had been too poor to do so at the time.

Daddy was not outwardly a religious man though he did more good for the people in his community than any Christian anywhere. At his death, a longtime friend, Zell Hearnsberger, compared him to Jesus in his endless devotion to helping others in every way possible—not only as a doctor.

But I well remember one night about 9:30, Daddy called Mother to his bedside, for it was one of the rare occasions when he was ill. She came in later and asked Sister and me to go get Mr. Hunter Parham, who lived about ten miles in the country in the Temperance Hill neighborhood, to come to our home to witness Daddy as he joined the church. In the meantime, Mother phoned the Methodist preacher and Mr. Roy Wise, who would be the second witness. As my sister and I arrived at the Parham home, all was dark, as they had gone to bed hours before. But Mr. Parham arose and said he would get dressed and come for he remembered the many times he had gotten Daddy out of bed to see a sick member of his family, a wife and ten children. The two friends and Mother witnessed this occasion as the minister performed it in the privacy of our sleeping porch with Daddy in bed. He must have been in his late 60's, and to my knowledge, he never went to church before or after this, though he lived to be eighty eight years old. He said he felt he was doing more good being in his office on Sunday morning, and every day of the week, year round, when he wasn't on house calls, to treat the sick, than he would do sitting in the church listening to some preacher.

He donated funds to *all* churches in our community, equally. He attended funerals of patients who died, if at all possible, and he loved going to 'graveyard workings' and 'dinner on the ground' meetings to be with his patients and friends of a lifetime.

PAT RHINE BROWN

PINE BLUFF, ARKANSAS

The very first thing that I remember—-it would have been in 1931 or 1932—were the high stacks of bolts of materials that were on our back porch. They were Red Cross materials and were there to be distributed by Mother and Daddy to needy families.

Two stories that have come down through the family, often repeated, have to do with sickness. As a little child, I would refuse to swallow the green tablets that were given for almost any malady. Mother began pinching off the tip of a banana, placing the pill in it and putting the tip back, offering the banana to me to eat, which I would do. The bitter taste of the pill didn't last long when you gobbled up the rest of the banana. I had also been hearing the Bible stories of Jesus and how he healed the sick, making the blind to see and the lame to walk. Because Daddy was a doctor, I was particularly interested in these stories. So, when I was sick one day and refusing to take the medicine or stay in bed, I looked at Selma and announced, "You know, I like Jesus' way of doing this a whole lot better than I do Daddy's."

All the children in the family and around town were having measles, except me. A neighbor, Mrs. Miles, asked me one day, "Pat, how come you didn't get the measles?" I answered, "I just tell you, Mrs. Miles, I didn't have time."

Daddy always enjoyed telling about Carlton Mays, the undertaker at Benton Funeral Home in Fordyce, commenting to people during the early 1940's, that, "Dr. Rhine signs more death certificates than all the other doctors put together." His intent was to say how hard Daddy worked, but it could be construed in another way.

Often, Daddy would put a jigsaw puzzle out on a card table in the living room. He would become totally involved in putting it together. During one of these times, a patient came in suffering from a kidney stone, he thought. Daddy asked him to sit down. He would see him shortly. He continued to work on the puzzle. The man would groan and say, "Doc, this pain is really killing me."

"Is that so? Now let me see. I believe this piece goes right here."

In a few minutes, the man would again try to get the doctor's attention. Again, "Here's where that piece goes." This went on for about thirty minutes. Finally, the man got up, came over and helped Daddy finish working the puzzle. Then he got his ailment looked after.

There was always a list of names by the telephone in the kitchen. These names were of women who were expecting babies so that when any of us took the call we would know what it was about. People were very reticent about telling children or even Mother the reason for the call if it was a pregnancy. This precaution was prompted by a man coming to the back door one day, asking for the doctor. Mother told the man that the doctor wasn't in, but she would take a message. The man replied, "We are having a little party, and we want Dr. Rhine to come." When Mother gave this message to Daddy, he realized that it was a delivery, and the man couldn't bring himself to tell Mother what the call really was about.

In his younger days, Claud Arnold, was always being lectured by Daddy about his bad habits of drinking and gambling. He would vow to Daddy that he had given up both. Because Daddy could tell when a person was not telling him the truth, and when Claud would 'fall off the wagon,' he tried very hard to avoid running into Daddy. He knew that a good 'tongue' lashing would be given to him. The way in which he kept from meeting Daddy at the Post Office was to hide behind large stacks of railroad crossties that were across the street from the Post Office. He would hide there until he saw Daddy get into his car and drive out into the country. Only then would Claud venture out to get his mail or go to the store. One

337

day, however, Daddy forgot some medicine and returned to his office, catching Claud, and grilling him once again on his behavior.

I was not subjected to Daddy's 'heavy handed' driving lessons. When I became sixteen, Susan spent a short while with me showing me how to shift gears. I spent an hour practicing going forward and backward in the road by our house. The next day, Daddy called home from the office requesting some vaccine that was in the refrigerator. Mother asked me if I thought I could drive the car to take it to him. Naturally, I answered "Yes," and I did. In a few days, Daddy came in from Hampton with a driver's license for me. In those days you were not required to take any kind of driving test, either written or demonstration.

I was in college at the University of Arkansas in Fayetteville when the Key book on Southern Politics was published. Daddy was cited in that book as an example of a citizen who could be influential in the outcome of elections. Also, the name Rhine was closely associated with the name Thornton. I was taking a political science course in local government from Dr. Henry Alexander, who was an authority on state and local government. Throughout the course, Dr. Alexander would call on Miss Thornton, but Miss Thornton never did respond. About halfway through the semester, I got my grade—a C. I went to talk to Dr. Alexander about it, because I felt that I had done better than that. He said to me, "But Miss Thornton, you don't answer questions." My grade did improve, and Miss Thornton began responding in class.

In the spring of 1949, I graduated from the University, and much to my surprise, Daddy decided to come along with Mother on an overnight trip for the graduating ceremony. This was a last minute decision and there was no time to spread the word of his absence. "Happy" McManus, who was not known to be terribly truthful and loved to tell 'tall tales,' took it upon himself to inform the doctor's patients, as they came to the office, that "The doctor is out of town for a few days."

This being something that had never happened before, and knowing "Happy's" reputation, people acknowledged the news, went into the office and took a seat. After a long time of waiting, and no doctor, they would go outside where "Happy" was silently chuckling to himself, enjoying telling the truth, and ask again when would the doctor be in, this time thinking perhaps that it was so, and leaving to verify it at either the Post Office or Mr. Lionel's store.

At the time when Ed and I began to be interested in building a new home, we contacted an architect in Hot Springs, I. Granger McDaniel, whom we did not know. He came for an initial visit to talk about our ideas and to get acquainted. One of Daddy's close medical friends and a family friend as well, Dr. Jack Stell, practiced in Hot Springs. He had a daughter, Ann, who through the years we had kept up with because her aunt, Mrs. May Thornton, lived next door to us.

As Irving talked about his work and his family, it became apparent to me that his wife, Ann, did many of the things I remembered Ann Stell

338

having done. So I asked him, "Is your wife Ann, by any chance, Ann Stell?"

"Yes. How did you know?"

"Her father and my father were good friends from way back."

"You must have come from Fordyce?"

"Almost. I grew up in Thornton. My father was Dr. Rhine."

With that, he literally fell off the sofa onto the floor. "Dr. Rhine is a household word around our home! I have wanted for a long time to know some of his family. How on earth was he able to educate you girls? I know about his feelings regarding charges and sending bills—or not sending bills. I have often wondered how he managed. I have spent many evenings discussing with young doctors the pros and cons of practicing medicine his way. How did he do it?"

Vacations were unknown in a country doctor's life. There was no one to 'cover' for him. Daddy did take one pleasure trip in 1904 to the St. Louis World's Fair. He was away from his practice for a week when he attended the American Medical Association meeting in Washington, D.C., in 1949, but that was not entirely pleasure, although it had some memorable moments. He enjoyed telling reporters of his last visit to that city in 1918.

One of the social events of that Convention was a cocktail party held in the Ballroom of the Mayflower Hotel, hosted by Mr. B. T. Fooks (the Grapette bottler of Camden, Arkansas) and the Arkansas Medical Society. This function was given to honor Distinguished Arkansans, most of whom were in the government in Washington, at that time. The hundreds of guests, mostly doctors, were amused and disbelieving to overhear the country doctor's reply when a walter offered him a cocktail. "Martini, Sir?" "Martini? Martini who?" Among that worldly and sophisticated group, he was an oddity and became an instant celebrity.

Just a few years ago, I was in Thornton visiting at Tommy and Pat Trammel's store, and an elderly black woman came in. She found out who I was and came over to speak to me. She said, "I'll never forget Dr. Rhine. I had a niece who got sick. I was living in Bearden, and she lived out in the country. The family sent for me to come, and when I got there I saw that she was about to have a baby! I sent someone for Dr. Rhine. He came, delivered the child, and as he was leaving, I told him that I only had five dollars to pay him. He said, "That is all that you owe me." The woman then said that several times in later years she had tried to pay him more for that particular visit, but he would never accept any more money from her.

When Daddy returned home from the hospital after the last bout of exhaustion and the ensuing pneumonia, I went down to spend the afternoon with him and Mother on Friday. He was up and talking about seeing patients again at home the next week. He had, however, had Mother to go to his office and locate the information about some new medical books he had ordered. He had her to cancel that order.

Just before I left to come home, Mother and I were in the kitchen, he came into the room, took both of us into his arms, and with tears in his eyes and in his voice, said, "I want to thank both of you for being so wonderful to me all these years." We responded by saying to him that he had been wonderful to us, too.

That was my last time to talk with him, but not the last time I would communicate with him. On the night before he died, after he had had a severe seizure, I sat by his bed, alone with him. Mother and Gin had gone out into the waiting room. I took his hand in mine and laid my head upon the hospital bed. In a few minutes I felt such a surge of strength coming from his hand into mine that I sat bolt upright with astonishment. I realized that he was conferring upon me the strength that he had always possessed and used to sustain others. I squeezed his hand to let him know that I understood what he had given to me.

"We closed the doors on a country doctors's practice, a way of life, which we will never see again."

MILTON STARK

I first met Dr. Rhine in August of 1948, just prior to Susan and me getting married. I was a student at the University of Southern California, and my brother and I had gotten a ride with a school teacher from Los Angeles to Arkansas. Actually, Gene had gotten off in Texas, and I had come to Ruston, Louisiana. From there I rode a bus to Camden, Arkansas, where Susan and Virginia met me. They brought me up to the Rhine home in Thornton, arriving in the afternoon. We went up on the back screened porch, where Susan and I met Dr. Rhine. Susan said, "Daddy, I'd like for you to meet Milton."

I stuck out my hand, and said, "How are you, Sir?"

His answer was a very gruff, "Hard boiled!" and he walked off.

The wedding was especially difficult for him. Susan was his first child to be married, and furthermore, she was marrying a complete stranger from California. Even so, Dr. Rhine was very generous in his gifts to the newlyweds, and he continued to be this way during the entire rest of his life.

Over the next sixteen years, Susan and I returned to the Rhine home to visit on a number of occasions, the first time alone and after that with the children as they came along. Dr. Rhine always seemed very pleased with the pictures I took of him and the children. He was an excellent photographic subject. One of the series of pictures which I liked very much was taken while he was talking to a drug salesman in his office. It recorded many of his typical expressions.

Each time we visited, I would drive him around the country on his house calls. As we would pass through the small rural communities or by farmhouses, no matter what time, day or night, his standard greeting was, "Mornin', old folks!"

341

He seemed to love to tell me about each of the places we visited, about how he had difficulty driving his horse and buggy up this hill, or how his Model-T would get stuck in this low spot, or to get to this location, he would have to ride the train to a certain spot and then walk the rest of the way. During these trips, he was a back seat driver, telling me, "Now, go slow here" or "Be sure to get over to the right as far as you can to miss that soft spot." He can certainly be forgiven for that, because he knew all of those back roads better than anybody.

Each time we would visit the Rhine's in Thornton, I would try to bring along as many tools as I could practically carry in the station wagon, because I learned right away that Dr. Rhine was no craftsman. As his daughter Susan says, "He couldn't hammer a nail into a plank without bending the nail." So each time we visited, I would attempt to repair something around the house. It seemed that either they could not find anyone who could do these repairs, or simply didn't consider it important enough, or certainly, Dr. Rhine could not fix them.

Dr. Rhine, over the years, had always received some payment for services in vegetables and other produce. In the Depression years, he received almost nothing else, if he got paid at all. In these better economic times, he was still given watermelons, peaches, strawberries or whatever. Better this than not getting paid at all, which probably happened with more than one-third of his patients.

This one very hot day, when we were visiting, a man brought in a bushel of roastin' ears. Dr. Rhine could never see anything go to waste, so, even though the temperature was 105 degrees and about ninety-five percent humidity, Dr. Rhine was determined to go out in the backyard and shuck this corn. Well, I thought if this eighty-seven-year-old man could do it, I could, too, so I proceeded out to help him. Not being used to the humidity and spending most of my time by the air conditioning unit, I thought I was going to die, but we did get the corn shucked, and he went on about seeing his sick folks, as usual, without any complaint.

Dr. Rhine had a reputation for being a great fox hunter. When we first started visiting there, he had a yard full of old hound dogs, which every morning he would go out and take care of, feed and so forth. One time we happened to be there when a representative of the magazine, *The Hunter's Horn* showed up, and lo and behold, he wanted a photograph of Dr. Rhine's family. We got about four or five of these dogs out there, and Dr. Rhine put a rope through their collars. I had one end of the rope, and he had the other end. Susan was holding Amy, and Mrs. Rhine was standing with us. Son of a gun, I looked like I belonged more in the picture than anybody else, even though I didn't know a thing about what I was doing.

Later, because of Dr. Rhine's interest in fox hunting, they felt it would be very appropriate for his son-in-law to go on a fox hunt. The following is my recollection of the fox hunt.

We went up to Sheridan, out in the country, to an old Baptist church. They had a meeting on the grounds. This was in the early evening. While the women were preparing the food and so forth, the fox hunters themselves had their dogs in cages on the back of their pick-up trucks. They were going around talking to each other about how good a dog they had, and how bad the other fellows dog was and trying to make deals about breeding dogs. One fellow had a pick-up truck load of horns. These are horns with mouthpieces on them—usually cow horns, but sometimes other horn material. These fox hunters would go over and try them out. They would put one to their mouth and blow a loud blast on it. (To this day, I have never been able to make much of a noise on those horns.) We had the dinner on the ground, very delicious food, barbequed meat, vegetables and all the trimmings.

About nine-thirty at night came the time to turn the hounds loose. One fellow, the leader of the Central Arkansas Fox Hunters' Association, turned his five or six hounds out in the woods. They started out on the trail, and they'd give a general yip, yip-yip. In a little bit they'd caught a little fresher smell of a fox, and they would go yip, yip, yip-yip-yip. Then all of a sudden, they caught a real fresh smell, and they cut loose with this yowling. That was the signal for all the other hunters to let their dogs out. They turned their dogs loose and joined the other dogs in the chase of this fox. It was a very wooded area. In fact, the underbrush was so thick you could hardly get through it. The dogs and the fox seemed to manage to get underneath the brush and ran back and forth in the woods.

The people I was with, Allen Lightfoot and his friends, would get out on the highway and drive the truck or cars up and down the highway, and we would get out and sit and listen to these dogs running this fox through the woods. Those guys could sit there and tell me which dog was leading the pack, which one was in the middle and which was coming up the rear, just by listening to their mouth or bark. They would say something to the effect, "Hear that coarse mouth" or "Hear that fine mouth." "Coarse mouth, he's leading the pack up there now!"

One of their favorite jokes, and if I heard it once, I heard it ten times, was about the city fellow they brought out to listen to all those hounds out there, and one fox hunter said to the other one, "Boy howdy, listen to that purty music." The city fellow says, "I can't hear no music for all them hounds barking." These people would crack up and slap their legs and thought it was the funniest thing they ever heard. I'm sure they were talking about me because I felt the same way.

Those hounds would chase that fox all night long. We were out there 'til the wee, small hours of the morning. When the dogs treed the fox, the leader of the Central Arkansas Fox Hunters' Association went out and blew the hounds out of the woods. That was with the hunting horns they were practicing blowing on earlier. Now when those hounds came out of the woods, the owners would try to collect them and put them back in the cages in the back of their pick-ups, but a lot of times, the dogs would get lost. They had a collar, and many of them from down around Thornton all had Dr. Rhine's collars, because everybody knew Dr. Rhine. Dr. Rhine had a telephone, and a lot of people out in the country didn't have telephones.

Maybe a day or so later, somebody would call up Dr. Rhine and say, "Dr. Rhine, we've got a hound up here that's got white markings on his side and a black spot on his back."

"Oh yeah, that belongs to Allen Lightfoot out here. I'll notify him." Dr. Rhine would get word to the owner and the owner would pick the dog up and bring him home. That was my experience with fox hunting.

Susan and I, together with our four children, returned to Arkansas in September of 1964 for Dr. Rhine's funeral. This was a tremendously emotional experience for everyone because the family and the community suffered a really serious loss with his passing. There was a tremendous outpouring of grief and sympathy from a great many people. However, I think the thing which touched the family most was that the morning after the funeral, we found placed in the door of his medical office a plain fruit jar filled with some miscellaneous garden flowers. I really feel that Dr. Rhine would have appreciated this tribute more than almost anything else that happened the day of the funeral.

A day or two after the funeral, Virginia, Susan and I took it upon ourselves to clear out his office. Some supposedly authoritative person told us that really the only thing we had to worry about was any narcotics, and we knew that Dr. Rhine had never kept narcotics in his office, because the office door was never locked.

Before I talk about clearing out the office, there are a few things I should explain.

First, Dr. Rhine rarely wrote a prescription. He usually made up his own and gave to the patients in an old envelope or in a medicine bottle with a cap, so he kept a large supply of medicines in his office.

Second, he had practiced medicine in this office beginning about 1926. [His first office was in the back of the Stout Lumber Company Commissary building, behind the drug store, which was operated by Dr. C. T. Black. When the mill shut down, he moved his office to the Bank building, where he had his office for the rest of his life.]

Third, he did not have a nurse or receptionist at any time, and patients never made appointments. All telephone calls were taken by Dr. Rhine, Mrs. Rhine or one of the family, since the home phone and the office phone were on the same line. If patients wanted to see the doctor, they would either come to his office and sit until Dr. Rhine showed up, or if too sick to make the trip to Thornton, they would call and ask him to make a house call, which he made a great many of every day. He practiced medicine seven days a week from ten to fourteen hours a day, and was awakened at night many, many times.

The office was on the first floor of a brick building, which also housed the post office. Above his office was the meeting place for the Thornton Masonic Lodge. The street in front of the office was graveled, and the sidewalk was brick, long ago grown over with grass and weeds. The office had fourteen foot ceilings, and the wall paper was peeling off of the walls.

On the left, as you entered, was a large roll-top desk, the top of which was usually covered with unopened medical publications. It seemed that he subscribed to all medical publications available, but only read two of them. So when he came in from the post office each morning, if he had got one of these publications which he did not read, he tossed it onto the roll-top desk.

Lola Matlock, the woman who worked for the Rhines, was sent over to the office ever so often to clean up these publications and mop the floor and so forth. In front of the desk were a number of 'ice cream parlor' chairs and wooden chairs for patients to sit on while waiting for the doctor to return to see them. For winter heat, there was a small butane heater. On the right was a desk which was next to a series of bookcases which extended back to his examining room door. The bookcases were loaded with medical books and ledgers. The desk was covered with letters, papers, and books. The bookcases had become unglued and were literally falling apart. A portable typewriter was on the desk, relatively new, having replaced an old Oliver typewriter which he had purchased early in his practice.

The back part of the office had a long table on which and under which were many two gallon, brown glass jugs filled with tonics. From the jugs that were labeled, it would appear that some held vitamin and mineral formulas for the elderly patients, while others held dog medicines. The back door opened out onto an unkept backyard.

Upon entering the examining room, to the right of the main office, you found, to the left of the door, a built-in table on which there was a wooden bucket, which held water, and on the end of the table was a centrifugal machine. There apparently was no running water in the office at all. The table also held a device which looked like a small miter box, together with a sharp butcher knife. The last was used to cut bandages, precisely the width he desired. He bought bandages in rolls which were thirty-nine inches wide. Under this table was at least a bushel of corks of different sizes, which he apparently had been caught with when manufacturers had changed from medicine bottles with corks to medicine bottles with caps. Across the entire back wall was an open cabinet lined with large bottles of prescription and non-prescription drugs. Some of these had been opened and others still sealed, as they had come from the drug houses. In the middle of the room was a very heavy iron dental chair, which could be flattened out like a bed. This was his examining table, and a place where he would catch a few winks of sleep in the afternoon when he would grow a little tired. At the head of the dental chair was a table holding the old sterilizer, in which he had his medical instruments and some hypodermic needles, which he currently used. To the right of the door was a table holding a cabinet with six drawers. It held a miscellaneous assortment of medical tools, dose books and medicines, which apparently had not been used since shortly after World War I. Beyond that was a glass-doored cabinet which held more medical tools and paraphernalia.

We felt that the best thing to do was to throw out all the bottles which were unlabeled or contained deteriorated medicines. These, we had Claud Arnold haul off and dispose of, he said by pouring down a deep hole. The doctors samples, of which there were many, we placed into a cardboard carton, which we planned to give to a hospital. The unopened prescription medicines, we planned to return to the drug firms for credit, and we planned to contact the pharmacy in Fordyce to determine whether they could use the opened bottles of medicine. All of the furniture we moved over to the house, along with the books and the medical instruments. We also tried to save the old medicines, such as gravel root or tincture of lobelia, etc., hoping that someone, someday would be interested in having all of these items in a medical museum.

As we were busy cleaning up the office, a number of people dropped by saying something to the effect that, "Dr. Rhine gave me these pills, and I've been doing pretty good on them. I wonder if you could give me some more." They would show us these pills in the palm of their hand. We would politely decline and refer them to the doctors in Fordyce. Later we got calls from a pharmacy in Fordyce asking if they could get a particular type of medicine, which Dr. Rhine prescribed, and they did not have it in stock.

One man came by telling us a story. "I went to see Dr. Rhine once and while sitting there waiting for Dr. Rhine to return, this big, black man came in with a bad toothache. The man was carrying on so that I told him, 'The only thing is to pull that tooth and I can do that.' So I took him in the back room, got a pair of Dr. Rhine's dental pliers, grabbed ahold of that bad tooth, pulled it out, and then I sent him on his way." I don't know if Dr. Rhine ever knew about it or not.

In going through his books and papers, we found his ledgers of payment for services dating back to 1899. It was very clear that he charged the same fees for services in 1964 as he did in 1899. These ranged from fifty cents to two dollars depending upon how much service he felt he had performed. He did have to charge a little more for the medications he gave out because the cost had definitely gone up. Sometime during World War II, he had increased the charge for prenatal care and delivery from ten dollars to fifty dollars.

After we were satisfied that we had gotten things in pretty good order, Virginia and I went home for lunch. As we were sitting at the table with the rest of the family, there was a knock at the back door. A young man came in who identified himself as Mr. Gray, from the State Health Department, and indicated he would like to see Dr. Rhine's medicines. Virginia and I about dropped our teeth. He apparently came prepared to examine a few medicines, which the ordinary doctor might carry in a bag or have available in an examining room. He was totally unprepared for the volumes of medicines which we had on hand.

With his coming on the scene, our total game plan, as far as the medicines went, was changed. We had to put all bottles in cartons, which were sealed. They were separated as to opened and unopened, with the plan to sell the unopened ones back to drug firms and possibly sell the opened ones to hospitals or nearby pharmacies or destroy them. He made me take the box of doctor's samples to the backyard, douse with kerosene and burn. Included in these samples were a small number of glass tear-shaped sealed vials of medicine. These apparently contained injectible fluids, which, when the fire got going good, started exploding sending glass in all directions.

This was an experience I will never forget, not only because of the problems we encountered, but mainly, because it was closing the door on a medical practice which spanned sixty-six and a half years, years in which Dr. Rhine had dedicated his life to the health and welfare of his many, many patients. We closed the door on a country doctor's practice, a way of life which we will never see again.

DR. DON MILLER

PINE BLUFF, ARKANSAS

I am director of the University of Arkansas for Medical Sciences, Area Health Education Center in Pine Bluff. The AHEC program here has specific training rotations for medical students from the University of Arkansas Medical School in Little Rock and the Family Practice Residency Program. It is a three year training program for graduate physicians. We train them to become family physicians. In connection with our total program, in the AHEC building, is a well-equipped library. The Melville Library serves an obvious function of providing resource material and educational matter and a place to study for these students and residents, and also other people in the community in various medical and paramedical training situations or professions.

So the opportunity to acquire, in 1979, materials, such as the Rhine Collection, which are of interest as medical historical significance, and a logical place to put it seemed to be in the library where it would be highly visible to the many people who might be interested in some medical history. It has proved to be so. Since the materials have been here, it serves as an educational tool for younger students and residents and physicians as to how things really were in a more primitive area and time, especially back in the early 1900's. The loan to the library by the Rhine family has been most appreciated and well used. The many items of interest that we have that belonged to Dr. Rhine, that he used in his practice or in association with his practice, enable us to have rotating exhibits, so there is an opportunity to change things around and keep it interesting.

347

JULIE BRIDGFORTH

PINE BLUFF, ARKANSAS

I am librarian at the Melville Library. When we received all of the pieces of equipment, books, medicines and such from Dr. Rhine, we were so enamored and intrigued with them that we immediately bought two huge, expensive books. One was on antique medical instruments, and the other was on the history of medicine in the United States because there were so many things that we couldn't identify—what they were and what they had been used for. It was fun to look them up in that book and find out what they really were. Some things had not changed very much. Surprisingly, a lot of his objects were not that different than the ones used today, such as some obstetrical forceps. Some of the residents were laughing about the ones used here in the hospital that were very similar to those in the exhibit.

Everyone who comes into the library enjoys the exhibit. We sometimes have children who come to the library with a parent. They love to see the things. Any time that we do tours of the library, we always take them over to the exhibit and show them Dr. Rhine's picture making house calls on his horse. That is how we introduce them to the exhibit. We don't have a 'Do Not Touch' policy at all. We actually have the objects out so people can pick them up to look at them and read the medicine labels. That is a favorite thing—the medicines, gravel root, witch hazel and the herbal kinds that he used. You wonder how much medicinal value that they had. So many of them had a high alcoholic content. I'm sure they probably made the patient feel better, but I'm not sure they really cured them of what ailed them.

I think, too, that there are so many pictures of him and articles about him, that he seems like a real person. It's not like it's an exhibit that is made up of a lot of materials. We actually have pictures of him and information about him.

A thing that happened after we got the exhibit up, so many doctors came in and enjoyed looking at it, and had things of their own. They may have had a father or grandfather who was a physician. We obtained a lot of other nice things because they saw and thought this would be a good way to show their old things. Dr. Dent Tisdale brought us one of the original EKG machines that was made especially for his father. It was in the box with his father's name on it, and the whole thing—packing, too.

Another funny thing that happened—one day, right after we had gotten the books out, Dr. Tom Ed Townsend had done a conference, and he and a group of the residents came into the library. Some of the books were lying near my desk. He picked up a book that was entitled, *A Textbook of the Diseases of Children*. The copyright was 1894. The subject of the Conference had been 'Tuberculosis In Children.' The treatment outlined in the textbook was life in the fresh air and sunshine; food was a broth of milk, egg and meat; medicines which they gave were cod liver oil and arsenic, which improved the general nutrition; they bathed them and

348

rubbed them to stimulate the general metabolism. They were all laughing about how far things have come. People have enjoyed looking up topics they were researching to see how they were done in the early 1900's.

One day, Dr. Miller received a letter from a physician in Little Rock, who was coordinating an effort between St. Vincent's Infirmary and the Museum of Science and History. They were going to have an antique medical exhibit there at the museum, and he was soliciting materials from all over the state. We thought about that and decided we should probably call and offer our collection. At least let them look at the things and see if they might be interested in using some of them. We contacted Jerry Shultz at the Museum of Science and History, and I think he didn't realize how much we had because he said, "Why don't you send me some photographs of what you have?" Needless to say, that took several rolls of film, and we sent them up. He called immediately and did use a large number of things. In fact, he probably had more of Dr. Rhine's things there than anyone else. He used them in setting up an exhibit that actually resembled an old doctors office. The exhibit was so popular that after the original three months were over, he asked if he could extend the loan for six more months, and we agreed to do that.*

The Dr. Rhine Collection has been a great addition to the library, and everyone—all ages—enjoys looking at and touching the items.

*A similar exhibit, sponsored by St. Michael's Hospital in Texarkana, U.S.A. was shown at the Texarkana Historic Museum from November 1984 through February 1985. Many items from the Dr. Rhine Collection of the Melville Library were included in this exhibit. PRB

Personal Papers and Letters of T. E. Rhine, M.D.

MEMPHIS HOSPITAL MEDICAL COLLEGE EXAMINATION

Circa 1897–99

Anatomy   by E. E. FRANC

1. Locate the heart, describe its valves and give their location?
2. Give origin, cause and relations of the right common carotid artery?
3. State origin, ending, divisions and branches of the subclavian artery?
4. Describe the circle of Willis.
5. If the inferior Vena Cava was constricted where it passes through the diaphram, how would the blood get back to the heart?
6. Give origin, course and distribution of the Phrenic nerve?
7. Describe the Brachial Plexus of nerves.
8. Name the structure supplied by the median nerve.
9. Name the structure supplied by the obturator nerve.
10. Name and describe the ligaments of the Knee Joint.

1. Describe the three states of matter—Solid, Liquid and Gas.
2. Define the term "Specific Gravity", and cite an illustration.
3. What is Sound?
4. Define the terms, Temperature, Specific Heat, and Latent Heat.
5. What do you understand by "Reflection of Light", and what is the law governing this phenomenon?
6. How may magnets be produced artificially?
7. How would you construct an electric battery?
8. Give occurence, preparation, physical and chemical properties, and uses of Oxygen.
9. Ditto Hydrochloric Acid.
10. Ditto Sulphur.
11. Ditto Carbon Dioxide.
12. Ditto Calcium Sulphate.
13. Give some essential points to be considered in keeping a residence and its surroundings sanitary.

14. If you obtain a precipitate on heating a specimen of Urine, what might it be, and how would you prove what it is?
15. Define—a. An Extract.
         b. A Fluid Extract.
         c. A Tincture.
         d. An Emulsion.

CONDUCT OF NORMAL LABOR

(Read before the Council District Medical Society in 1906 at Camden, Arkansas, by Dr. T. E. Rhine.)

What is labor? Labor is the expulsion of a viable foetus through the natural passage of the mother. If engaged to deliver a woman, we should invariably visit them unless impossible, then should have her husband report to us, finding out symptoms of present pregnancy and anything needing treatment should have it. If a multipara and not acquainted with her post child bearing history, you should ascertain that, as to length of labor, difficult or not, hemorrhages, eclampsia, etc., as that may put you on the lookout and treat her for bad symptoms. Bowels and liver should be kept acting. Coscara Sagrado is the best laxative for bowels and is also tonic to stomach, for liver and occasional purgative should be given. Kidneys should be watched especially if some disease existed before pregnancy. Urine should be examined regularly to ascertain conditions as near as possible. Keep acting, if not, give bland diuretics. Regulate diet, bathing, plenty of light, outdoor exercise. Some may do hard labor without injury, others cannot. As pleasant surroundings as possible, uterine tonics with general tonics if needed. Give them instructions as to what they need and how to arrange everything so as to be in readiness when needed. Also to assistants, nurses. Too many helpers are in the way. One or two old ladies are sufficient.

When summoned to attend a labor case I attend as soon as possible, because we cannot tell what may happen before we arrive. I take with me my medicine case which contains all medicines needed. My hypodermic case with necessary tablets is always in my pocket. My obstetric bag contains 1 oz. absorbent cotton, 1 yd. Bichto Gauze, pocket case which contains instruments needed to repair lacerations etc., antiseptic soap, nail brush, umbilical scissors, boric acid, chloroform, 4 oz. fountain syringe, Kelly pad, elastic catheter, forceps Elliots small.

When I arrive, if no rush, I pass a few minutes in pleasantry with the attendants, then turn my attention to the woman to be delivered. If I have not seen her (which we often do not or even know anything about the case until called) I question her concerning present pregnancy as to whether any bad symptoms had developed, which would put us on our guard as worse might develop before labor was over. Condition of bowels, if not moving well, later on use enema to unload; whether passed water freely or not, as it might be necessary to use catheter; to past labors if a multipara. Ask concerning pains as to frequency, severity, character, duration. If any flow, if any, what kind. Has bag of water broke.

When I have plenty of time, I have them be prepared as near as possible like I do when full instructions are given beforehand. If I have not time, I try to have everything as clean as possible. The bed is prepared by putting a mattress on a bedstead without a feather bed if I can prevent it and will not allow springs at all in long labors. Put on mattress a sheet, on that a good oilcloth large enough to cover bed, on that another sheet, then a folded sheet to catch the discharges, then another clean cloth to catch the bulk of discharges which can be removed as soon as baby is born and will be out of the way and first folded sheet to remain to catch the remainder of discharges. When my pad is suitable for use, I use it, which catches most of the discharges and saves a great deal of work. Before using I wash it with carbolic water. The cover and pillows are fixed to suit the patient.

Preparation of patient where instructions are given. I have her to take a general warm bath and especially scrub abdomen, genitals, thighs, with soap and water. When she intends going to bed, to put on an underskirt and gown. The gown can be pulled high up under arms, not getting soiled which will save removing after labor is over, which is quite a help. The skirt will protect limbs etc. and can be easily removed when soiled bed apparel is. Where no time is to be had, I have them dressed and bathed according to my rule, and especially bathed, as it saves them a spell of septicemae, because some are dirty and you cannot deliver a child without touching them and getting your hands again soiled.

After my verbal examination, if patient is not in bed, I ask her to lie down so I can examine her. I call for hot water and a clean towel, scrub my hands well with antiseptic soap and nail brush, trim off my nails and cleanse out under them well with my knife, again scrub them. Now to examine the abdomen, to try and make out the presentation and perhaps the position of the child. Listen for the heart sounds which may help you locate position of child, if heard, insures live child, so far. After my abdominal examination, if I have positively made out the presentation and position of child, but a great number of times I cannot, especially in fat patients, poly hydramnios, etc. I again wash my hands in some antiseptic water. I prefer carbolic acid or creolin; anoint my index finger with antiseptic vaseline and proceed to make my vaginal examination, have my patient lie on back with knees flexed and far apart, slip up skirt out of way, place finger in palm of hand so as not to touch anything. If uterus is high, put other hand on abdomen and push down. Also, let other fingers extend over perineum as that gives better reach than if flexed in palm. What do we examine for to find out the condition of vagina and it's orifice as regards latency, freedom from obstruction, sensibility as to tenderness, moisture, condition of it's thickness, elasticity and amount of dilatation; whether pregnant or not; whether labor has begun, how far advanced; whether bag of water has ruptured; what the presentation and position is; whether pelvis is normal or deformed, (if deformed, to what extent would complicate labor); whether rectum or bladder are distended with their natural contents or not, if so could use enemata or catheter to release. After your examination, if you find everything all right, you should tell your patient so to keep her in good spirits. Do not give a positive opinion as to time of delivery, but say, if nothing happens, it will be over in so many hours, saying some women get along faster than others and some women faster at one time than at another. If you find your patient in the first stage of labor, it is not necessary for her to stay in bed. If she desires, she may sit up or walk about the rooms. The physician can do as he sees fit. As few examinations as possible should be made throughout labor. During first stage, you may give a little chloral-hydrate or hypodermic of morphia to relieve so much suffering. It also helps to relax parts. As complete dilatation of cervix shows second stage approaching, if woman has not laid down, should do so, for if bag of water has not ruptured, may do so at any moment and wash down cord which may cause considerable trouble replacing or may cause death of child by obstruction to circulation, or a precipitate labor. Always after rupture of membrane in the advanced stage, make an examination to be sure of your presentation and position. During last part of first and second stage if no obstruction exists and pains are not sufficient to expel child, I give something to strengthen them, Quinine cinicufugia, mistle toe, hypodermic of strychnia and nitroglycerin, and once in a while, I give small doses of ergot. If anterior lip of cervix becomes caught between head and pubic bone and becomes edematous and impedes labor, I try to push up over occiput when pain starts. During last part of second stage, when head presses against perineum and flexion not complete, I put a finger in rectum and push backward against forehead and pull occiput forward as much as possible so as to help nature complete flexion which lessens force on perineum and lessens chances of rupture. Also, pull perineum upward to protect it. Do not let head descend too fast against it before it has time to relax. Also ask patient not to bear down any more than she can help and can govern the expulsion of head, almost feeling out head between pains. Do not let face be born before you have the neck hugging the pubic bone and occiput laying on top of pubis and you lessen to a great extent the chances for rupture. As soon as head is born, feel for cord around neck and if wound around neck try to slip it over head. If you can't, over shoulders. If wound too tight to remove, you may have to cut if cord is too short for child to be born. When pains start, elevate head so lower shoulder can be born first and if large and need help from any cause, introduce finger in vagina and in axila and by doing so aid the expulsion materially. Still bear in mind the shoulders may rupture the perineum which has escaped at birth of head. Then lower body for upper shoulders to be born, hips are usually born with pain that expels last shoulder. Manage a breech on best of judgment. After baby is born, wrap with something to keep from getting cold and trying to breathe before head is born. If after coming head is not born immediately, pass finger into vagina and into mouth with child on arm and put other hand on neck and push down and elevate and extract. If face is upward, you will have to lower child. You may have to use forceps on after coming head. Always hold child in axis of vaginal canal while being born. When born, I lay on his back, out of discharges, then put a hand on womb to make it follow the child so as to prevent hemorrhage. Then I wipe mouth, eyes, etc. with a clean cloth to remove mucus etc. from them. If he does not breathe by this time, I gently press on his heart, sprinkle with cold water. If it breathes, I wait until cord quits pulsating before tieing and cutting. If it doesn't breathe, I ligate and cut immediately so I can better resusitate. I tie cord with cord of some soft thread soaked in carbolic acid water and use pair of umbilical scissors to cut cord kept in same solution. If he does not breathe by this time, bathe it in warm water with a dash of cold water on breast at intervals, artificial respiration, pull out tongue and blow into mouth filling lungs with air. If no breathing so far, I catch under arms and throw over my shoulder and bring down and repeat again and again. Do not despair in a few minutes, as some have been reported resussitated two hours after birth. When all right, I hand to a nurse who has a warm article of clothing of some kind to wrap it in. Have her to anoint it with lard well, which I think removes the vernix coseosa best. After waiting a few minutes, have her to wipe it off well with a clean, soft cloth which removes most of the secretions on body. Then to bathe with warm water and soft soap. Of course, I vary from this rule in very feeble infants not strong enough to bear so much handling. While she is bathing the child, I attend to the mother. I wash my hands well and deliver the placenta by slight traction on cord and compressing the uterus and having the woman to bear down as if she was having a pain. If too much force is needed to extract by cord, I introduce my fingers and catch hold of it and remove, always examining it to see if I can tell whether all is removed. Of course, if the case demands it, I deliver placenta immediately after severing the cord. If not, I wait ten to twenty minutes. If it is attached, I again wash my hands and annoint and intro- duce into uterus and feel it with my hand. I always examine for rupture of perineum immediately after delivery of placenta. I never use a douche immediately after labor unless to control hemorrhage or have introduced my hand into uterus. I always give a teaspoon of ergot after delivery of placenta to keep up contractions. Also, knead uterus through abdomen for several minutes afterwards to be sure it does not relax and at intervals for an hour or so care to make sure.

Now the baby is bathed and ready for cord to be dressed which I always do. I dust boric acid well over cord and abdomen, pull stump of cord through a hole in a piece of absorbent cotton and again dust it with boric

357

acid. The cotton absorbs the moisture from cord better than anything else. Fold the cotton over stump and then put on an abdominal binder, not tight enough to impede circulation, as I believe jaundice is thereby caused. Look it over for any deformity which may exist. Have nurse dust boric acid all over body and rub in well, which I think soothes the delicate skin. Do not put too many clothes on them and almost smother them.

By this time the Mother has rested somewhat. Then I have the nurse, if reliable, scrub her hands as I would myself, and have her bathed and all soiled articles removed, leaving her perfectly clean. Also, her bed. If perineum is ruptured, I repair. I have them slip a clean folded sheet under her to catch the discharges and remove as soon as soiled and another one replaced. I put an abdominal binder on. That's the last thing I do if they wish to wear one. Unless they are made correctly, they are of no use but wearrisome. They should be made to come below the femoral trochanter and up to the ribs. They should have grooves in them to make them fit. You can pin from below upward or the other way, just as you like. Everything all right now, I go home. The management of mother and child after delivery is so closely connected, I will have to mention a few things. Give the mother as long a rest as possible before disturbing her, as she needs a rest. Let the child nurse as soon as mother rests. Have mother to wash nipples after each nursing with something to toughen and to avoid fissures. Be sure and dry after each nursing. For the lochial discharge, I have them to use pads if prepared. If not, just clean cloths to catch the flow, and replace by another one when soiled. These save the patients clothes and bed from getting so soiled. If they won't use cloths or have not them, I always have them bathe with sterile water and a clean cloth several times a day which removes the adherent discharges, lessens chances of septic troubles and gives them a great deal of comfort. Change patients clothes as well as bed clothing as often as needed. For after pains, if due to relaxation and formation of clots, give ergot, viburim comp. Remove clots with finger or hot douches, hemalgic morphine, gelsumun, chorsil, quinine. Reflex from over distended bowel or bladder relieves each. If mother's urine is not voided in eight hours, hot fomentation over bladder. If no avail, use catheter. Bowels should move in twenty-four hours unless open free before delivery. You can use enemata. Castor oil is best, but can use any laxative desired.

Diet should be light, but nutritious. Do not starve. For first few days if baby gets hungry, you may feed a little, before mother's milk appears, but do not give it heavy diet such as sugar tits, meat, pure milk etc. as you are almost sure of some gastrointestinal trouble.

If it's bowels do not move in twenty-four hours, give a laxative. Castor oil first, or other laxative. Kidneys may not act for several days, because they do not secrete, especially in boys. The reason I do not know, perhaps for want of liquids. If bladder becomes full and will not void it's contents, give it a hot bath or cold over region of bladder, or if that does not suffice, can use small elastic catheter.

Chapped nipples often gives considerable trouble as to curing and pain to mother, while allowing child to nurse. Prevention is by getting mother to harden nipples before delivery by using tannic acid, alum, borax, alcohol and by bathing and drying them after each nursing. Curative, best in my hands, is to annoint nipple, except fissure to protect nipple from the medicine and apply nitrate silver 20 to 30 gr. to 1 oz. to fissure after cocaine, then dust with boric acid and abstain from nursing that breast for 24 to 36 hours, using breast pump to extract milk. The Benzoin comp. used in same way is useful. Many other things are useful. Fordye Barker uses Nitrate Lead Unguent.

Sunken nipples, draw out with hand, breast pump or dry cup, having baby ready to nurse.

For the exuberant granulation of the umbilicus, burnt alum, calomel will remove them. Have bathed and dusted with boric acid twice daily.

Second day hemorrhage, after cord has fallen off, use styptics. If of no avail, use figure of eight ligature by using any small pieces of steel or iron as small wire knitting needles, hair pin, hat pin, etc.

One thing which has given me considerable trouble is inflammation of breasts to keep abscess from forming. Many things are useful, as hot applications belladonna, applied, lead and opium wash, antiphogistine, tincture of iodine, strapping with adhesive strips. My favorite locally is equal parts of salt, camphor and glycerine applied warm on absorbent cotton covered well and bound by adhesive strips with bowels freely open, light diet, bedside pot and phytolacca internally. Of course, if abscess forms, incise freely and drain.

The mother should stay in bed until she is able to be up. No rule will apply to all cases, as some can be up twice as soon as others without perceptible injury. Err on the safe side and run no risk.

T. E. Rhine, M. D.
Thornton, Ark.
July 2, 1917

Miss Nita Raines
Little Rock, Ark.
Kind Friend: Was dumb almost to speechlessness when your letter drove up to our town. However I was elated over it as I am always over all mysterious happenings. Was sure glad to get the letter. Well I have some fine records now but not all I want. Here is a list of some I want. Edison of course. Forgotten. Carry me back to Old Virginy. Little grey home in the west. Sing me the Rosary. I hear you calling me. Somewhere a voice is calling. Rock me to sleep mother. Traumerei (Violincello by Gruppe). Violin piece by Spalding. Humoresque (Violin) by Spalding. I have Nightingale song that you had sung by Christine Miller and some song it is just as you used to sing it. Just had a big baptist meeting quite a number joined.

Hope you are having a joyous good time and wish I could get off for a few days and enjoy myself a little. Cornelias house is looking more like a place to stay than when you left. If I thought any one would care I would join the Army Medical Corp, but as all would be so glad to get rid of such a pest I will try and worry them a while yet. Have missed your music more than I could ever think of. When I was lonely and despondent it sure helped then. As you are tired of this preamble will disappear. Be a good old maidy and write again when you have nothing else to do or think about.

Your friend,
Ed

360

New York Polyclinic
New York, N. Y.
Apr 7, 1918

Miss Nita Raines,
Thornton, Ark.

Dear Friend Oh! how tired tonight worked til eleven o'clock last night doing all kinds of operations on a dead man recalling all of my old familiar stunts on the cadaver its fun and a pleasure to think how quickly those seemingly forgotten things I learned years ago loom up so quickly. Today is Sunday and wish I could drop over and see old M. J. with a stick of candy and tell him about all I saw today or rather try as to tell all I saw would be impossible. visited Riverside Drive, Grants Tomb ship dock rode the subway. Saw the water supply of N. Y. City in lake. A portion of Central Park a most beautiful place and will be more so when summer comes. In the park is the Museum of fine arts no one cannot tell of it so any can even imagine its immensity and instructiveness. Saw an Egyptian pyramid made 1600 B. C. Menagerie. Will return and see the National Museum of History later. This is the easiest place to travel around with a map of the city I even say can't get lost if you know where you stay at. Just study the city map and learn how to pick you the street car you want whether surface, elevated or subway those subways certainly go fast and the locals stop every 3 to 6 streets and the express ones only stop at very important points can ride at least 30 miles for a nickel Saw many costly homes of the millionaires. I wish I had my old Ford up here so I could go where I wanted to plenty of them here. Sure a lot of fine cars here the prettiest things I ever saw. When I have time to am going to look for an Edison house and see if I can find some records I want. If I find some songs will send a few also. Well where I am taking my meals for a few days there is a goodlooking girl you see and look at her out of my right eye as she eats at my side. Have a very quiet room in a big apartment house. We have met an awful nice doctor from Kentucky here where we are stopping and we three go together all the time. Well I can hear them singing at a church close by. If I have any friends down there give them my best regards. But don't suppose I have. Well we'll disappear at this time. Write if you have no serious objections.

Your friend,
Ed Rhine

Hoboken, New Jersey
Dec. 22, 1918

Dear Friend: Enjoy Xmas for me as I suppose I will have to work as lots of

361

the boys are coming in now. They have a lot of interesting experiences to relate others sad. Quite a number has some soverniers of different kinds. Have not seen any one I even knew since I left Camp Greenleaf, but have met some that are from Ark. both doctors and soldiers. Have had some few experiences but not enough to balance by far the comforts of home and friends and being a free man and not a servant. Poor privates my sympathies goes out to them I tell you. I would like to get my discharge but am somewhat doubtful of it just now unless my friends get quite busy and help me out. Hope you have a nice time Little Rock. I have only been over to New York twice since I came back. Don't care for any shows as I have to be very careful about my expenses to come out without getting money from home everybody sticks us all they can. What a shame. They must not have any moral conscience. Some of the boys are badly maimed but cheerful. Saw one boy totally blind was just as cheerful as could be more so than I was. They are sure glad to get back calling it a sure enough country God's country. Well I smiled at a few nurses this morning that was on the ship I helped to unload. Got them some Red Cross candy. Now the Red Cross is a great charitable institution far better than the Y. M. C. A. while the Y.M.C.A. has done wonderful things for the boys. All the war activities has done a lot for the boys. They speak well of the Salvation Army. I am broke so you need not expect any xmas present this xmas as I am giving no one any not even my mother. Tell Mary Sue I hope Santa brings her a package of popcorn. Regards to rest of your uncle's family.

Your friend,
Lt. T. E. Rhine

T. E. Rhine, M.D.
Thornton, Ark.
May 22, 46

Dear Virginia: Its been one of the greatest pleasures of my life to have you all home for my day and you all added so much pleasure to the occasion. Its just wonderful what great girls you all are. Its impossible to express myself in what I care for you girls, you all are so great to me. I hope you all can slightly grasp how much I love you all and what great women I want you all to make. women respected by all who know you whether great or small, high or low as all are created by the almighty Parent. So it behooves us to be nice and courteous to all and costs nothing. Hope you are rested by now and your examinations are off and you are again enjoying your school work. Those days were great to me. Write us often if nothing but a postal card saying am all right.

Your dad.

Unusual Occurances in 59 Years of Practice

Hydatiform mole afterbirth at 13 months
Two cords tied with a knot in them
Three transverse births
Twins, one dead, the other in transverse position
Two accidental hemorrhages, one mother never menstruated after that
 even though she was only twenty three years old
Two small after births passed after normal labor, one 30 days after full term
 delivery, the other, one week after full term delivery
Two sets of triplets, one, all breach, the other one normal
One case with both breasts cancerous
Woman had a baby and had not menstruated in fifteen months. She was 49
 years old
Negro girl had a baby at 12½ years and had never menstruated
Negro girl had a baby at 11½ years and had another before she was 13 years
Cephalic after coming head. Stuck a hole in the ear to let the water out
Woman who menstruated all nine months of pregnancy
Delivered 13 babies for three mothers
Delivered an 18 pound baby by podalic version
Delivered a 20 pound baby by normal delivery
Baby born with measles. The mother was sick with measles when the child
 was born, so it was covered with the rash
 Baby born of a smallpox patient in the pustular stage. The baby, also, had
 the eruptions in the pustular stage

In late 1948, while Mother was gathering information for the scrap
book that was to document his qualifications for the nomination for Doctor
of the Year, Mother and Daddy were listening to the radio. The program
was probably "This is Your Life," and a doctor was on the show. They were
making much over the fact that he had doctored on some families for three
generations. This struck Daddy as being insignificant, because he could

363

easily recall families he had doctored on four or five generations. That started the mental hunt for "families." For the next nine years, Daddy would remember names of families he had practiced for and they would record them. In 1957, when they stopped, this is the statistical account:

17 families in which he delivered three generations
18 families in which he had delivered both parents and the children
20 families in which he had practiced for six generations
150 families in which he had practiced for five generations
250 families in which he had practiced for four generations

"Mail-order" Doctoring

This letter is typical of this particular patient's epistles, which he received frequently, probably every other week.

Dear Doc: I thought I would let you know how I am today. Doc, my right side had got a little better than it was until late yesterday and last night. My side hurt me all night below my ribs and all up in my side, all in my ribs and in my back, clear up under my shoulder. I know it's my liver. It comes from my back around my side down to my bowels. My bowels moved out this morning, loose. Looked like they had cold in it or infection. They weren't right. That I guess is why my liver and right side is worse. I just believe Doc if we could just get my liver to act a little bit, I would get better. Is there anything in them tabs you are giving me to work on the liver? I thought maybe if there was that might be the reason my bowels moved like they did this morning and making my liver and side hurt so. Hope it is the medicine. You give me some of them malarial capsules before when I had jonders. Do you think they would help this time? I imagine I am so nervous this time tho I couldn't stand them.

My side is hurtin worse last night and today so I thought I would let you know how I was. I'm taking the little tablets you sent me, one two times a day, night and morning.

You just do for me what you think best for me.

Your friend Harvey

August 20, 1963

Dear Dr. Rhine:

Since you have neither seen nor heard of me prior to the receipt of this letter, I am afraid you will think, "She certainly has her nerve!", and just

365

toss this letter into the trash basket. However, taking this risk, I will go ahead and finish.

I became "acquainted" with you through one of your patients, a Mr. Bill B_____ , who lives here in El Dorado, the early part of 1961, shortly after the birth of my son. Hearing Mr. B_____'s story about his extreme weight problem and seeing how much good you had done for him, I finally persuaded him to let me try some of the capsules you had given him for weight reduction—they were solid red at one end, and had tiny multi-colored granules in the other. I had taken almost every reducing pill known, but none of them worked—till I took your capsules. Now, at nearly the end of August, 1963, I have maintained the weight I lost down to, except for about six pounds. I have been trying to lose this extra poundage for about two months now, but to no avail whatsoever.

It is for this reason I am writing you at this time—to see if perhaps you will take pity and let me have some of your pills. I would come to see you, but it would be very difficult as I have a regular job and then a son to raise when I am not working...My husband is attending x-ray school at the University of Arkansas Medical Center in Little Rock.

If you would please see fit to let me have some of your pills, I would very sincerely appreciate it. If you will, please let me know how much the charge is and I will send you the amount in advance. If possible, I would like to have a sixty day supply.

Hoping to hear from you at your earliest possible convenience,

I am,

Kansas City, Missouri
January 26, 1961

Dear Dr. Rhine,

Please forgive me if this is not the way to spell your name. I've never seen it written.

I am writing you to see if you would sell me some medicine.

I am Jewel and Gurt James niece (by marriage) and a couple of years ago while I was visiting them my son, then eight, got a real sore throat. I brought him to you and the medicine you gave worked like magic. I would love to keep some on my medicine shelf all the time. He has had several sore throats this winter and to be frank I don't care too much for the Doctor's here compared to what you gave him.

If you do not wish to mail the medicine (let me know how much to send if you do), would you send the prescription?

Thank you
Sincerely

New Edinburg,
Arkansas
June 3, 1964

Dear Dr. Rhine,
    I am sending you $5.00 on my bill. I owe you $6.00 but I can't send but
$5.00 today and I want you to send me some more pills please send them by
mail. What it be I will pay on this end for the mailing and the packing.

Chula Vista, California
July 16, 1958

Dear Dr. Rhine, I am writing to ask you if you could give me the name of the
high blood pressure medicine you have been giving me so that I can get the
same here or should I keep on taking anything for high blood pressure. I
haven't had a test but feel like I still have high blood as this neuralgia is still
with me.
Words can't express my thanks to you for what you have done for us over
the years and especially Dick's last illness. If you should come to California
be sure to come to see Sidney's family at Chula Vista and oblige.

P.S. The tablets you have been giving me are red and yellow.

Rt. 2, Fordyce, Arkansas
September 9, 1964

Dr. T. E. Rhine:
Dear Sir: I am sending you $5.00 on my account with you. I would have
sent it before now but I could not get around to sent it because I have been
down in my back and could not walk very far.
                                        Yours truly,

N.B. Dr. Rhine, I have taken all of the pink tablets. I do not have nuthing
now, but the white ones you gave me.

Palmdale, California
April 20, 1964

Dr. T. E. Rhine
Thornton, Ark.
Dear Dr. Rhine,

How are you? I have been hearing about you this month. I am glad you are able to be on the go.

I am feeling better now. I saw a doctor and I received some medication for my blood pressure which is 150 over 80.

My nose bled some several times between Friday and Tuesday. I began taking the brown tablet you prescribed "Theolaphen" and I felt better. The doctor gave me a prescription to buy more. I could not find them. Then the doctor prescribed Esidrix K 25/500. My nose had not bled any more, and I think my blood pressure is normal. I will have it checked soon.

On March 25, I sent you a letter. I did not hear from you. I sent a check for not more than five dollars. It was Mr. and Mrs._____'s check. If you can help me, I need the following:

1. One Elastic Stocking
2. Theolaphen—brown tablets (Blood pressure)
3. Rauwolfia—blood pressure
4. Something for kidney and bladder trouble. I sent a capsule in last letter.

The Rauwolfia is a red tablet. Some one gave me this once. I remember that it made me feel better and I wrote the name of it in a book.

I am sending a bill for my last stocking. If you can not get it cheaper, I will order one.

Yesterday was a cold windy day in Palmdale. Winter coats fit very well.

Thanking you in advance, I am

Yours truly,

Making Life Successful

Many things closely combined contribute to making life worth living. By a successful life I do not mean the accumulation of wealth, but a life that will be pointed out as a life to pattern after or partly so at least. A starting point when laying the foundation for the success of ones future life, which should be begun early in life, is forming good habits and the best education that opportunity affords.

Education is the foundation for the future on which we can learn to think and concentrate the mind by this cultivation. Next to concentrated thoughts is purpose, preseverance, energy, industry, integrity, opportunity, control of temper, judgment, character, patience, cheerfulness, politeness, honesty, economy, kindness, contentment, self-reliance, good manners, and lastly but not the least, close attention to the little things.

Learn to think, for the keen intellect cuts its way smoothly, gracefully and rapidly. The dull one wears its life out against the simplest problems. To perceive accurately and think correctly is the aim of mental training. We cannot exaggerate the importance of clear, correct thinking. For undigested learning is as oppressive as undigested food. Thought is to the brain what gastric juice is to the stomach, a solvent to reduce whatever is received to a condition in which all that is nutritive and wholesome may be appropriated. The stomach is to the frame what the memory is to the brain, to learn in order to be wise makes the mind active and powerful. Some of the great advantages of thinking are: first, it transfers and conveys thoughts of others to ourselves so as to make them property of our own; secondly, it enables us to distinguish truth from error and reject the wrong from everything we have read, seen or heard; thirdly, by it we fix in our memory only what we best approve, without loading it with all we read; lastly, by properly meditating on what comes within the view of our minds, that we may improve upon the thoughts of others and acquire a reputation by improving on the labors of others. The mental superiority of one man over another usually originates in the habit of thinking, for it is not mere reading, but thinking, that gives us possession of knowledge. If you take away thought from the life of man, what remains is a dismal future.

Remember to think before you speak; consider before you promise; take time to deliberate before advising. In the morning, think what you have to do today, but at night ask yourself, "What have I done, and have I done it well?" Think not of the things that concern us not, but fill your head and heart with good thoughts that there will be no room for the bad, for today as never before, there is need for much individual thought for too many of us yield to the opinions of others without careful consideration on our part, for we need not fear we will exhaust our brain in thought, if we will only draw our inspiration from actual human life. Oliver Wendell Holmes says success is the result of a mental attitude and the right mental attitude will bring success in everything you undertake. Men who succeed have faith in themselves and faith in their fellows. Doubt either and you are doomed.

The man who does his work so well that he needs no supervision has already succeeded. Men who act their thoughts and think little of their acts are the ones who win. There is no such word in all the bright lexicon of speech as 'failure' unless you yourself have written it there. Dr. Acheson, one of the great inventors of today, when asked "What is the one thing most essential to make notable achievements?" unhesitatingly replied, "Train yourself to concentrate your thoughts on a subject for a protracted period, allowing nothing else to obtrude into your mind until you have thought out the thing completely from beginning to end. Think things through. I have often spent an entire night concentrating my mind on just one subject, perhaps ten hours at an unbroken stretch. Everything must be thought out before it can be carried out." He says it is not hard to acquire the habit of concentration, protracted thought. Then he gives an illustration. Look about you and select some object. Bring into clear vision the various steps involved in their production and realize what embodies the act. For example, you see your mother sewing with a piece of thread. This is a very simple act, but think what was necessary to be done to enable her to perform this act. Go back to the iron mines; see the iron extracted from the ore after being taken from Mother Earth, perhaps hundreds of feet underneath it's surface; the conversion of the cast iron into steel; the drawing the steel into wire; and the final formation of the needles. Go back to the cotton fields and follow the processes of suitable preparation, planting, growing, gathering, ginning, spinning and the final manufacture of the thread. Such a line of thought may be extended over not only minutes but hours. But you can and should educate yourself to have the necessary patience to concentrate your mind. Have beside you a good encyclopedia and an unabridged dictionary and the best selection of reference books you can afford. If you don't know much about a subject, for instance, the cultivation of cotton, read about it, keeping your mind intently on what you are reading. If you have never seen a blast furnace in operation, turn to your encyclopedia or reference books which will give you full information. For education is not at all a matter of going to school. I had only three years in school, and whatever I have learned has been the result mainly of reading and of concentration, sustained thinking. So don't let your minds get lazy, but keep them active. The rewards of thought come to men who keeps his mind working day and night, at home and abroad, in season and out of season and everlastingly getting new ideas and applying them to his job.

Purpose

We must have a definite purpose in view and direct our entire efforts to that idea, for we can never estimate the power of purpose, for it takes hold of the heart of life and spans our whole manhood. It enters into our hopes, aims and prospects and holds its scepter over our business careers and gives us that indomitable will, that inflexible purpose, of looking into the future through good and evil and gives us greater confidence and commands success by keeping your eye fixed on a certain point. The man that starts in life with a determination to reach a certain high position and adheres unwaveringly to his purpose, rarely fails to reach his desired goal. Every man must pursue his views steadily and should not be turned from his views by other objects, ever so attractive, for life is not long enough for any man to accomplish everything. Few, at best, accomplish more than one thing well, for the most of us really accomplish nothing worthy. But when endowed with average intelligence, we should attempt to accomplish one thing useful, important or worthy. We have men in our country endowed with superior mental ability for any pursuit and make it successful, but life is too short, even with a mastermind, to make eminent success in varied vocations, for he must unite his efforts and energies on one profession to attain near perfection.

Perseverance, Industry, Energy, Integrity, Judgment

Next to purpose, comes the closely connected in being successful. In speaking of perseverance, I refer to all connected. For they are which builds, constructs and accomplishes whatever is good, great, and valuable. They built the Pyramids of Egypt, erected the gorgeous Temple of Jerusalem, built a wall around the Chinese Empire, scaled the stormy, cloud-capped Alps. But the greatest achievement of interest to us was opening up the great highway through the watery wilderness of the mighty Atlantic, leveling the forests of the New World and rearing in their stead a community of states and the greatest nation now known. That nation is our great U.S.A. of which we are all immensely proud.

They have put in motion millions of spindles, winged as many flying shuttles, harnessed thousands of iron steeds and many more thousand freighted cars are hitched to them and set flying from town to town and nation to nation. The many great ships that sail the great oceans, tunneling mountains of granite, and annihilating space with lightening speed. The wonderful system of telegraph, telephone and the wonderful Atlantic cable connecting nations, but the more wonderful wireless telephone and telegraphy. Just think of those inventors! How many days, even years, of patient toil, nights of weariness, months and years of vigilant, powerful effort was spent to perfect what the world has bowed to in reverance. We might ask ourselves why have their works power, names a charm, and deeds a glory. Because they were the sons of perseverance, unremitting industry and toil. Because from childhood to age, they knew no such word as 'fail', for defeat only gave them power, difficulty taught them the necessity of redoubled exertions, and dangers gave them more courage, and the sight of labor inspired in them corresponding energy. So it has been with all men who have been eminently successful in any profession. Success has always been wrought out by persevering industry and not by natural powers alone. Talent is desirable, but perseverance more, as it strengthens the natural powers, especially when strengthened by cultivation.

Honest industry procures friends in all parts of the civilized world. Men of business put their confidence in men who falter not, but toil against every barrier between them and success, but shuns the lazy, indolent and faltering. Remember, to win you must be steady and true to yourself, and be sure your trade or profession is a laudable one. Then plan, work and live for it, throwing your mind, might, strength, heart and soul into your acts. Then success will crown your efforts.

If you plan to be great or small, the same perseverance is necessary. For everyone admires an iron determination and comes to the aid of those who direct it for good. Opposing circumstances often creates within us strength both mental and physical, overcoming all obstacles, giving us greater powers of resistance by learning to labor patiently, if we would succeed. For the noblest thing in all the world is honest labor, and never suffer your energies to degenerate. Our most formidable rivals are those earnest, determined minds which reckon every hours value and achieve eminence by persistant application, for there is always room at the front for a man with force, but remember you cannot dream yourself into a character or reputation, but must hammer and forge yourself one. So don't live in hopes with your arms folded, for fortune only smiles on those who roll up their sleeves and put their shoulders to the wheel and push, for there is nothing impossible for those who try.

Success in life comes to those who make perseverance a bosom friend, yet the lack of perseverance, the refusal to profit by experience, and the lack of faith and steadfast hope, has caused many aspirants in the race to fall by the wayside. But those who use experience as a wise councilor, caution as an elder brother, and hope as a guardian genius, rarely fail to succeed.

Cheerfulness, Kindness, Courtesy, Politeness

Stand over and above all other social traits. For being cheerful and content, all nature smiles with us and the air seems more balmy, the sky more clear, the ground has a brighter green, the trees a richer foliage, the flowers a more fragrant smell, birds sing sweeter, the sun, moon and stars appear more beautiful. Whoever possesses such a noble nature carries sunshine and happiness wherever they go. Such a face enlivens every other face it meets, spreading joy and gladness in its pathway. Look on the bright side of life, but do not let the shadows of failure, misfortune, fall across your pathway. For being cheerful is the only happy life. Times may be hard, but it makes them no easier to wear a gloomy, sad look, for the harder the task, the need of more singing, for it is the sunshine that makes the flowers and not the clouds. There is no investment that pays larger dividends than the above four words and costs so little.

Little Things

Remember the little things in life are what counts, for the careful attention to the little things and small details are what leads to the mighty, reminding us to never pass up the little things lightly. Recall how small the nerve to a tooth is and often it runs a man distracted with pain. It is said a mosquito makes an elephant absolutely mad. The moments are the golden sands of time, and every day is a little life. Our whole life is but a day repeated, therefore we must not dare lose or misspend one. Everything has a small beginning, for the spring starts the river, combining the small things produces the great and powerful, for the nails and small bolts hold the parts together that constructs our massive skyscrapers, so don't lose sight of the small things. Little acts are the elements of true greatness for they raise life's values like the little figures over the larger ones in arithmetic to its highest powers. They are the real tests of character. There are no such things as trifles in the biography of man. Acorns cover the land with oaks, and the accumulation in youth of small deeds proves a great character in age.

You may not be a great river bearing large vessels of blessings to the world, but you can be a little spring by the wayside of life singing merrily all day and night, giving a cup of cold water to every weary, thirsty passer-by, for life is made up of small deeds. If we travel over the country, we must do it step by step. Writers of books do it sentence by sentence. If you learn science, you do it fact by fact, principle by principle. What is the happiness of life made up of? Little courtesies, kindnesses, pleasant words, genial smiles, friendly greetings, good wishes and deeds of charity. The greatest men are those who carefully improve and develop the little things and a careful observation of the little things are the secret of their success in business.

What is knowledge? It is but the accumulation of small facts collected and passed from man to man.

Hard work is the key to the door of success, and you yourself must turn the key that unlocks the door. Then do your work, not only well, but unusually well. The biggest thing about big success is the price; it takes a big man to pay it. You can measure in advance the size of your success by how much you are willing to pay for it, not in money, but in time, thought, energy, economy, purpose, devotion, study, sacrifice, patience and care that a man must give to his life work before he can make it amount to anything.

I wish to mention a few really great successful men with poor advantages and no capital in youth, but carefully guarded the little things, made use of every spare moment—Columbus, Daniel Webster, Henry Clay, A. Lincoln, A. Carnegie, John Jacob Astor, Cornelius and Commodore Vanderbilt, G. Washington, Herbert Hoover and Henry Ford.

Opportunities

Sages of the world have preached always of the phantom opportunity. This conversation has arisen from the graves of action. Allow this trailing of the subject, because it really would appear that he who talks incessantly without taking a breath of reason seldom encounters realism. It is possible then to consider rightly that the false doctrine of procrastination has been the real mother trouble of the world. The thought that procrastination was conceived for the sake of humanity would seem to parent an effort to apologize for indolence. The weight of judgment rules that promptness and decision, while quick to exact tribute, nevertheless is an economic jewel, because the one motion suffices to clear the field and allow the procession to proceed. Procrastination breeds a greater weight of indolence than the world is entitled to bear, because each exhibit adds to the derangements and mutilates the symmetry of principles and purpose in life. We cannot wait or stand still with a bludgeon to smite opportunity on the head to capture it, but requires constant effort. To work diligently is to manufacture opportunity. There is no necessity then of waiting for it. It can be immediately grasped by going to the root and foundation of its class and kind anywhere in the field of endeavor. It lives in occupation not speculation. Craft-wise, it may not be who best can wait, but in the essence of realism, who best can work. Opportunity comes no more often to the man born under a lucky star, than to the simple fellow who boasts no star attraction.

How to Capture Life's Greatest Values

*(A speech delivered by Dr. T. E. Rhine at Locust
Bayou High School graduation exercises
probably in the early 1940's.)*

It seems to me there are four simple, provable and practicable secrets of capturing the greatest values of life, four ways of making a greater success and at the same time, of achieving real happiness. First, decide what you want most of all out of life. Then write down your goals and a plan to reach them. Most people go through their years with vague notions of their ultimate aims. One survey showed nine out of ten persons had no definite plan in life. In their careers they leave too much to the happenstances of the jobs they are offered and to the willy-nilly turn of events. They lack a sense of direction so essential to keeping on a true course.

A Greek philosopher counseled, "Know thyself". So appraise your talents, personally, your inner drives, to the things you can do and like to do best. Size up the weaknesses you have to overcome. There is no average citizen, there is no common person. Do you consider yourself average or common? Do you believe that you were turned out in mass production as like to a majority of humans as peas in a pod, or that you think and dream and act like all other millions of Americans. Of course you don't. The very suggestion that you are like every one else makes you indignant. For you feel that you are different and you are. No one else in this world has exactly the same likes and dislikes that you have. No one else is moved to joy or pity, anger, desire, fear, remorse or rebellion just as you are moved or by the same occasions. Nor is any one else's character based on the same pattern. No one else has your same sources of courage or honesty or friendliness. No one has your deeply hidden fears or dreams. For all these various parts of your nature are uniquely colored by the elements which make you.

Your plan for work and happiness should be big, imaginative and daring. Strike out boldly for the things you honestly want more than any thing else in the world. The mistake is to put your sights too low, not to raise them too high. The definite far-away goal will supercharge your whole body and spirit. It will awaken your mind and creative imagination and put meaning into otherwise lowly, step-by-step tasks you must go through in order to attain the final success you desire.

The great psychologist William James said, men habitually use only a small part of the powers they possess and which they might use under appropriate circumstances. You can release human energy and spirit as wondrous as the physical scientist frees atomic energy. Use the great powers that you can tap through faith in God and the hidden energies of your soul. Over and over, in an infinite number and variety of proofs in the lives of people, it has been seen how man can draw upon the Higher Power and the soul within him.

Faith is the key to unlocking limitless powers of the mind, the heart, the soul-faith in God; faith that right triumphs over wrong; faith that you can win over disasters and setbacks; faith that smashes fear; faith in the ultimate realization of your hopes.

Again and again I have seen the tremendous power of faith. Only a faith that it could be done led to the construction of Bonneville Dam on the lower Columbia River in Oregon. We were warned that the raging waters of the Columbia River would rise 20 to 30 feet within a day or two, ripping to shreds any puny works of man to dam it. The native Indians had a legend that no man would ever walk across the Columbia River. Government engineers were doubtful that it could be done. The bonding companies refused to take the risk of the hazardous project. But undaunted faith answered the skeptics and proved that what man can dare and imagine, they can find a way to accomplish.

All things are possible to him that believeth. What a man can imagine in his mind, he can accomplish.

Love people and serve them. Respect yourself, others and the law. This is practical. I can think of hundreds of successful persons whose careers prove it. A fundamental love of people—all people—is an unfailing mark of the finest characters. Whereas an ingrained attitude of "What will I get out of it?" leads up a blind alley to failure. In a job you are simply filling human wants. You get ahead in direct relation to how well you offer services others need. If your aim is high, you may search for new services that will fill the needs of others. Even as James Watt developed steam power and ushered in the industrial age, or the Wright Brothers invented the airplane and pierced vistas into the air age, the opportunities to develop products and services are as boundless as the ideas and desires of mankind.

Your achievements may be directly limited or expanded by how well you get along with others. Alone, you are only one individual with your own set of capacities. But associate yourself with others and you can have the power of teamwork to do much greater things. You can put teamwork not only in your own career, but into your personal contribution to democracy—democracy both of government and industrial relations—and teamwork into the part you may play in world affairs. The same spirit that can make greatness in a person can forge new greatness for a people and a nation.

376

In order to make the most out of your own life, you must give and give and give of yourself to others. Tis the hardest thing in the world to give everything, even though tis usually the only way to get everything. Your greatness is measured by your kindness; your education and intellect by your modesty; your real caliber is measured by the consideration and tolerance you have for others.

Work. You can find life so packed with the joy and adventure of discovery that you will throw all you have into your work. The secret of work is a fourth and all-essential ingredient of the happy life of achievement. We need a lifework that forever keeps us growing. No wonder some people find only drudgery in their jobs, when they are not fired by the vision that today's work can be a stepping stone to greater work. In working and growing we can find ways of always keeping young, forever learning, always accepting new challenges and opportunities.

Live daringly, fearlessly. Taste the relish to be found in competition— in having to put forth the best within you to match the deeds risk-taking, hard-working competitors. Take the well considered risk instead of the sure thing that fails to call forth the most you have to offer.

Each one of us should form in his own mind a daily prayer to God that we learn to give free rein to our tremendous powers of believing, serving and working.

Keep my vision always clear to see the goals,
Help me tap the hidden powers within and above me,
Give me strength to work with all the energies of mind and body,
Help me to practice the love of people and service to others,
Keep me forever with a smile on my face for the whole human race.

In conclusion, I wish to give my formulae for a happy and successful life. Live well, laugh often, enjoy the respect and companionship of good and intelligent men and women, and have a love for little children. I consider this philosophy of life to be correct. After all, the great values in life are not what we have materially, but those finer qualities which are developed in character building—the possession of virtues which creates a spirit of brotherhood and helps us to be intensely interested in the welfare of others.

DIARY KEPT BY NANITA RHINE DURING PART OF THE YEAR 1931

(This diary was kept in a Physician's Year Book, compliments of Reed and Carnick, pioneers in endocrine therapy.)

RESOLUTIONS FOR 1931
1. Keep a diary each day.
2. Read something worthwhile each day.
3. Spend some time with my music each day.
4. Spend some time with V. E. music each day.
5. Spend some time in physical exercise each day.
6. Spend some time in facial exercise each day.
7. Keep a budget.

READING FOR 1931
World Classics
Jan.—Oriental Literature, Vol. I, Persia
      3 volumes, Harvard Shelf of Fiction

READING FOR 1932
Delphian Books

January 1, Thursday
Indolence:
Too often vanquishes the best, and turns
To naught the noblest, firmest resolution.
          Firdusi.   Shah Nameh

Selma's day off. Work hard all day. Mr. Geo. Gray dies at 2:30 p.m. Give V. E.'s music lesson, but have no time for my music, reading or self improvement.

January 2, Friday
whoever
Proudly neglects the worship of his God
Brings desolation on his house and home.
            Firdusi.   Shah Nameh

Spend most of day sewing, making dress for myself out of spring coat. Talk to Mary Sue in afternoon. She has tonsilitis. Dr. attends Mr. Gray's funeral. See to children baths and tend to part of their lessons & music. Read a little.

January 3, Saturday
Place not thy trust upon a world like this
Where nothing fixed remains.
            The Caravan
Goes to another city, one today,
The next, tomorrow, each observes it's turn,
And time appointed, mine has come at last,
And I must travel on the destined road.
            Shah Nameh

Go to Mary Sue's. Mr. & Mrs. Stewart Gardner & Vick Cone. Find M.S. much better than expected.

January 4, Sunday
Such are the freaks of Fortune, friend & foe
Alternate, wear the crown. The world itself
Is an ingenuous juggler, every moment
Playing some novel trick; exalting one
In pomp and splendour, crushing down another,
As if in sport, and death, the end of all.
            Shah Nameh   Firdusi

Rains all day. Much disturbed over the England, Ark. call for food. In afternoon receive letter from Holder Raines. Food riot at England, Ark. Situation serious everywhere.

January 5, Monday
Time sweep's o'er all things; why then should the wise
Mourn o'er events which roll resistless on,
And set at nought all mortal opposition?
            Shah Nameh

Dr. has two babies—Will Bass and Hugh Nance. Spend day in sewing mostly. Give V. E. her music and read some in Rubaiyat. Enjoy it but shall read it again before copying quotations.
Weight—self, 137 lbs. V.E., 66 lbs. S.E., 52½ lbs. Pat, 30 lbs.

January 6, Tuesday
> When Sun and Moon o'er heaven refulgent blaze
> Shall little stars obtrude their feeble rays?
>> Shah Nameh

Ironed in the morning. Had a caller, cut up lard, made sausages and sewed in the afternoon. Edna H. sent us one of her pictures. Dr. goes fox hunting. Help children with their lessons and get them to bed. Take time to read and memorize a few verses in Rubaiyat. To bed at 10:00.

January 7, Wednesday
> Come, fill the cup, and in the fire of Spring
> Your winter-garment of Repentance fling;
> The Bird of Time has but a little way
> To flutter—and the Bird is on the wing.

Very bad day. Dr. gone all day. Go for children. Finish tweed dress. Have meat to work with. Read a little in "The Divan", Hafiz.

January 8, Thursday
> A Book of Verses underneath the Bough.
> A jug of Wine, a loaf of Bread and Thou
> Beside me, singing in the Wilderness,
> Ah, Wilderness, were Paradise anow!

Cloudy and cold. The weather bad & times worse. Bank stilled closed. Dr. attends Red Cross meeting at Hampton & made representative in this township. Have hopes of getting Bank re-organized.

January 9, Friday
> The Worldly Hope men set their hearts upon
> Turns Ashes, or it prospers; and anon,
> Like Snow upon the Desert's dusty Face,
> Lighting a little hour or two—is gone.

Day is bad. Not feeling good. V.E. comes down with stomach trouble and cold. I read of so much distress in our Southland and the whole country for that matter and our own folks are in such a deplorable condition that it gets me. Walkers write they are coming. We are so blue and worried. Dr. wires them to postpone their visit. Am glad for don't feel in humor for that kind of company. Mary Sue calls at night. Says they can come Sunday so will slay the old turkey hen tomorrow. Cow sick.

January 10, Saturday
> I sometimes think that never blows so red
> The rose as where some buried Caesar bled:

Nita comes home with Dr. to spend the night. V.E. is in bed all day. I feel better myself except sleepy from having to be up so much with V.E. last night. Clean house good. Selma prepares turkey for dinner tomorrow. Mrs. Thornton gives me some pumpkin for pies and also tells me a "True Story" that leaves me thankful for the many blessings I have. Dr. Peters comes to see the cow.

January 11, Sunday
Why, if the Soul can fling the Dust aside,
And naked on the Air of Heaven ride,
Were't not a Shame—were't not a Shame for him
In this clay carcass to abide?

Mary Sue and George come and spend the day. Children have a good time together tho V.E. is still feeling bad. Dinner is not so good. It rains all day. Am going to read some now and then get the bunch to bed. Distress is so great in our state till I can think of nothing else.

January 12, Monday
'Tis but a Tent where takes his one day's rest
A Sultan to the realm of Death addrest;
The Sultan rises and the dark Ferrash
Strikes, and prepares it for another Guest.

V.E. stays home in the morning. Do a little mending in the aft. Children get to bed late. Dr. goes to Bearden on call with Dr. Byrd after supper. Read Chapter 1 of The Goulistan by Sadi. To bed at ten.

January 13, Tuesday
And fear not lest Existance closing your
Account, and mine, should know the like no more;
The Eternal Saki from the Bowl has pour'd
Millions of Bubbles like us, and will pour.

Ironed and did my mending. Dr. quite busy. Mrs. Cargyle buried in Fordyce. Too tired to read.

January 14, Wednesday
Certain tis that sins of others none shall write upon they scroll.
Be my deeds or good or evil, look thou to thyself alone:
All men, when their work is ended, reap the harvest they have sown.
                    The Divan, Hafiz

Selma takes the day off. Get along nicely with work but am so tired and nervous after dinner that I can hardly stand it. Cut out dress blouse for Pat. Dr. looking after Red Cross applicants. Situation very serious.

January 15, Thursday
   Whoever brings you, and sums up the faults of others, will doubtless
   expose your defects to them.
            Gulistan, Sa-di

   Feel some better today. Dr. makes two trips to see Mr. Barner below
   Bearden. Selma still off. Busy with the usual housework. Read a little
   after children get to bed.

January 16, Friday
   So much can support you, but in whatever you exceed that you must
   support it.   Gulistan, Sa-di

   Selma comes back so work hard all day making little jumper dress for
   Pat. Go to Mrs. Condray's for a little while in the afternoon.

January 17, Saturday
   Eat ye and drink ye, but not to an excess.
            Koran

   Rains hard all day. Help children with their Valentines. Make blouse
   for Pat's jumper dress.

January 18, Sunday
   Riches are intended for the comfort of life, and not life for the
   purpose of hoarding riches.   Gulistan, Sa-di

   Pat doesn't seem well. Fever 101½ in the late afternoon. Seems to have
   a light case of flu.

January 19, Monday
   Reveal not every secret you have to a friend, for how can you tell
   but that friend may hereafter become an enemy?

   Entertain Pat all day. Plays some in the morning, but fever comes up in
   the afternoon. Dr. goes to Fordyce on business. Red Cross work taking a
   great deal of his time. Fox hunting now.

January 20, Tuesday
   Keep to yourself any intelligence that may prove unpleasant til
   some person else has disclosed it.

   Iron and mend. Pat still cross. Walked down to Mrs. Condray's for a
   little while in afternoon.

January 21, Wednesday
   Patience accomplishes its object, while hurry speeds to its ruin.

Look over music and find three musical recitations for the children. They are very much interested in singing now and I enjoy playing for them to sing.

January 22, Thursday
Nothing is so good for an ignorant man as silence, and if he knows this he would no longer be ignorant. Levity in a nut is a sign of its being empty.

Pat is playful but still weak. Don't get much done. Mr. Condray gives the children one of his paintings, "The Christmas Star".

January 23, Friday
All that we are is the result of what we have thought.
Dharmapada

Accomplish very little. Get garden seed and plant early tomatoe seed in pan. Mrs. Reece Holmes calls in afternoon. Dr. spends most of day doing Red Cross work. Read a little after supper.

January 24, Saturday
Thoughts, well guarded, brings happiness.
Dharmapada

January 25, Sunday
He who does not arouse himself when it is time to rise, though young and strong is full of sloth, whose will and thought are weak, that lazy and idle man never finds the way to knowledge.
Dharmapada, Buddha

Went to see Alex's new baby in the afternoon. Baby pretty as can be and just as fat. They seem to be doing very well for times to be so terrible. Dr. put on committee for Government loans.

January 26, Monday
Mountains & ocean waves around me lie;
Forever the mountain-chains tower to the sky;
Fixed is the ocean immutably;
Man is a thing of nought, born but to die.
Anon.

Don't accomplish very much since Patricia is still cross from her little sick spell.

January 27, Tuesday
Iron. Dr. sells First National Bank stock in order to pay up here. Selma has finger lanced. V.E. doing good in her music.

January 28, Wednesday

Selma sick. Have all work to do. Go to P.T.A. Arrangements are made to provide soup for undernourished children.

January 29, Thursday

Selma still away because of her finger. Have all of the work to do. Go to call on Mrs. Cone who has been sick quite a while. Stop at Mrs. Peterson's. Merchants & Planters Bank, Camden, closes.

January 30, Friday

Recollections Of My Children

Ne'er a melon can I eat
But call to mind my children dear
Ne'er a chestnut crisp and sweet
But makes the loved ones seem more near.
Whence did they come, my life to cheer?
Before mine eyes they seem to sweep,
So that I may not even sleep.
What use to me the gold & silver hoard?
What use to me the gems, most rich and rare?
Brighter by far, aye! bright beyond compare
The joys my children to my heart afford.
Yamaganu-No-Okure

January 31, Saturday

Go to Fordyce. Buy dress goods for myself & sox for children.

February 1, Sunday

Start to Sunday School. Take a class and am to have charge of the music in the Primary Dept. Dr. goes to Wheelan Springs to see Mr. Payne's little girl.

February 2, Monday

Try to sew but have company. So many come with cries of distress til my mind is so torn up that I can hardly think. Give Mrs. Strong peas, beans, tomato for G.W.

February 3, Tuesday

Mrs. Strong and I make 8 gallons of soup for school. Do a little gardening. Dr. is at the American Legion meeting in Fordyce tonight. Have children all in bed and am going to try to get caught up in my reading if I can stay awake.

February 4, Wednesday

Iron in morning and mend afternoon. Start to P.T.A. but Mrs. C. comes in. Children bring home report cards. Both extra good.

February 5, Thursday
Go to Camden with Dr. Take children to picture show. Get home at midnight. Quite a task to break the children's routine but feel like it did all of us good to get out a little.

February 6, Friday
Suffer with my usual nervous headache. Do very little but entertain Pat. Have a nervous jimmy-fit. Wish I could control myself better.

February 7, Saturday
Patricia's third birthday. Have cake and candles for her. She gets quite a thrill from blowing out the candles. I am still feeling bad so don't have much celebration.

February 8, Sunday
Bad weather. Don't go to the S.S. and the day seems dreadfully long. Dr. gone as usual. Give girls cold tablets. They are very proud to be able to swallow one.

February 9, Monday
Finish little red dresses for the girls. Mrs. C. comes in afternoon. Dr. at home during the evening.

February 10, Tuesday
Iron and make Susan a dress. Dr. goes to Carthage to Legion meeting.

February 11, Wednesday
Spend all my spare time trying to plan to buy clothing for the entire family on our limited income.

February 12, Thursday
Dr. working so hard and most of it for nothing.

February 13, Friday
Rains hard all day. Mrs. C. gives me two old dresses to make up for the children.

February 14, Saturday
Do regular cleaning. Try to sew but don't accomplish much.

February 15, Sunday
Patricia not very well. We drive to Camden late in afternoon. M.S. not at home. Go to hospital with Dr. to see Mrs. Charles Higgs. Spend a while with the Cathey's.

February 16, Monday
Stay in all day giving Pat medicine for cold. Have got her to taking it in a

banana & for the first time in her life I am able to get enough down her to do her some good.

February 17, Tuesday
Pat better but still give medicine. Tired as if I had done a full days work.

February 18, Wednesday
Iron. Mary Sue comes. We discuss clothes & M.S. makes black silk jacket for me. Nita goes to school with children.

February 19, Thursday
Patricia feels much better in the evening and I get some sewing done. Also cut out several garments after supper.

February 20, Friday
Spend most of spare time sewing and studying catalog to see where I can save a penny.

February 21, Saturday
Didn't feel so well. Dr. was in and out all night and sleep was broken. Finish children's dresses.

February 22, Sunday
Planned to go to S.S. but couldn't as it started raining. Rained all afternoon.

February 23, Monday
Sewed a little. Get sewing stand from woman for price of meat. Taking bad cold. Raining now.

February 24, Tuesday
Iron, mend and do quite a bit of sewing.

February 25, Wednesday
Get my new dress from Ward's but have to send it back as it is too large.

February 26, Thursday
Get children's oxfords from Ward's.

February 27, Friday
Tired tonight. Dr. gone on calls til late.

February 28, Saturday
Go to Fordyce to buy some groceries. My first time to buy out of town. Do not feel very well. Working hard but worried more.

March 1, Sunday
Feel too bad to go to S.S. J.D. Thornton store burglary. Mr. T. shoots one. They find him in old boiler room today.

March 2, Monday
Spend most of my spare time studying catalogs and advertisements to see where I can buy most economically.

March 3, Tuesday
Ironing and mending day.

March 4, Wednesday
Spent most of day cutting out underwear for myself and dresses for children. Mrs. C. gives Susan brown crepe dress to be made over.

March 5, Thursday
Go to Mary Sue's after school. Dr. attends Medical Society. 1:00 am getting home.

March 6, Friday
Pat cross from trip last night but gets long nap in the afternoon. Spend my 37th birhday very quietly. Calion bridge opening.

March 7, Saturday
Make my first trip to Fordyce to buy groceries at a cash store. Treat the family to grapefruit. Find that I can save money but dislike buying away from home.

March 8, Sunday
Another bad Sunday. We have had only one pretty Sunday this year.

March 9, Monday

March 10, Tuesday
While ironing receive message that Aunt Fanny Morgan is to be buried at Kingsland in afternoon. Call Mary Sue and we go together. See relatives I have not seen since a girl. Cousin Marcia Pearce & "Barney" who gives Mary Sue the bear hug intended for me.

March 11, Wednesday
Do remainder of ironing

March 12, Thursday
Sew.

March 13, Friday

March 14, Saturday
    Go to Fordyce again. Mrs. Hardman, Kenneth & Edna come.

March 15, Sunday
    Prepare dinner for Hardman's. Mrs. H. looks so bad. Worry seems to be
    her trouble.

March 16, Monday

March 17, Tuesday
    Do an extra big ironing. Am not getting much solid reading done, as I
    have only a short time every evening after the children are put to bed
    and it takes most of that time making my orders.

March 18, Wednesday

March 19, Thursday
    Do a little gardening. Folks seem to be perking up a little bit now since
    Spring is around the corner. Wash mine and Pat's hair. Pretty day.

March 20, Friday
    Kirkpatricks call for more help. Dr. eats fish with the Harry Wrights'
    tonight. V.E. is busy composing songs & music while Susan & Pat are
    busy with paper dolls. Rained all day.

March 21, Saturday
    Go to Fordyce.

March 22, Sunday

March 23, Monday

March 24, Tuesday

March 25, Wednesday
    Egypt is the gift of the Nile

March 26, Thursday

March 27, Friday

March 28, Saturday

March 29, Sunday
    Aunt Sudie, Uncle Vasco, Mary Sue, George & Nita Raines here for the
    day. Certainly enjoy having them.

March 30, Monday

March 31, Tuesday

April 1, Wednesday
Children bring home report cards. V.E. makes A in everything. Susan's report good also.

April 2, Thursday
Dr. 55th birthday. Mrs. Wright bakes him an angel food cake.

April 3, Friday
Children practicing for Easter program. Finish their dresses.

April 4, Saturday
Cornelia's family arrive from Memphis.

April 5, Sunday
Drive out to see Cornelia for little while. Pat's eye infected so don't get to go to Easter program. Dr. goes to Fordyce to Legion meeting. Lonesome and blue. Drive out in Hopeville neighborhood with Dr.

April 6, Monday
Celia sick. Aunt Arberry does washing.

April 7, Tuesday
Virginia Elizabeth comes home from school sick. Suffering with sciatica so have quite a time.

April 8, Wednesday
V.E. some better. Get some new cantilever shoes.

April 9, Thursday
Try to do a little reading after supper. Seems that my time is all taken and yet I don't seem to accomplish a thing. Dr. working hard.

April 10, Friday
V.E. still in bed with flu.

April 11, Saturday
Miss Edna comes for the day. Have quite a time. V.E. begging to read when she should not.

April 12, Sunday
Go for a little ride late in afternoon but V.E. is still weak.

April 13, Monday
V.E. goes to school in afternoon.

April 14, Tuesday

April 15, Wednesday
Poor little V.E. will work as hard on her lesson and she doesn't feel like doing so, but that medal looks so big.

April 16, Thursday

April 17, Friday

April 18, Saturday
Go to Camden to buy hat. Get me a blue that looks well with my blue dress. Have a pleasant time but am all tired out.

April 19, Sunday
Baccalaureate sermon—Dr. Queen. Go but with Pat and sciatica can't stay through the sermon.

April 20, Monday
Susan has picnic.

April 21, Tuesday
V.E. has picnic. Made her "daisy" dress for program.

April 22, Wednesday
Take Pat to school to practice for her first appearance on the stage.

April 23, Thursday
Children's program—Susan looks beautiful as a fairy and does her dance much more gracefully than I expected. V.E. does her part exceptionally well and can be heard in back of auditorium. Pat & Mimi Robertson as flower girls are cute as can be. Am just too proud of my three girlies.

April 24, Friday
Closing exercises. V.E. wins the 3rd grade medal for which she has been working so hard all year. She has done *well*, especially since having the flu.

April 25, Saturday

April 26, Sunday
Go to Sunday School. Am trying to go regularly now.

April 27, Monday
   Clean pantry. Suffer severely with sciatica all afternoon.

April 28, Tuesday
   Spooks comes. Children play all day. I iron in the morning and we do
   part of our kitchen cleaning in afternoon.

April 29, Wednesday
   Mary Sue comes and starts the children in rhythmic expression. Susan
   goes home with her for the first time away from home.

April 30, Thursday
   Finish housecleaning. Call to see how Susan is making it & find she is
   having a great time.

April 31, Friday
   Susan & Nita get back. Selma not here so have all the work to do. Dr.
   goes to Rison to Legion meeting.

May 2, Saturday
   Take Nita back home in the afternoon. Spend a pleasant afternoon with
   Mary Sue.

May 3, Sunday
   Sunday School.

May 4, Monday
   Trying to keep V.E. interested in her music, but am making no attempt
   at anything of the kind with Susan on account of her eyes. Dr. goes to
   Pine Bluff to Legion meeting and I am sitting here trying to catch up
   with reading, writing, etc.

May 5, Tuesday

May 6, Wednesday

May 7, Thursday
   This is a month of adjustment, getting the children's hours regulated.
   Both the older ones are doing some piano.

May 10, Sunday
   Have joint session of Sunday School at Baptist Church.

May 15, Friday
   Am reading Pride & Prejudice by Jane Austen.

May 17, Sunday
Go to Locust Bayou to singing. Enjoy the hospitality of Dr. and Mrs. Davis.

May 19, Tuesday
Am now reading Vanity Fair, Thackeray. 4th volume in Harvards Shelf of Fiction.

May 21, Thursday
Children doing well in music.

May 22, Friday
Am feeling good now. Still taking oxayl-iodide together with salts and lemons.

May 23, Saturday
Doing all my work half the time.

May 24, Sunday
Feeling bad today.

May 26, Tuesday
Walk up to the Cottage to see Bess Holmes. Children spend the day there.

Address delivered at Dr. Rhine Day
May 17, 1946, by John Strait

This is one of the happy occasions of my life, to be here with all you folks to help pay tribute to one of our country's great citizens, my uncle, Dr. Rhine.

I have written down what I want to say, not because I don't remember, but because I am so darn frightened at this enormous gathering of grateful friends and neighbors of 'Uncle's' that I probably would become tongued-tied. You know I am a life insurance peddler and not president of one of our country's big utility companies like Mr. Moses is. Who ever heard of a life insurance man making a *few* remarks? In the remarks I make it will be necessary for me to use the personal pronoun frequently, but I trust you will understand that I must do so to give you my viewpoint of this great man. The way he has looked to me and the view I still have of him. He did so much for me. I am now and have always been most grateful to him. I will never live long enough to repay him.

Farming is a grand and noble work, but from childhood I didn't like it and only for Uncle Ed, I might have had to be one. I never liked picking cotton—it hurt my back! I like life insurance work. In fact, I enjoy it tremendously. After 25 years at it, I had darn sight better enjoy it or else. Social Security doesn't pay much and that is a long time away.

I know there must be a big committee to handle a gathering like this. I am not aware of all their names as my correspondence has been with Roy Wise and these details were not mentioned, but I am sure of one thing—that they have been busy men and I am sure they deserve the most grateful thanks from not only Uncle Ed, but each and every one of us.

As you know I live in what used to be the nation's capitol. It is now the world's capitol. It is overgrown and most people are overworked. It is full of congressmen and diplomats, most, if not all, of whom are trying to impress each other along with everybody else whom they come in contact with—from the shoe shine boy to the manager of the hotel. The shoe shine boy isn't the shoe shine boy anymore. He is more apt to be the owner of several pieces of real estate, and the hotel manager isn't easily impressed. It isn't what you know in Washington, it's who you know.

I know lots of people in Washington. I call over 500 men by their first name. You see being an Arkansas country boy, I didn't have any better sense than to treat everybody nice and be sociable. I find they all like it, even the congressman and the diplomat. After a game of golf, in the shower room, we all look somewhat alike, anyway. . . . . .

This idea of a party for Uncle is a wonderful tribute from his friends and neighbors and will be to him a life-long pleasant memory. I am sure he will never be able to express in words his great appreciation to all.

To me he is and always has been my ideal. In 1910 he took me away from a cotton farm down in Cleveland County and too, it was a farm that his father had given to me in reward for my mother, Uncle Ed's older sister, Betty, naming me after him.

Uncle had me live in his home here in Thornton as most of you know. I did the usual chores around the home that other boys of those years did, but I was never allowed to feed his 75 or 100 foxhounds. This job was positively reserved for his leisure. I never knew how many dogs he had. I am not sure he was exact as to the count himself. Maybe Zell Hearnsberger knew. Besides this, I swept out the big old school house that stood here then. My pay was $5.00 per month. On Saturday, I worked in the mill. My pay there was $1.65 per day: the hours were 7 am to 11 pm. Who said a work day was 8 hours? John L. Lewis would throw a fit if he ever hears of this.

All this money was turned over to Uncle—to buy shoes—and I did wear shoes then—clothes, books and my allowance for Coca-Colas and the Sunday School collection.

In the summer I worked steady in the mill. This money was also turned over to his care. During the school months my job at nights, *orders* "were to study your lessons and when you go out at nights during the week, I'll take you." He did, too, on occasion take me out, and I mean out—in white tie and tails to a dance. In those days as a lot of you know, Uncle was quite the town dude. A good dresser and a free spender—but few people knew about his spending because that was done on the Q.T. and it wasn't spending as we know it today. It was giving and the giving was to the poor and needy. And it was done because of—not publicity he might receive—but of the satisfaction in doing something for the men and women less fortunate. No change in him as of today in this respect. In dancing—well, I'd say there has been *some* change.

In his practice, country calls came on bad nights as on good ones, and I was young then and full of pep. On bad nights when he had long country calls to make I was routed out of bed to accompany him. Not his doing, tho'. It was Mammy's, as she was affectionately known to all, his mother, who would urge him to let me go along. Maybe he might get stalled and I would be of some help. Farm houses were not so close together in those days—and on some occasions, I was a help. Country roads had a lot of sand in them in spots and auto tires were small and smooth, and bitter weeds had a way of growing in the middle of roads to conceal stumps that were a menace to autos. Auto lights were not so dependable as today, either, but a good lantern was dependable then as now. A little push was all an auto needed to help it through the sand and a little pre-wading was all you needed to know how deep the branch was.

One occasion I won't forget soon. His buggy team ran away with him, the tongue dropped, split all to pieces, tossed the buggy and him out and over. He gave himself some of his own medicine and crawled a half mile to a telephone and called home. Mammy sent me post haste to his rescue. I rode old Bill, one of his two fine saddle horses and I rode him the nine miles out in 35 minutes. Not many saddle horses can make this statement. Uncle was not banged up much tho; and with other help, we got him home o.k.

During my school days in Thornton, we had a baseball team. Uncle, bless his generous heart, bought the equipment for the team. I could not play baseball very good, but I was put on the team, away out in right field where I would do the team the least damage. After all, I was Dr. Rhine's nephew, wasn't I? And baseball equipment costs money, doesn't it? The same was true about basketball. Everybody had in those days love and respect for this great man as they do today which this gathering testifies to.

Through Uncle's unselfish efforts, we were given a course in manual training at the school and I won the gold medal for making a library table and the medal I have today, my mother having kept it for me all these years. I am not handy with tools today. Now I am not saying that again I won because I was Dr. Rhine's nephew. One essay we were required to write and in competition, too, we were asked to, instead of using our names on the paper, to number them. I numbered mine 13 and I won. Maybe the principal knew my handwriting. Uncle was the president, vice-president, secretary and treasurer of the school, I believe.

There were advantages in being Dr. Rhine's nephew. Price Shaddock and I had girl friends, but Aunt Ethel helped us keep that quiet. Remember, Uncle had plans for me and I was supposed to work the plan.

My stay in Thornton finally came to a close with my graduation in the spring of 1914. Of course, my ambition was to study medicine and follow my uncle, and these were his plans for me, too. We conferred and the decision was this—I was to go to Ouachita College for two years and then to medical school. And for that summer vacation, I was sent to Hampton to take the examination for a school teacher's license. I passed and that summer taught school at Clio in Cleveland County. That fall I was off to Ouachita with the best looking dark blue suit of clothes that Uncle could buy, which was, as I see it now, a "God-speed-you" gift. I believe down in his heart he wanted to see me dressed up because when he was in medical school he had only one complete matched suit and that was the one he graduated in and, too, he graduated with the second highest grade that had been made at that school. I found that out 30 years after I left Thornton.

After one year at Ouachita the horrible realization of the First World War was at hand.

That summer and fall, I worked in a drug store in Rison and lived with my mother for the first time in a long time.

I went to war as Uncle did. Our paths never crossed during those two years, though. He was a 1st Lt. and I was a 2nd. He was in Europe and I was in America. After the war, lots of changes had been made, and some of these affected the study of medicine.

Again I am in the presence of this great man seeking his advice. Finally it was decided that I should go to business school. The best one in the U.S. was sought out, and it turned out I should go to Poughkeepsie, N.Y. to Eastman Business College. Soon I appreciated the fact I didn't care for office work. Maybe the war changed me some, and I sought a selling job and within about one year I found myself in life insurance work. Six years in Poughkeepsie, ten in Boston and now ten years in the most publicized city in the world, our nation's capitol. As I have said, I like my work. After the doctor comes, then the minister, then the undertaker, and then last, but by far not the least, the insurance man comes and provides the money to pay all these bills. *But* there is nothing in life that would have given me more pleasure than to have followed in my Uncle's footsteps, a more noble work has never been performed, fate did not decree it so. I salute you Dr. Rhine. I am fortunate and proud to be your nephew. My love and respect you have always had. Your advice has been most helpful and you have my lifelong gratitude. Our only regret today, as we have gathered here to honor you, is that in these world troubled times that there are not more men like you, Uncle Ed.

Thank you

If you have enjoyed this Arkansas book
from August House, Inc., publishers,
write for our full list of 47 Arkansas books
and records. Please enclose $2 to cover
mailing and handling costs.

August House, Inc., publishers
Post Office Box 3223
Little Rock, Arkansas 72203-3223